国外优秀数学著作
原版系列

偏微分方程全局吸引子的特性
（英文）

Properties of Global Attractors of Partial Differential Equations

[苏] A. V. 巴宾（A. V. Babin）
[苏] 维施内克（M. I. Vishik）著

哈尔滨工业大学出版社
HARBIN INSTITUTE OF TECHNOLOGY PRESS

黑版贸审字 08-2017-118 号

Special Edition for People's Republic of China distribution only. This edition has been authorized by the American Mathematical Society for sale in People's Republic of China only and is not for export therefrom.

This work was originally published by the American Mathematical Society under the title Properties of Global Attractors of Partial Differential Equations, © 1992 by the American Mathematical Society. The present edition was created by Harbin Institute of Technology Press under authority of the American Mathematical Society and is published under license.

图书在版编目(CIP)数据

偏微分方程全局吸引子的特性=Properties of Global Attractors of Partial Differential Equations:英文/(苏)A. V. 巴宾(A. V. Babin),(苏)维施内克(M. I. Vishik)著. —哈尔滨:哈尔滨工业大学出版社,2019.1

ISBN 978-7-5603-7545-8

Ⅰ.①偏… Ⅱ.①A…②维… Ⅲ.①偏微分方程-全局-吸引子-特性-研究-英文 Ⅳ.①O175

中国版本图书馆 CIP 数据核字(2018)第 167046 号

策划编辑	刘培杰
责任编辑	张永芹　聂兆慈
封面设计	孙茵艾
出版发行	哈尔滨工业大学出版社
社　　址	哈尔滨市南岗区复华四道街 10 号　邮编 150006
传　　真	0451-86414749
网　　址	http://hitpress.hit.edu.cn
印　　刷	哈尔滨市工大节能印刷厂
开　　本	787mm×1092mm　1/16　印张 12　字数 350 千字
版　　次	2019 年 1 月第 1 版　2019 年 1 月第 1 次印刷
书　　号	ISBN 978-7-5603-7545-8
定　　价	108.00 元

(如因印装质量问题影响阅读,我社负责调换)

Contents

Editors' Preface	i
Asymptotic Expansion at Infinity of a Strongly Perturbed Poiseuille Flow A. V. BABIN	1
Unbounded Attractors of Evolution Equations V. V. CHEPYZHOV and A. YU. GORITSKIĬ	85
Attractors of Singularly Perturbed Parabolic Equations, and Asymptotic Behavior of Their Elements M. YU. SKVORTSOV and M. I. VISHIK	129
The Asymptotics of Solutions of Reaction-Diffusion Equations with Small Parameter V. YU. SKVORTSOV and M. I. VISHIK	149
编辑手记	173

Editors' Preface

A global attractor of an evolution equation is a set of trajectories describing the behavior of a dynamical system for very large values of time. It is important to note that a point of the attractor of a system of partial differential equations is an element of a certain function space; such a point is a function of the space variables and also depends on the parameters that appear in the equations. To any limiting regime (as $t \to +\infty$) of a physical system with dissipation described by an evolution equation corresponds a trajectory lying in the attractor. Such regimes are often of great interest from the physical point of view. For example, according to the conjectures of Landau and Ruelle-Takens, it is precisely the nontrivial dynamics on the attractors of Navier-Stokes systems that determine the presence of turbulence. Thus, obtaining information as complete as possible about attractors is both important from the physical viewpoint and interesting as a mathematical problem.

The articles in the present volume are concerned with the existence of attractors and their use in the description of the behavior of solutions as $t \to +\infty$. However, the key point is the detailed analysis of functions belonging to the attractor. The dependence of these functions on the space variables, as well as on the parameters, is studied.

In the article *Asymptotic expansion at infinity of a strongly perturbed Poiseuille flow* by A. B. Babin, functions lying on attractors of two-dimensional and three-dimensional Navier-Stokes systems in unbounded domains having the shape of a canal or tube are considered. In the absence of external forces, for small fluxes of the liquid in the tube the established regime is described by the stationary stable Poiseuille flow. If a large external force decaying at infinity acts on the liquid, then experiments show that the turbulence created by this force does not travel to infinity. The article gives a mathematical justification of this fact. Namely, the nonstationary solution $u(t, x)$ lying on the attractor exponentially tends to a stable stationary flow as $|x| \to \infty$. In other words, at infinity nontrivial dynamics on the attractor rapidly disappear, which corresponds to the absence of turbulence at infinity. The asymptotic expansion at infinity of functions lying on the attractor is presented.

In the paper *Attractors of singularly perturbed parabolic equations, and asymptotic behavior of their elements* by M. Yu. Skvortsov and M. I. Vishik, second order parabolic equations with fourth order singular perturbation of the form $\varepsilon^2 \Delta^2 u$, where Δ is the Laplace operator and ε is a small parameter, are studied. The key point is the behavior of functions lying on the attractor as $\varepsilon \to 0$. In the description of the asymptotic behavior near the boundary of the domain, a boundary layer naturally arises.

In the paper *The asymptotics of solutions of reaction-diffusion equations with small parameter* by V. Yu. Skvortsov and M. I. Vishik, systems of two parabolic reaction-diffusion equations, one of which has small parameter as the coefficient at the derivative with respect to time, i.e., the term $\varepsilon \partial_t u_1$ occurs in this equation. The asymptotic behavior as $\varepsilon \to 0$ of the solutions of this system for all $t \geq 0$ is described in terms of solutions lying in the attractor of the limit system, with one equation becoming stationary.

The paper *Unbounded attractors of evolution equations* by V. V. Chepyzhov and A. Yu. Goritskiĭ is devoted to the study of attractors for equations that have no bounded attracting sets, i.e., equations that are not dissipative in the narrow sense. Such equations have no compact global attractors. However, for certain sufficiently wide classes of such equations, it is possible to introduce a reasonable notion of attractor, prove the existence of attractors, and describe their properties. These attractors are neither compact nor bounded, but they are locally compact and finite-dimensional. The general theory is illustrated by specific examples.

The authors tried to make the exposition as self-contained as possible, referring only to those facts that can be found in easily accessible books; for all other statements detailed proofs are given.

Translated by S. SOSSINSKY

Asymptotic Expansion at Infinity of a Strongly Perturbed Poiseuille Flow

A. V. BABIN

Introduction

The velocity field $v(t, x) = v(t, x_1, x_2, x_3)$ of a flow of an incompressible viscous fluid in a tube $\Omega = \omega \times \{-\infty < x_3 < +\infty\}$ is a solution of the Navier-Stokes system

$$\partial_t v + B(v, v) - \nu \Delta v + \nabla p = f,$$
$$\operatorname{div} v = 0, \quad v|_{\partial \Omega} = 0. \tag{I.1}$$

Here

$$B(u, v) = (u \cdot \nabla) v = \sum_{i=1}^{3} u_i \partial_i v. \tag{I.2}$$

We denote by ω a bounded domain in $\mathbb{R}^2$ with a smooth boundary $\partial \omega$. The Poiseuille flow $v = V$ is a solution of the form $V = (0, 0, V_3(x_1, x_2))$, where the function V_3 is a solution of the equation

$$\partial_1^2 V_3 + \partial_2^3 V_3 = \nu^{-1} p', \quad V_3|_{\partial \omega} = 0, \tag{I.3}$$

the number p' describing the rate of growth of p along the tube. Obviously, V is a solution of (I.1) if $f = 0$.

In this paper we shall consider strongly perturbed Poiseuille flows which are solutions of (I.1) with nonzero (and not small) external force f. We assume that $f = f(t, x)$ satisfies the condition

$$\int_T^{T+1} \int_\Omega (1 + |x_3|^2)^\gamma |f(t, x)|^2 \, dx \, dt \leq M \quad \forall T, \tag{I.4}$$

with $\gamma > 0$. This means that $f(t, x)$ decays, as $|x| \to \infty$, more rapidly than functions from $L_2(\Omega)$. We consider the solutions of (I.1) of the form

$$v = V + u, \tag{I.5}$$

1991 *Mathematics Subject Classification.* Primary 58F12, 58F39, 76D05.

where the perturbation $u = u(t, x)$ is defined for all $t \in \mathbb{R}$ and

$$\int_\Omega |\nabla u(t, x)|^2 \, dx \leq C \qquad \forall t \in \mathbb{R}, \tag{I.6}$$

$$\int_T^{T+1} \int_\Omega |\Delta u(t, x)|^2 \, dx \, dt \leq C_1 \qquad \forall T \in \mathbb{R}. \tag{I.7}$$

Solutions defined for all t and satisfying estimates similar to (I.6), (I.7) naturally arise in the process of describing the limit behavior as $t \to +\infty$ of regular solutions of the initial-value problem for (I.1) (see, for example, [10]). In the two-dimensional case such solutions lie on the attractor of the system (I.1) (see [6, 10, 12, 15, 25] and §9). We shall consider the situation when the original Poiseuille flow satisfies the energy stability condition (see §7). This condition is satisfied if the Reynolds number for the original Poiseuille flow is not large. For example, in the case when ω is a circle of radius r, it is sufficient that $\text{Re} \leq 17$, where the Reynolds number $\text{Re} = V_{\max} r/\nu$, $V_{\max}$ is the maximal velocity of the original Poiseuille flow. (Note that the maximal value of the velocity of the perturbed flow may be arbitrarily large.)

Obviously, the function u defined by (I.5) satisfies the following system, analogous to (I.1):

$$\begin{aligned} &\partial_t u + B(u, u) - \nu \Delta u + L_0 u + \operatorname{grad} p = f, \\ &\operatorname{div} u = 0, \quad u|_{\partial \Omega} = 0 \quad (L_0 u = B(V, u) + B(u, V)). \end{aligned} \tag{I.8}$$

The main result of this paper is the existence of the expansion

$$u(t, x) = \sum_{k=1}^n z_k(t, x) + \omega_{n+1}(t, x). \tag{I.9}$$

Here the terms z_k are uniquely determined by f. The equation for z_1 is

$$\begin{aligned} &\partial_t z_1 - \nu \Delta z_1 + L_0 z_1 + \operatorname{grad} p_1 = f, \quad -\infty < t < \infty, \\ &\operatorname{div} z_1 = 0, \quad z_1|_{\partial \Omega} = 0. \end{aligned} \tag{I.10}$$

The functions $z_2, z_3, \ldots$ are defined recurrently as the solutions of the equations

$$\begin{aligned} &\partial_t z_k - \nu \Delta z_k + L_0 z_k + \sum_{i+j=k} B(z_i, z_j) + \operatorname{grad} p_k = 0, \\ &\operatorname{div} z_k = 0, \quad z_k|_{\partial \Omega} = 0. \end{aligned} \tag{I.11}$$

The terms z_k of (I.9) are the solutions of (I.10) and (I.11) satisfying the conditions of the type of (I.6), (I.7). The existence of such solutions is proved in §5. Moreover, these solutions satisfy the estimates

$$\int_\Omega (1 + |x|^2)^{k\gamma} (|\nabla z_k(t, x)|^2 + |z_k|^2) \, dx \leq C_k \qquad \forall t, \tag{I.12}$$

$$\int_T^{T+1} \int_\Omega (1 + |x|^2)^{k\gamma} (|\Delta z_k|^2 + |z_k|^2) \, dx \, dt \leq C_k \qquad \forall T, \tag{I.13}$$

where C_k does not depend on t and T. If f does not depend on t, neither do z_k. In §6 the following estimates of the remainder are established:

$$\int_\Omega (1+|x|^2)^{\gamma(n+1)}(|\nabla\omega_{n+1}|^2+|\omega_{n+1}|^2)dx \leqslant C_{n+1}, \qquad (I.14)$$

$$\int_T^{T+1}\int_\Omega (1+|x|^2)^{\gamma(n+1)}(|\Delta\omega_{n+1}|^2+|\omega_{n+1}|^2)dx\,dt \leqslant C_{n+1}. \qquad (I.15)$$

Note that the estimates (I.12)–(I.15) show that the solution $v(t,x)$ of (I.11) tends to the laminar Poiseuille flow $V(x)$ as $|x|\to\infty$. The difference $u = v - V$ decays more rapidly when γ is greater, i.e., f decays more rapidly.

It is important to notice that a solution of equation (I.8) satisfying (I.6), (I.7) may be nonunique. Nevertheless, all the terms z_k of the asymptotic expansion are the same for any such a solution. It is proved in §4 that if u_1 and u_2 are any solutions of (I.8), (I.6), (I.7), then their difference $u_1 - u_2$ decays exponentially as $|x_3| \to \infty$; hence there exists a $\gamma_1 > 0$ such that

$$\int_\Omega e^{\gamma|x_3|}|\nabla(u_1-u_2)|^2 dx \leqslant C \qquad \forall t. \qquad (I.16)$$

In the case when f does not depend on t, there exists a regular steady-state solution $u = u_1$ of (I.8), (I.6), (I.7) independent of t. Estimate (I.16) implies that any time-dependent solution $u_2(x,t)$ of (I.8), (I.6), (I.7) exponentially tends to $u_1(x)$ as $|x|\to\infty$. Therefore all the dynamics described by regular solutions of (I.1), (I.6), (I.7) exponentially decays at infinity. From the viewpoint of the theory of dynamical systems, turbulence is generated by complicated dynamics on the attractor of the system (see [17, 22]). The attractor of the system (I.1) consisting of regular solutions contains solutions $v = V + u$ satisfying (I.6), (I.7). By (I.16), the parameters of any time-dependent flow $u_2(t,x)$ measured in a neighborhood of a point $x = x^0$, $|x^0| \gg 1$, are exponentially close to the parameters of the steady-state flow $u_1(x)$ and actually do not depend on t when $|x^0|$ is sufficiently large. So the time-dependent component of $u_1(t,x)$ decays much more rapidly than its time-independent components. Therefore the measurement at a point x_0 lying at a large distance along the tube will practically describe a time-independent flow given by the terms z_k. That means that the turbulence does not propagate to infinity along the tube and is located in a bounded part of the tube.

Note that since $f = f(x)$ may be taken arbitrarily large in a bounded part of the tube Ω, the dynamics on the attractor can be very complicated and becomes trivial only at infinity.

It is well known (see [17]) that the physical turbulence generated by finite perturbations of a Poiseuille flow with a small Reynolds number does not propagate along the tube at a large distance. Our mathematical results are in a good correspondence with such a picture.

Note that in the 3-dimensional case the attractor consisting of regular solutions may not coincide with the attractor consisting of weak solutions. Nevertheless it seems natural to consider solutions satisfying (I.6), (I.7) as solutions representing settled flows (both in the autonomous and the nonautonomous cases). If a global attractor (in any sense) exists, such a solution lies on the attractor.

Note that in the two-dimensional case, the global attractor consists of regular solutions (see, for example, [6, 15, 25]).

In the two-dimensional case, the attractor of the Navier-Stokes system in a bounded domain was constructed in [14]. The existence of an attractor and the finiteness of its Hausdorff dimension was proved in [1, 2] for the case of a strip and a channel-like unbounded domain, respectively. The asymptotic expansion of functions lying on the attractor was obtained in [2, 3]; it has the same form as (I.9)–(I.11).

In §8 we consider the initial-value problem for (I.1). The asymptotic expansion of regular solutions analogous to (I.9)–(I.11) is obtained in this case also.

The proofs of the results mentioned above are based on weighted estimates for solutions of linear Stokes and nonlinear Navier-Stokes systems in a cylindrical domain. Such equations in unbounded domains were considered by many authors (see, for example, [13, 7, 19, 23]). Weighted estimates also were useful in many applications (see, for example, [8, 11, 20, 21]). Here we try to make the exposition self-contained and we use without proof only well-known results concerning equations in bounded domains proved in standard books on the subject ([9, 13, 24]).

The paper includes this introduction and nine sections. In §0 notation and preliminary results concerning properties of the Stokes equation and divergence-free vector fields in an unbounded cylindrical domain are presented.

In §1 the weighted functions that we systematically use are introduced and properties of the operators of multiplication by such functions are discussed.

§2 is devoted to the investigation of commutators of the projection onto the space of divergence-free vector fields and the operator of multiplication by the weight function.

In §3 we obtain an estimate in a weighted norm of a regular global solution of the Navier-Stokes system.

In §4 we prove that any two regular global solutions of (I.1) are exponentially close at infinity.

In §5, terms of an asymptotic expansion at infinity are constructed.

§6 is devoted to obtaining an estimate of the error of approximation by the nth sum of the asymptotic expansion obtained in the preceding section.

In §7 sufficient conditions on the original steady-state Poiseuille flow providing validity of the above results are given.

In §8 some generalizations are considered. First, solutions of the initial-value problem for the Navier-Stokes system are considered and results similar to those formulated above are obtained. Second, the problem (I.1) in a half-tube is considered. All the above results hold in this case also.

In §9 the problem (I.1) is considered in the two-dimensional case when Ω is a strip and ω is an interval. The existence of a global attractor is proved. Properties of functions lying on the attractor are investigated. Their behavior as $|x| \to \infty$ is of the kind described above in the three-dimensional case.

§0. Notation and preliminary results on the Stokes equation in an unbounded cylindrical domain

In this section we shall introduce some notation used throughout the paper and formulate results well known in the case of a bounded domain. We shall formulate and prove these results in the case of a cylindrical domain to make the exposition self-contained. We give the proof only when the unboundedness of Ω makes a difference and when we could not find the proof in standard books.

In this paper we shall consider equations in the unbounded domain Ω,

$$\Omega = \{x = (x_1, x_2, x_3) \in \mathbb{R}^3, \ (x_1, x_2) \in \omega, \ x_3 \in \mathbb{R}\}, \qquad (0.1)$$

that is, $\Omega = \omega \times \mathbb{R} \subset \mathbb{R}^3$, $\omega \subset \mathbb{R}^2$. The domain ω is assumed to be bounded and to have an infinitely smooth boundary $\partial \omega$. By $D(\Omega)$ and $D(\overline{\Omega})$ we shall denote the spaces of infinitely differentiable functions in Ω and $\overline{\Omega}$ with compact support. The Sobolev spaces $H_l(\Omega)$ are equipped with norms $\|u\|_l$, defined by

$$\|u\|_l^2 = \sum_{|\alpha| \leq l} \int_\Omega |\partial^\alpha u(x)|^2 \, dx. \qquad (0.2)$$

We use the standard notation $\alpha = (\alpha_1, \ldots, \alpha_3)$, $\partial^\alpha = \partial_1^{\alpha_1} \cdots \partial_3^{\alpha_3}$, $|\alpha| = \alpha_1 + \alpha_2 + \alpha_3$, $\partial_i = \partial/\partial x_i$. The closure in $H_l(\Omega)$ of the set $D(\Omega)$ is denoted by $H_l^0(\Omega)$. The set $D(\overline{\Omega})$ is dense in $H_l(\Omega)$, and $D(\Omega)$ is dense in $H_l^0(\Omega)$. By $H_l(\Omega)^3$ we denote spaces of vector fields $u = (u_1, u_2, u_3)$ on Ω; the norm in $H_l(\Omega)^n$ is also denoted by $\|\cdot\|_l$ and is defined by (0.2), where $|v| = (v_1^2 + \cdots + v_n^2)^{1/2}$. We shall often use the notation

$$uv = u_1 v_1 + \cdots + u_3 v_3, \qquad u, v \in \mathbb{R}^3,$$
$$\nabla u \nabla v = \partial_1 u \, \partial_1 v + \cdots + \partial_3 u \, \partial_3 v.$$

The last notation is used both for scalar and vector-valued functions. For vector-valued functions u we have

$$|\nabla u|^2 = \sum_{i,j} |\partial_i u_j|^2.$$

The space dual to $H_l^0(\Omega)$ is denoted by $H_{-l}(\Omega)$. The duality between $H_l^0(\Omega)$ and $H_{-l}(\Omega)$ is denoted by $(\ ,\ )$. The same notation is used for the inner product in $H = L_2(\Omega)$

$$(u, v) = \int_\Omega uv\, dx, \qquad \|u\| = \sqrt{(u, u)}.$$

The space of distributions dual to $D(\Omega)$ is denoted by $D'(\Omega)$; the duality between $D(\Omega)$ and $D'(\Omega)$ is also denoted by $(\,,\,)$.

We denote by $(\,,\,)_{\partial\Omega}$ and $(\,,\,)_\omega$ the inner products in $L_2(\partial\Omega)$ and $L_2(\omega)$ respectively, and write $(\,,\,)$ instead of $(\,,\,)_\Omega$.

PROPOSITION 0.1. *For $u \in H_s(\Omega)$, $s \in \mathbb{N}$, a trace $lu = u|_{\partial\Omega}$ is defined on $\partial\Omega$ and the operator $l: u \to u|_{\partial\Omega}$ from $H_s(\Omega)$ to $H_{s-1/2}(\partial\Omega)$ is bounded.*

PROOF. This property is proved in the case of half-space in any standard book on PDE's (see, for example, [18]). The case of a cylindrical domain Ω is reduced to that of the half-space in the same way as for a bounded domain, since all the cut-off functions and changes of variables can be taken independently of x_3. The spaces $H_s(\mathbb{R}^n)$ and $H_s(\mathbb{R}^{n-1})$ are defined for real s in [18], and $H_s(\partial\Omega)$ is defined in the same way as the space $H_s(\Gamma)$ for compact manifolds Γ, since $\partial\Omega = \omega \times \mathbb{R}$ and all changes of variables and partitions of unity can be chosen independently of x_3.

PROPOSITION 0.2. *Let $g_j \in H_{m-j-1/2}(\partial\Omega)$, $j = 0, 1, \ldots, m-1$. The bounded operator*

$$R: \prod_{j=0}^{m-1} H_{m-j-1/2}(\partial\Omega) \to H_m(\Omega)$$

is defined, $\partial^j/\partial n^j(Rg)|_{\partial\Omega} = g_j$, $j = 1, \ldots, m$, $\partial u/\partial n$ is the derivative of u in the direction of an outer normal to $\partial\Omega$.

PROOF. A construction of R in the cases of half-space and bounded domain can be found in [18]. Since $\Omega = \omega \times \mathbb{R}$, this construction can be applied to the case under consideration without changes.

PROPOSITION 0.3. *The space $H_l^0(\Omega)$ coincides with the subspace of functions $u \in H_l(\Omega)$ satisfying zero boundary conditions*

$$\left.\frac{\partial^j u}{\partial u^j}\right|_{\partial\Omega} = 0, \qquad j = 0, \ldots, l-1.$$

PROOF. This fact in the cases of half-space and bounded domain is proved in [18]; in the case $\Omega = \omega \times \mathbb{R}$ no essential change of the proof is needed.

We shall sometimes mollify functions $u(x_1, x_2, x_3)$ with respect to x_3. Let

$$\chi \in D(\mathbb{R}), \quad \chi(t) \geq 0, \quad \int_{-\infty}^{+\infty} \chi(t)dt = 1, \quad \chi(t) = 0 \text{ when } |t| \geq 1.$$

Let $u \in L_2(\Omega)$, $\delta > 0$. The mollified function u_δ is defined by the convolution

$$u_\delta(x_1, x_2, x_3) = \frac{1}{\delta} \int_\Omega u(x_1, x_2, \xi) \chi\left(\frac{x_3 - \xi}{\delta}\right) d\xi. \tag{0.3}$$

PROPOSITION 0.4. *Let $u \in L_2(\Omega)$, u_δ be defined by (0.3). Then $\partial_3^k u \in L_2(\Omega)$ for any $k \in \mathbb{N}$,*

$$\|u - u_\delta\| \to 0 \quad \text{as } \delta \to 0. \tag{0.4}$$

If $u \in H_l(\Omega)$, then $\partial_3^k u \in H_l(\Omega)$ for any k,

$$\|u_\delta\|_l \leq C\|u\|_l, \qquad \|u - u_\delta\|_l \to 0 \quad \text{as } \delta \to 0. \tag{0.5}$$

If $u \in H_l^0(\Omega)$, then $\partial_3^k u \in H_l^0(\Omega)$. If $u \in D'(\Omega)$, $u \in H_l(\omega \times I_R)$ for any R, then $\partial^\alpha \partial_3^k u_\delta \in H_{l-|\alpha|}(\omega \times I_R)$ for any R and $|\alpha| \leq l$,

$$\partial_3^k(\partial^\alpha u)_\delta = \partial_3^k \partial^\alpha u_\delta \tag{0.6}$$

(derivatives are understood in the sense of distributions).

PROOF. All the properties of u_δ are standard consequences of properties of the convolution.

Now consider the Laplace operators

$$\Delta = \partial_1^2 + \partial_2^2 + \partial_3^2, \qquad \Delta_2 = \partial_1^2 + \partial_2^2.$$

PROPOSITION 0.5. *For any $v \in D(\Omega)$, we have*

$$(-\Delta v, v) \geq \lambda_1 \|v\|^2, \qquad \lambda_1 > 0. \tag{0.7}$$

PROOF. The Laplace operator Δ_2 with Dirichlet boundary conditions on $\partial\omega$ has a positive first eigenvalue $\lambda_1 > 0$. By using the Fourier method, it can be easily verified that (0.7) holds with the same $\lambda_1 > 0$.

Now consider the Dirichlet problem

$$\Delta u = f, \qquad u|_{\partial\Omega} = 0. \tag{0.8}$$

PROPOSITION 0.6. *Let $f \in H_{-1}(\Omega)$. Then there exists a unique solution $u \in H_1^0(\Omega)$ of (0.8),*

$$\|u\|_1 \leq C\|f\|_{-1}. \tag{0.9}$$

If $f \in H = L_2(\Omega)$, then $u \in H_2(\Omega)$,

$$\|u\|_2 \leq C\|f\|. \tag{0.10}$$

PROOF. The existence of $u \in H_1^0(\Omega)$ follows from the inequality (0.7) and the Friedrichs theorem. If $f \in H$, the solution u belongs to $H_2(\omega \times I_R)$, $I_R = [-R, R]$, for any R. Indeed, consider the cut-off function $\chi \in D(\mathbb{R})$, $\chi = 1$ when $|t| \leq R$, $\chi = 0$ when $|t| \geq R+1$. The function $u_1 = \chi u$ is the solution of the problem

$$\Delta u_1 = \chi f + 2\nabla u \nabla \chi + u \Delta \chi,$$
$$u_1|_{\partial\Omega_R} = 0, \qquad \omega \times I_{R+1} \subset \Omega_R \subset \omega \times I_{R+2}, \tag{0.11}$$

Ω_R has a smooth boundary. The Dirichlet problem (0.8) in a bounded domain admits a solution $u_1 \in H_2(\Omega_R)$,

$$\|u_1\|_2 \leq C \|\chi f\| + C \|\nabla u \nabla \chi\| + C \|u \Delta \chi\|. \tag{0.12}$$

Hence $u_1 \in H_2(\omega \times I_R)$.

Using the mollification (0.3) with respect to x_3, we obtain by (0.6) the equation for u_δ,

$$\Delta u_\delta = f_\delta, \qquad u_\delta|_{\partial \Omega} = 0. \tag{0.13}$$

The function $\partial_3 u_\delta$ belongs to $H_1^0(\Omega)$ by Proposition 0.4 and satisfies the equation

$$\Delta(\partial_3 u_\delta) = \partial_3 f_\delta, \qquad \partial_3 u_\delta|_{\partial \Omega} = 0. \tag{0.14}$$

Since (0.14) is of the form (0.8), the estimate (0.9) with u and f replaced by $\partial_3 u_\delta$ and $\partial_3 f_\delta$, is valid. The constant C in (0.9) does not depend on δ, $\|\partial_3 f_\delta\|_{-1} \leq C\|f_\delta\| \leq C_1 \|f\|$; hence $\|\partial_3 u_\delta\|_1$ is bounded uniformly as $\delta \to 0$. We choose a weakly convergent subsequence $\partial_3 u_\delta \to v$ in H_1^0, $\delta \to 0$. Since $\partial_3 u_\delta \to \partial_3 u$ in H, we have $v = \partial_3 u$. Therefore,

$$\|\partial_3 u\|_1 \leq C \|f\|. \tag{0.15}$$

Rewrite equation (0.8) in the form

$$\Delta_2 u = f - \partial_3^2 u, \qquad u|_{\partial \omega} = 0, \tag{0.16}$$

for almost all $x_3 \in \mathbb{R}$. Here $u = u(x_1, x_2, x_3)$ depends on x_3 as a parameter. Since $u \in H_2(\omega \times I_R)$, the restriction to $\omega \times \{x_3 = t\}$ belongs to $H_{3/2}(\omega) \subset H_1(\omega)$. Hence the solution of (0.16) is unique and satisfies the estimate

$$\|u\|_{H_2(\omega)}^2 \leq C(\|f\|_{L_2(\omega)}^2 + \|\partial_3^2 u\|_{L_2(\omega)}^2) \tag{0.17}$$

(see, for example, [16]). Integrating (0.17) in x_3, we get the estimate

$$\sum_{\alpha_1 + \alpha_2 \leq 2} \int_R \int_\omega |\partial_1^{\alpha_1} \partial_2^{\alpha_2} u|^2 \, dx_1 dx_2 dx_3 \leq C_1 (\|f\|^2 + \|\partial_3 u\|_1^2).$$

By (0.15) the right-hand side is bounded by $C\|f\|^2$, and using (0.15) to estimate derivatives involving $\partial_3 u$, we obtain (0.10).

Let $u \in L_2(\Omega)$, $\text{div } u \in L_2(\Omega)$ and

$$\|u\|_E^2 = \|u\|^2 + \|\text{div } u\|^2. \tag{0.18}$$

The space of all $u \in L_2(\Omega)^3$ satisfying $\|u\|_E < \infty$ is denoted by E; obviously, E is a Hilbert space. Note that $D(\Omega)$ is dense in E (for the proof see [24]).

Denote by l_n the operator $u \cdot n|_{\partial \Omega}$, where $u = (u_1(x), \ldots, u_3(x))$, n is an outer normal to Ω at a point x.

PROPOSITION 0.7. *The operator l_n is defined on E and is a bounded operator from E to $H_{-1/2}(\partial\Omega)$.*

PROOF. Green's formula

$$(u, \nabla w) + (\operatorname{div} u, w) = (l_n u, w) \qquad (0.19)$$

is valid for $u \in D(\overline{\Omega})^3$, $w \in H_1(\Omega)$. Since the terms on the left-hand side continuously depend on $u \in E$, this gives the possibility to define $l_n u$ for $u \in E$. Details can be found in [24] in the case of a bounded domain. Since $\Omega = \omega \times \mathbb{R}$ is cylindrical and Propositions 0.2 and 0.3 are valid, the proof is the same in the case under consideration.

Denote by $\mathscr{V}$ the space of smooth compactly supported divergence-free vector fields,

$$\mathscr{V} = \{v \in D(\Omega) : \operatorname{div} v = 0\}. \qquad (0.20)$$

The closure of $\mathscr{V}$ in $H = L_2(\Omega)^3$ is denoted by H_0. (Note that $H_0 \neq H_0(\Omega)$.)

PROPOSITION 0.8. *Let $u \in H_0$. Then $\operatorname{div} u = 0$ (in the sense of distributions), $l_n u = 0$.*

PROOF. The operator div is continuous in the sense of distributions and $\operatorname{div} u = 0$ for $u \in \mathscr{V}$. Hence $\operatorname{div} u = 0$ for $u \in H_0$. Further, $l_n u = 0$ for $u \in \mathscr{V}$. Obviously, $\|u\|_E = \|u\|$ for $u \in \mathscr{V}$. Therefore the closure of $\mathscr{V}$ in H coincides with the closure of $\mathscr{V}$ in E. Hence, by Proposition 0.7, we have $l_n u = 0$ for any $u \in H_0$.

Denote by Π the orthogonal projection from H onto H_0, $\Pi H = H_0$. Put $\pi_0 = I - \Pi$, where I denotes the identity operator.

PROPOSITION 0.9. *The space $\pi_0 H$ coincides with the set of gradients ∇p of distributions $p \in D'(\Omega)$ such that $\nabla p \in H$.*

PROOF. A vector $g \in \pi_0 H$ if $(g, v) = 0$ for any $v \in H_0 = \overline{\mathscr{V}}$. Since $\mathscr{V}$ is dense in $\overline{\mathscr{V}}$, this is equivalent to $(g, v) = 0$ for any $v \in \mathscr{V}$. If $g = \nabla p$, $p \in D'(\Omega)$, then $(\nabla p, v) = -(p, \operatorname{div} v) = 0$ by the definition of distributions. Hence the set $U = \{\nabla p \in H : p \in D'(\Omega)\}$ is a subset of $\pi_0 H$, $U \subset \pi_0 H$. Conversely, let $g \in H$, $(g, v) = 0$ for any $v \in \mathscr{V}$. The inner product in H defines a functional on $\mathscr{V}$, $(g, v) = \langle g, v \rangle$, $v \in D(\Omega)$. Since $\langle g, v \rangle = 0$ for any $v \in \mathscr{V}$ and $g = \nabla p$, we have $p \in D'(\Omega)$ (see [24, Proposition I.1.1]). Therefore $\pi_0 H \subset U$ and $\pi_0 H = U$.

Denote by H_1 the closure of $\mathscr{V}$ in $H_1(\Omega)^3$. Since $\mathscr{V} \in D$, we have

$$H_1 \subset (H_1^0(\Omega))^3.$$

By Proposition 0.8, $\operatorname{div} u = 0$ for any $u \in H_1$. Denote by V_1 the set of functions $v \in (H_1^0(\Omega))^3$ with compact support that satisfy $\operatorname{div} v = 0$.

PROPOSITION 0.10. *The space H_1 coincides with the closure $\overline{V}_1$ of V_1 in $H_1(\Omega)^3$.*

PROOF. Since $\mathscr{V} \subset V_1$, we have $H_1 = \overline{\mathscr{V}} \subset \overline{V}_1$. Conversely, let $p \in D'(\Omega)$, $\nabla p \in H_{-1}(\Omega)^3$. Then $p \in L_2(\Omega_1)$ for any bounded subdomain Ω_1 of Ω. Let $v \in V_1$. Then $(\nabla p, v) = -(p, \operatorname{div} v) = 0$. Hence $(\nabla p, v) = 0$ for any $v \in \overline{V}_1$. Finally, let G be a functional on $\overline{V}_1$. Since $\overline{V}_1$ is closed in $(H_1^0)^3$, G can be represented as (g, v), $v \in \overline{V}_1$, $g \in H_{-1}(\Omega)^3$. If G equals zero on $\mathscr{V}$, then $g = \nabla p$. Therefore $(g, v) = (\nabla p, v) = 0$ for any $v \in \overline{V}_1$, and $\overline{V}_1 \subset \overline{\mathscr{V}} = H_1$.

Now consider the problem

$$\operatorname{div} v = g, \qquad v|_{\partial \Omega} = 0. \tag{0.21}$$

We suppose that the function $g \in L_2(\Omega)$ satisfies the condition

$$\int_\omega g(x_1, x_2, x_3)\, dx_1 dx_2 = 0 \tag{0.22}$$

for almost all $x_3 \in \mathbb{R}$.

To find a solution of (0.21), we consider the Neumann problem in the domain ω

$$\Delta_2 z = h, \qquad \partial_n z|_{\partial \omega} = 0. \tag{0.23}$$

The following fact is well known.

PROPOSITION 0.11. *Let $h \in L_2(\omega)$ satisfy the condition*

$$\int_\omega h\, dx_1 dx_2 = 0. \tag{0.24}$$

Then there exists a unique solution $z \in H_2(\Omega)$ of the problem (0.23) satisfying

$$\int_\omega z\, dx_1 dx_2 = 0, \tag{0.25}$$

and the inequality

$$\|z\|_{H_{l+2}(\omega)} \leq C \|h\|_{H_l(\omega)} \tag{0.26}$$

holds for $l = 0, 1, \ldots$, $C = C_l$ as $h \in H_l(\omega)$.

Note that the boundary $\partial \omega$ of the domain ω is a smooth closed curve Γ. If $n = (n_1, n_2)$ is an outer normal to Γ at some point, then the vector $\tau = (-n_2, n_1)$ is tangent to Γ at this point. As usual, we denote by $\partial_n u$ and $\partial_\tau u$ the normal and the tangential directional derivatives.

Now consider the problem with biharmonic operator:

$$\Delta_2^2 w + w = 0, \qquad w|_{\partial \omega} = 0, \qquad \partial_n w|_{\partial \omega} = \partial_\tau h_1|_{\partial \omega}. \tag{0.27}$$

PROPOSITION 0.12. *Let $h_1 \in H(\omega)$. Then there exists a unique solution $w \in H_{l+2}(\omega)$ ($l = 0, 1, \ldots$) and*

$$\|w\|_{l+2} \leq C \|h_1\|_{l+2}. \tag{0.28}$$

In Propositions 0.12, 0.13, we use the notation $\|\cdot\|_l$ for the norm in $H_l(\omega)$ and $H_l(\omega)^n$.

PROOF. The problem (0.27) is elliptic, therefore it has finite-dimensional kernel and cokernel (see [18]). The kernel is zero. Indeed, after setting $h_1 = 0$, multiplying (0.27) by w and integrating by parts, we find that $w = 0$. Since the problem (0.27) is selfadjoint, the cokernel is zero too. So this problem has a unique solution. Since

$$\|\partial_\tau h_1\|_{l+3/2} \leqslant C\|h_1\|_{l+2},$$

using the theorem on the regularity of solutions of the Dirichlet problem (0.27) (see [18]), we obtain (0.28).

PROPOSITION 0.13. *Let* $h \in H_l(\omega)$, $l = 0, 1, \ldots,$ *satisfy* (0.24), *let* z *be a solution of* (0.27), *and* w *be a solution of* (0.27) *with* $h_1 = z$. *Then the vector field*

$$v' = (v_1, v_2) = (\partial_1 z, \partial_2 z) + (\partial_2 w, -\partial_1 w) \tag{0.29}$$

satisfies the equation

$$\partial_1 v_1 + \partial_2 v_2 = h, \qquad v'|_{\partial\omega} = 0, \tag{0.30}$$

and the following estimate

$$\|v'\|_{l+1} \leqslant C\|h\|_l \tag{0.31}$$

holds.

PROOF. Obviously, by (0.23),

$$\partial_1 v_1 + \partial_2 v_2 = \partial_1^2 z + \partial_2^2 z + \partial_1\partial_2 w - \partial_2\partial_1 w = h.$$

To verify the boundary condition on v', we multiply v' by n at $\partial\omega$

$$v'n = n_1\partial_1 z + n_2\partial_2 z + n_1\partial_2 w - n_2\partial_1 w = \partial_n z + \partial_\tau w = \partial_\tau w.$$

Since $w = 0$ on $\partial\omega$, we have $\partial_\tau w = 0$ and $v'n = 0$. Multiplying v' by τ at $\partial\omega$ we obtain

$$v'\tau = -n_2\partial_1 z + n_1\partial_2 z - n_2\partial_2 w - n_1\partial_1 w = \partial_\tau z - \partial_n w = \partial_\tau z - \partial_\tau h_1 = 0$$

since $h_1 = z$ in (0.27). Hence $v' = 0$ on $\partial\omega$, and (0.30) is valid.

Applying estimates (0.26) and (0.28), we see that

$$\|v'\|_{l+1} \leqslant C(\|\nabla z\|_{l+1} + \|\nabla w\|_{l+1})$$
$$\leqslant C_1(\|z\|_{l+2} + \|w\|_{l+2}) \leqslant C_2(\|h\|_l + \|z\|_{l+2}) \leqslant C_3\|h\|_l$$

which yields (0.31).

Denote by $E_0(\omega)$ the space of functions $h \in L_2(\omega)$ satisfying (0.24). By Proposition 0.13, the operator G_2 is defined on $E_0(\omega)$,

$$G_2 h = v', \qquad G_2 : E_0(\omega) \to (H_1^0(\omega))^2, \tag{0.32}$$

where v' satisfies (0.30) and (0.31) holds.

Denote by $E_0(\Omega)$ the space of functions $g \in L_2(\Omega)$ satisfying (0.22). We define the operator G_3 acting from $E_0(\Omega)$ into the space of vector fields on Ω by the formula

$$(G_3 g)(x_1, x_2, x_3) = (G_2 g(\cdot, \cdot, x_3)(x_1, x_2), 0). \tag{0.33}$$

PROPOSITION 0.14. *The operator G_3 is bounded from $E_0(\Omega) \cap H_l(\Omega)$ to $(H_l(\Omega))^3 \cap L_2(\mathbb{R}, H_1^0(\omega)^3)$, and*

$$\operatorname{div} G_3 g = g, \qquad G_3 g|_{\partial \Omega} = 0 \tag{0.34}$$

for any $g \in E_0(\Omega)$, and for $l = 0, 1, 2, \ldots$

$$\|G_3 g\|_{L_2(\mathbb{R}, H_{l+1}(\omega)^3)}^2 + \|G_3 g\|_l^2 \leq C \|g\|_l^2. \tag{0.35}$$

PROOF. Since $G_3 g = (v_1, v_2, 0)$ and $(v_1, v_2) = v'$ satisfies (0.30), we obtain (0.34). Note that the norm in $H_l(\Omega)$ can be written in the form

$$\|u\|_l^2 = \sum_{i=0}^{l} \int_{-\infty}^{+\infty} \|\partial_3^i u(\cdot, \cdot, x_3)\|_{H_{l-i}(\omega)}^2 dx_3. \tag{0.36}$$

The norm in $L_2(\mathbb{R}, H_{l+1}(\omega))$ of the function $u(x_1, x_2, x_3)$ is defined by

$$\|u\|_{L_2(\mathbb{R}, H_{l+1}(\omega))}^2 = \int_{-\infty}^{+\infty} \|u(\cdot, \cdot, x_3)\|_{H_{l+1}(\omega)}^2 dx_3. \tag{0.37}$$

Hence, integrating $\|G_2 g(\cdot, \cdot, x_3)\|_{H_{l+1}(\omega)}^2$ with respect to x_3 and using (0.31), we obtain

$$\|G_3 g\|_{L_2(\mathbb{R}, H_{l+1}(\omega)^3)}^2 \leq C \int_{-\infty}^{+\infty} \|h(\cdot, \cdot, x_3)\|_l^2 dx_3 \leq C_1 \|h\|_l^2. \tag{0.38}$$

Since $G_2 g(\cdot, \cdot, x_3)$ depends on x_3 as a parameter and G_2 is linear, (0.33) and (0.38) imply

$$\partial_3^i G_3 g = G_3 \partial_3^i g \tag{0.39}$$

for $g \in H_l(\Omega)$, $i \leq l$. Using (0.36), (0.39), (0.31), we obtain (0.35).

PROPOSITION 0.15. *Let $u \in H_1^0(\Omega)^3$, $\operatorname{div} u = 0$. Then*

$$\int_\omega u_3(x_1, x_2, x_3) dx_1 dx_2 = 0 \quad \text{for any } x_3 \in \mathbb{R}. \tag{0.40}$$

PROOF. By Green's formula for $u \in H_1^0(\Omega)^3$ we have

$$\int_{\omega \times [a,b]} \operatorname{div} u \, dx = \int_\omega (u_3(x_1, x_2, b) - u_3(x_1, x_2, a)) dx_1 dx_2. \tag{0.41}$$

This is evident if $u \in D(\Omega)$, and holds for $u \in H_1^0(\Omega)^3$ since both sides of (0.41) depend continuously on $u \in H_1(\Omega)^3$. Obviously,

$$\int_{-\infty}^{+\infty} \|u_3(\cdot, \cdot, x_3)\|_{L_2(\omega)}^2 dx_3 \leq \|u\|^2.$$

Therefore for any $\varepsilon > 0$ and $R > 0$ there exists an $x_3 > R$ such that
$$\|u_3(\cdot, \cdot, x_3)\|_{L_2(\omega)} \leqslant \varepsilon.$$
Since $\operatorname{div} u = 0$, relation (0.41) and this estimate imply
$$\left|\int_\omega u_3(x_1, x_2, a)\, dx_1 dx_2\right| \leqslant C\varepsilon$$
for any $\varepsilon > 0$. Since a is arbitrary, this yields (0.40).

PROPOSITION 0.16. *The space H_1 coincides with the subspace V of $H_1^0(\Omega)^3$ consisting of divergence-free functions.*

PROOF. Obviously $H_1 \subset V$. Conversely, let $v \in V$. Let $\chi(x_3)$ be a smooth cut-off function, $\chi(x_3) = 1$ as $|x| \leqslant 1$, $\chi(x_3) = 0$ as $|x_3| \geqslant 2$. Let $\chi_\delta(x_3) = \chi(\delta x_3)$. Obviously $\chi_\delta v = w \in H_1^0(\Omega)^3$ and
$$\operatorname{div} w = v_3 \partial_3 \chi_\delta = h. \tag{0.42}$$
By (0.40), since χ_R does not depend on x_1, x_2, we have
$$\int_\omega v_3 \partial_3 \chi_\delta\, dx_1 dx_2 = 0 \quad \text{for any } x_3 \in \mathbb{R}. \tag{0.43}$$
Let $u = G_3(v_3 \partial_3 \chi_\delta)$. Since $v_3 \partial_3 \chi_\delta = 0$ when $|x_3| \geqslant 2/\delta$, (0.33) implies that
$$u(x_1, x_2, x_3) = 0 \quad \text{when } |x_3| \geqslant 2/\delta.$$
By (0.42) and (0.34),
$$\operatorname{div}(w - u) = 0.$$
By Proposition 0.14, $u \in H_1^0(\Omega)^3$. Therefore $w - u \in H_1^0(\Omega)^3$, $w - u = 0$ when $|x_3| \geqslant 2/\delta$. Obviously, $v = w - u + (1 - \chi_\delta)v + u$. The function $w - u$ belongs to the space V_1 considered in Proposition 0.10. It can be easily verified that
$$(1 - \chi_\delta)v \to 0 \quad \text{in } H_1(\Omega)^3 \quad \text{as } \delta \to 0.$$
Next, by Proposition 0.14,
$$\|u\|_1^2 \leqslant C\|v_3 \partial_3 \chi_\delta\|_1^2 \leqslant C\delta \|v\|_1.$$
Therefore $w - u \to v$ as $\delta \to 0$ and $v \in \overline{V}_1$. By Proposition 0.10 this yields $v \in H_1$.

Now consider the Stokes problem
$$\Delta u + \nabla p = f,$$
$$\operatorname{div} u = 0, \quad u|_{\partial \Omega} = 0. \tag{0.44}$$

PROPOSITION 0.17. *For any $f \in H_{-1}(\Omega)^3$ there exists a solution u, p of the problem (0.44), $u \in H_1$, $p \in D'(\Omega)$, $\nabla p \in H_{-1}(\Omega)^3$, u is unique, p is unique modulo constants, and the estimate*
$$\|u\|_1 + \|\nabla p\|_{-1} \leqslant C \|f\|_{-1} \tag{0.45}$$
holds.

PROOF. The proof of this proposition may be found in [13, 24]. We restrict ourselves to deducing (0.45). Multiplying (0.44) by u, we obtain

$$(\Delta u, u) + (\mathrm{grad}\, p, u) - (f, u) = -(\nabla u, \nabla u) - (f, u).$$

Hence
$$\|\nabla u\|^2 \leq \|f\|_{-1} \|u\|_1.$$

By (0.7) $\|u\|_1 \leq C\|\nabla u\|$ for $u \in H_1^0(\Omega)$, therefore $\|u\|_1 \leq C\|f\|_{-1}$. Since $\|\Delta u\|_{-1} \leq C\|u\|_1$, we get $\|\nabla p\|_{-1} \leq \|\Delta u\|_{-1} + \|f\|_{-1} \leq C_1 \|f\|_{-1}$, which yields (0.45).

PROPOSITION 0.18. *Let* $f \in H = L_2(\Omega)^3$. *Then the solution of* (0.44) *belongs to* $H_2(\omega \times]-R, R[)$, $p \in H_1(\omega \times]-R, R[)$ *for any* $R > 0$.

PROOF. Let $\chi_\delta(x_3)$ be the same as in the proof of Proposition 0.16. Multiplying (0.44) by $\chi = \chi_\delta$, we obtain

$$\begin{aligned}\Delta(\chi u) + \nabla(\chi p) &= \overline{f}, & \overline{f} &= \chi f + 2\nabla\chi \nabla u + \Delta\chi u + p\nabla\chi, \\ \mathrm{div}(\chi u) &= u_3 \partial_3 \chi, & \chi u|_{\partial\Omega} &= 0.\end{aligned} \quad (0.46)$$

Note that if Ω' is a bounded domain with smooth boundary, then the solution of the problem

$$\Delta v + \mathrm{grad}\, p = \overline{f}, \quad \mathrm{div}\, v = \overline{g}, \quad v|_{\partial\Omega'} = 0, \quad (0.47)$$

where
$$\int_{\Omega'} g\, dx = 0, \quad (0.48)$$

exists, is unique (p is unique modulo constants) and satisfies the estimate

$$\|v\|_{H_2(\Omega')^3} + \|p - p_0\|_{H_1(\Omega')} \leq C_0(\|f\|_{L_2(\Omega')^3} + \|g\|_{H_1(\Omega')}), \quad (0.49)$$

where
$$p_0 = |\Omega'|^{-1} \int_{\Omega'} p(x)\, dx, \quad (0.50)$$

$|\Omega'|$ is the volume of Ω' (see, for example, [9, 24]). Since $g = u_3 \partial_3 \chi$ satisfies (0.43) with v replaced by u, (0.49) is applicable. For Ω we take a domain with a smooth boundary such that

$$\omega \times]-R-1, R+1[\subset \Omega' \subset \omega \times]-R-2, R+2[. \quad (0.51)$$

Noticing that $\|\chi u\|_l = \|\chi u\|_{H_l(\Omega')}$, we obtain

$$\|\chi u\|_2 + \|\chi p - (\chi p)_0\|_{H_1(\Omega')} \leq C(\|\overline{f}\| + \|u_3 \partial_3 \chi\|_1). \quad (0.52)$$

By the definition of $\overline{f}$ in (0.46), we have

$$\|\overline{f}\| \leq C(\|f\| + \|\nabla u\| + \|u\| + \|p\|_{L_2(\Omega')}). \quad (0.53)$$

We have also
$$\|p\|_{L_2(\Omega')} \leq C\|\nabla p\|_{H_{-1}(\Omega')} \leq C\|\nabla p\|_{-1}. \quad (0.54)$$

Using (0.52), (0.53), (0.54) and (0.45) we obtain the needed assertion.

PROPOSITION 0.19. *Let $f \in H = L_2(\Omega)^3$, let $u \in H_1$, $p \in D(\Omega')$ be a solution of* (0.44). *Then $u' = \partial_3 u$, $p' = \partial_3 p$ are solutions of* (0.44) *with u, p, f replaced by u', p', $\partial_3 f$ respectively and*

$$\|\partial_3 u\|_1 + \|\nabla \partial_3 p\|_{-1} \leqslant C \|f\|. \tag{0.55}$$

PROOF. Denote by ∂_3^h the finite difference operator

$$\partial_3^h v(x) = (v(x_1, x_2, x_3 + h) - v(x_1, x_2, x_3))/h.$$

Applying ∂_3^h to (0.44), we obtain, since $\Omega = \omega \times \{x_3 \in \mathbb{R}\}$,

$$\Delta \partial_3^h u + \nabla \partial_3^h p = \partial_3^h f, \\ \operatorname{div} \partial_3^h u = 0, \quad \partial_3^h u \big|_{\partial \Omega} = 0. \tag{0.56}$$

From (0.45) it follows that

$$\|\partial_3^h u\|_1 + \|\nabla \partial_3^h p\|_{-1} \leqslant C \|\partial_3^h f\|_{-1}. \tag{0.57}$$

For $g \in D(\Omega)$, using a change of a variable, we obtain

$$|(\partial_3^h f, g)| = \left| \int_\Omega f(g(x_1, x_2, x_3 - h) - g(x_1, x_2, x_3)) \, dx/h \right|$$

$$= \left| \int_\omega \int_\mathbb{R} f(x', x_3) \int_0^h \partial_3 g(x', x_3 - t) \, dt \, dx_3 \, dx' \right| |h|^{-1}$$

$$\leqslant \left(\int_0^h \int_\Omega f^2(x) \, dx \, dt \right)^{1/2} \left(\int_0^h \int_\Omega |\partial_3 g(x', x_3 - t)|^2 \, dx \, dt \right)^{1/2} |h|^{-1}$$

$$\leqslant \|f\| \|\partial_3 g\|.$$

Hence

$$\|\partial_3^h f\|_{-1} \leqslant C \|f\|, \tag{0.58}$$

where C does not depend on h. Therefore $\partial_3^h u$ and $\nabla \partial_3^h p$ are uniformly bounded in H_1 and $H_{-1}(\Omega)$ respectively. For any $v \in D'(\Omega)$

$$\partial_3^h v \to \partial_3 v \quad \text{in } D'(\Omega) \quad \text{as } h \to 0.$$

Hence (0.57) yields (0.55).

PROPOSITION 0.19'. *Let $f \in H$, let $u \in H_1$, $p \in D'(\Omega)$ be a solution of* (0.44). *Then the first and second components u_1, u_2 of u satisfy the estimate*

$$\|u_1\|_2 + \|u_2\|_2 \leqslant C \|f\|, \tag{0.59}$$

and p satisfies the estimate

$$\|\partial_1 p\| + \|\partial_2 p\| \leqslant C \|f\|. \tag{0.60}$$

PROOF. Transposing terms with $\partial_3 u$ to the right-hand side of (0.44), we rewrite the equations for u_1, u_2 in the form

$$\Delta_2 u_1 + \partial_1 p = f_1 - \partial_3^2 u_1, \quad \Delta_2 u_2 + \partial_2 p = f_2 - \partial_3^2 u_2, \\ \partial_1 u_1 + \partial_2 u_2 = g, \quad g = -\partial_3 u_3, \quad u_1|_{\partial \omega} = u_2|_{\partial \omega} = 0. \tag{0.61}$$

Here we regard x_3 as a parameter. By Proposition 0.18, all the terms in (0.61) are defined for almost all x_3. The system (0.61) is a nonhomogeneous two-dimensional Navier-Stokes system, and the solution $u' = (u_1, u_2)$ of this system in the bounded domain ω satisfies the estimate

$$\|u'\|_{H_2(\omega)^2} + \|p - p_0\|_{H_1(\omega)}^2$$
$$\leq C(\|f_1 - \partial_3^2 u_1\|_{L_2(\omega)}^2 + \|f_2 - \partial_3^2 u_2\|_{L_2(\omega)}^2 + \|\partial_3 u_3\|_{H_1(\omega)}^2) \quad (0.62)$$

(see [22]). Here

$$p_0 = \int_\omega p\, dx_1 dx_2 \, |\omega|^{-1}. \quad (0.63)$$

Note that adding any constant independent of x_1, x_2 to p does not change the system (0.61). So we can choose this constant so that $p_0 = 0$ in (0.60) and in (0.63). The value of $\nabla_2 p = (\partial_1 p, \partial_2 p)$ remains the same after such a change, so after integrating (0.62) with respect to x_3, we obtain

$$\sum_{\alpha_1 + \alpha_2 \leq 2} \int_\Omega |\partial_1^{\alpha_1} \partial_2^{\alpha_2} u'|^2 dx + \int_\Omega (|\partial_1 p|^2 + |\partial_2 p|^2) dx$$
$$\leq C(\|f\|^2 + \|\partial_3 u\|_1^2). \quad (0.64)$$

Note that by (0.55) $\|\nabla \partial_3 u\|$ is bounded. Using (0.55) to etimate $\partial_3^2 u'$, $\partial_1 \partial_3 u'$, and $\partial_2 \partial_3 u'$, we obtain (0.59) and (0.60).

PROPOSITION 0.20. *Let $f \in H$, let $u \in H_1$, $p \in D'(\Omega)$ be a solution of (0.44). Then $\partial_3 p \in L_2(\Omega)$, and*

$$\|\partial_3 p\| \leq C \|f\|. \quad (0.65)$$

PROOF. Let Ω_0 be a domain with smooth boundary,

$$\{\omega \times]-2, 2[\} \subset \Omega_0 \subset \{\omega \times]-3, 3[\},$$
$$\Omega_k = \Omega_0 + ke_3, \quad e_3 = (0, 0, 1), \quad k \in \mathbb{R}. \quad (0.66)$$

Let 1_{Ω_0} be the characteristic function of the set Ω_0. Since $D(\Omega_0)$ is dense in $L_2(\Omega_0)$, there exists an $h_0 \in D(\Omega_0)$ such that

$$\int_\Omega |h_0 - 1_{\Omega_0}|^2 dx \leq \frac{1}{2} |\Omega_0|^{1/2}. \quad (0.67)$$

Let $x' = (x_1, x_2)$. Consider the function

$$r(t) = \int_\Omega \partial_3 p(x) h_0(x', x_3 - t) dx' dx_3. \quad (0.68)$$

We claim that

$$\int_{-\infty}^{+\infty} |r(t)|^2 dt \leq C \|f\|^2. \quad (0.69)$$

To prove this inequality, we use the well-known property of the convolution of two functions g and h of one real variable:

$$\int_{-\infty}^{+\infty}\left|\int_{-\infty}^{+\infty} g(x_3)h(x_3-t)\,dx_3\right|^2 dt \leq \|g\|_{L_2(\mathbb{R})}\|h\|_{L_1(\mathbb{R})}. \qquad (0.70)$$

Computing $\partial_3 p$ from (0.44), we obtain

$$r(t) = \int_\Omega (f_3 - \Delta u_3) h_0(x', x_3 - t)\,dx'dx_3$$
$$= \int_\Omega f_3 h_0(x', x_3 - t)\,dx'dx_3 + \int_\Omega \nabla u_3 \nabla h_0(x', x_3 - t)\,dx'dx_3. \qquad (0.71)$$

Obviously

$$\left|\int_\Omega f_3 h_0(x', x_3 - t)\,dx'dx_3\right|$$
$$\leq \int_{-\infty}^{+\infty} \left(\int_\omega |f_3|^2 dx'\right)^{1/2} \left(\int_\omega |h_0(x', x_3 - t)|^2 dx'\right)^{1/2} dx_3, \qquad (0.72)$$

$$\left|\int_\Omega \nabla u_3 \nabla h_0(x', x_3 - t)\,dx'dx_3\right|$$
$$\leq \int_{-\infty}^{+\infty} \left(\int_\omega |\nabla u_3|^2 dx'\right)^{1/2} \left(\int_\omega |\nabla h_0(x', x_3 - t)|^2 dx'\right)^{1/2} dx_3. \qquad (0.73)$$

Integrating in t inequalities (0.72) and (0.73) squared and using (0.70), we obtain an upper bound for the norm of the left-hand side of (0.71) in $L_2(\mathbb{R})$

$$\int_{-\infty}^{+\infty} |r(t)|^2 dt \leq C(\|f\|^2 + \|\nabla u\|^2).$$

This by (0.45) implies (0.69).

Note that

$$\|\partial_3 p - (\partial_3 p)_k\|_{L_2(\Omega_k)} \leq C\|\nabla \partial_3 p\|_{H_{-1}(\Omega_k)}, \qquad (0.74)$$

where $(\partial_3 p)_k$ is defined by

$$(\partial_3 p)_k = |\Omega_0|^{-1} \int_{\Omega_k} \partial_3 p(x)\,dx \qquad (0.75)$$

and $|\Omega_0| = |\Omega_k|$ is the volume of Ω_0 (see, for example, [9]). Note that for any $i \in \mathbb{Z}$ there exists a $t_i \in [i, i+1)$ such that

$$\left|\int_\Omega \partial_3 p h_0(x', x_3 - t_i)\,dx\right|^2 \leq 2\int_i^{i+1}\left|\int_\Omega \partial_3 p h_0(x', x_3 - t)\,dx\right|^2 dt. \qquad (0.76)$$

Let $k = k(i) = t_i$, where t_i are the same as in (0.76). By (0.66), the union of all the Ω_k, $k = k(i)$, $i \in \mathbb{Z}$, covers Ω. Hence

$$\|\partial_3 p\|^2 \leq \sum_k \|\partial_3 p\|^2_{L_2(\Omega_k)}. \qquad (0.77)$$

Obviously, by (0.67) and (0.75),

$$\|(\partial_3 p)_k\|_{L_2(\Omega_k)} = |\Omega_0|^{-1/2} \left|\int_{\Omega_k} \partial_3 p\, dx\right|$$

$$\leq |\Omega_0|^{-1/2} \left(\left|\int_{\Omega_k} \partial_3 p h_0(x', x_3 - k)\, dx\right|\right.$$

$$\left. + \left|\int_{\Omega_k} \partial_3 p(1 - h_0(x', x_3 - k))\, dx\right|\right)$$

$$\leq |\Omega_0|^{-1/2} \left|\int_{\Omega} \partial_3 p h_0(x', x_3 - k)\, dx\right| + \frac{1}{2}\|\partial_3 p\|_{L_2(\Omega_k)}.$$

Using this inequality and (0.74), we obtain

$$\|\partial_3 p\|^2_{L_2(\Omega_k)} \leq C \|\nabla \partial_3 p\|^2_{H_{-1}(\Omega_k)} + C\left|\int \partial_3 p h_0(x', x_3 - k)\, dx\right|^2. \quad (0.78)$$

By (0.76) and (0.68), we have

$$\|\partial_3 p\|^2_{L_2(\Omega_k)} \leq C \|\nabla \partial_3 p\|^2_{H_{-1}(\Omega_k)} + C \int_i^{i+1} |r(t)|\, dt. \quad (0.79)$$

Here $k = k(i)$. To estimate the norm of $\nabla \partial_3 p$ in $H_{-1}(\Omega_k)$, consider the expression $(\nabla \partial_3 p, h)$, where $h \in D(\Omega_k)^3$ is a test function. By (0.44)

$$(\nabla \partial_3 p, h) = -(\nabla p, \partial_3 h) = (\Delta u - f, \partial_3 h) = (-f, \partial_3 h) + (\nabla \partial_3 u, \nabla h).$$

Therefore

$$|(\nabla \partial_3 p, h)| / \|h\|_1 \leq \|f\|_{L_2(\Omega_k)} + \|\nabla \partial_3 u\|_{L_2(\Omega_k)}.$$

Hence

$$\|\nabla \partial_3 p\|^2_{H_{-1}(\Omega_k)} \leq 2\|f\|^2_{L_2(\Omega_k)} + 2\|\nabla \partial_3 u\|^2_{L_2(\Omega_k)}. \quad (0.80)$$

Using (0.78), (0.79), (0.80), we obtain

$$\|\partial_3 p\|^2_{L_2(\Omega_k)} \leq C\left(\int_i^{i+1} |r(t)|^2\, dt + \|f\|^2_{L_2(\Omega_k)} + \|\nabla \partial_3 u\|^2_{L_2(\Omega_k)}\right). \quad (0.81)$$

Note that by the definition of $k = k(i)$ and Ω_k, any point $x_3 \in \mathbb{R}$ belongs to no more than 7 different sets Ω_k. Summing (0.81) with respect to i and $k = k(i)$, and taking into consideration (0.77) and the above remark, we conclude that

$$\|\partial_3 p\|^2 \leq C_1 \left(\int_{-\infty}^{+\infty} |r(t)|^2\, dt + \|f\|^2 + \|\nabla \partial_3 u\|^2\right).$$

Using (0.55) and (0.69), we obtain (0.65).

PROPOSITION 0.21. *Let $f \in H$, let $u \in H_1$, $p \in D'(\Omega)$ be a solution of (0.44). Then*

$$\|u\|_2 + \|\nabla p\| \leq C \|f\|. \quad (0.82)$$

PROOF. We already have the estimates (0.59), (0.60) and (0.65), so it suffices to estimate $\|u_3\|_2$. The equation for u_3 in the system (0.44) is of the form
$$\Delta u_3 = f_3 - \partial_3 p, \qquad u_3|_{\partial\Omega} = 0.$$
Proposition 0.6 implies the estimate
$$\|u_3\|_2 \leqslant C \left(\|f_3\| + \|\partial_3 p\|\right). \tag{0.83}$$
From (0.83), (0.65), (0,59) and (0.60) it follows that (0.82) is valid.

PROPOSITION 0.22. *Let Π be the orthogonal projection from H onto H_0. Then the operator $\Pi\Delta$ is defined and bounded on $H_2(\Omega)^3 \cap H_1 = H_2$, $\Pi\Delta H_2 = H_0$ and for any $u \in H_2$ we have*
$$\|u\|_2 \leqslant C \|\Pi\Delta u\|, \tag{0.84}$$
where $\|\cdot\|_2$ is the norm in $H_2(\Omega)^3$.

PROOF. Obviously $\Delta u \in H$ if $u \in H_2(\Omega)^3$. By Proposition 0.9,
$$\Delta u = \Pi\Delta u - \nabla p, \tag{0.85}$$
where $p \in D'(\Omega)$, $\nabla p \in L_2(\Omega)^3$, $\nabla p = -\pi_0(\Delta u)$. The equation (0.85), where $u \in H_1$, is equivalent to (0.44) for $f = \Pi\Delta u$ and by Proposition 0.21 the estimate (0.84) holds. Since (0.44) has a solution $u \in H_2$ for any $f \in H$ by Propositions 0.17 and 0.21, the operator $\Pi\Delta$ maps H_2 on $H_0 = \Pi H$.

§1. Projections and multiplications by weight functions

In this section properties of the projection Π onto the space H_0 of divergence-free vector fields are investigated. By Propositions 0.8 and 0.9,
$$H_0 = \{u \in H \colon \operatorname{div} u = 0, \ l_n u = 0\}. \tag{1.1}$$
This space can be also obtained as the closure in H of the set V defined by (0.20) and consisting of smooth divergence-free vector fields with compact support in Ω. The closure of V in $H_1(\Omega)$ is denoted by H_1. By Propositions 0.16 and 0.3,
$$H_1 = \{u \in H_1(\Omega)^3 \colon \operatorname{div} u = 0, \ u|_{\partial\Omega} = 0\}. \tag{1.2}$$
Note that by (0.7)
$$-(\Delta v, v) = \|\nabla v\|^2 \geqslant \lambda_1 \|v\|^2 \tag{1.3}$$
for any $v \in H_1^0(\Omega)$. Hence the norm $\|v\|_1$ is equivalent to $\|\nabla v\|$.

We denote by H_2 the space
$$H_2 = \{u \in H_2(\Omega)^3 \colon \operatorname{div} u = 0, \ u|_{\partial\Omega} = 0\}. \tag{1.4}$$
By Propositions 0.22, 0.16 and 0.3, this space coincides with $(\Pi\Delta)^{-1} H_0$.

Now we introduce weight functions, which will be systematically used below. By $\varphi = \varphi(x, \varepsilon, \rho, \gamma)$ we shall denote a function of one variable $x_3 \in \mathbb{R}$ depending on the parameters $\varepsilon > 0$, $\rho \geq 0$ and $\gamma \in \mathbb{R}$. It is assumed everywhere below that the following conditions

$$\varphi(x, \varepsilon, \rho, \gamma) \geq 1, \qquad \varphi(x, \varepsilon, \rho, \gamma) = \varphi(\varepsilon x, 1, \rho, 1)^{\gamma}, \qquad (1.5)$$

$$\left.\begin{array}{l}\varphi(x, 1, \rho, \gamma) \text{ does not depend on } \rho \text{ for } |x_3| \leq \rho, \\ \varphi(x, 1, \rho, \gamma) = \varphi(\rho + 1, 1, \rho, \gamma) \text{ as } |x_3| \geq \rho + 1,\end{array}\right\} \qquad (1.6)$$

$$|(\partial^{\alpha}\varphi(x, \varepsilon, \rho, \gamma))| \leq C\varepsilon^{|\alpha|}\varphi(x, \varepsilon, \rho, \gamma), \qquad (1.7)$$

hold, where $|\alpha| \leq 3$, C does not depend on x, ρ and ε. The dependence on ρ is assumed to be monotone:

$$\varphi(x, \varepsilon, \rho_1, \gamma) \geq \varphi(x, \varepsilon, \rho_2, \gamma) \text{ when } \rho_1 \geq \rho_2 \geq 1, \ \gamma \geq 0. \qquad (1.8)$$

Henceforth for brevity we shall use the notation

$$\varphi = \varphi(x, \varepsilon, \rho, \gamma).$$

By (1.6) there exists a limit function

$$\Phi(x, \varepsilon, \gamma) = \lim_{\rho \to +\infty} \varphi(x, \varepsilon, \rho, \gamma). \qquad (1.9)$$

We shall often suppose that the following property holds

$$C'\Phi(x, \varepsilon, \gamma) \leq \Phi(x, 1, \gamma) \leq C\Phi(x, \varepsilon, \gamma), \qquad (1.10)$$

where C does not depend on x.

In the case when (1.10) holds, we denote by $H_{l,\gamma}$, $\gamma \geq 0$, the space with the norm

$$\|u\|_{l,\gamma}^2 = \sum_{|\alpha| \leq l} \int_{\Omega} \Phi^2(x, 1, \gamma)|\partial^{\alpha}u(x)|^2 \, dz. \qquad (1.11)$$

If $\gamma = 0$, $H_{l,\gamma}$ coincides with $H_l(\Omega)$. By (1.10) the norm in $H_{l,\gamma}$ with $\Phi(x, 1, \gamma)$ replaced by $\Phi(x, \varepsilon, \gamma)$ is equivalent to the original norm.

The main example of weights is the weights Φ defined by

$$\Phi(x, 1, \gamma) = (1 + |x_3|^2)^{\gamma/2}. \qquad (1.12)$$

All the results of the paper are valid with such Φ.

Obviously (1.10) holds for such Φ. The existence of φ satisfying (1.5)–(1.9) will be proved below in Lemma 1.0 for the case of (1.12) and in more general case in Lemma 1.8.

REMARK 1.1. All the results of the paper are valid for any function φ satisfying (1.5)–(1.10). One more example of the corresponding function Φ is

$$\Phi(x, 1, \gamma) = \exp\left[\gamma \ln^q(1 + |x_3|^2)\right], \qquad 1 \geq q \geq 0. \qquad (1.12')$$

This can be seen after comparing the statements of Theorems 3.1 and 3.2.

REMARK 1.2. Some results of the paper can be specialized to the case when instead of (1.7) we assume

$$|\partial^\alpha \varphi(x, \varepsilon, \rho, \gamma)| \leq C\varepsilon^{|\alpha|}\varphi(x, \varepsilon, \rho, \gamma'), \tag{1.13}$$

where $\gamma' \leq \gamma$, γ' depends only on γ (see, for example, Theorem 2.1 for the example of such a specification).

Everywhere in this paper we shall take $0 < \varepsilon < \varepsilon_0 \leq 1$, where ε_0 is sufficiently small, $\rho \geq 1$ and later ρ will tend to $+\infty$. All constants which do not depend on ε and ρ we denote by the letter C with indices; this letter with the same index may denote different constants in different inequalities. We shall denote by φ the operator of multiplication by the function φ, this operator is bounded and invertible by (1.6) and (1.5) in the spaces $H_l(\Omega)$, $l = 0, 1, 2, 3$.

LEMMA 1.0. *There exists a function φ satisfying (1.5)–(1.8) and (1.10), (1.12).*

PROOF. Let $\chi \in C^\infty(\mathbb{R})$, $\chi(\tau) \geq 0$ for any τ,

$$\chi(\tau) = 0 \quad \text{when } \tau \leq 0, \qquad \chi(\tau) = 1 \quad \text{when } \tau \geq 1, \tag{1.14}$$

$$\chi'(\tau) \geq 0 \quad \text{for any } \tau. \tag{1.15}$$

Let $\rho \geq 1$. For $r \geq 0$ put

$$g_\rho(r) = (1 + r^2)(1 - \chi(r - \rho)) + (1 + \rho^2)\chi(r - \rho). \tag{1.16}$$

Obviously, $g_\rho(r)$ is infinitely differentiable with respect to r when $r \geq 0$, and by (1.14)

$$g_\rho(r) = 1 + r^2 \quad \text{when } r \leq \rho, \qquad g_\rho(r) = 1 + \rho^2 \quad \text{when } r \geq \rho + 1. \tag{1.17}$$

Note that

$$\partial g_\rho(r)/\partial \rho \geq 0 \quad \text{when } \rho \geq 1, \qquad r \geq 0. \tag{1.18}$$

Indeed, by (1.16)

$$\partial_\rho g_\rho(r) = (1 + r^2)\chi'(r - \rho) + 2\rho\chi(r - \rho) - (1 + \rho^2)\chi'(r - \rho)$$
$$= 2\rho\chi(r - \rho) + \chi'(r - \rho)(r^2 - \rho^2).$$

Since $\chi \geq 0$, $\chi' \geq 0$ and $\chi'(r - \rho) = 0$ when $r - \rho \leq 0$, this implies (1.18).

A weight function $\varphi(x, \varepsilon, \rho, \gamma)$ is defined by

$$\varphi(x) = \varphi(x, \varepsilon, \rho, \gamma) = (g_\rho(|\varepsilon x_3|))^{\gamma/2}. \tag{1.19}$$

Obviously, (1.5) is valid, (1.17) implies (1.6), (1.8) follows from (1.18). Now we shall prove (1.7). Since φ depends on εx_3, it is sufficient to prove (1.7) for $\varepsilon = 1$. We have

$$\partial_i \varphi = (\gamma/2)g_\rho(|x_3|)^{\gamma/2-1}\partial_i(g_\rho(|x_3|)), \tag{1.20}$$

$$\partial_i\partial_j\varphi = (\gamma/2)g_\rho(|x_3|)^{\gamma/2-1}\partial_i\partial_j(g_\rho(|x_3|))$$
$$+ (\gamma/2)(\gamma/2 - 1)\partial_i(g_\rho(|x_3|))\partial_j(g_\rho(|x_3|))g_\rho(|x_3|)^{\gamma/2-2}. \quad (1.21)$$

It can easily be seen that (1.7) for $\gamma = 1$ implies (1.7) for all γ. Therefore we restrict ourselves to the case $\gamma = 1$. Since φ is even, we shall consider only $x_3 \geq 0$. By (1.16),

$$\partial_3 g_\rho(x_3) = \partial_3[(1 + x_3^2)(1 - \chi(x_3 - \rho)) + (1 + \rho^2)\chi(x_3 - \rho)]$$
$$= 2x_3(1 - \chi(x_3 - \rho)) + (\rho^2 - x_3^2)\chi'(x_3 - \rho).$$

Therefore

$$|\partial_3 g_\rho(x_3)| \leq 2x_3 + |x_3 - \rho|(x_3 + \rho)|\chi'(x_3 - \rho)|$$
$$\leq 2(1 + x_3^2)^{1/2} + |x_3 - \rho| + (x_3 + \rho)|\chi'(x_3 - \rho)|.$$

Since $\chi'(|x_3| - \rho)$ may be nonzero only if $\rho < |x_3| < \rho + 1$, this implies the estimate

$$|\partial_3 g_\rho(|x_3|)| \leq 2(1 + |x_3|^2)^{1/2} + |x_3 + \rho||\chi'(x_3 - \rho)|$$
$$\leq C(1 + |x_3|^2)^{1/2} \quad (1.22)$$

for $|x_3| \leq \rho + 1$. For $|x_3| \geq \rho + 1$, we have $\partial_3 g_\rho(|x_3|) = 0$. If $\rho \leq |x_3| \leq \rho + 1$ and $\rho \geq 1$, then $|x_3| \leq 2\rho$,

$$g_\rho(|x_3|) \geq 1 + \rho^2 \geq 1 + |x_3|^2/4 \geq (1 + |x_3|^2)/4. \quad (1.23)$$

By this inequality and by (1.17) we get

$$|\partial_3 g_\rho(|x_3|)| \leq Cg_\rho(|x_3|)^{1/2}. \quad (1.24)$$

By using (1.20) and (1.24) we obtain

$$|\partial_3\varphi| \leq C_1\gamma g_\rho(|x_3|)^{\gamma/2-1} g_\rho(|x_3|)^{1/2}. \quad (1.25)$$

This implies (1.7) for $|\alpha| = 1$.

Now if we differentiate $\partial_3 g_\rho$ with respect to x_3, we obtain

$$\partial_3^2 g_\rho(x_3) = 2(1 - \chi(x_3 - \rho)) - 4\chi'(x_3 - \rho)x_3$$
$$+ (\rho^2 - x_3^2)\chi''(x_3 - \rho). \quad (1.26)$$

Note that $\chi'(x_3 - \rho)$ and $\chi''(x_3 - \rho)$ equal zero if $|x_3| < \rho$ and $|x_3| > \rho + 1$. Therefore it is sufficient to consider the case $\rho < |x_3| < \rho + 1$. For such $x_3 > 0$ we have

$$|(\rho^2 - |x_3|^2)| \leq 2\rho + 1 \leq 4(1 + |x_2|^2)^{1/2}.$$

Hence by (1.26)

$$|\partial_3^2 g_\rho(x_3)| \leq 2 + C_0(1 + |x_3|^2)^{1/2} + C(1 + |x_3|^2)^{1/2}$$
$$\leq C_1(1 + |x_3|^2)^{1/2} \leq C_2 g_\rho(x_3)^{1/2}, \quad (1.26')$$

when $0 \leqslant |x_3| \leqslant \rho + 1$. By using (1.21), (1.24), (1.26') we obtain the inequality

$$|\partial_3^2 \varphi| \leqslant C_1 g_\rho(x_3)^{\gamma/2 - 1/2}. \quad (1.26'')$$

This implies (1.7) for $|\alpha| = 2$. In the case $|\alpha| = 3$, we obtain (1.7) after differentiating $\partial_3 g_\rho$ in a similar way.

Obviously, the function Φ defined by (1.9) equals $(1 + |x_3|^2)^{\gamma/2}$. Further, we clearly have

$$(1 + |x_3|^2)^{\gamma/2} \geqslant (1 + |\varepsilon x_3|^2)^{\gamma/2} \geqslant \varepsilon^{\gamma/2}(1 + |x_3|^2)^{\gamma/2},$$

when $\gamma \geqslant 0$, and an analogous inequality is valid for $\gamma < 0$. Therefore (1.10) is valid and Lemma 1.9 is proved.

REMARK 1.3. The function $\varphi(x, \varepsilon, \rho, \gamma)$ constructed in Lemma 1.9 satisfies the following inequality, which is stronger than (1.7),

$$|\partial^\alpha \varphi(x, \varepsilon, \rho, \gamma)| \leqslant C\varepsilon^{|\alpha|} \varphi(x, \varepsilon, \rho, \gamma - 1).$$

This inequality coincides with (1.13), where $\gamma' = \gamma - 1$. This follows directly from (1.25) and (1.26'').

Now several technical propositions will be formulated.

PROPOSITION 1.1.

$$C^{-1} \|u\|_1 \leqslant \|\nabla u\| \leqslant C \|u\|_1 \quad \forall u \in H_1^0(\Omega),$$
$$C^{-1} \|u\|_2 \leqslant \|\Delta u\| \leqslant C \|u\|_2 \quad \forall u \in H_1^0(\Omega) \cap H_2(\Omega).$$

PROOF. Obviously

$$\|u\|_1^2 = \|u\|^2 + \|\nabla u\|^2.$$

Using (1.3), we obtain the first inequality. Proposition 0.6 implies the second inequality.

PROPOSITION 1.2. Let ε be small, $\varphi = \varphi(x, \varepsilon, \rho, \gamma)$. Then

$$C^{-1} \|\nabla(\varphi u)\| \leqslant \|\varphi \nabla u\| \leqslant C \|\nabla(\varphi u)\| \quad \forall u \in H_1^0(\Omega), \quad (1.27)$$

$$\|\varphi \nabla u\| + \|\varphi u\| \leqslant C \|\varphi \nabla u\| \quad \forall u \in H_1^0(\Omega), \quad (1.28)$$

$$\sum_{|\alpha| \leqslant 2} \|\varphi \partial^\alpha u\| \leqslant C \|\varphi \Delta u\| \quad \forall u \in H_1^0(\Omega) \cap H_2(\Omega), \quad (1.29)$$

$$C^{-1} \|\varphi \Delta u\| \leqslant \|\Delta(\varphi u)\| \leqslant C \|\varphi \Delta u\| \quad \forall u \in H_1^0(\Omega) \cap H_2(\Omega). \quad (1.30)$$

PROOF. Obviously

$$\varphi \nabla u = \nabla(\varphi u) - u \nabla \varphi. \quad (1.31)$$

Therefore by (1.7),

$$\big| \|\varphi \nabla u\| - \|\nabla(\varphi u)\| \big| \leqslant \|u \nabla \varphi\| \leqslant C\varepsilon \|\varphi u\|. \quad (1.32)$$

Inequality (1.3) implies

$$\|\varphi u\| \leqslant C \|\nabla(\varphi u)\|. \quad (1.33)$$

From (1.32) and (1.33) we get

$$\left|\|\varphi \nabla u\| - \|\nabla(\varphi u)\|\right| \leq C_1 \varepsilon \|\nabla(\varphi u)\|. \tag{1.34}$$

This implies (1.27) if ε is small. Now (1.33) and (1.27) imply (1.28). Setting φu instead of u we obtain from (0.10)

$$\|\partial^\alpha(\varphi u)\| \leq C \|\Delta(\varphi u)\|, \qquad |\alpha| \leq 2. \tag{1.35}$$

Taking $|\alpha| \leq 1$ and using (1.28) and (1.27), we obtain:

$$\|\varphi \nabla u\| + \|\varphi u\| \leq C \|\nabla(\varphi u)\| \leq C_1 \|\Delta(\varphi u)\|. \tag{1.36}$$

Obviously

$$\partial_i \partial_j (\varphi u) = \varphi \partial_i \partial_j u + \partial_i \varphi \partial_j u + \partial_j \varphi \partial_i u + u \partial_i \partial_j \varphi. \tag{1.37}$$

Using (1.7) and (1.28), we obtain:

$$\|\varphi \partial_i \partial_j u - \partial_i \partial_j (\varphi u)\| \leq C \varepsilon \|\varphi \nabla u\| + C \varepsilon^2 \|\varphi u\| \leq C_1 \varepsilon \|\varphi \nabla u\|. \tag{1.38}$$

Hence by (1.35) and (1.36), we have

$$\|\varphi \partial^\alpha u\| \leq \|\partial^\alpha(\varphi u)\| + C_1 \varepsilon \|\varphi \nabla u\| \leq C_2 \|\Delta(\varphi u)\|. \tag{1.39}$$

Inequality (1.38) implies

$$\left|\|\varphi \Delta u\| - \|\Delta(\varphi u)\|\right| \leq C \varepsilon \|\varphi \nabla u\|. \tag{1.40}$$

From (1.39) and (1.40) we get

$$\sum_{|\alpha| \leq 2} \|\varphi \partial^\alpha u\| \leq C_3 \|\varphi \Delta u\| + C_4 \varepsilon \|\nabla u\|.$$

Since ε is small, this implies (1.29). Inequality (1.30) follows from (1.40) and (1.36).

PROPOSITION 1.3. *Let ε be small, $u \in H_l(\Omega)$, $l = 0, 1, 2$. Then*

$$C^{-1} \sum_{|\alpha| \leq l} \|\partial^\alpha(\varphi u)\| \leq \sum_{|\alpha| \leq l} \|\varphi \partial^\alpha u\| \leq C \sum_{|\alpha| \leq l} \|\partial^\alpha \varphi u\|. \tag{1.41}$$

PROOF. This inequality follows from (1.32) and (1.38) since ε is small. Now put

$$\pi_0 = I - \Pi, \tag{1.42}$$

where Π is the projection from H onto H_0.

The following theorem is the main result of this section.

THEOREM 1.1. *Let $\varphi = \varphi(x, \varepsilon, \rho, \gamma)$. Then*

$$\|\varphi \pi_0 h\| \leq C \|\varphi h\| \qquad \forall h \in H. \tag{1.43}$$

The proof of this theorem is based on several lemmas that we state and prove below.

Let us consider the Dirichlet problem

$$\Delta p_0 = \operatorname{div} h, \qquad p_0|_{\partial \Omega} = 0, \tag{1.44}$$

where $h \in H$. This problem has a unique solution $u \in H_1^0(\Omega)$ by Proposition 0.6. So the operator

$$Q_0: h \to p_0 \tag{1.44'}$$

is well defined.

LEMMA 1.1. *The operator Q_0 from H to $H_1^0(\Omega)$ is bounded. Moreover*

$$\|\varphi \nabla Q_0 h\| + \|\varphi Q_0 h\| \leq C \|\varphi h\| \quad \forall h \in H. \tag{1.45}$$

PROOF. By multiplying (1.44) by $\varphi^2 p_0$, we obtain:

$$-(\nabla p_0, \nabla(\varphi^2 p_0)) = -(h, \nabla(\varphi^2 p_0)).$$

Hence, by (1.7) and (1.28), we obtain

$$|(\varphi^2 \nabla p_0, \nabla p_0)| \leq |(\nabla p_0, p_0 \nabla \varphi^2)| + |(h, (\nabla \varphi^2) p_0)| + |(h, \varphi^2 \nabla p_0)|$$
$$\leq C\varepsilon \|\varphi \nabla p_0\| \|\varphi p_0\| + \|\varphi h\|(\|\varphi \nabla p_0\| + C\varepsilon \|\varphi p_0\|)$$
$$\leq C_1 \varepsilon \|\varphi \nabla p_0\|^2 + C_2 \|\varphi h\| \|\varphi \nabla p_0\|$$
$$\leq C_1 \varepsilon \|\varphi \nabla p_0\|^2 + (1/3) \|\varphi \nabla p_0\|^2 + C_3 \|\varphi h\|^2.$$

Since ε is small, $C_1 \varepsilon \leq 1/3$ and we have

$$(1/3) \|\varphi \nabla p_0\|^2 \leq C_3 \|\varphi h\|^2.$$

Using (1.28), we obtain (1.45).

Consider now the Neumann problem

$$\Delta p_2 - p_2 = 0, \quad \partial_n p_2 |_{\partial \Omega} = l_n \overline{g}. \tag{1.46}$$

Here and below we denote by ∂_n the derivative in the direction of the outward normal n to the boundary $\partial \Omega$, and by $l_n g$ the operator of scalar multiplication of a vector $g \in \mathbb{R}^3$ by the normal n, $n \perp \partial \Omega$.

LEMMA 1.2. *Let $\overline{g} \in E$, where E is defined by (0.18). Then the operator $Q_2: E \to H_1(\Omega)$ is defined for such $\overline{g}$, for $\overline{g} \in D(\overline{\Omega})$ the function $p_2 = Q_2 \overline{g}$ is a solution of (1.46) and the following estimate holds for any $\overline{g} \in E$*

$$\|\varphi p_2\| + \|\varphi \nabla p_2\| \leq C (\|\varphi \overline{g}\| + \|\text{div } \overline{g}\|). \tag{1.47}$$

PROOF. Since $D(\overline{\Omega})$ is dense in E and the functions φ and φ^{-1} are smooth and bounded, it is sufficient to construct Q_2 and to prove (1.47) for $\overline{g} \in D(\overline{\Omega})$. The smooth solution p_2 can be obtained by using the Fourier transform F with respect to x_3 as in the proof of Lemma 2.7. The function $\overline{p} = p(x', \xi_3)$, $x' = (x_1, x_2)$, satisfies the equation

$$\Delta_2 \overline{p}_2 - (1 + \xi_3^2) \overline{p}_2 = 0, \quad \partial_n \overline{p}_2 |_{\partial \omega} = l_n \overline{g}. \tag{1.48}$$

There exists a unique smooth solution of this problem, which decays rapidly as $|\xi_3| \to \infty$. Thus $p_2 = F^{-1} \overline{p}_2$ is a smooth rapidly decaying as $|x_3| \to \infty$

solution of (1.46) (p_2 decays as $|x_3| \to \infty$ since $\bar{p}_2$ is smooth with respect to ξ_3).

Multiply (1.46) by $-\varphi p_2$. Using Green's formula, we obtain

$$(\nabla p_2, \nabla(\varphi^2 p_2)) + \|\varphi p_2\|^2 = \int_{\partial\Omega} \partial_n p_2 \varphi^2 p_2 \, d\sigma. \tag{1.49}$$

Using Green's formula again, we obtain

$$\int_{\partial\Omega} \partial_n p_2 \varphi^2 p_2 \, d\sigma = \int_{\partial\Omega} l_n \bar{g} \varphi^2 p_2 \, d\sigma = \int_{\Omega} \operatorname{div}(\bar{g}\varphi^2 p_2) \, dx$$
$$= \int_{\Omega} \bar{g} \nabla(\varphi^2 p_2) \, dx + \int_{\Omega} \operatorname{div} \bar{g} \varphi^2 p_2 \, dx. \tag{1.50}$$

Therefore (1.49) by (1.7) implies

$$\|\varphi \nabla p_2\|^2 + \|\varphi p_2\|^2 \leq C\varepsilon \|\varphi \nabla p_2\| \|\varphi p_2\| + \|\varphi \bar{g}\| \|\varphi \nabla p_2\|$$
$$+ C\varepsilon \|\varphi \bar{g}\| \|\varphi p_2\| + C\|\varphi \operatorname{div} \bar{g}\| \|\varphi p_2\|.$$

This gives (1.47).

Denote by S the operator of averaging with respect to $(x_1, x_2) \in \omega$:

$$Sh(x_3) = |\omega|^{-1} \int_\omega h(x_1, x_2, x_3) \, dx_1 \, dx_2, \tag{1.51}$$

where $|\omega|$ denotes the area of the domain ω.

We have

$$\|\varphi Sh\|_{L_2(\mathbb{R})} \leq C \|\varphi h\|. \tag{1.51'}$$

Indeed,

$$\int_{-\infty}^{+\infty} |\varphi Sh|^2 \, dx_3 \leq \int_{-\infty}^{+\infty} |\omega|^{-2} \left(\int_\omega |h| \, dx_1 dx_2\right)^2 \varphi^2(x_3) \, dx_3$$
$$\leq |\omega|^{-1} \int_{-\infty}^{+\infty} \int_\omega |h|^2 \, dx_1 dx_2 \, \varphi^2(x_3) dx_3 = |\omega|^{-1} \|\varphi h\|^2.$$

On E define the operator Q_4 by the formula

$$Q_4 \bar{g} = S(g_3 - \partial_3 Q_2 \bar{g}), \tag{1.52}$$

where Q_2 is defined in Lemma 1.2, $\bar{g} = (g_1, g_2, g_3)$. By (1.51') and (1.47), Q_4 is a bounded operator from E into $L_2(\mathbb{R})$.

LEMMA 1.3. *The operator Q_4 from H_0 to $L_2(\mathbb{R})$ is bounded. Moreover*

$$\int_{-\infty}^{+\infty} |\varphi Q_4 \bar{g}|^2 \, dx_3 \leq C \|\varphi \bar{g}\|^2. \tag{1.53}$$

The function $p_4' = Q_4 \bar{g}$ satisfies (in the sense of distributions) the equation

$$\partial_3 p_4' + Sp_2 = 0, \tag{1.54}$$

where $p_2 = Q_2 \bar{g}$ is the solution of (1.46).

PROOF. Since V is dense in H_0, it suffices to consider $\bar{g} \in V$. Note that if $\bar{g}_n \to \bar{g}$ in H_0, $\bar{g}_n \in V$, then $\bar{g}_n \to g$ in E since $\operatorname{div} \bar{g}_n = 0$. By

Lemma 1.2, the operator $\partial_3 Q_2$ from E to $L_2(\Omega)$ is bounded, and therefore by the above argument is continuous from E to $L_2(\Omega)$. Using (1.51') we see that the operator (1.52) from H_0 to $L_2(\mathbb{R})$ is bounded.

Differentiating (1.52) with respect to x_3 and using the fact that $\operatorname{div}\overline{g} = 0$ when $\overline{g} \in V$, we obtain

$$\partial_3 p_4' = |\omega|^{-1} \int_\omega (\partial_3 g_3 - \partial_3^2 p_2) \, dx_1 dx_2$$
$$= -|\omega|^{-1} \int_\omega [\partial_1 g_1 + \partial_2 g_2 - (\partial_1^2 + \partial_2^2) p_2] \, dx_1 dx_2$$
$$+ |\omega|^{-1} \int_\omega p_2 \, dx_1 dx_2. \qquad (1.55)$$

By Green's formula the first summand in (1.55) equals

$$\int_{\partial\omega} (g_1 n_1 + g_2 n_2 - \partial_1 p_2 n_1 - \partial_2 p_2 n_2) \, ds = \int_{\partial\omega} (l_n \overline{g} - \partial_n p_2) \, ds = 0.$$

Hence (1.54) holds for $\overline{g} \in V$. Since the operators SQ_2 and Q_4 from H_0 into $L_2(\mathbb{R})$ are continuous, and ∂_3 is continuous from $L_2(\mathbb{R})$ into $D'(\mathbb{R})$, we obtain (1.54) for any $\overline{g} \in H_0$.

To prove (1.53), note that by (1.51')

$$\int_{-\infty}^{+\infty} |\varphi Q_4 \overline{g}|^2 \, dx_3 \leq C(\|\varphi \overline{g}\|^2 + \|\varphi \partial_3 Q_2 \overline{g}\|^2). \qquad (1.56)$$

From this inequality and (1.47), where $\operatorname{div}\overline{g} = 0$ (since $\overline{g} \in V$), we get (1.53), and Lemma 1.3 is proved.

Now consider the equation for $p_3 = p_3(x_1, x_2, x_3)$

$$\Delta p_3 + p_2 - Sp_2 = 0, \quad Sp_3 = 0, \quad \partial_n p_3|_{\partial\Omega} = 0, \qquad (1.57)$$

where S is defined by (1.51), p_2 is a function from $L_2(\Omega)$.

LEMMA 1.4. *The equation* (1.57) *has a unique solution* $p_3 \in H_2(\Omega)$, *so the operator* Q_3, $Q_3 p_2 = p_3$, $Q_3: L_2(\Omega) \to H_2(\Omega)$ *is well defined on* $L_2(\Omega)$. *Moreover*

$$\sum_{|\alpha| \leq 2} \|\varphi \partial^\alpha p_3\| \leq C \|\varphi p_2\| \qquad (1.58)$$

for any $p_2 \in L_2(\Omega)$.

PROOF. Let us use the Fourier method. Let $e_0 = |\omega|^{-1/2}$, e_i, $i = 1, 2, \ldots$, be orthonormal eigenfunctions of the Laplace operator $\Delta_2 = \partial_1^2 + \partial_2^2$ with the Neumann boundary condition on $\partial\omega$, $\partial_n e_j|_{\partial\omega} = 0$,

$$-\Delta_2 e_j = \lambda_j e_j, \quad 0 = \lambda_0 < \lambda_1 \leq \lambda_2 \leq \cdots. \qquad (1.59)$$

The solution of (1.57) is of the form

$$p_3 = \sum_{j=1}^\infty a_j(x_3) e_j(x_1, x_2). \qquad (1.60)$$

The coefficients a_j satisfy the equations

$$\partial_3^2 a_j - \lambda_j a_j = -b_j, \tag{1.61}$$

where

$$b_j(x_3) = (p_2, e_j), \quad j = 1, 2, \ldots. \tag{1.62}$$

Obviously

$$p_2 = \sum_{j=1}^{\infty} b_j(x_3) e_j(x_1, x_2) + Sp_2. \tag{1.63}$$

Since $p_2 \in L_2(\Omega)$, we have $b_j \in L_2(\mathbb{R})$. Equation (1.61) has a unique solution $a_j \in H_2(\mathbb{R})$. Multiplying (1.61) by $\varphi^2 a_j$ and integrating by parts, we obtain

$$-\int_{-\infty}^{+\infty} (\partial_3 a_j \partial_3(\varphi^2 a_j) + \lambda_j \varphi^2 a_j^2) dx_3 = \int_{-\infty}^{+\infty} b_j \varphi^2 a_j \, dx_3.$$

By using (1.7) with small ε, $\varepsilon \ll \lambda_1$, we obtain:

$$\int_{-\infty}^{+\infty} (\varphi^2 |\partial_3 a_j|^2 + \lambda_j \varphi^2 a_j^2) dx_3 \leq C \int_{-\infty}^{+\infty} \varphi^2 b_j^2 \, dx_3, \tag{1.64}$$

where C does not depend on j.

Multiplying (1.61) by $\varphi^2 \partial_3^2 a_j$ and using (1.7), we get:

$$\int_{-\infty}^{+\infty} (\varphi^2 |\partial_3^2 a_j|^2 + \lambda_j \varphi^2 |\partial_3 a_j|^2) \, dx$$

$$\leq \int_{-\infty}^{+\infty} \left[\frac{1}{2} \varphi^2 |\partial_3^2 a_j|^2 + \frac{1}{2} \varphi^2 b_j^2 + C\varepsilon \lambda_j \varphi^2 |\partial_3 a_j|^2 + \varphi^2 |a_j|^2 \right] dx_3. \tag{1.65}$$

Since ε is small, from (1.64) and (1.65) we deduce the inequality

$$\int_{-\infty}^{+\infty} \varphi^2 \left[|\partial_3^2 a_j|^2 + \lambda_j |\partial_3 a_j|^2 + \lambda_j |a_j|^2 \right] dx_3 \leq \int_{-\infty}^{+\infty} \varphi^2 b_j^2 \, dx_3. \tag{1.66}$$

Using (1.61) and (1.66), we obtain

$$\int_{-\infty}^{+\infty} \varphi^2 \lambda_j^2 a_j^2 \, dx_3 \leq C \int_{-\infty}^{+\infty} \left[\varphi^2 |\partial_3 a_j|^2 + \varphi^2 |b_j|^2 \right] dx_3$$

$$\leq C_1 \int_{-\infty}^{+\infty} \varphi^2 b_j^2 \, dx_3. \tag{1.67}$$

Therefore we have

$$\int_{-\infty}^{+\infty} \varphi^2 \left[|\partial_3^2 a_j|^2 + \lambda_j |\partial_3 a_j|^2 + \lambda_j^2 |a_j|^2 \right] dx_3 \leq C \int_{-\infty}^{+\infty} \varphi^2 |b_j|^2 \, dx_3, \tag{1.68}$$

where C does not depend on j.

Note that by (1.60)

$$\|\varphi \partial^\alpha p_3\| \leq \sum_{j=1}^{\infty} \int_{-\infty}^{+\infty} |\partial_3^{\alpha_3} a_j|^2 \varphi^2 \int_{\omega} |\partial_1^{\alpha_1} \partial_2^{\alpha_2} e_j|^2 dx_1 dx_2 dx_3. \tag{1.69}$$

The solution of the Neumann problem

$$\Delta_2 u = g, \quad \partial_n u|_{\partial\omega} = 0, \quad Su = 0, \qquad (1.70)$$

where $Sg = 0$, S is defined by (1.51), satisfies the estimate

$$\sum_{|\beta|\leq 2}\int_\omega |\partial_1^{\beta_1}\partial_2^{\beta_2} u|^2 dx_1 dx_2 \leq C \int_\omega |g|^2 dx_1 dx_2. \qquad (1.71)$$

Since (1.59) is of the form (1.70) with $g = -\lambda_j e_j$, we deduce from (1.69) and (1.68) when $\alpha_3 = 0$, $\alpha_1 + \alpha_2 \leq 2$ that

$$\|\varphi\partial^\alpha p_3\|^2 \leq C\sum_{j=1}^\infty \int_{-\infty}^{+\infty} |a_j|^2 \varphi^2 \lambda_j^2 dx_3 \leq C_1 \sum_{j=1}^\infty \int_{-\infty}^{+\infty} \varphi^2 |b_j|^2 dx_3. \qquad (1.72)$$

Taking into account (1.63), we obtain

$$\|\varphi(p_2 - Sp_2)\|^2 = \sum_{j=1}^\infty \int_{-\infty}^{+\infty} \varphi^2 b_j^2(x_3) dx_3 \qquad (1.73)$$

for any $p_2 \in L_2(\Omega)$. Hence (1.72) implies the inequality

$$\|\varphi\partial^\alpha p_3\|^2 \leq C\|\varphi(p_2 - Sp_2)\|^2 \qquad (1.74)$$

if $\alpha_3 = 0$. If $\alpha_3 \leq 2$, $\alpha_1 = 0$, $\alpha_2 = 0$, we have

$$\|\varphi\partial^\alpha p_3\|^2 \leq C\sum_{j=1}^\infty \int_{-\infty}^{+\infty} \varphi^2 |\partial_3^\alpha a_j|^2 dx_3.$$

Using (1.68) and (1.73), we obtain (1.74) in this case also. Let $\nabla_2 p_3 = (\partial_1 p_3, \partial_2 p_3)$. Obviously,

$$\int_\omega \nabla_2 e_i \nabla_2 e_j \, dx_1 dx_2 = -\int_\omega \Delta_2 e_i e_j \, dx_1 dx_2.$$

Hence

$$\|\varphi \nabla_2 \partial_3 p_3\|^2 = -\sum_{i,j=1}^\infty \int_{-\infty}^{+\infty} |\partial_3 a_j|^2 \varphi^2 \int_\omega \Delta_2 e_i e_j \, dx_1 dx_2 dx_3$$

$$= \sum_{j=1}^\infty \int_{-\infty}^{+\infty} |\partial_3 a_j|^2 \varphi^2 \lambda_j \, dx_3.$$

Using this formula, (1.68) and (1.73), we obtain (1.74) in the case $\alpha_3 = 1$, $\alpha_2 + \alpha_1 = 1$. Therefore (1.74) holds for $|\alpha| \leq 2$ and this yields (1.58).

LEMMA 1.5. *The operator* $I - \nabla Q_0$ *from H into E is bounded and*

$$\|\varphi(h - \nabla Q_0 h)\|_E \leq C\|\varphi h\|.$$

PROOF. Let $h \in D(\overline{\Omega})^3$. By Lemma 1.1

$$\|\varphi(h - \nabla Q_0 h)\| \leq C\|\varphi h\|.$$

By (1.44)
$$\operatorname{div}(\varphi(h - \nabla Q_0 h)) = \nabla\varphi \cdot (h - \nabla Q_0 h) + \varphi(\operatorname{div} h - \Delta Q_0 h)$$
$$= \nabla\varphi \cdot (h - \nabla Q_0 h).$$

By (0.18) and (1.7) we conclude that
$$\|\varphi(h - \nabla Q_0 h)\|_E \leq C\|\varphi h\| + C\varepsilon\|\varphi(h - \nabla Q_0 h)\| \leq C_1 \|\varphi h\|$$

for $h \in D(\overline{\Omega})^3$. Since $D(\overline{\Omega})^3$ is dense in H, this yields the assertion of the lemma.

LEMMA 1.6. *Let π_0 be defined by (1.42). Then π_0 may be written in the form*
$$\pi_0 h = \nabla(Q_0 h) + \nabla(Q_1 h)$$
$$+ S(h_3 - \partial_3 Q_0 h - \partial_3 Q_1 h) e_3 + \nabla(Q_3 Q_1 h). \quad (1.75)$$

Here and everywhere below
$$Q_1 h = Q_2(h - \nabla(Q_0 h)), \qquad e_3 = (0, 0, 1) \in \mathbb{R}^3, \quad (1.75')$$

the operator Q_1 is bounded from H into $H_1(\Omega)$ and
$$\|\varphi Q_1 h\|_1 \leq C \|\varphi h\| \quad (1.75'')$$

for any $h \in H$.

PROOF. By Lemma 1.5, the operator $I - \nabla Q_0$ from H into E is bounded. Using Lemma 1.2, we conclude that $Q_1 = Q_2(I - \nabla Q_0)$ is bounded. From (1.47) and Lemma 1.5 it follows that
$$\|\varphi Q_1 h\|_1 \leq C \|\varphi(h - \nabla Q_0 h)\|_E \leq C_1 \|\varphi h\|,$$

i.e., (1.75'') holds.

Note that both sides of (1.75) depend continuously on $h \in H$ by Lemmas 1.1, 1.4 and by (1.51'). Hence it suffices to prove (1.75) for $h \in D(\Omega)^3$ since $D(\Omega)^3$ is dense in H.

Let $h \in D(\Omega)^3$. By Proposition 0.9
$$h = v + \nabla p, \qquad v \in H_0, \ \nabla p \in H, \ p \in D'(\Omega). \quad (1.76)$$

The function p is defined modulo constants.

Computing the divergence of both sides of (1.76), we obtain the equation
$$\Delta p = \operatorname{div} h. \quad (1.77)$$

Let $p_0 = Q_0 h$ be defined by (1.44). Then $p_1 = p - p_0$ is a solution of the equation
$$\Delta p_1 = 0 \quad (1.78)$$

and
$$\nabla p_1 = g, \qquad g = h - v - \nabla p_0. \quad (1.79)$$

Obviously $\nabla p_1 = \nabla p - \nabla p_0 \in H$. Hence by (1.78), $\nabla p_1 \in E$ (see (0.18) for the definition of E). Proposition 0.7 implies that $l_n \nabla p_1 = \partial_n p_1$ is defined. By (1.44), we have div $g = 0$ and $g \in E$. Hence, $l_n g$ is defined and by (1.79)

$$\partial_n p_1|_{\partial\Omega} = l_n g = l_n(h - \nabla p_0); \qquad (1.80)$$

here we use the fact that $l_n v = 0$ by Proposition 0.8.

Let $p_2 = Q_2(h - \nabla p_0)$ be the solution of (1.46) where $g = h - \nabla p_0$. Combining (1.46), (1.79) and (1.80), we obtain the following equation for $p_5 = p_1 - p_2$

$$\Delta p_5 + p_2 = 0, \qquad \partial_n p_5|_{\partial\Omega} = 0.$$

Let $p_4' = Q_4 g$, where $g = h - \nabla p_0$, Q_4 be defined by (1.52), and

$$p_4 = S(p_5|_{x_3=0}) + \int_0^{x_3} p_4'(\xi)\, d\xi, \qquad p_3 = p_5 - p_4.$$

Obviously, $Sp_3 = 0$ when $x_3 = 0$. We have

$$\partial_3 Sp_3 = S(\partial_3 p_1 - \partial_3 p_2) - SQ_4 g.$$

Using (1.52), the equality $S^2 = S$ and (1.79), we obtain

$$\partial_3 Sp_3 = S(\partial_3 p_1 - \partial_3 p_2) - S^2(g_3 - \partial_3 p_2) = S(\partial_3 p_1 - g_3) = 0.$$

By (1.54), $\Delta p_4 = \partial_3^2 p_4 = -Sp_2$ and p_3 satisfies (1.57). Note that the function $p_3 = Q_3 p_2$ satisfies (1.57) by Lemma 1.4. We now prove that the solution of (1.57) such that $\nabla p_3 \in H$ is unique.

Let p_3', p_3'' be two solutions of (1.57). Then $u = p_3' - p_3''$ satisfy the equation

$$\Delta u = 0, \qquad Su = 0, \qquad \partial_n u|_{\partial\Omega} = 0. \qquad (1.81)$$

By (0.19), the boundary condition in (1.81) means that

$$(\nabla u, \nabla w) + (\Delta u, w) = 0$$

for any $w \in D(\overline{\Omega})$. Therefore

$$(\nabla u, \nabla w) = 0$$

for any such w. Green's formula implies

$$(\nabla u, \nabla w) = (u, \partial_n w)_{\partial\Omega} - (u, \Delta w).$$

This is obvious for $u \in D(\overline{\Omega})$. If the support of w lies in $\omega \times (-R, R)$ this holds for $u \in H_1(\omega \times (-R, R))$ by continuity. Since $\nabla u \in H$ implies $u \in H_1(\omega \times (-R, R))$ for any R, we have

$$(u, \Delta w) = 0 \quad \text{if } \partial_n w|_{\partial\Omega} = 0 \qquad (1.82)$$

for $w \in H_2(\Omega)$. Put $w(x_1, x_2, x_3) = b(x_3)e_j(x_1, x_2)$, where the e_j are the same as in (1.59), $b \in H_2(\mathbb{R})$. Obviously

$$\Delta w = (\partial_3^2 b - \lambda_j b)e_j.$$

Consider the ordinary differential equation
$$\partial_3^2 b - \lambda_j b = h, \qquad h \in D(\mathbb{R}).$$

Since $\lambda_j > 0$, there exists a solution $b \in H_2(\mathbb{R})$ of this equation. Using it, we deduce from (1.82) that
$$(u, he_j) = \int_{-\infty}^{+\infty} (u(\cdot, \cdot, x_3), e_j)_\omega h(x_3)\, dx_3 = 0$$

for any $h \in D(\mathbb{R})$, $j = 1, 2, \ldots$. Since $Su = 0$, this gives $u = 0$. Therefore the solution of (1.57) is unique, $p_3 = Q_3 p_2$. So we have
$$\nabla p = \nabla(p_0 + p_2 + p_4 + p_3), \tag{1.83}$$

where
$$p_0 = Q_0 h, \qquad p_2 = Q_2(h - \nabla p_0) = Q_1 h,$$
$$\nabla p_4 = p_4' e_3 = S(g_3 \partial_3 p_2) e_3 = S(h_3 - \partial_3 p_0 - \partial_3 p_2) e_3, \tag{1.84}$$
$$\nabla p_3 = \nabla(Q_3 p_2) = \nabla(Q_3 Q_1 h).$$

Hence by (1.83) we obtain (1.75).

Now let us prove Theorem 1.1. By (1.75)
$$\|\varphi \pi_0 h\| \leq \|\varphi \nabla Q_0 h\| + \|\varphi \nabla Q_1 h\|$$
$$+ \|\varphi S(h_3 - \partial_3 Q_0 h - \partial_3 Q_1 h)\| + \|\varphi \nabla (Q_3 Q_1 h)\|.$$

By using (1.45), (1.75″), (1.51′), (1.58), we obtain:
$$\|\varphi \pi_0 h\| \leq C \|\varphi h\| + C(\|\varphi h_3\| + \|\varphi \nabla Q_0 h\| + \|\varphi \nabla Q_1 h\|) + C\|\varphi Q_1 h\|$$
$$\leq C_2 \|\varphi h\|.$$

Therefore (1.43) holds and Theorem 1.1 is proved.

LEMMA 1.7. *Let* $h \in H_1(\Omega)^3$. *Then* $\Pi h \in H_1(\Omega)^3$,
$$\|\Pi h\|_1 \leq C \|h\|_1. \tag{1.85}$$

PROOF. Since $D(\overline{\Omega})$ is dense in $H_1(\Omega)$, we restrict ourselves to the case $h \in D(\overline{\Omega})^3$. By Proposition 0.6 the solution of the Dirichlet problem (1.44) satisfies the estimate
$$\|p_0\|_2 \leq C \|\operatorname{div} h\| + C_1 \|p_0\| \tag{1.86}$$

and we obtain by (1.45), where $\varphi = 1$,
$$\|\nabla Q_0 h\|_1 \leq C_2 \|h\|_1. \tag{1.87}$$

The solution p_2 of the Neumann problem (1.46) satisfies the estimate
$$\|p_2\|_2 \leq C\|l_n g\|_{H_{1/2}(\partial \Omega)} + C_1 \|p_2\|. \tag{1.88}$$

The proof of this estimate is standard, it can be carried out as in the case of a bounded domain in [16, 18]. The corresponding estimates in a half-space are proved there. The reduction to the case of the half-space must be done by using changes of variables and cut-off functions independent of x_3. Another way of proving (1.88) for the case $\Omega = \omega \times R$ considered is to use the corresponding estimate for ω in a way similar to the proof of Proposition 0.6. See also Lemma 2.7.

Hence we have by (1.47) and by continuity of the trace operator from $H_1(\Omega)$ to $H_{1/2}(\partial\Omega)$,

$$\|\nabla Q_2 g\|_1 \leqslant C_2 \|g\|_1. \tag{1.89}$$

By using (1.42), (1.75), (1.75'), (1.87), (1.89) and (1.58), where $\varphi = 1$, we obtain

$$\begin{aligned}\|\Pi h\|_1 &\leqslant \|h\|_1 + C\|\mathrm{div}\, h\| + C\|h\|_1 + C\|Q_0 h\|_1 \\ &\quad + \|S(h_3 - \partial_3 Q_0 h - \partial_3 Q_1 h)\|_1 + C\|Q_1 h\|. \end{aligned} \tag{1.90}$$

By using (1.51) we get

$$\|Sv\|_1 \leqslant C\|v\|_1. \tag{1.91}$$

Hence, using (1.75'), (1.87), (1.89) we conclude that

$$\|\Pi h\|_1 \leqslant C\|h\|_1 + C(\|\nabla Q_0 h\|_1 + \|\nabla Q_1 h\|_1) \leqslant C_1 \|h\|_1.$$

LEMMA 1.8. *Let $h(t)$, $t \geqslant 1$, be an infinitely differentiable function, $h(t) \geqslant 0$ when $t \geqslant 0$, $C \geqslant h'(t) \geqslant 0$ when $t \geqslant 1$, $|h''(t)| + |h'''(t)| \leqslant C$ when $t \geqslant 1$. Let*

$$\varphi(x, \varepsilon, \rho, \gamma) = \exp(\gamma h(g_\rho(|\varepsilon x_3|)^{1/2})), \tag{1.92}$$

where g_ρ is defined by (1.16). Then (1.5)–(1.8) hold.

PROOF. Relation (1.5) is obvious, (1.6) follows from (1.17). By (1.92),

$$\begin{aligned}\partial \varphi/\partial \rho &= (1/2) \exp(\gamma h(g_\rho(|\varepsilon x_3|)^{1/2})) \gamma h'(g_\rho(|\varepsilon x_3|)^{1/2}) \\ &\quad \times g_\rho(|\varepsilon x_3|)^{-1/2} \partial g_\rho(|\varepsilon x_3|)/\partial \rho.\end{aligned}$$

Therefore (1.8) follows from (1.18). To prove (1.7), note that

$$\partial_3 \varphi = \varphi \gamma h' \partial_3 (g_\rho(|\varepsilon x_3|)^{1/2}), \tag{1.93}$$

$$\begin{aligned}\partial_3^2 \varphi &= \varphi(\gamma h' \partial_3 g_\rho(|\varepsilon x_3|)^{1/2})^2 + \varphi \gamma h''(\partial_3 g_\rho(|\varepsilon x_3|)^{1/2})^2 \\ &\quad + \varphi \gamma h' \partial_3^2 (g_\rho(|\varepsilon x_3|)^{1/2}).\end{aligned} \tag{1.94}$$

By (1.25) and (1.26") (with $\gamma = 1$) we get

$$|\partial_3 (g_\rho(|\varepsilon x_3|)^{1/2})| \leqslant C\varepsilon, \qquad |\partial_3^2 (g_\rho(|\varepsilon x_3|)^{1/2})| \leqslant C\varepsilon^2. \tag{1.95}$$

Since h' and h'' are bounded, we deduce inequality (1.7) from (1.93), (1.94) and (1.95). Third derivatives are estimated in a similar way.

REMARK 1.3. All the conditions of Lemma 1.10 are fulfilled for $h(t) = t^q$, $0 < q \leqslant 1$ or for $h(t) = \ln^p(t+2)$, $p > 0$.

LEMMA 1.9. *Let $\varphi = \varphi(x, \varepsilon, \rho, \gamma)$ satisfy (1.4)–(1.8), and Φ be defined by (1.9). Then the following assertions hold.*

(i) *Suppose $u \in L_2(\Omega)$, $\|\varphi u\| \leq M$ for any $\rho \geq 1$. Then*
$$\|\Phi u\| \leq M.$$

(ii) *Suppose $u \in H_1^0(\Omega)$, $\|\varphi \nabla u\| \leq M$ for any $\rho \geq 1$. Then*
$$\int_\Omega \Phi^2(u^2 + |\nabla u|^2) dx \leq CM.$$

(iii) *Suppose $u \in H_1^0(\Omega) \cap H_2(\Omega)$, $\|\varphi \Delta u\| \leq M$ for any $\rho \geq 0$. Then*
$$\sum_{|\alpha| \leq 2} \int_\Omega \Phi^2 |\partial^\alpha u|^2 dx \leq CM.$$

PROOF. Obviously
$$\|\varphi u\|^2 = \int_\Omega \varphi^2 |u|^2 dx.$$

By (1.8) $\varphi(x, \varepsilon, \rho, \gamma)$ increases as ρ increases. Therefore, applying Fatou's lemma, we obtain the assertion (i).

By Proposition 1.2
$$\int \varphi^2(u^2 + |\nabla u|^2) dx \leq C \|\varphi \nabla u\|^2.$$

Using Fatou's lemma, we deduce assertion (ii) from this inequality. Assertion (iii) follows from Proposition 1.2 in a similar way.

§2. Estimates of norms of the commutators of π_0 and φ

Let $h \in L_2(\Omega)^3$. Let π be defined by (1.42),
$$Kh = \pi_0 \varphi h - \varphi \pi_0 h = (\varphi \Pi - \Pi \varphi) h \qquad (2.1)$$
where $\varphi = \varphi(x, \varepsilon, \rho, \gamma)$ satisfies (1.5)–(1.8). Everywhere below we assume $0 < \varepsilon \leq \varepsilon_0$, ε_0 is sufficiently small.

LEMMA 2.1. *Let $\varphi_1 = \varphi(x, \varepsilon, \rho, \gamma_1)$. Then*
$$\|\varphi_1 Kh\| \leq C \|\varphi_1 \varphi h\| \qquad (2.2)$$
for any $h \in H = L_2(\Omega)^3$.

PROOF. Since $D(\overline{\Omega})^3$ is dense in H and in E, it suffice to prove (2.2) for $h \in D(\Omega)$ and use the fact that both sides of (2.2) depend continuously on $h \in H$. By Theorem 1.1, in which φ is replaced by φ_1,
$$\|\varphi_1 \pi_0 \varphi h\| \leq C \|\varphi_1 \varphi h\|. \qquad (2.3)$$
Denote
$$\varphi_2 = \varphi_1 \varphi, \qquad \varphi_2 = \varphi(x, \varepsilon, \rho, \gamma + \gamma_1). \qquad (2.4)$$

By Theorem 1.1 in which φ is replaced by φ_2,

$$\|\varphi_1 \varphi \pi_0 h\| = \|\varphi_2 \pi_0 h\| \leq C\|\varphi_2 h\|. \tag{2.5}$$

Relations (2.3) and (2.5) imply (2.2). The main result of this section is the estimate given in the following theorem, which is much stronger than (2.2).

THEOREM 2.1.

$$\|\varphi_1 K h\|_1 \leq C\varepsilon \|\varphi_2 h\| \tag{2.6}$$

for any $h \in H$, where C depends only on γ, γ_1. If (1.13) holds instead of (1.7), then $\varphi_2 = \varphi_1 \varphi'$, where $\varphi' = \varphi(x, \varepsilon, \rho, \gamma')$, γ' is the same as in (1.13).

The proof of Theorem 2.1 is based on several lemmas which are stated and proved below.

Everywhere below we shall use the notation (2.4) for brevity. Put

$$K_i h = \nabla Q_i \varphi h - \varphi \nabla Q_i h, \qquad i = 0, 1, 2, 3. \tag{2.7}$$

Here Q_i are the same as in Lemmas 1.1, 1.2, 1.4, 1.6. Since φ and its derivatives are bounded, $\varphi h \in H$ if $h \in H$, $\varphi h \in E$ if $h \in E$, therefore all expressions in (2.7) are well defined for $h \in E$.

LEMMA 2.2. *Let $h \in E$. Then*

$$Kh = K_0 h - (S(K_0 h)_3)e_3 + K_1 h - (S(K_1 h)_3) e_3 + \nabla Q_3 K_1^0 h + K_3 Q_1 h, \tag{2.8}$$

where $(K_i h)_3$ is the third component of $K_i h$, $e_3 = (0, 0, 1)$, S is defined by (1.51),

$$K_1^0 h = Q_1 \varphi h - \varphi Q_1 h = K_2^0 (h - \nabla Q_0 h) - Q_2 K_0 h, \tag{2.9}$$

$$K_2^0 h = Q_2 \varphi h - \varphi Q_2 h. \tag{2.10}$$

PROOF. Using (1.75), we obtain

$$Kh = \nabla Q_0 \varphi h + \nabla Q_1 \varphi h + S\left(\varphi h_3 - \partial_3 Q_0 \varphi h - \partial_3 Q_1 \varphi h\right) e_3$$
$$+ \nabla Q_3 Q_1 \varphi h - \varphi \nabla Q_0 h - \varphi \nabla Q_1 h$$
$$- \varphi S\left(h_3 - \partial_3 Q_0 h - \partial_3 Q_1 h\right) e_3 - \varphi \nabla Q_3 Q_1 h.$$

Since $S(U_3) = (SU)_3$ and $S\varphi = \varphi S$, we obtain (using notation (2.7))

$$Kh = K_0 h + \left(S(-K_0 h - K_1 h)\right)_3 e_3 + K_1 h$$
$$+ \nabla Q_3 \left(Q_1 \varphi h - \varphi Q_1 h\right) + \nabla Q_3 \varphi Q_1 h - \varphi \nabla Q_3 Q_1 h.$$

Hence, by using (2.9), (2.10), we get

$$Kh = K_0 h - (SK_0 h)_3 e_3 + K_1 h - (SK_1 h)_3 e_3 + \nabla Q_3 K_1^0 h + K_3 Q_1 h \tag{2.11}$$

which coincides with (2.8).

Later we shall use the following representation of the operator K_1

$$\begin{aligned}
K_1 h &= \nabla Q_2 (\varphi h - \nabla Q_0 \varphi h) - \varphi \nabla Q_2 (h - \nabla Q_0 h) \\
&= K_2 h + \varphi \nabla Q_2 \nabla Q_0 h - \nabla Q_2 \nabla Q_0 \varphi h \\
&= K_2 h - K_2 \nabla Q_0 h - \nabla Q_2 (\varphi \nabla Q_0 h - \nabla Q_0 \varphi h) \\
&= K_2 (h - \nabla Q_0 h) - \nabla Q_2 K_0 h.
\end{aligned} \qquad (2.12)$$

Now we estimate the weighted norms of the operators involved in (2.8). We shall use the weight function $\varphi_1 = \varphi(x, \varepsilon, \rho, \gamma_1)$. Since $D(\overline{\Omega})^3$ is dense in H and in E, it suffices to consider $h \in D(\overline{\Omega})^3$ instead of $h \in H$ and $h \in E$ in all the proofs below.

LEMMA 2.3. *Let* $h \in H$. *Then*

$$\|\varphi_1 K_0 h\|_1 \leqslant C\varepsilon \|\varphi_2 h\|. \qquad (2.13)$$

PROOF. Put $Q_0 \varphi h = p_{0\varphi}$. According to (1.44), (1.44′), the function $p_{0\varphi} \in H_1^0(\Omega)$ is a solution of the equation

$$\Delta p_{0\varphi} = \text{div}\,(\varphi h), \qquad p_{0\varphi}|_{\partial \omega} = 0. \qquad (2.14)$$

Obviously,

$$K_0 h = \nabla p_{0\varphi} - \varphi \nabla p_0 = \nabla(p_{0\varphi} - p_0 \varphi) + p_0 \nabla \varphi. \qquad (2.15)$$

Therefore, using Proposition 1.2 and (1.7), we obtain

$$\begin{aligned}
\|\varphi_1 K_0 h\|_1 &\leqslant \|\varphi_1 \nabla(p_{0\varphi} - \varphi p_0)\|_1 + \|\varphi_1 (\nabla \varphi) p_0\|_1 \\
&\leqslant C \|\varphi_1 \Delta(p_{0\varphi} - \varphi p_0)\| + C\varepsilon \|\varphi_1 \varphi \nabla p_0\|.
\end{aligned} \qquad (2.16)$$

The function φp_0 is a solution of the equation

$$\Delta(\varphi p_0) = \varphi \Delta p_0 + 2\nabla \varphi \nabla p_0 + p_0 \Delta \varphi = \varphi \,\text{div}\, h. \qquad (2.17)$$

Therefore $w = p_{0\varphi} - \varphi p_0$ is a solution of the equation obtained by subtracting (2.17) from (2.14),

$$\Delta w = h \nabla \varphi + 2 \nabla p_0 \nabla \varphi + p_0 \Delta \varphi, \qquad w|_{\partial \Omega} = 0. \qquad (2.18)$$

Hence, by (1.7),

$$\|\varphi_1 \Delta w\| \leqslant C\varepsilon \left(\|\varphi_2 h\| + \|\varphi_2 \nabla p_0\| + \|\varphi_2 p_0\| \right).$$

Using Proposition 1.2 and Lemma 1.1, we deduce that

$$\|\varphi_1 \Delta w\| \leqslant C\varepsilon \left(\|\varphi_2 h\| + \|\varphi_2 \nabla p_0\| \right) \leqslant C_1 \varepsilon \|\varphi_2 h\|. \qquad (2.19)$$

Using (2.16) and (2.19), and Lemma 1.1, we obtain

$$\|\varphi_1 K_0 h\|_1 \leqslant C\varepsilon \left(\|\varphi_2 h\| + \|\varphi_2 \nabla p_0\| \right) \leqslant C_1 \varepsilon \|\varphi_2 h\|. \qquad (2.20)$$

This implies (2.13).

LEMMA 2.4. *Let* $h \in E$. *Then*

$$\|\varphi_1 K_2 h\|_1 \leq C\varepsilon\|\varphi_2 h\| + C\varepsilon\|\varphi_2 \operatorname{div} h\|. \quad (2.21)$$

PROOF. Similarly to (2.16), we obtain

$$\|\varphi_1 K_2 h\|_1 \leq \|\varphi_1 \nabla w\|_1 + C\varepsilon\|\varphi_2 p_2\|_1, \quad (2.22)$$

where $p_2 = Q_2 h$ is a solution of (1.46), where $g = h$, while $w = p_{2\varphi} - \varphi p_2$ is a solution of the equation analogous to (2.18)

$$\Delta w - w = 2\nabla p_2 \nabla \varphi + p_2 \Delta \varphi. \quad (2.23)$$

Since a normal vector to $\partial\Omega$ is orthogonal to the x_3-axis and φ depends only on x_3 we have

$$\varphi \partial_n p_2|_{\partial\Omega} = \partial_n (\varphi p_2)|_{\partial\Omega} = l_n \varphi g = \partial_n p_{2\varphi}|_{\partial\Omega}.$$

Hence

$$\partial_n w|_{\partial\Omega} = 0. \quad (2.24)$$

Note that the solution of the problem

$$\Delta v - v = g, \qquad \partial_n v|_{\partial\Omega} = 0, \quad (2.25)$$

satisfies the estimate

$$\|v\|_2 \leq C\|g\|. \quad (2.26)$$

(See Lemma 2.7 below.)

Multiplying (2.23) by φ_1, we easily deduce the equation for $\varphi_1 w$:

$$\Delta(\varphi_1 w) - \varphi_1 w = \varphi_1 (2\nabla p_2 \nabla \varphi + p_2 \Delta \varphi) + 2\nabla \varphi_1 \nabla w + w\Delta \varphi_1,$$
$$\partial_n \varphi_{1w}|_{\partial\Omega} = 0. \quad (2.26')$$

By using (2.26) where $v = \varphi_1 w$ and (1.7), we obtain

$$\|\varphi_1 w\|_2 \leq C\varepsilon\|\varphi_2 \nabla p_2\| + C\varepsilon\|\varphi_2 p_2\| + C\varepsilon\|\varphi_1 \nabla w\| + C\varepsilon\|\varphi_1 w\|. \quad (2.27)$$

Using Proposition 1.3 and the fact that ε is small we get

$$\|\varphi_1 w\|_2 \leq C_1 \varepsilon \left(\|\varphi_2 p_2\| + \|\varphi_2 \nabla p_2\|\right). \quad (2.27')$$

Using Lemma 1.2 to estimate $p_2 = Q_2 h$, and Proposition 1.3, we obtain

$$\|\varphi_1 \nabla w\|_1 \leq C\varepsilon \left(\|\varphi_2 h\| + \|\varphi_2 \operatorname{div} h\|\right).$$

Using this estimate and Lemma 1.2, we deduce from (2.22) the estimate (2.21).

LEMMA 2.5. *Let* $v \in L_2(\Omega)$. *Then*

$$\|\varphi_1 K_3 v\|_1 \leq C\varepsilon \|\varphi_2 v\|. \quad (2.28)$$

PROOF. Similarly to (2.16), we obtain

$$\|\varphi_1 K_3 v\|_1 \leq \|\varphi_1 \nabla(p_{3\varphi} - \varphi p_3)\|_1 + C\|\varphi_1 p_3 \nabla \varphi\|_1, \quad (2.29)$$

where $p_{3\varphi} = Q_3(\varphi v)$, $p_3 = Q_3 v$. By (1.57), the function $w = p_{3\varphi} - \varphi p_3$ is a solution of the equation

$$\Delta w = S(\varphi v) - \varphi v - (\varphi S v - \varphi v) + 2\nabla\varphi \nabla p_3 + p_3 \Delta\varphi.$$

Since $\varphi = \varphi(x_3)$, we have $S\varphi = \varphi S$ and this equation takes the form

$$\Delta w = -g, \quad g = 2\nabla\varphi \nabla p_3 + p_3 \Delta\varphi. \tag{2.30}$$

Two more conditions on w following from (1.57) take the form

$$S(p_{3\varphi}) - \varphi S p_3 = S(p_{3\varphi} - \varphi p_3) = Sw = 0, \tag{2.31}$$

$$(\partial_n(p_{3\varphi}) - \varphi \partial_n p_3)|_{\partial\Omega} = \partial_n w|_{\partial\Omega} = 0 \tag{2.32}$$

(we use the fact that φ depends only on x_3). Since $Sp_{3\varphi} = 0$, $S(p_3) = 0$, and $\nabla\varphi$, $\Delta\varphi$ depend only on x_3, we have

$$Sg = 2\nabla\varphi S\nabla p_3 + \Delta\varphi Sp_3 = 2\partial_3\varphi S\partial_3 p_3 = 2\partial_3\varphi\partial_3 Sp_3 = 0$$

and therefore

$$-g = -(g - Sg). \tag{2.33}$$

Using (1.58), where p_3 is replaced by w and p_2 by g, we obtain

$$\sum_{|\alpha|\leq 2} \|\varphi_1 \partial^\alpha w\|_2 \leq C\|\varphi_1 g\|.$$

By Proposition 1.3 and (1.7) this implies

$$\|\varphi_1 \nabla w\|_1 \leq C\varepsilon \left(\|\varphi_2 \nabla p_3\| + \|\varphi_2 p_3\|\right). \tag{2.34}$$

From (2.29), (2.34) and (1.58), where φ is replaced by φ_2 and p_2 by v, we obtain (2.28).

LEMMA 2.6. *Let $h \in E$. Then*

$$\|\varphi_1 K_2^0 h\|_2 \leq C\varepsilon \|\varphi_2 h\| + C\varepsilon \|\varphi_2 \operatorname{div} h\|. \tag{2.35}$$

PROOF. We have

$$\|\varphi_1 K_2^0 h\|_2 = \|\varphi_1(p_{2\varphi} - \varphi p_2)\|_2 = \|\varphi_1 w\|_2, \tag{2.36}$$

where $p_{2\varphi} = Q(\varphi h)$, $p_2 = Q_2 h$, $w = p_{2\varphi} - \varphi p_2$. Using (2.27') and Lemma 1.2, we obtain (2.35).

In Ω consider the problem

$$\Delta v - v = g_1, \quad \partial_n v|_{\partial\Omega} = l_n g_2. \tag{2.37}$$

LEMMA 2.7. *Let $g_1 \in L_2(\Omega)$, $g_2 \in H_1(\Omega)$. Then there exists a unique solution $v \in H_2(\Omega)^2$ satisfying*

$$\|v\|_2 \leq C \left(\|g_2\|_1 + \|g_1\|\right), \tag{2.38}$$

$$\sum_{|\alpha|\leq 2} \|\varphi_1 \partial^\alpha v\| \leq C \left(\|\varphi_1 g_2\|_1 + \|\varphi_1 g_1\|\right). \tag{2.39}$$

PROOF. Since $D(\overline{\Omega})$ is dense in $H_l(\Omega)$, it suffices to prove the existence of solutions of (2.37) satisfying (2.38), (2.39) for $g_1, g_2 \in D(\overline{\Omega})$. Denote by $\overline{v}(x', \xi_3)$ the Fourier transform of $v(x', x_3)$ with respect to x_3. Obviously $\overline{v}$ satisfies

$$\Delta_2 \overline{v} - (|\xi_3|^2 + 1)\overline{v} = \overline{g}_1, \qquad \partial_n \overline{v}|_{\partial \omega} = l_n \overline{g}_2, \qquad (2.40)$$

where $\xi_3 \in \mathbb{R}$ is a parameter. Multiplying this equation by $\overline{v}^*$, where $\overline{v}^*$ denotes the complex conjugate to $\overline{v}$, and using Green's formula, we obtain

$$\|\nabla_2 \overline{v}\|^2_{L_2(\omega)} + (|\xi|^2 + 1)\|\overline{v}\|^2_{L_2(\omega)}$$
$$\leq \|g_1\|_{L_2(\omega)} \|\overline{v}\|_{L_2(\omega)} + \|\nabla_2 g_2\|_{L_2(\omega)} \|\overline{v}\|_{L_2(\omega)} + \|g_2\|_{L_2(\omega)} \|\nabla_2 \overline{v}\|_{L_2(\omega)}. \qquad (2.41)$$

Multiplying this equation by $1 + |\xi_3|^2$, we get

$$(1 + |\xi_3|^2) \|\nabla_2 \overline{v}\|^2_{L_2(\omega)} + (|\xi_3|^2 + 1)^2 \|\overline{v}\|^2_{L_2(\omega)}$$
$$\leq C(\|g_1\|^2_{L_2(\omega)} + \|\nabla_2 g_2\|^2_{L_2(\omega)}) + C(1 + |\xi_3|^2) \|g_2\|^2_{L_2(\omega)}. \qquad (2.42)$$

Equation (2.40), with $|\xi_3|^2 \overline{v}$ transposed to the right-hand side yields the estimate

$$\|\overline{v}\|_{H_2(\omega)} \leq C((|\xi|^2 + 1)\|\overline{v}\|^2_{L_2(\omega)} + \|\overline{g}_1\|^2_{L_2(\omega)} + \|l_n \overline{g}_2\|^2_{H_{1/2}(\partial \omega)}). \qquad (2.43)$$

Since the trace operator l_n from $H_1(\omega)$ into $H_{1/2}(\partial \Omega)$ is bounded, we deduce from (2.41) and (2.43)

$$\|\overline{v}\|^2_{H_2(\omega)} \leq C \|\overline{g}_1\|^2_{L_2(\omega)} + C \|\overline{g}_2\|^2_{H_1(\omega)} + C(1 + |\xi_3|^2) \|g_2\|^2_{L_2(\omega)}.$$

Combining this inequality with (2.42), integrating with respect to ξ_3, and using the fact that the Fourier transform of $\partial_3^k v$ equals $(i\xi_3)^k \overline{v}$, we obtain (2.38).

To get (2.39), note that $\varphi_1 v$ is a solution of the problem

$$\Delta(\varphi_1 v) - \varphi_1 v = \varphi_1 g_1 - 2\nabla \varphi_1 \nabla v - \Delta \varphi_1 v,$$
$$\partial_n |\varphi_1 v|_{\partial \Omega} = l_n \varphi_1 g_2.$$

Using (2.38) with v replaced by $\varphi_1 v$, we obtain

$$\|\varphi_1 v\|_2 \leq C \left(\|\varphi_1 g_2\|_1 + \|\varphi_1 g_1\| + \|\nabla \varphi_1 \nabla v\| + \|\Delta \varphi_1 v\| \right).$$

By (1.7) and Proposition 1.3 we deduce (2.39) from this estimate.

PROOF OF THEOREM 2.1. Let $h \in D(\overline{\Omega})^3$. By Lemma 2.2

$$\|\varphi_1 Kh\|_1 \leq \|\varphi_1 K_0 h\|_1 + \|\varphi_1 SK_0 h\|_1 + \|\varphi_1 K_1 h\|_1$$
$$+ \|\varphi_1 S(K_1 h)\|_1 + \|\varphi_1 \nabla Q_3 K_1^0 h\|_1 + \|\varphi_1 K_3 Q_1 h\|_1.$$

Since $\nabla(Sv) = \partial_3 Sv = S\partial_3 v$, it follows that (1.51') and (1.7) imply

$$\|\varphi Sv\|_1 \leq C \|\varphi v\|_1. \qquad (2.44)$$

Using this inequality, (1.58) and (2.28), we obtain

$$\|\varphi_1 K h\|_1 \leq C \|\varphi_1 K_0 h\|_1 + C \|\varphi_1 K_1 h\|_1 + C \|\varphi_1 K_1^0 h\| + C\varepsilon \|\varphi_2 Q_1 h\|. \quad (2.45)$$

Hence, using (2.13), (2.9), (2.12) and (1.75'), we get

$$\begin{aligned}\|\varphi_1 K h\|_1 &\leq C\varepsilon \|\varphi_2 h\| + C \|\varphi_1 K_2 (h - \nabla Q_0 h)\|_1 + C \|\varphi_1 \nabla Q_2 K_0 h\|_1 \\ &+ C \|\varphi_1 K_2^0 (h - \nabla Q_0 h)\|_1 + C \|\varphi_1 Q_2 K_0 h\|_1 \\ &+ C\varepsilon \|\varphi_2 Q_2 (h - \nabla (Q_0 h))\|. \end{aligned} \quad (2.46)$$

Now we shall estimate separately all the terms on the right-hand side of (2.46). We shall use the estimate

$$C(\|\varphi v\| + \|\varphi \operatorname{div} v\|) \leq C \|\varphi v\|_E \leq C^{-1}(\|\varphi_0\| + \|\varphi \operatorname{div} v\|). \quad (2.47)$$

It follows from (0.18) and (1.7) when ε is small, since $\varphi \operatorname{div} v = \operatorname{div}(\varphi v) - v \nabla \varphi$. Using (2.21), (2.47) and Lemma 1.5, we obtain

$$\|\varphi_1 K_2 (I - \nabla Q_0) h\|_1 \leq C\varepsilon \|\varphi_2 (I - \nabla Q_0) h\|_E \leq C_1 \varepsilon \|\varphi_2 h\|. \quad (2.48)$$

Since the equation (1.46) for $p_2 = Q_2 g$ is of the form (2.37) with $g_1 = 0$, we can use Lemma 2.7 and Proposition 1.3 to obtain

$$\|\varphi_1 \nabla Q_2 K_0 h\|_1 \leq C \|\varphi_1 K_0 h\|_1. \quad (2.49)$$

Hence by (2.13),

$$\|\varphi_1 \nabla Q_2 K_0 h\|_1 \leq C_1 \varepsilon \|\varphi_2 h\|. \quad (2.50)$$

By (2.35), (2.47), and Lemma 1.5,

$$\|\varphi_1 K_2^0 (h - \nabla Q_0 h)\|_1 \leq C\varepsilon \|\varphi_2 (h - \nabla Q_0 h)\|_E \leq C_1 \varepsilon \|\varphi_2 h\|. \quad (2.51)$$

From (1.47) and (2.13), we get

$$\|\varphi_1 Q_2 K_0 h\|_1 \leq C \|\varphi_1 K_0 h\|_1 \leq C_1 \varepsilon \|\varphi_2 h\|. \quad (2.52)$$

By (1.47), (2.47), and Lemma 1.5,

$$\|\varphi_2 Q_2 (h - \nabla Q_0 h)\| \leq C \|\varphi_2 (h - \nabla Q_0 h)\|_E \leq C_1 \|\varphi_2 h\|. \quad (2.53)$$

By applying estimates (2.48), (2.50), (2.51), (2.52) and (2.53) to find the bound of the right-hand side of (2.46), we obtain (2.6).

Note that if (1.13) holds rather than (1.7), then in all the estimates of this section, we can take

$$\varphi_2 = \varphi(x, \varepsilon, \rho, \gamma_1) \varphi(x, \varepsilon, \rho, \gamma') = \varphi(x, \varepsilon, \rho, \gamma_1 + \gamma')$$

with $\gamma_1 + \gamma' \leq \gamma_1 + \gamma$. No changes in proofs are needed in this case. Theorem 2.1 is proved.

LEMMA 2.8. *Let* $u \in H_2$. *Then*

$$\|\varphi u\|_2 \leqslant C \|\Pi\Delta(\varphi u)\|. \tag{2.54}$$

PROOF. Consider the equation

$$\Pi\Delta(\varphi u) = f, \qquad f \in H_0. \tag{2.55}$$

By Proposition 0.9, this is equivalent to

$$\Delta(\varphi u) + \nabla p = f. \tag{2.56}$$

Since $u \in H_2$, we have by (1.4)

$$\begin{aligned}\varphi u \in (H_1^0(\Omega))^3 \cap (H_2(\Omega))^3, \\ \operatorname{div}(\varphi u) = u\nabla\varphi, \qquad \varphi u|_{\partial\Omega} = 0.\end{aligned} \tag{2.57}$$

We have used that φ and its derivatives are bounded. Since $\varphi u \in H_2(\Omega)^3$, we have $\Delta(\varphi u) \in H$ and

$$\nabla p = (I - \Pi)(\Delta(\varphi u)) \in H = L_2(\Omega)^3. \tag{2.58}$$

By Proposition 0.15, relation (0.40) holds and

$$\int_\omega u\nabla\varphi \, dx_1 dx_2 = 0, \qquad x_3 \in \mathbb{R}, \tag{2.59}$$

since $\nabla\varphi$ does not depend on x_3. Applying Proposition 0.14 to the function $g = u\nabla\varphi$, we find the function $v = G_3(u\nabla\varphi)$ satisfying

$$\operatorname{div} v = u\nabla\varphi, \qquad v|_{\partial\Omega} = 0, \tag{2.60}$$

$$\|v\|_2 \leqslant C\|u\nabla\varphi\|_2. \tag{2.61}$$

Using (1.7) and Proposition 1.3, we obtain

$$\|v\|_2 \leqslant C\varepsilon\|\varphi u\|_2. \tag{2.62}$$

Let $w = \varphi u - v$. By (2.56) and (2.60), ω is a solution of the system

$$\Delta w + \nabla p = f - \Delta v. \tag{2.63}$$

By Proposition 0.21

$$\|w\|_2 \leqslant C\|f\| + C\|v\|_2.$$

Using (2.62), we obtain

$$\|w\|_2 \leqslant C\|f\| + C_1\varepsilon\|\varphi u\|_2. \tag{2.64}$$

Since $\|\varphi u\|_2 \leqslant \|v\|_2 + \|w\|_2$, by (2.62) and (2.64), we get

$$\|\varphi u\|_2 \leqslant C\|f\| + C_2\varepsilon\|\varphi u\|_2.$$

Since ε is small, $C_2\varepsilon \leqslant 1/2$ and this estimate for the solution of (2.55) implies (2.54).

THEOREM 2.2. *Let* $u \in H_2$. *Then*

$$\|\varphi u\|_2 \leqslant C \|\varphi \Pi \Delta u\|. \tag{2.65}$$

PROOF. Obviously,

$$\varphi \Pi \Delta u = (\varphi \Pi - \Pi \varphi) \Delta u + \Pi \varphi \Delta u = K \Delta u + \Pi \Delta (\varphi u) - \Pi (2 \nabla \varphi \nabla u + u \Delta \varphi)$$

where K is defined by (2.1). By Theorem 2.1, (1.7), and Proposition 1.2 we obtain

$$\|\varphi \Pi \Delta u\| \geqslant \|\Pi \Delta (\varphi u)\| - C\varepsilon \|\varphi \Delta u\| - 2\|\nabla \varphi \nabla u\| - \|u \Delta \varphi\|$$
$$\geqslant \|\Pi \Delta (\varphi u)\| - C_1 \varepsilon \|\varphi \Delta u\|.$$

From this inequality, Proposition 1.3, and (2.54), it follows that

$$\|\varphi u\|_2 \leqslant C \|\varphi \Pi \Delta u\| + C\varepsilon \|\varphi u\|_2.$$

Since ε is small, this implies (2.65).

REMARK 2.1. We used the estimate

$$\|K \Delta u\| \leqslant C\varepsilon \|\varphi \Delta u\|, \qquad u \in H_2,$$

which follows from (2.6). The stronger estimate

$$\|\varphi_1 K \Delta u\| \leqslant C\varepsilon \|\varphi_2 \nabla u\|^{1-b} \|\varphi_2 \Delta u\|^b, \qquad u \in H_2,$$

with $b \in]1/2, 1[$, is valid. We shall not use this estimate here, so we omit the proof.

§3. Weighted estimates for regular solutions of the Navier-Stokes system

After excluding the pressure by projection onto H_0, the Navier-Stokes system (I.1) (see the introduction) takes the form

$$\partial_t u - \nu \Pi \Delta u + \Pi L_0 u + \Pi B(u, u) = \Pi f, \tag{3.1}$$

where we assume $u(t) \in H_1$ for any t,

$$B(u, v) = \sum_{i=3}^{3} u_i \partial_i v, \tag{3.2}$$

$$L_0 u = B(V, u) + B(u, V), \tag{3.3}$$

where $V = V(x)$ is the Poiseuille flow described in the introduction. It is assumed that for $u \in H_1$

$$(L_0 u, \varphi^2 u) \geqslant -\nu' \|\varphi \nabla u\|^2 - C\varepsilon \|\varphi \nabla u\|^2, \tag{3.4}$$

$$\|\varphi L_0 u\| \leqslant C \|\varphi \nabla u\|, \tag{3.5}$$

where

$$0 \leqslant \nu' \leqslant \nu - \nu'', \qquad \nu'' > 0, \tag{3.6}$$

$\varphi = \varphi(x, \varepsilon, \rho, \gamma)$ satisfies (1.5)–(1.8) and (1.10) (sufficient conditions for (3.4), (3.5) to hold are given in §7).

We suppose that u ($t = u(t, x)$) is a solution of (3.1) defined for all $t \in \mathbb{R}$ and satisfying the estimates

$$J_{1,0}^{\infty}(u) \leqslant M_0, \tag{3.7}$$

$$J_{2,0}^{2}(u) \leqslant M_1. \tag{3.8}$$

Here and below we use the notations

$$J_{l,\gamma}^{\infty} = \sup\{\|u(t)\|_{l,\gamma}, \, t \in \mathbb{R}\}, \tag{3.9}$$

$$J_{l,\gamma}^{2} = \sup\left\{\int_{T}^{T+1} \|u(t)\|_{l,\gamma}^{2} dt, \, T \in \mathbb{R}\right\}^{1/2}. \tag{3.10}$$

Here $\|u\|_{l,\gamma}$ is defined by (1.11).

We suppose that $f = f(t, x)$ satisfies the estimate

$$J_{0,\gamma}^{2}(f) \leqslant M_f, \qquad \gamma > 0. \tag{3.11}$$

THEOREM 3.1. *Under the conditions imposed, there exists an M_2 depending on M_0, M_1 and M_f in (3.11) such that*

$$J_{1,\gamma}^{\infty}(u) + J_{2,\gamma}^{2}(u) + J_{0,\gamma}^{2}(\partial_t u) \leqslant M_2. \tag{3.12}$$

THEOREM 3.2. *If all the conditions of Theorem 3.1 but (1.10) hold, then there exists an $\varepsilon > 0$ such that*

$$\sum_{|\alpha| \leqslant 1} \|\Phi \partial^{\alpha} u(t)\| \leqslant M_2 \qquad \forall t \in \mathbb{R}, \tag{3.13}$$

$$\int_{T}^{T+1} \left(\sum_{|\alpha| \leqslant 2} \|\Phi \partial^{\alpha} u\|^2 + \|\Phi \partial_t u\|^2\right) dt \leqslant M_2 \qquad \forall T \in \mathbb{R}, \tag{3.14}$$

where $\Phi = \Phi(x, \varepsilon, \gamma) = \varphi(x, \varepsilon, \infty, \gamma)$ is defined by (1.9); in (1.11) Φ is also assumed to be $\Phi(x, \varepsilon, \gamma)$ rather than $\Phi(x, 1, \gamma)$.

The proof of Theorems 3.1 and 3.2 is based on a sequence of lemmas.

LEMMA 3.1. *Let (3.7), (3.8) hold. Then*

$$J_{0,0}^{2}(\partial_t u) \leqslant C. \tag{3.15}$$

PROOF. By (3.1), since Π is bounded in $H = (L_2(\Omega))^3$,

$$\|\partial_t u\| \leqslant \|\Delta u\| + \|B(u, u)\| + \|f\|. \tag{3.16}$$

By (3.8) and (3.11),

$$J_{0,0}^{2}(\partial_t u) \leqslant M_1 + M_f + J_{0,0}^{2}(B(u, u)). \tag{3.17}$$

By the Ladyzhenskaya-Gagliardo-Nirenberg inequality (see [16]), we have

$$\|u_i \partial_i v\| \leqslant \|u\|_{L_4} \|\partial_i v\|_{L_4} \leqslant C \|u\|^{1/4} \|u\|_1^{3/4} \|v\|_1^{1/4} \|v\|_2^{3/4}. \tag{3.18}$$

Hence

$$\int_{T}^{T+1} \|B(u, u)\|^2 dt \leqslant C \int_{T}^{T+1} \|u\|^{1/2} \|u\|_1^{2} \|u\|_2^{3/2} dx \leqslant C M_0^{5/2} M_1^{3/2}. \tag{3.19}$$

Using this inequality and (3.17), we obtain (3.15).

LEMMA 3.2. *Let* $0 < \eta \leq 1$, *let* u *satisfy* (3.7), (3.8). *Then for almost all* $t \in \mathbb{R}$

$$(\partial_t u - \nu \Pi \Delta u, \varphi^2(u + \eta \partial_t u))$$
$$\geq (\eta - \eta \varepsilon)\|\varphi \partial_t u\|^2 + (\nu - \varepsilon)\|\varphi \nabla u\|^2 + (1/2)\partial_t \|\varphi u\|^2 \quad (3.20)$$
$$+ (\eta \nu / 2)\partial_t \|\varphi \nabla u\|^2 - C\varepsilon \|\varphi \Delta u\|^2.$$

All the terms in (3.20) *belong to* $L_1([-T, T], \mathbb{R})$ *for any* T, *derivatives are understood in the sense of distributions.*

PROOF. At first, let us prove (3.20) for $u \in C^1([-T, T], H_2)$, for any $T > 0$. For such u the left-hand side of (3.20) is equal to

$$(1/2)\partial_t \|\varphi u\|^2 + \eta \|\varphi \partial_t u\|^2 - \nu(\varphi^2 \Pi \Delta u, u + \eta \partial_t u). \quad (3.21)$$

Since $\Pi = I - \pi_0$, where I is the identity operator, then by (2.6)

$$\varphi \Pi - \Pi \varphi = K, \quad \|\varphi_1 K h\|_1 \leq C\varepsilon \|\varphi_2 h\|, \quad (3.22)$$

for any $h \in H$; here

$$\varphi_2 = \varphi_1 \varphi. \quad (3.23)$$

For $w \in H_1$ we have

$$-(\Pi \Delta u, \varphi^2 w) = -(\Pi \varphi^2 \Delta u, w) - (K' \Delta u, w)$$
$$= -(\varphi^2 \Delta u, w) + (K' \Delta u, w)$$
$$= (\nabla u, \nabla(\varphi^2 w)) + (\varphi^{-1} K' \Delta u, \varphi w), \quad (3.24)$$

where

$$K' = \varphi^2 \Pi - \Pi \varphi^2. \quad (3.25)$$

Using (1.7), (3.22), and Proposition 1.2, we obtain

$$|(\nabla u, \varphi^2 \nabla w) + (\Pi \Delta u, \varphi^2 w)| \leq C\varepsilon \|\varphi \Delta u\| \|\varphi w\| + C\varepsilon \|\varphi \nabla u\| \|\varphi w\|$$
$$\leq C_1 \varepsilon \|\varphi \Delta u\| \|\varphi w\|. \quad (3.26)$$

Using (3.26) with $w = u + \nu \partial_t u$ to get a bound for (3.21) from below, we obtain

$$(\partial_t u - \nu \Pi \Delta u, \varphi(u + \eta \partial_t u))$$
$$\geq (1/2)\partial_t \|\varphi u\|^2 + \eta \|\varphi \partial_t u\|^2 + \nu(\varphi \nabla u, \varphi(\nabla u + \eta \partial_t \nabla u)) \quad (3.27)$$
$$- C\varepsilon \|\varphi \Delta u\| \|\varphi u\| - C\varepsilon \eta \|\varphi \Delta u\| \|\partial_t u\|.$$

Using Proposition 1.2 and the inequality $2ab \leq \delta a^2 + \delta^{-1} b^2$, we see that the right-hand side is bounded from below by

$$(\nu - \varepsilon)\|\varphi \nabla u\|^2 + (\nu \eta / 2)\partial_t \|\nabla u\|^2 + (1/2)\partial_t \|\varphi u\|^2$$
$$+ (\eta - \eta \varepsilon)\|\varphi \partial_t u\|^2 - C_1 \varepsilon \|\varphi \Delta u\|^2. \quad (3.28)$$

From (3.27), using the bound (3.28), we conclude that (3.20) holds for functions $u(t)$, smooth in t.

Let now u satisfy (3.7), (3.8). By Lemma 3.1, $\partial_t u$ satisfies (3.15). Using a mollifying of u with respect to t (a formula similar to (0.3) may be used) we obtain the sequence $u_n(t)$, $u_n \in C^2([-T, T], H_2)$ for any T,

$$u_n \to u \quad \text{in } L_2([-T, T], H_2), \tag{3.29}$$
$$\partial_t u_n \to \partial_t u \quad \text{in } L_2([-T, T], H_0), \tag{3.30}$$
$$u_n \text{ are bounded in } L_\infty([-T, T], H_1) \tag{3.31}$$

for any $T > 0$. Note that $u_n = (u_{1n}, u_{2n}, u_{3n})$, we denote by $\mathrm{div}(\varphi \nabla u_n)$ the vector $\sum \partial_i(\varphi \partial_i u_n)$. Obviously,

$$(1/2)\partial_t \|\varphi \nabla u_n\|^2 = (\varphi^2 \nabla u_n, \partial_t \nabla u_n) = (-\mathrm{div}(\varphi^2 \nabla u_n), \partial_t u_n). \tag{3.32}$$

The passage to the limit is possible here in the sense of distributions and in $L_1([-T, T], \mathbb{R})$ for any T. Indeed, by (3.29), we have $\nabla u_n \to \nabla u$ in $L_2([-T, T], H)$. Since φ and its derivatives are bounded, we have $\varphi \nabla u_n \to \varphi \nabla u$ in $L_2([-T, T], H)$. For $h \in D(\mathbb{R})$, by (3.29)

$$\int \partial_t \|\varphi^2 \nabla u_n\|^2 h\, dt = \int \|\varphi^2 \nabla u_n\|^2 \partial_t h\, dt$$
$$\to \int \|\varphi^2 \nabla u\|^2 \partial_t h\, dt \quad (n \to \infty). \tag{3.33}$$

Therefore the left-hand side of (3.32) tends to $(1/2)\partial_t \|\nabla u\|^2$. The function $(\mathrm{div}(\varphi^2 \nabla u_n)(t), \partial_t u_n(t))$ of the variable t depends continuously in $L_1([-T, T], \mathbb{R})$ on $\mathrm{div}(\varphi^2 \nabla u_n) \in L_2([-T, T], H)$ and on $\partial_t u_n \in L_2([-T, T], H)$. Using (3.29) and (3.30), we obtain

$$(-\mathrm{div}(\varphi^2 \nabla u_n), \partial_t u_n) \to -(\mathrm{div}\, \varphi^2 \nabla u, \partial_t u) \quad \text{in } L_1([-T, T], \mathbb{R}).$$

Hence
$$(1/2)\partial_t \|\nabla u\|^2 = -(\mathrm{div}\, \varphi^2 \nabla u, \partial_t u), \tag{3.34}$$

and both sides belong to $L_1([-T, T], \mathbb{R})$ for any T.

Analogously,
$$\partial_t \|\varphi u\|^2 = 2(\varphi^2 u, \partial_t u) \tag{3.35}$$

belongs to $L_1([-T, T], \mathbb{R})$ for any t and is a limit in $L_1([-T, T], \mathbb{R})$ of $\partial_t \|\varphi u_n\|^2 = 2(\varphi^2 u_n, \partial_t u_n)$. By (3.30)

$$\|\varphi \partial_t u_n\|^2 \to \|\varphi \partial_t u\|^2 \quad \text{as } n \to \infty$$

in $L_1([-T, T], \mathbb{R})$. By (3.29) $\varphi \nabla u_n \to \varphi \nabla u$ in $L_2([-T, T], H(\Omega)^3)$ and

$$\|\varphi \nabla u_n\|^2 \to \|\varphi \nabla u\|^2 \quad \text{as } n \to \infty$$

in $L_1([-T, T], \mathbb{R})$. Hence the right-hand side of (3.20) is the limit as $n \to \infty$ of the right-hand side of (3.20) with u replaced by u_n.

By (3.29) and (3.30),
$$\partial_t u_n - \nu\Pi\Delta u_n \to \partial_t u - \nu\Pi\Delta u,$$
$$\varphi^2(u_n + \eta\partial_t u_n) \to \varphi^2(u + \eta\partial_t u)$$
in $L_2([-T, T], H)$. Hence the left-hand side of (3.20) is the limit as $n \to \infty$ of the left-hand side of (3.20) with u_n substituted for u. Therefore (3.20) holds and Lemma 3.2 is proved.

LEMMA 3.3. *Let $B(u, v)$ be defined by (3.2) and let u satisfy (3.7). Then for $u \in H_2$*
$$|(\Pi B(u, u), \varphi^2 u)| \leq C\varepsilon M_0 \|\varphi\nabla u\| \|\varphi u\|. \tag{3.36}$$

PROOF. Obviously $\Pi u = u$ and
$$(\Pi B(u, u), \varphi^2 u) = (B(u, u), \Pi\varphi^2 u)$$
$$= (B(u, u), \varphi^2 u) + (B(u, u), K'u), \tag{3.37}$$
where K' is the same as in (3.25). Using the relations $u|_{\partial\Omega} = 0$, $\operatorname{div} u = 0$ and $\varphi = \varphi(x_3)$, we obtain
$$(B(u, u), \varphi^2 u) = \frac{1}{2}\sum_i (u_i, \partial_i(u\varphi^2 u)) - \frac{1}{2}(u_3 u, u\partial_3\varphi^2)$$
$$= -(\varphi u_3 u, u\partial_3\varphi). \tag{3.38}$$

By Sobolev's embedding theorem, Proposition 1.2 and (1.7), we have
$$|(B(u, u), \varphi^2 u)| \leq C\varepsilon(|u|^2, \varphi^2|u|) \leq C\varepsilon\|\varphi u\|_{L_4}\|u\|_{L_4}\|\varphi u\|$$
$$\leq C_1\varepsilon\|u\|_1 \|\varphi u\| \|\varphi u\|_1. \tag{3.39}$$

By Theorem 2.1 where φ is replaced by φ^{-1}, we obtain for $u, v \in H_1$
$$|(B(u, v), K'v)| = \left|\left(\varphi\sum u_i v, \varphi^{-1}\partial_i K'v\right)\right|$$
$$\leq C\|u\|_{L_4}\|\varphi v\|_{L_4}\|\varphi^{-1}K'v\|_1$$
$$\leq C_1\varepsilon\|u\|_{L_4}\|\varphi v\|_{L_4}\|\varphi^{-1}\varphi^2 v\|. \tag{3.40}$$

By Sobolev's embedding theorem and Proposition 1.2, we obtain
$$|(B(u, u), K'u)| \leq C_1\varepsilon\|u\|_1 \|\varphi u\|_1 \|\varphi u\| \leq C_1\varepsilon M_0\|\varphi\nabla u\|\|\varphi u\|.$$
Using this inequality, (3.39), and Proposition 1.2, we obtain (3.36).

LEMMA 3.4. *Let $u, v \in H_2$, $\omega \in H$. Suppose $1/3 \leq \theta \leq 2/3$ and $0 \leq s_1, s_2, s_1 + s_2 \leq 1$. Then*
$$|(\Pi B(u, v), \varphi\omega)| \leq C\|\varphi^{1-s_1-s_2}\omega\|\|\varphi^{s_1}\Delta v\|^{3(1-\theta)/2}\|\varphi^{s_1}\nabla v\|^{(3\theta-1)/2}$$
$$\times \|\varphi^{s_2}\nabla u\|^{3\theta/2}\|\varphi^{s_2}u\|^{(2-3\theta)/2}, \tag{3.41}$$
$$\|\varphi\Pi B(u, v)\| \leq C\|\varphi^{s_1}\Delta v\|^{3(1-\theta)/2}\|\varphi^{s_1}\nabla v\|^{(3\theta-1)/2}$$
$$\times \|\varphi^{1-s_1}\nabla u\|^{3\theta/2}\|\varphi^{1-s_1}u\|^{(2-3\theta)/2}. \tag{3.42}$$

PROOF. Obviously,

$$|(\Pi B(u, v), \varphi\omega)| \leq |(B(u, v), \varphi\omega)| + \|(\varphi^s B(u, v), \varphi^{-s} K\omega)\|$$
$$\leq \|\varphi^s B(u, v)\|(\|\varphi^{1-s}\omega\| + \|\varphi^{-s} K\omega\|), \quad (3.43)$$

where $K\omega = \Pi\varphi\omega - \varphi\Pi\omega$. By Theorem 2.1

$$\|\varphi^{-s} K\omega\| \leq \varepsilon C \|\varphi^{1-s}\omega\|. \quad (3.44)$$

Setting $s = s_1 + s_2$, from (3.43), (3.44), and (3.2), we deduce

$$|(\Pi B(u, v), \varphi\omega)| \leq C \|\varphi^{1-s}\omega\| \|\varphi^{s_1+s_2} B(u, v)\|$$
$$\leq C_1 \|\varphi^{1-s}\omega\| \|\varphi^{s_1}\nabla v\|_{L_{2p}} \|\varphi^{s_2} u\|_{L_{2q}}, \quad (3.45)$$

where $1/p + 1/q = 1$. When $1 \leq p \leq 3$, by the Ladyzhenskaya-Gagliardo-Nirenberg inequality we have

$$\|\varphi^{s_1}\nabla v\|_{L_{2p}} \leq C \|\varphi^{s_1}\nabla v\|_1^{\theta_1} \|\varphi^{s_1}\nabla v\|^{1-\theta_1}, \quad (3.46)$$

$$\|\varphi^{s_2} u\|_{L_{2q}} \leq C \|\varphi^{s_2} u\|_1^{\theta_2} \|\varphi^{s_2} u\|^{1-\theta_2}, \quad (3.47)$$

where

$$\theta_1 = \frac{3}{2} - \frac{3}{2p}, \qquad \theta_2 = \frac{3}{2} - \frac{3}{2q}. \quad (3.48)$$

(If $p = 1$, we set $q = \infty$, and $\|\varphi_n\|_{L_\infty} \leq C \|\varphi_n\|_2^{1/2} \|\varphi_n\|_n^{1/2}$.) Set $1/p = \theta$, then $1/q = 1 - \theta$, $\theta_1 = (3/2)(1 - \theta)$, $\theta_2 = 3\theta/2$. By Propositions 1.2 and 1.3 we obtain

$$\|\varphi^{s_1}\nabla v\|_{L_{2p}} \|\varphi^{s_2} u\|_{L_{2q}} \leq C \|\varphi^{s_1}\Delta v\|^{3(1-\theta)/2} \|\varphi^{s_1}\nabla v\|^{(3\theta-1)/2}$$
$$\times \|\varphi^{s_2}\nabla u\|^{3\theta/2} \|\varphi^{s_2} u\|^{1-3\theta/2}. \quad (3.49)$$

From (3.45) and (3.49) we deduce (3.41). Inequality (3.42) follows from (3.41) where $s_1 + s_2 = 1$.

LEMMA 3.5. *Let* $y \in C([T_0, +\infty[)$ *be a nonnegative real-valued function*, $\partial_t y$ *be the derivative of* y *in the sense of distributions and assume that* $\partial_t y \in L_1[T_0, T_1]$, $\forall T_1 > T_0$. *Suppose that for almost all* $t \geq T_0$, y *satisfies the inequality*

$$\partial_t y + \alpha y \leq \beta(t) y + \gamma(t), \quad (3.50)$$

where the functions $\beta, \gamma \geq 0$ *and the number* $\alpha > 0$ *satisfy the following conditions. The functions* γ *and* β *are integrable on any bounded interval and there exists a* $\tau > 0$ *such that for any* $T_1 \geq T_0$

$$\int_{T_1+\tau i}^{T_1+\tau(i+1)} \beta(t) \, dt \leq \beta_0 \tau, \quad (3.51)$$

$$\int_{T_1+\tau i}^{T_1+\tau(i+1)} \gamma(t) \, dt \leq \gamma_0 \tau, \quad (3.52)$$

where
$$\alpha > \beta_0. \tag{3.53}$$

Then for all $t \geq T \geq T_0$ we have
$$y(t) \leq C_0 y(T) e^{-(\alpha - \beta_0)(t-T)} + C_1 \gamma_0, \tag{3.54}$$

where C_0 and C_1 depend only on α, β and τ.

PROOF. Let us consider at first the case when β and γ are continuous. Let
$$y_1(t) = y(t) \exp\left(\int_T^t (\alpha - \beta(\xi)) \, d\xi\right). \tag{3.55}$$

Obviously,
$$\partial_t y_1(t) \leq \gamma(t) \exp\left(\int_T^t (\alpha - \beta(\xi)) \, d\xi\right). \tag{3.56}$$

Therefore
$$y_1(t) \leq y_1(T) + \int_T^t \gamma(\eta) \exp\left(\int_T^\eta (\alpha - \beta(\xi)) \, d\xi\right) d\eta. \tag{3.57}$$

Hence by (3.55),
$$y(t) \leq y(T) \exp\left(\int_T^t (\beta(\xi) - \alpha) \, d\xi\right) + \int_T^t \gamma(\eta) \exp\left(\int_\eta^t (\beta(\xi) - \alpha) \, d\xi\right) d\eta. \tag{3.58}$$

For all $t \geq T \geq T_0$, we have
$$\int_T^t \beta(\xi) \, d\xi \leq C + \beta_0(t - T). \tag{3.59}$$

Indeed, let i be an integer, $i \geq 0$, such that
$$T + i\tau \leq t \leq T + (i+1)\tau. \tag{3.60}$$

By (3.51), where $T_1 = T$,
$$\int_T^t \beta \, d\xi \leq (i+1)\beta_0 \tau.$$

By (3.60), $i\tau \leq t - T$. Hence (3.59) holds with $C = \beta_0 \tau$. Using (3.59) to estimate the right-hand side of (3.58), we obtain
$$y(t) \leq y(T) \exp\left(C + \beta_0(t - T) - \alpha(t - T)\right) + \int_T^t \gamma(\eta) \exp\left(C + \beta(t - \eta) - \alpha(t - \eta)\right) d\eta. \tag{3.61}$$

If (3.60) is satisfied, we have by (3.52)

$$\int_T^t \gamma(\eta) \exp\left((\beta_0 - \alpha)(t - \eta)\right) d\eta$$

$$\leq \sum_{k=0}^{k=i} \int_{T+k\tau}^{T+(k+1)\tau} \gamma(\eta) \exp\left((\beta_0 - \alpha)(t - \eta)\right) d\eta$$

$$\leq \sum_{k=0}^{k=i} \gamma_0 \tau \exp\left((\beta_0 - \alpha)(t - T - k\tau)\right)$$

$$\leq \gamma_0 \tau \exp\left((\alpha - \beta_0)(T - t)\right) (e^{(\alpha-\beta_0)(i+1)\tau} - 1)(e^{(\alpha-\beta_0)\tau} - 1)^{-1}$$

$$\leq C\gamma_0 \tau \exp\left[-(\alpha - \beta_0)i\tau + (\alpha - \beta_0)(i+1)\tau\right] \leq C_1 \gamma_0.$$

This inequality and (3.61) imply (3.54).

Consider now the case when β and $\partial_t y$ are not continuous and belong to $L_1(-T, T)$ for any T. In this case, y and $\int_T^t \beta \, d\xi$ coincide almost everywhere with continuous functions. To obtain (3.54), it is sufficient to have (3.57), because futher computations do not depend on the continuity of β. To deduce (3.56) from (3.50), we use the formula

$$\partial_t(uv) = u\partial_t v + v\partial_t u. \tag{3.62}$$

We now prove that this formula is valid on $[-T_2, T_2]$ for

$$u, v \in C\left([-T_2, T_2]\right), \qquad \partial_t u \in L_1\left([-T_2, T_2]\right)$$

for any T in the sense of distributions. Let $h \in C_0^\infty\left([-T_2, T_2]\right)$.

Obviously for smooth u, v

$$-\int u_n v_n \partial_t h \, dt = \int u_n \partial_t v_n h \, dt + \int v_n \partial_t u_n h \, dt. \tag{3.63}$$

Functions u, v can be approximated by smooth u_n, v_n

$$\begin{aligned} u_n \to u, \quad & v_n \to v \quad \text{in } C([-T_2, T_2]), \\ \partial_t u_n \to \partial_t u, \quad & \partial_t v_n \to \partial_t v \quad \text{in } L_1([-T_2, T_2]). \end{aligned} \tag{3.64}$$

Obviously it is possible to pass to the limit in both sides of (3.63) as $n \to \infty$, and we obtain (3.62).

Another formula used in obtaining (3.56) is

$$\partial_t \exp(v(t)) = \exp(v(t)) \partial_t v(t). \tag{3.65}$$

Obviously, for smooth v_n and $h \in D(\mathbb{R})$, we have

$$-\int \exp(v_n(t)) \partial_t h \, dt = \int \exp(v_n(t)) \partial_t v_n(t) h \, dt.$$

Using v_n satisfying (3.64) we obtain (3.65). Using (3.62) with $u = y$ and $uv = y_1$ defined by (3.55), and also using (3.65) with

$$v(t) = -\int_T^t \beta \, d\xi,$$

we deduce (3.56) from (3.50). To deduce (3.57) from (3.56), we need the formula

$$\int_T^t \partial_t y \, dt = y(t) - y(T). \tag{3.66}$$

Since $u = y$ can be approximated by $u_n = y_n$ satisfying (3.64), and (3.66) holds for u_n, we obtain (3.66) by passing to the limit as $n \to \infty$. Using (3.66), we obtain (3.57). Therefore (3.54) is proved under the conditions of Lemma 3.5, and this lemma is proved.

PROOF OF THEOREMS 3.1 AND 3.2. Multiplying (3.1) by $\varphi^2(u + \eta \partial_t u)$ and using Lemma 3.2 and (3.4), we obtain

$$\eta(1 - \varepsilon)\|\varphi \partial_t u\|^2 + (\nu - \nu' - C\varepsilon)\|\varphi \nabla u\|^2$$
$$+ (1/2)\partial_t \|\varphi u\|^2 + (\eta \nu/2)\partial_t \|\varphi \nabla u\|^2$$
$$\leq |(\Pi f, \varphi^2(u + \eta \partial_t u))| + C\varepsilon \|\varphi \Delta u\|^2$$
$$+ |(\Pi B(u, u), \varphi^2 u)| + C\eta \|\varphi \nabla u\| \|\varphi \partial_t u\|$$
$$+ |(\varphi^2 L_0 u, \varphi^{-1} K' u)| + \eta \|\varphi \Pi B(u, u)\| \|\varphi \partial_t u\|, \tag{3.67}$$

where K' is defined by (3.25). Using (3.5), Lemma 3.3 and Theorem 2.1, we see that the right-hand side of (3.67) is not greater than

$$C\delta^{-1}\|\varphi \Pi f\|^2 + \delta \|\varphi u\|^2 + \delta \eta \|\varphi \partial_t u\|^2 + C\varepsilon \|\varphi \Delta u\|^2$$
$$+ C\varepsilon M_0 \|\varphi \nabla u\| \|\varphi u\| + C\eta \|\varphi \nabla u\| \|\varphi \partial_t u\|$$
$$+ C\varepsilon \|\varphi \nabla u\| \|\varphi u\| + \eta \|\varphi \Pi B(u, u)\|^2 + \|\varphi \partial_t u\|^2 (\eta/2). \tag{3.68}$$

Here $\delta > 0$ is arbitrary and we have used the inequality

$$2ab \leq \delta^{-1} a^2 + \delta b^2. \tag{3.69}$$

By using Proposition 1.2, Theorem 1.1, (3.41) with $s_1 = 0$, $\theta = 1/2$ and (3.69), from (3.67) and (3.68) we deduce

$$\partial_t(\|\varphi u\|^2 + \eta \nu \|\varphi \nabla u\|^2) + \eta(1 - 2\varepsilon)\|\varphi \partial_t u\|^2 + 2(\nu'' - C\varepsilon)\|\varphi \nabla u\|^2$$
$$\leq C_1 \delta^{-1} \|\varphi f\|^2 + C_1 \delta \|\varphi \nabla u\|^2 + C_1 \varepsilon M_0 \|\varphi \nabla u\|^2 + \eta \delta_1 \|\varphi \partial_t u\|^2$$
$$+ C_1 \delta_1^{-1} \eta \|\varphi \nabla u\|^2 + C_1 \varepsilon \|\varphi \nabla u\|^2 + C\varepsilon \|\varphi \Delta u\|^2$$
$$+ M_0^{1/2} C_1 \eta \|\Delta u\|^{3/2} \|\varphi \nabla u\|^{3/2} \|\varphi u\|^{1/2}. \tag{3.70}$$

Here $\nu'' > 0$ by (3.6).

By Theorem 2.2

$$\|\varphi \Delta u\|^2 \leq C \|\varphi \Pi \Delta u\|^2. \tag{3.71}$$

Since u is a solution of (3.1),

$$\|\varphi \Pi \Delta u\|^2 \leq C(\|\varphi \partial_t u\|^2 + \|\varphi \Pi L_0 u\|^2 + \|\varphi \Pi B(u, u)\|^2 + \|\varphi \Pi f\|^2).$$

Using Theorem 1.1, (3.5) and (3.42) (with $\theta = 1/2$, $s_1 = 0$), and Proposition 1.2, we get

$$\|\varphi \Delta u\|^2 \leq C(\|\varphi \partial_t u\|^2 + \|\varphi \nabla u\|^2 \\ + M_0^{1/2}\|\Delta u\|^{3/2}\|\varphi \nabla u\|^2 + \|\varphi f\|^2). \quad (3.72)$$

From (3.70) and (3.72), setting

$$\delta_1 = 1/2, \quad \delta = \nu''/(4C_1), \quad 0 < \eta \leq \nu''/(4C_1 \delta_1^{-1})$$

we deduce that

$$\partial_t(\|\varphi u\|^2 + \eta \nu \|\varphi \nabla u\|^2) + \eta(1/2 - 2\varepsilon - C_2\varepsilon\eta^{-1})\|\varphi \partial_t u\|^2 \\ + ((3/2)\nu'' - C_1\varepsilon M_0 - 2C_3\varepsilon)\|\varphi \nabla u\|^2 \\ \leq C_4 \|\varphi f\|^2 + C_5(\eta + \varepsilon)M_0^{1/2}\|\Delta u\|^{3/2}\|\varphi \nabla u\|^2. \quad (3.73)$$

Let

$$y(t) = \|\varphi u(t)\|^2 + \eta \nu \|\varphi \nabla u(t)\|^2. \quad (3.74)$$

By Lemma 3.2, $y \in L_1([-T, T])$ for any $T > 0$. After changing y on a set of zero Lebesgue measure, we can regard y as a continuous function. Since $\varepsilon \leq \varepsilon_1$ and ε_1 is small, (3.73) implies

$$\partial_t y + (\eta/4)\|\varphi \partial_t u\|^2 + \nu''\|\varphi \nabla u\|^2 \\ \leq C_4 \|\varphi f\|^2 + C_5(\eta + \varepsilon)M_0^{1/2}\|\Delta u\|^{3/2}\|\varphi \nabla u\|^2. \quad (3.75)$$

Obviously, by Proposition 1.2

$$Cy \geq \nu'' \|\varphi \nabla u\|^2 \geq \alpha y, \quad \alpha > 0. \quad (3.76)$$

Hence (3.75) imply

$$\partial_t y + \alpha y \leq C_5(\varepsilon + \eta)M_0^{1/2}\|\Delta u\|^{3/2} y + C_4 \|\varphi f\|^2. \quad (3.77)$$

This inequality is a form of relation (3.50), where

$$\beta = C_5(\varepsilon + \eta)M_0^{1/2}\|\Delta u\|^{3/2}, \quad \gamma = C_4 \|\varphi f\|^2. \quad (3.78)$$

By (3.8) and (3.11), inequalities (3.51), (3.52) hold with $\tau = 1$:

$$\beta_0 = C_5(\eta + \varepsilon)M_0^{1/2}M_1^{3/2}, \quad \gamma_0 = C_4 M_f^2. \quad (3.79)$$

If ε_2 and η are small, then $\beta_0 < \alpha/2$, the condition (3.53) is fulfiled, and the estimate (3.54) holds for any T, t, $t \geq T$. Therefore

$$y(t) \leq C_0 y(T) e^{-\alpha(t-T)/2} + C_1, \quad (3.80)$$

where C_0 and C_1 do not depend on t and T. By (3.7), since $\varphi \leq C(\rho)$ when $\rho < \infty$, we obtain

$$y(T) \leq C(\rho) M_0 \quad \forall t \in \mathbb{R}. \quad (3.81)$$

By letting T tend to $-\infty$ and using (3.81), we deduce from (3.80) that

$$y(t) \leqslant C_1 \quad \forall t \in \mathbb{R}, \tag{3.82}$$

where C_1 does not depend on t and ρ. Now integrating (3.75) with respect to t and using (3.82), (3.11), (3.8), we obtain

$$\eta \int_T^{T+1} \|\varphi \partial_t u\|^2 dt \leqslant C_2 \tag{3.83}$$

for any $T \in \mathbb{R}$.

Integarating (3.72) with respect to t over $[T, T+1]$ and using (3.82), (3.76), (3.8), (3.7) and (3.11) to find a bound for the right-hand side, we conclude that

$$\int_T^{T+1} \|\varphi \Delta u\|^2 dt \leqslant C_1. \tag{3.84}$$

Since the bounds in (3.82), (3.83), (3.84) do not depend on ρ, we can apply Lemma 1.9. Using this lemma, we obtain (3.12) in the case when (1.10) holds. This implies the assertion of Theorem 3.1. If we do not apply (1.10), then Lemma 1.9 implies (3.13) and (3.14) and the assertion of Theorem 3.2 holds.

§4. Exponential proximity at infinity of any two regular global solutions of the Navier-Stokes system

Let

$$\Phi_1(x, \varepsilon, \gamma) = \exp(\gamma(1 + |\varepsilon x_3|^2)^{1/2}). \tag{4.1}$$

Let u_1, u_2 be two solutions of (3.1) satisfying conditions (3.7), (3.8). It is assumed that the function f satisfies (3.11) and the function $\Phi = \Phi_f$ in the definition of the norm $\|f\|_{0,\gamma}$ in (1.11) is a function for which the condition

$$\lim_{|x| \to \infty} \Phi_f(x) = +\infty \tag{4.2}$$

holds. It is supposed also, that the corresponding function φ satisfies (1.5)–(1.8). By Theorem 3.2 both u_1 and u_2 satisfy (3.13) and (3.14), where $\varepsilon = \varepsilon_1$. In this section ε_1 will be fixed.

The main result of this section is a theorem showing that u_1 and u_2 are exponentially close one to another as $|x_3| \to \infty$. To formulate this statement accurately, denote by $J'^\infty_{0,\gamma}(u)$ and $J'^2_{2,\gamma}(u)$ the values defined by (3.9) and (3.10), where $\|u\|_{l,\gamma}$ is replaced by $\|u\|'_{l,\gamma}$,

$$(\|u\|'_{l,\gamma})^2 = \sum_{|\alpha| \leqslant l} \int_\Omega |\partial^\alpha u|^2 \Phi_1(x, \varepsilon, \gamma) \, dx, \tag{4.3}$$

and Φ_1 is defined by (4.1).

THEOREM 4.1. *Let* u_1, u_2 *be two solutions of* (3.1) *described above. Then there exist* $\varepsilon > 0$ *and* $C > 0$ *such that*

$$J'^{\infty}_{1,\varepsilon}(u_1 - u_2) + J'^{2}_{2,\varepsilon}(u_1 - u_2) + J'^{2}_{0,\varepsilon}(\partial_t(u_1 - u_2)) \leq C. \tag{4.4}$$

We shall consider also the situation when u_1 and u_2 are solutions of (3.1) with different right-hand sides f_1 and f_2 respectively. It is assumed that u_1 and u_2 satisfy (3.7), (3.8) and f_1, f_2 satisfy (4.2).

THEOREM 4.2. *Assume that*

$$J'^{2}_{0,\beta}(f_1 - f_2) \leq C_0 \tag{4.4'}$$

with some $\beta > 0$. *Then there exist* $\varepsilon > 0$ *and* $C > 0$ *such that* (4.4) *holds*.

To prove Theorems 4.1 and 4.2 we need notation and some lemmas. Let $w = u_1 - u_2$. Obviously w satisfies the equation

$$\partial_t w - \nu\Pi\Delta w + \Pi L_0 w + \Pi B(u_1, w) + \Pi B(w, u_2) = f_3, \tag{4.5}$$

where $f_3 = f_1 - f_2$. Let $\chi_1 \in D(\mathbb{R})$, $\chi_1 \geq 0$, $|\chi_1| \leq 1$,

$$\begin{aligned}\chi_1(x_3) &= 1 \quad \text{when } |x_3| \leq 1, \\ \chi_1(x_3) &= 0 \quad \text{when } |x_3| \geq 2,\end{aligned} \tag{4.6}$$

$$\chi(x_3) = \chi_1(\sigma x_3), \quad 0 < \sigma \leq 1. \tag{4.7}$$

Rewrite (4.5) in the form

$$\partial_t w - \nu\Pi\Delta w + \Pi L_0 w + \Pi L_1 w = f, \tag{4.8}$$

where

$$L_1 w = B((1-\chi)u_1, w) + B(w, (1-\chi)u_2), \tag{4.9}$$

$$f = -\Pi B(\chi u_1, w) - \Pi B(w, \chi u_2) + f_3. \tag{4.10}$$

LEMMA 4.1. *There exists a function* $\varphi(x, \varepsilon, \rho, \gamma)$ *such that* (1.5)–(1.8) *hold and* (1.9) *holds with* $\Phi(x, \varepsilon, \gamma) = \Phi_1(x, \varepsilon, \gamma)$, *where* Φ *is defined by* (4.1).

PROOF. Since the function $h(t) = t$ satisfies all the assumptions of Lemma 1.8, then the function φ defined by (1.92) satisfies (1.5)–(1.8) and also (1.9) with $\Phi = \Phi_1$.

Henceforth in this section we shall denote by φ the function defined in Lemma 4.1, $\varepsilon \leq \varepsilon_0$, where ε_0 is small.

LEMMA 4.2. *For any* $\sigma > 0$, $\gamma > 0$, $\gamma \leq \beta$ *there exists* C *such that for any* ε, $0 < \varepsilon \leq \varepsilon_0$,

$$J'^{2}_{0,\gamma}(f_1) \leq C. \tag{4.11}$$

PROOF. According to (4.10),

$$\|\varphi f\| \leq C\|\varphi\Pi B(\chi u_1, w)\| + C\|\varphi\Pi B(w, \chi u_2)\| + \|\varphi f_3\|. \tag{4.12}$$

By (3.42), where $\theta = 1/2$, $s_1 = 0$, we have

$$\|\varphi\Pi B(\chi u, w)\|^2 \leq C \|\Delta(w)\|^{3/2} \|\nabla w\|^{1/2} \|\varphi\nabla(\chi u_1)\|^{3/2} \|\varphi\chi u_1\|^{1/2}.$$

Since χ has a compact support when $\sigma > 0$, we get

$$\|\varphi\Pi B(\chi u_1, w)\|^2 \leq C_1 \|w\|_2^{3/2} \|w\|^{1/2} \|u_1\|_1^2. \tag{4.13}$$

Analogously, using (3.42) with $\theta = 1/2$, $s_1 = 1$, we obtain

$$\|\varphi\Pi B(w, \chi u_2)\| \leq C\|u_1\|_2^{3/2} \|u_1\|_1^{1/2} \|w\|_1^2. \tag{4.14}$$

Integrating (4.13) end (4.14) with respect to t, using (4.4') and taking into account the fact that u_1, u_2 and $w = u_1 - u_2$ satisfy (3.7) and (3.8), we obtain (4.11) after passing to the limit as $\rho \to +\infty$. The constant C in (4.11) does not depend on $\varepsilon \leq \varepsilon_0$, since Φ_1 decreases when ε decreases.

LEMMA 4.3. *Let L_1 be defined by (4.9). Then for any $w \in H_1^0(\Omega)^3$,*

$$\|\varphi\Pi L_1 w\|^2 \leq \beta_1(t) \|\varphi\nabla w\|^2, \tag{4.15}$$

where

$$\int_T^{T+1} \beta_1(t)\, dt \leq Cr(\sigma) \quad \forall T \in \mathbb{R}, \tag{4.16}$$

where $r(\sigma) \to 0$ as $\sigma \to 0$.

PROOF. Obviously

$$\|\varphi\Pi L_1 w\|^2 \leq 2\|\varphi\Pi B(w, (1-\chi)u_2)\|^2 + 2\|\varphi\Pi B((1-\chi)u_1, w)\|^2. \tag{4.17}$$

By (3.42) (with $\theta = 1/2$, $s_1 = 1$), we have

$$\|\varphi\Pi B(w, (1-\chi)u_2)\|^2$$
$$\leq C \|\Delta((1-\chi)u_2)\|^{3/2} \|\nabla((1-\chi)u_2)\|^{1/2} \|\varphi\nabla w\|. \tag{4.18}$$

(Here we used Proposition 1.2.) By Theorem 1.1,

$$\|\varphi\Pi B((1-\chi)u_1, w)\|^2 \leq C \|(1-\chi)u_1\|_{L_\infty} \|\varphi\nabla w\|.$$

By the multiplicative inequality and Propositions 1.2 and 1.3,

$$\|(1-\chi)u_1\|_{L_\infty}^2 \leq C\|(1-\chi)u_1\|_2 \|(1-\chi)u\|_1$$
$$\leq C_1 \|\Delta((1-\chi)u_1)\| \|\nabla((1-\chi)u_1)\|.$$

Hence

$$\|\varphi\Pi B((1-\chi)u_1, w)\|^2$$
$$\leq C \|\varphi\nabla w\| \|\Delta((1-\chi)u_1)\| \|\nabla((1-\chi)u_1)\|. \tag{4.19}$$

Obviously

$$\|\Delta((1-\chi)u_2)\| \leq \|(1-\chi)\Delta u_2\| \\ + 2\|\nabla(1-\chi)\nabla u_2\| + \|u_2\Delta(1-\chi)\|. \quad (4.20)$$

Let

$$r_1(t) = \sup\{\Phi_f(x_3, 1, \gamma)^{-1}, |x_3| \geq t\}.$$

Obviously $r_1(t)$ is monotonically decreasing and by (4.2)

$$r_1(t) \to 0 \quad \text{as } t \to +\infty. \quad (4.21)$$

By (4.6), (4.7) $|1-\chi| \leq 1$,

$$(1-\chi) = 0 \quad \text{when } |x_3| \geq \sigma^{-1}. \quad (4.22)$$

Therefore, we obtain

$$\|(1-\chi)\Delta u_i\|^2 = \int (1-\chi)^2 \Phi^{-2}(x, \varepsilon_1, \gamma) \Phi^2(x, \varepsilon_1, \gamma) |\Delta u_i|^2 dx$$
$$\leq \|\Phi \Delta u_i\|^2 \sup\{\Phi^{-2}(x, \varepsilon_1, \gamma) : |x_3| \geq \sigma^{-1}\}$$
$$\leq \|\Phi \Delta u_i\|^2 r_1(\varepsilon_1 \sigma^{-1})^2. \quad (4.23)$$

Here $\Phi = \Phi_f(x, \varepsilon_1, \gamma)$, ε_1 is such that (3.13), (3.14) hold with $\varepsilon = \varepsilon_1$. Finding bounds for the second and the third terms on the right-hand side of (4.20) in a similar way, we obtain

$$\|\Delta((1-\chi)u_i)\| \leq C r_1(\varepsilon_1 \sigma^{-1})(\|\Phi \Delta u_i\| + \|\Phi \nabla u_i\| + \|\Phi u_i\|). \quad (4.24)$$

In the same way, we obtain

$$\|\nabla((1-\chi)u_i)\| \leq C r_1(\varepsilon_1 \sigma^{-1})(\|\Phi \nabla u_i\| + \|\Phi u_i\|), \quad (4.25)$$

where $i = 1, 2$.

Combining (4.17), (4.18), (4.19) and using (3.13) (with u replaced by u_1 and u_2), we obtain

$$\|\Pi L_1 w\|^2 \leq C r_1(\varepsilon_1 \sigma^{-1}) \|\varphi \nabla w\|^2 (C + \|\Phi \Delta u_2\|^{3/2} + \|\Phi \Delta u_1\|). \quad (4.26)$$

Using (3.14) for u_1 and u_2, after integrating (4.26) with respect to t over $[T, T+1]$, we obtain (4.15), (4.16), where $r(\sigma) \to 0$, since $r_1(\varepsilon_1 \sigma^{-1})^2 \to 0$ as $\sigma \to 0$ by (4.21).

PROOF OF THEOREM 4.2. Multiplying (4.8) by $\varphi^2(w + \eta \partial_t w)$, using Lemma 3.2, and (3.4), in the same way as (3.67) we obtain

$$(\eta - \eta \varepsilon)\|\varphi \partial_t w\|^2 + (\nu - \nu' - C\varepsilon)\|\varphi \nabla w\|^2$$
$$+ (1/2)\partial_t \|\varphi w\|^2 + (\eta \nu/2)\partial_t \|\varphi \nabla w\|^2 - C\varepsilon \|\varphi \Delta w\|^2$$
$$\leq C\|\varphi(w + \eta \partial_t w)\|(\|\varphi \Pi f\| + \|\varphi \Pi L_1 w\|)$$
$$\leq \delta_1 \|\varphi w\|^2 + (\eta/2)\|\varphi \partial_t w\|^2$$
$$+ C\delta_1^{-1}\|\varphi \Pi f\|^2 + C_1 \|\varphi \Pi L_1 w\|^2. \quad (4.27)$$

Similarly to (3.72), using (4.15), we obtain

$$\|\varphi\Delta w\|^2 \leq C(\|\varphi\partial_t w\|^2 + \|\varphi\nabla w\|^2 + \beta_1(t)\|\varphi\nabla w\|^2 + \|\varphi\Pi f\|^2).$$

Let

$$y = \|\varphi w\|^2 + \eta\nu\|\varphi\nabla w\|^2. \tag{4.28}$$

Using Lemmas 4.2 and 4.3, setting $\delta_1 = \nu''/2$, using that by Proposition 1.2

$$Cy \geq \|\varphi\nabla w\| \geq \alpha y, \qquad \alpha > 0,$$

from (4.27) we deduce like in the proof of Theorem 3.1, that

$$\partial_t y + \mu y \leq C\beta_1(t)y + C\|\varphi\Pi f\|^2, \tag{4.29}$$

where $\mu > 0$. If σ is chosen small enough, then by (4.16)

$$\int_T^{T+1} C\beta_1(t)\,dt \leq \frac{\mu}{2}. \tag{4.30}$$

Fixing such a $\sigma = \sigma_1$ and using Lemma 4.2, we conclude that all the conditions of Lemma 3.5 for $\tau = 1$ are fulfilled. Applying Lemma 3.5 as in the proof of Theorems 3.1 and 3.2, we conclude that (3.82) is valid. Theorem 4.2 is deduced from (3.82) just like Theorem 3.2 in §3.

Theorem 4.1 immediately follows from Theorem 4.2, since $f_2 - f_1 = 0$ in this case.

REMARK 4.1. Let the external force f in (I.1) and in (3.1) be independent of t and satisfy (3.11) for some choice of Φ. Then there exists a stationary solution z of (3.1), independent of t,

$$-\nu\Pi\Delta z + \Pi L_0 z + \Pi B(z, z) = \Pi f, \tag{4.31}$$

$z \in H_2$. (For the existence and regularity of such a solution see, for example, [24].) Obviously (3.7) and (3.8) hold. Such a solution z may be nonunique, but by Theorem 4.1 the difference $z_1 - z_2$ of any such solutions decays exponentially as $|x| \to \infty$. Moreover, if $u(t)$ is any time-dependent solution of (3.1) satisfying (3.7) and (3.8), then $z - u(t)$ by (4.4) decays exponentially as $|x| \to \infty$. This shows, in particular, that $\partial_t u(t)$ decays exponentially as $|x| \to \infty$. Note that these assertions are valid if f decays at infinity slightly more rapidly than a function from $L_2(\Omega)^3$, that is $\Phi = \Phi_f$ may be any function satisfying (4.2) for which $\varphi = \varphi_f$ satisfies (1.5)–(1.9).

REMARK 4.2. Let $f = f_1 + g$, where f_1 is independent of t and is of the kind described in the preceding remark, and g satisfies (4.4') with $f_1 - f_2$ replaced by g. Let $u(t)$ be a solution of (3.1) satisfying (3.7), (3.8). Then by Theorem 4.2

$$u(t) = z + w(t),$$

where z is a time-independent regular solution and $w(t, x)$ decays exponentially as $|x| \to \infty$.

§5. Asymptotic expansion at infinity of regular global solutions

In this section we shall determine the terms of the asymptotic expansion as $|x| \to \infty$ of solutions of (3.1). This expansion can be formally written in the form

$$u(t, x) = \sum_{k=1}^{\infty} z_k(t, x) \qquad (5.0)$$

(this series is not convergent, this is asymptotical). In this section we shall write the equations for z_k and study properties of z_k. In the next section an estimate of the remainder of an approximation of u by a partial sum of the series (5.0) will be obtained.

Consider the equation

$$\partial_t z_1 - \nu \Pi \Delta z_1 + \Pi L_0 z_1 = \Pi f. \qquad (5.1)$$

It is assumed that f satisfies (3.11), L_0 is defined by (3.3) and satisfies (3.4), (3.5).

Consider also the equations for z_k, $k = 2, 3, \ldots$,

$$\partial_t z_k - \nu \Pi \Delta z_k + \Pi L_0 z_k + \sum_{i+j=k} \Pi B(z_i, z_j) = 0. \qquad (5.2)$$

Here B is defined by (3.2).

THEOREM 5.1. *Let φ satisfy (1.5)–(1.8), (1.10). Let f satisfy (3.11). Then there exists a solution z_1 of equation (5.1) and solutions z_k, $k = 2, 3, \ldots$, of the equation (5.2). These solutions $z_k(t, x)$, $t \in \mathbb{R}$, $x \in \Omega$ belong to $L_2([-T, T], H_2) \cap L_\infty([-T, T], H_1)$ for any $T > 0$. Moreover,*

$$J_{1, k\gamma}^{\infty}(z_k) + J_{2, k\gamma}^{2}(z_k) + J_{0, k\gamma}^{2}(\partial_t z_k) \leq M_k'. \qquad (5.3)$$

Such solutions are unique.

Theorem 5.1 shows that the greater the number k of the term z_k, the greater the order of decrease $k\gamma$ of this term.

The proof of Theorem 5.1 is based on several lemmas.

Consider the initial-value problem

$$\partial_t v - \nu \Pi \Delta v + \Pi L_0 v = h, \qquad (5.4)$$

$$v|_{t=\tau} = v_0. \qquad (5.5)$$

LEMMA 5.1. *Let $h \in L_2([-\tau, T_0], H_0)$ for any $T_0 > 0$, let $v_0 \in H_1$, $T \geq \tau$. Then there exists a unique solution*

$$v \in L_2([\tau, T], H_2) \cap L_\infty([\tau, T], H_1)$$

such that $\partial_t v \in L_2([\tau, T], H)$.

PROOF. The existence of a unique solution

$$v \in L_2([\tau, T], H_1) \cap L_\infty([\tau, T], H_0)$$

is proved, for example, in [24], Chapter 3, in the case when $L_0 = 0$, and Ω is bounded. In the case considered here, the proof remains the same. The proof is based on Galerkin's method for the equation (5.4), and since the conditions (3.4), (3.5) hold with $\varphi = 1$, all the estimates for Galerkin approximations are the same. The estimate

$$\int_\tau^T \|\partial_t v\|^2 dt \leq C\left(\int_\tau^T \|h\|^2 dt + \|v(\tau)\|^2\right) \quad (5.6)$$

also can be obtained in the same way as in [24].

Since $\nu \Pi \Delta v = \partial_t v - h$, we have for almost all t the estimate resulting from Proposition 0.22:

$$\|v\|_2^2 \leq C(\|\partial_t v\|^2 + \|h\|^2). \quad (5.7)$$

Integrating this estimate with respect to t and using (5.6), we obtain the estimate

$$\int_\tau^T \|v\|_2^2 dt \leq C \int_\tau^T \|h\|^2 dt. \quad (5.8)$$

Since

$$\partial_t(\nabla v, \nabla v) = 2(\partial_t v, \Delta v),$$

inequalities (5.8) and (5.9) imply that $\|\nabla v\|$ is bounded in $L_\infty(\tau, T)$, and $v \in ([\tau, T], H_1)$.

LEMMA 5.2. *Let* $J_{0,0}^2(h) < \infty$. *Then there exists a unique solution* $u(t)$, $t \in \mathbb{R}$, *of the equation* (5.4) *such that* $J_{2,0}^2(u) + J_{1,0}^\infty(u) + J_{0,0}(\partial_t u) < \infty$, *and the estimate*

$$J_{2,0}^2(u) + J_{1,0}^\infty(u) + J_{0,0}^2(\partial_t u) \leq C J_{0,0}^2(h) \quad (5.9)$$

holds.

PROOF. Let v_0 be some function from H_1, for example, $v_0 = 0$, let $\tau = -n$, $n = 1, 2, \ldots$. Let $u = u_n$ be a solution of (5.4), (5.5). Multiplying (5.4) by $u + \eta \partial_t u$ and using Lemma 3.2 and (3.4), where $\varphi = 1$, $\varepsilon = 0$, we obtain

$$\eta \|\partial_t u\|^2 + (\nu - \nu') \|\nabla u\|^2 + (1/2)\partial_t \|u\|^2 + (\eta \nu/2)\partial_t \|\nabla u\|^2$$
$$\leq \|h\|(\|u\| + \eta \|\partial_t u\|) + C\eta \|\nabla u\| \|\partial_t u\|$$
$$\leq (\eta/2)\|\partial_t u\|^2 + \delta^{-2} C_1 \|h\|^2 + C_1 \eta \|\nabla u\|^2 + \delta \|u\|^2,$$

where $\delta < 1$. Using Proposition 2.1 and choosing $\delta \ll \nu - \nu'$, we obtain

$$\partial_t(\|u\|^2 + \eta \nu \|\nabla u\|^2) + \eta \|\partial_t u\|^2 + (\nu'' - C\eta)\|\nabla u\|^2 \leq C_1 \|h\|^2. \quad (5.10)$$

Let η be so small that $C\eta = \nu''/2$ and let
$$y = \|u\|^2 + \eta\nu\|\nabla u\|^2.$$
Obviously $Cy \leq \|u\|_1^2 \leq C^{-1}y$. We have
$$\partial_t y + \mu y \leq C\|h\|^2.$$
Applying Lemma 3.5, where $\delta = 1$, $\beta_0 = 0$, $\alpha = \mu$, we obtain from (3.54)
$$\|u(t)\|_1^2 \leq C\|v_0\|_1^2 e^{-\mu(t-\tau)} + CJ_{0,0}^2(h)^2. \tag{5.11}$$
Integrating (5.10) with respect to t, using (5.11) for $T \geq \tau = -n$, we obtain
$$\int_T^{T+1} \|\partial_t u\|^2 dt \leq CJ_{0,0}(h)^2 + C\|u(T)\|_1^2$$
$$\leq C_1 J_{0,0}^2(h) + C_1\|v_0\|^2 e^{-\mu(T+n)}. \tag{5.12}$$
Integrating (5.7), where $v = u$, with respect to t over $[T, T+1]$, $T \geq -n$ we obtain
$$\int_T^{T+1} \|u\|_2^2 dt \leq CJ_{0,0}^2(h)^2 + C_1\|v_0\|_1^2 e^{-\mu(T+n)}. \tag{5.13}$$
Note that bounds for the norms of $u = u_n$ are independent of n. Let $n \to \infty$. We can choose a weakly convergent subsequence u_n (we use the same indices), $u_n \to u$ weakly in $L_2([-T,T], H_2)$, $\partial_t u_n \to \partial_t u$ weakly in $L_2([-T,T], H)$, $T = 1, 2, \ldots$. It can be easily verified in a standard way that since u_n are solutions of (5.4) on $[-T,T] \times \Omega$ for large n, then u is a solution of (5.4). This solution is defined for all $t \in \mathbb{R}$ and satisfies estimates (5.11), (5.12), (5.13), where n is arbitrarily large. Hence u satisfies (5.9).

To prove the uniqueness of u, consider two solutions u_1 and u_2 with bounded $J_0^\infty(u)$. Let $u = u_1 - u_2$, $v_0 = u(\tau)$, $\tau = -n$. Obviously $u_1 - u_2$ is a solution of (5.9) with $h = 0$, and $\|v_0\|$ is uniformly bounded with respect to τ. Passing to the limit in (5.11) as $\tau \to -\infty$, we see that $u(t) = 0$ and $u_1 = u_2$.

LEMMA 5.3. *Let $J_{0,\gamma}^2(h) \leq \infty$, $\gamma > 0$. Then the solution of the equation (5.4), constructed in Lemma 5.2, satisfies the estimate*
$$J_{0,0}^\infty(\varphi\nabla v) + J_{0,0}^2(\varphi\Delta v) + J_{0,0}^2(\varphi\partial_t v) \leq CJ_{0,0}^2(\varphi h). \tag{5.14}$$

Here $\varphi = \varphi(x, \varepsilon, \rho, \gamma)$ is a weight function satisfying (1.5)–(1.8), *C does not depend on ε, ρ and h.*

PROOF. Multiplying (5.4) by $\varphi^2(u + \eta\partial_t u)$, we see as in (3.73), with some simplifications due to absence of $B(u, u)$, that the following estimate is valid
$$\partial_t(\|\varphi v\|^2 + \eta\nu\|\varphi\nabla v\|^2) + \eta(3/2 - 2\varepsilon - C\varepsilon\eta^{-1})\|\varphi\partial_t v\|^2$$
$$+ ((3/2)\nu'' - 2C\varepsilon)\|\varphi\nabla v\|^2 \leq C\|\varphi h\|^2. \tag{5.15}$$

In the same way as (3.77) was deduced from (3.73), from (5.15) we deduce for $y = \|\varphi v\|^2 + \eta\gamma\|\varphi\nabla v\|^2$ the inequality

$$\partial_t y + \mu y \leq C\|\varphi h\|^2. \tag{5.16}$$

Lemma 3.5 implies that

$$y(t) \leq C_0 y(T) e^{-\mu(t-T)} + C_1 J_{0,0}^2(\varphi h)^2.$$

Since $p < \infty$, φ is bounded, and $J_{0,1}^\infty(v) \leq C_1$ implies $J_{0,0}^\infty(\varphi v) \leq C$. Therefore $y(T)$ is bounded uniformly with respect to T. Letting T tend to $-\infty$, we obtain

$$\|\varphi v\|^2 + \|\varphi\nabla v\|^2 \leq Cy \leq C_1 J_{0,0}^2(\varphi h)^2. \tag{5.17}$$

Integrating (5.15) with respect to t and using (5.17), we obtain, since ε is small,

$$\int_T^{T+1} \|\varphi\partial_t v\|^2 dt \leq C J_{0,0}^2(\varphi h)^2. \tag{5.18}$$

From (5.4) and (3.5) it follows that

$$\|\varphi\Pi\Delta u\|^2 \leq C(\|\varphi h\|^2 + \|\varphi\nabla v\|^2 + \|\varphi\partial_t v\|^2).$$

Using (5.17), (5.18), Theorem 2.2, and Proposition 1.2, we conclude that

$$\int_t^{T+1} \|\varphi\Delta v\|^2 dt \leq C J_{0,0}^2(\varphi h)^2. \tag{5.19}$$

Now (5.9) follows from (5.17), (5.18), (5.19).

PROOF OF THEOREM 5.1. We shall use an inductive argument. For the first step of the induction let $k = 1$. The solution of the equation (5.1) exists by Lemma 5.2. The estimate (5.14) with $v = z_1$, $h = \Pi f$ holds for any $p > 1$.

Using Lemma 1.9 and using the fact that the right-hand side of (5.14), where $h = \Pi f$, is bounded by $J_{0,\gamma}(f)$ in view of Theorem 1.1, we obtain (5.3) for $k = 1$.

Suppose now that (5.3) holds for $k = 1, \ldots, l - 1$. Let $k = l$. The equation (5.2) is of the form (5.4) with $v = z_k$,

$$h = h_k = -\sum_{i+j=k} \Pi B(z_i, z_j). \tag{5.20}$$

To deduce (5.3) from (5.14), we must estimate

$$Q_{ij} = \int_T^{T+1} \|\varphi^k \Pi B(z_i, z_j)\|^2 dt. \tag{5.21}$$

Using Lemma 3.4 with $s_1 = j/k$, $s_2 = i/k$, $\theta = 1/2$, φ replaced by $\varphi^k = \varphi(x, \varepsilon, p, \gamma k)$, we obtain

$$\|\varphi^k \Pi B(z_i, z_j)\|^2 \leq C\|\varphi^j \Delta z_j\|^{3/2} \|\varphi^j \nabla z_j\|^{1/2} \|\varphi^i \nabla z_i\|^{3/2} \|\varphi^i z_i\|^{1/2}.$$

Hence, using Proposition 1.2, we obtain

$$Q_{ij} \leqslant C_1 J_{0,0}^2(\varphi^j \Delta z_j)^{3/2} J_{0,0}^\infty(\varphi^j \nabla z_j)^{1/2} J_{0,0}^\infty(\varphi^i \nabla z_i)^{3/2}. \tag{5.22}$$

Summing this estimate with respect to i, j, $i+j = k = l$ and using (5.3) values of k for smaller than l to find a bound for the right-hand side of (5.22), we obtain

$$J_{0,0}^2(\varphi^k h_k) \leqslant C. \tag{5.23}$$

Using this estimate, we deduce from Lemma 5.3 that (5.14) holds with v, φ, h replaced by z_k, φ^k, h_k, and the right-hand side of (5.14) is bounded uniformly with respect to ρ.

By Lemma 1.9, inequality (5.14) implies (5.3) and Theorem 5.1 is proved.

§6. Estimate of the error

Let z_k, $k = 1, \ldots,$ be the functions constructed in the preceding section, let u be the solution of (3.1). Put

$$w = w_{n+1} = u - S_n, \qquad S_n = z_1 + \cdots + z_n. \tag{6.1}$$

The following theorem shows that the error of approximation by S_n decays more rapidly than any of the terms involved in S_n.

THEOREM 6.1. *Let φ satisfy (1.5)–(1.8), (1.10), let f satisfy (3.11), let u be a solution of (3.1) satisfying (3.7), (3.8). Then*

$$J_{1,\gamma}^\infty(w) + J_{2,\gamma(n+1)}^2(w) + J_{0,\gamma(n+1)}^2(\partial_t w) \leqslant C_{n+1}. \tag{6.2}$$

PROOF. Substituting $u = S_n + w$ into (3.1), taking into account (5.1), (5.2), and the identity $B(u, u) - B(S_n, S_n) = B(u, w) + B(w, S_n)$, we see that $w = u - S_n$ satisfies the equation

$$\partial_t w - \nu \Pi \Delta w + \Pi L_0 w + \Pi B(u, w)$$
$$+ \Pi B(w, S_n) + \sum_{i+j \geqslant n+1} \Pi B(z_i, z_j) = 0. \tag{6.3}$$

Here $i, j \geqslant 1$, $i, j \leqslant n$. Let us prove that

$$J_{0,0}^\infty(\varphi^l \nabla w) + J_{0,0}^2(\varphi^l \Delta w) + J_{0,0}^2(\varphi^l \partial_t w) \leqslant C_l, \tag{6.4}$$

$l = 1, \ldots, n+1$. We shall use an inductive argument.

At the initial step $l = 1$, $s_1 = z_1$, $w = u - z_1$. Obviously, u satisfies (3.12) by Theorem 3.1, z_1 satisfies (5.3) with $k = 1$ by Theorem 5.1. Therefore, since $\varphi \leqslant \Phi$, their difference w satisfies (6.4) with $l = 1$.

Suppose now that (6.4) holds for $l = 1, \ldots, k-1$. We shall prove that it holds for $l = k$, $k \leqslant n+1$. Multiplying (6.3) by $\varphi^{2k}(w + \eta w)$ and using

Lemma 3.2 and Theorem 1.1, we obtain

$$(1/2)\partial_t(\|\varphi^k w\|^2 + \nu\eta\|\varphi^k \partial_t w\|^2) + (\nu'' - C\varepsilon)\|\varphi^k \nabla w\|^2$$
$$+ (\eta - \eta\varepsilon - \varepsilon)\|\varphi^k \partial_t w\|^2 - C\varepsilon\|\varphi^k \Delta w\|^2$$
$$\leq C(\|\varphi^{k-1} w\| + \eta\|\varphi^{k-1} \partial_t w\|)$$
$$\times (\|\varphi^{k+1} \Pi B(u, w)\| + \|\varphi^{k+1} \Pi B(w, S_n)\|)$$
$$+ \sum_{i+j \geq n+1} \|\varphi^k \Pi B(z_i, z_j)\|(\|\varphi^k w\| + \eta\|\varphi^k \partial_t w\|). \quad (6.5)$$

Now we shall obtain bounds for the terms in the right-hand side of (6.5). By Lemma 3.4, where $\theta = 1/2$, $s_2 = 1/(k+1)$, $s_1 = k/(k+1)$, we obtain

$$\|\varphi^{k+1} \Pi B(u, w)\|^2 \leq C\|\varphi^k \Delta w\|^{3/2} \|\varphi^k \nabla w\|^{1/2} \|\varphi \nabla u\|^{3/2} \|\varphi u\|^{1/2}. \quad (6.6)$$

Analogously, setting $s_2 = k/(k+1)$, $s_1 = 1/(k+1)$, we obtain

$$\|\varphi^{k+1} \Pi B(u, S_n)\|^2$$
$$\leq C\|\varphi \Delta S_n\|^{3/2} \|\varphi \nabla S_n\|^{1/2} \|\varphi^k \nabla w\|^{3/2} \|\varphi^k w\|^{1/2}. \quad (6.7)$$

Note that since $\varphi \geq 1$, we have $\varphi^k \leq \varphi^{i+j}$ when $i+j \geq n+1$, $k \leq n+1$. Hence, by Lemma 3.4 with $s_2 = i/(i+j)$, $s_1 = j/(i+j)$ we obtain

$$\|\varphi^k \Pi B(z_i, z_j)\| \leq \|\varphi^{i+j} \Pi B(z_i, z_j)\|$$
$$\leq C\|\varphi^i \Delta z_i\|^{3/2} \|\varphi^i \nabla z_i\|^{1/2} \|\varphi^j \nabla z_j\|^{3/2} \|\varphi^j z_j\|^{1/2}. \quad (6.8)$$

Using Proposition 1.2, Theorem 3.1, and Theorem 5.1, from (6.6) and (6.7) we deduce

$$\|\varphi^{k+1} \Pi B(u, w)\| + \|\varphi^{k+1} \Pi B(w, S_n)\|$$
$$\leq C\|\varphi^k \Delta w\|^{3/2} \|\varphi^k \nabla w\|^{1/2} + C\|\varphi \Delta S_n\|^{3/2} \|\varphi^k \nabla w\|^2. \quad (6.9)$$

Using Proposition 1.2 and Theorem 5.1, we obtain

$$\|\varphi^k \Pi B(z_i, z_j)\| \leq C\|\varphi^i \Delta z_i\|^{3/2}. \quad (6.10)$$

Using the inequality $2ab \leq \delta a^2 + \delta^{-1} b^2$, inequalities (6.9) and (6.10), and Proposition 1.2, we conclude that the right-hand side of (6.5) is bounded by

$$C(\delta^{-1} + \delta_1^{-1})(\|\varphi^{k-1} \nabla w\|^2 + \eta^2 \|\varphi^{k-1} \partial_t w\|^2)$$
$$+ \delta_1 \|\varphi \Delta S_n\|^{3/2} \|\varphi^k \nabla w\|^2 + \delta\|\varphi^k \Delta w\|^{3/2} \|\varphi^k \nabla w\|^{1/2}$$
$$+ C\delta^{-1} \sum \|\varphi^i \Delta z_i\|^{3/2} + \delta(\|\varphi^k \nabla w\|^2 + \|\varphi^k \partial_t w\|^2). \quad (6.11)$$

Here positive $\delta \leq 1$, $\delta_1 \leq 1$ are arbitrary.

Since w is a solution of (6.3), it follows from (3.12), (6.9), (6.10) and Theorem 2.2 that we have

$$\|\varphi^k \Delta w\|^2 \leq C(\|\varphi^k \partial_t w\|^2 + \|\varphi^{k-1}\Delta w\|^{3/2}\|\varphi^{k-1}\nabla w\|^{1/2})$$
$$+ C\sum \|\varphi^i \Delta z_i\|^{3/2} + C\|\varphi^k \nabla w\|^2. \quad (6.12)$$

Taking into account (6.11) and (6.12), from (6.5), using the inequality $a^{3/2}b^{1/2} \leq a^2 + Cb^2$, we get

$$\partial_t(\|\varphi^k w\|^2 + \nu\eta\|\varphi^k \nabla w\|^2) + (2\nu'' - C\varepsilon - C\delta)\|\varphi^k \nabla w\|^2$$
$$- \delta_1 \|\varphi \Delta S_n\|^{3/2}\|\varphi^k \nabla w\|^2 + (2\eta - 2\eta\varepsilon - C\varepsilon - C\delta)\|\varphi \partial_t w\|^2$$
$$\leq C(\delta^{-1} + \delta_1^{-1})\bigl(\|\varphi^{k-1}w\|^2 + \|\varphi^{k-1}\partial_t w\|^2$$
$$+ \sum \|\varphi^i \Delta z_i\|^{3/2} + \|\varphi^{k-1}\Delta w\|^2\bigr). \quad (6.13)$$

We take δ and ε sufficiently small, and (6.13) implies an estimate for

$$y = \|\varphi^k w\|^2 + \nu\eta\|\varphi^k \nabla w\|^2$$

which is of the form

$$\partial_t y + \nu''\|\varphi^k w\|^2 + \eta\|\varphi^k \partial_t w\|^2 \leq h + C\delta_1 \|\varphi \Delta S_n\|^{3/2} y, \quad (6.14)$$

where h is equal to the right-hand side of (6.13). Using (6.4) with $l = k - 1$ and Theorem 5.1, we conclude that

$$\int_T^{T+1} h(t)\,dt \leq C(1 + \delta_1^{-1}) \quad \text{for any } T. \quad (6.15)$$

From (6.14) it follows that

$$\partial_t y + \mu y \leq h + C\delta_1 \|\varphi \Delta S_n\|^{3/2} y, \quad \mu > 0. \quad (6.15')$$

By (5.3) there exists a $\delta_1 > 0$ such that

$$C\delta_1 \int_T^{T+1} \|\varphi \Delta S_n\|^{3/2}\,dt \leq \frac{\mu}{2}, \quad (6.15'')$$

for any T. Note that since $\rho \to \infty$, φ is bounded and $y = \|\varphi^k\|^2 + \nu\eta\|\varphi^k \nabla w\|^2$ is bounded for all t since $\|\nabla u\|$ and $\|\nabla S_n\|$ are bounded for all t. Applying Lemma 3.5, we obtain (as in the proof of Theorem 5.1 or Theorem 3.1)

$$\|\varphi^k \nabla w\|^2 \leq Cy(t) \leq C_1 \quad \text{for any } t \in \mathbb{R}. \quad (6.16)$$

Integrating (6.14) with respect to t and using (6.16) and (6.15), we get

$$\int_T^{T+1} \|\varphi^k \partial_t w\|^2\,dt \leq C. \quad (6.17)$$

Integrating (6.12) and using (6.16), (6.17), (6.4) for $l = k - 1$ and Theorem 5.1, we obtain
$$\int_T^{T+1} \|\varphi^k \Delta w\|^2 dt \leq C.$$
Hence (6.4) is proved for $l = k$ and therefore for $l = 1, \ldots, n + 1$. Using Lemma 1.9 and inequality (1.10) we deduce the inequality (6.2) from (6.4) with $l = n + 1$, and Theorem 6.1 is proved.

§7. Verification of the conditions on the original Poiseuille flow

The conditions (3.4), (3.5) impose some restrictions on the steady-state Poiseuille flow
$$V = (0, 0, V_3), \qquad V_3 = V_3(x_1, x_2), \tag{7.1}$$
where V_3 is a solution of (I.3). The solution of this equation satisfies the inequality
$$\|V_3\|_{C^2(\omega)} \leq C\nu^{-1}|p'|. \tag{7.2}$$
We shall show in this section that if $\nu^{-1}|p'|$ is sufficiently small, then (3.4) and (3.5) hold.

LEMMA 7.1. *Let* $V = (0, 0, V_3)$, V_3 *be a solution of* (1.3). *Then* (3.5) *holds.*

PROOF. By (3.3) and Hölder's inequality
$$\|\varphi L_0 u\| \leq \|\varphi B(V, u)\| + \|\varphi B(u, V)\|$$
$$\leq \|V_3\|_{C(\omega)} \|\varphi \nabla u\| + \|\varphi u\| \|V_3\|_{C^1(\omega)}.$$
This inequality and Proposition 1.2 imply (3.5).

Let
$$\lambda_1^0 = \inf \left\{ \frac{(B(u, V), u)}{\|\nabla u\|^2}, \ u \in H_1 \right\}. \tag{7.3}$$

LEMMA 7.2. *Let* $V = (0, 0, V_3)$, V_3 *be a solution of* (1.3). *Then* (3.4) *holds with* $\nu' = \lambda_1^0$.

PROOF. Since both sides of (3.4) depend continuously on $u \in H_1$ and V is dense in H_1, it suffices to prove (3.4) for $u \in V$. By (3.2) and (7.1)
$$(B(V, u), \varphi^2 u) = \int V_3 \partial_3 u \varphi^2 u \, dx$$
$$= \frac{1}{2} \int V_3 \varphi^2 \partial_3 |u|^2 \, dx = \frac{1}{2} \int |u|^2 V_3 \partial_3 \varphi^2 \, dx.$$
By (1.7)
$$|(B(V, u), \varphi^2 u)| \leq C\varepsilon \|\varphi u\|^2 \|V_3\|_{C(\omega)}.$$
Using (7.2) and Proposition 1.2, we obtain
$$|(B(V, u), \varphi^2 u)| \leq C_1 \varepsilon \|\varphi \nabla u\|^2. \tag{7.4}$$

By (3.2) and (7.1)
$$|(B(V, u), \varphi^2 u)| = \int (u_1 \partial_1 V_3 + u_2 \partial_2 V_3) \varphi^2 u_3 \, dx. \tag{7.5}$$

Obviously
$$|(B(u, V), \varphi^2 u)| = |(B(\varphi u, V), \varphi u)|.$$

Let
$$\lambda_1^1 = \inf \left\{ \frac{(B(\varphi u, V), \varphi u)}{\|\nabla(\varphi u)\|^2}, \ u \in H_1 \right\}. \tag{7.6}$$

From (7.4), (7.6) and (3.3) it follows that
$$(L_0 u, \varphi^2 u) \geq \lambda_1^1 \|\nabla(\varphi u)\|^2 - C\varepsilon \|\varphi \nabla u\|^2. \tag{7.7}$$

Now we proceed to estimate λ_1^1. Let $v = \varphi u$, $u \in H_1$. Since $u \in H_1^0(\Omega)^3$, then $v \in H_1^0(\Omega)^3$. Since $\operatorname{div} u = 0$ we have
$$\operatorname{div}(\varphi u) = u \nabla \varphi = u_3 \partial_3 \varphi. \tag{7.8}$$

By Proposition 0.15,
$$\int_\omega u_3 \partial_3 \varphi \, dx_1 dx_2 = \partial_3 \varphi \int_\omega u_3 \, dx_1 dx_2 = 0 \tag{7.9}$$

for any x_3. Let
$$w = G_3 (u_3 \partial_3 \varphi), \tag{7.10}$$

the operator G_3 being defined by (0.33). Let $z = \varphi u - w$. By (7.8) and (0.34)
$$\operatorname{div} z = 0, \quad z \in H_1^0(\Omega)^3. \tag{7.11}$$

By (0.35), (1.7) and Proposition 1.2,
$$\|\varphi u - z\|_1 \leq C \|u_3 \partial_3 \varphi\|_1 \leq C_1 \varepsilon (\|\varphi u\| + \|\varphi \nabla u\|)$$
$$\leq C_2 \varepsilon \|\varphi \nabla u\| \leq C_3 \varepsilon \|\nabla(\varphi u)\|. \tag{7.12}$$

Obviously,
$$\left| \frac{(B(\varphi u, V), \varphi u)}{\|\nabla(\varphi u)\|^2} - \frac{(B(z, V), z)}{\|\nabla z\|^2} \right|$$
$$\leq \frac{|(B(\varphi u, V), \varphi u) - (B(z, V), z)|}{\|\nabla(\varphi u)\|^2}$$
$$+ |(B(z, V), z)| \cdot \left| \|\nabla(\varphi u)\|^{-2} - \|\nabla z\|^{-2} \right|. \tag{7.13}$$

Since B is bilinear, using (7.12), we obtain
$$|(B(\varphi u, V), \varphi u) - (B(z, V), z)|$$
$$\leq |(B(\varphi u - z, V), \varphi u)| + |(B(z, V), \varphi u - z)|$$
$$\leq C\varepsilon \|\varphi u\| \|\nabla(\varphi u)\| + C\varepsilon \|z\| \|\nabla(\varphi u)\|$$
$$\leq C\varepsilon \|\nabla(\varphi u)\| \|\varphi u\| + C\varepsilon (\|z - \varphi u\| + \|\varphi u\|).$$

Using (7.12) and Proposition 1.2, we obtain

$$|(B(\varphi u, V), \varphi u) - (B(z, V), z)| \leq C\varepsilon \|\nabla \varphi u\|^2.$$

By (7.12),
$$|\|\nabla(\varphi u)\| - \|\nabla z\|| \leq C\varepsilon \|\nabla(\varphi u)\|. \tag{7.14}$$

By Proposition 1.2 and (7.2),
$$|(B(z, V), z)| \leq C\|\nabla z\|^2.$$

Hence
$$|(B(z, V), z)| \cdot |\|\nabla(\varphi u)\|^{-2} - \|\nabla z\|^{-2}|$$
$$\leq C|\|\nabla z\|^2 - \|\nabla(\varphi u)\|^2|\|\nabla \varphi u\|^{-2} \leq C_1\varepsilon. \tag{7.15}$$

Therefore
$$\left|\frac{(B(\varphi u, V), \varphi u)}{\|\nabla(\varphi u)\|^2} - \frac{(B(z, V), z)}{\|\nabla z\|^2}\right| \leq C\varepsilon,$$

for any $u \in H_1$, $z = \varphi u - G_3(u_3 \partial_3 \varphi)$. By (7.11) and (1.2), we have $z \in H_1$. Comparing (7.3) and (7.6), we see that

$$\lambda_1^1 \geq \lambda_1^0 - C\varepsilon. \tag{7.16}$$

Hence by (7.7)
$$(L_0 u, \varphi^2 u) \geq \lambda_1^0 \|\nabla(\varphi u)\|^2 - C_1 \varepsilon \|\varphi \nabla u\|^2.$$

By (1.34) this yields
$$(L_0 u, \varphi^2 u) \geq \lambda_1^0 \|\varphi \nabla u\|^2 - C\varepsilon \|\varphi \nabla u\|^2, \tag{7.17}$$

and Lemma 7.2 is proved.

LEMMA 7.3. *Let V be defined by (7.1), $u \in H_1$. Then*

$$|(B(u, V), u)| \leq (1/4) V_m \lambda_1^{-1/2} \|\nabla u\|^2, \tag{7.18}$$

where λ_1 is the least eigenvalue of the operator $-\partial_1^2 - \partial_2^2$ in ω with the Dirichlet boundary conditions,

$$V_m = \max\{|V_3(x)|, \; x \in \overline{\omega}\}.$$

PROOF. Suppose $p > 0$. It can be easily seen that since $\nu^{-1} p' > 0$, the solution V_3 of (1.3) is nonpositive by the maximum principle. Let

$$W = (0, 0, V_3 + V_m/2).$$

Obviously
$$|W(x_1, x_2)| = |W_3(x_1, x_2)| \leq V_m/2 \tag{7.19}$$

for any $(x_1, x_2) \in \omega$. Obviously
$$B(u, V) = B(u, W) \quad \text{for any } u. \tag{7.20}$$

Integrating by parts, we obtain

$$(B(u, W), u) = (u_1 \partial_1 W_3 + u_2 \partial_2 W_3, u_3)$$
$$= -(W_3, u_3 \partial_1 u_1 + u_1 \partial_1 u_3 + u_3 \partial_2 u_2 + u_2 \partial_2 u_3).$$

Since $\partial_1 u_1 + \partial_2 u_2 = -\partial_3 u_3$ and W does not depend on x_3,

$$-(W_3, (\partial_1 u_1 + \partial_2 u_2)) = (W_3, u_3 \partial_3 u_3) = (1/2)(W_3, \partial_3(u_3)^2) = 0.$$

Hence by (7.20)

$$|(B(u, V), u)| \leq |(W_3, u_1 \partial_1 u_3 + u_2 \partial_2 u_3)|$$
$$\leq (\delta/4)(\|W_3 u_1\|^2 + \|W_3 u_2\|^2) + \delta^{-1}(\|\partial_1 u_3\|^2 + \|\partial_2 u_3\|^2)$$
$$\leq (\delta V_m^2/16)(\|u_1\|^2 + \|u_2\|^2) + \delta^{-1}\|\nabla u_3\|^2. \qquad (7.21)$$

Since $u_i \in H_1^0(\Omega)$,

$$\lambda_1 \|u_i\|^2 \leq \|\nabla u_i\|^2, \qquad (7.22)$$

where $\lambda_1 > 0$ is the lower bound of the spectrum of the Laplace operator Δ in Ω with the Dirichlet boundary conditions. Using the Fourier method, we can easily see that λ_1 coincides with the first eigenvalue of the Laplace operator $-\Delta_2$ in ω with Dirichlet boundary conditions. Therefore (7.21) and (7.22) imply

$$|(B(u, V), u)| \leq (1/16)\delta V_m^2 \lambda_1^{-1}(\|\nabla u_1\|^2 + \|\nabla u_2\|^2) + \delta^{-1}\|\nabla u_3\|^2.$$

Setting here $\delta = 4\lambda_1^{1/2}/V_m$ we obtain (7.18).

LEMMA 7.4. *Let V be defined by (7.1). Then (3.4) holds with $\nu' = V_m \lambda_1^{-1/2}/4$, where λ_1 and V_m are the same as in (7.18). If $\nu^{-1}|p'|$ is small then (3.6) holds.*

PROOF. The assertion of this lemma is a direct consequence of Lemma 7.2, Lemma 7.3 and (7.2).

To illustrate the sufficient conditions obtained, consider the case when ω is a circle of the radius r_0,

$$\omega = \{(x_1, x_2) : x_1^2 + x_2^2 \leq r_0^2\}.$$

In this case the solution V_3 of (1.3) can be written explicitly

$$V_3 = \nu^{-1} p'(x_1^2 + x_2^2 - r_0^2)/4.$$

Obviously

$$V_m = \nu^{-1} p' r_0^2/4.$$

By Lemma 7.4 for condition (3.4) to hold it suffices to have

$$V_m \lambda_1^{-1/2}/4 < \nu. \qquad (7.23)$$

It is well known that in the case under consideration
$$\lambda_1^{1/2} = r_0^{-1}\mu_1^0,$$
$\mu_1^0 = 2.4048$ being the first zero of the special function J_0. Hence (7.23) holds if
$$\text{Re} = V_m r_0/\nu < 4\mu_1^0.$$
Here Re is the Reynolds number (see [1]) for the Poiseuille flow in a circular tube. So Re ≤ 9 is sufficient for all the results of this paper to hold. Of course, this condition is not precise (more detailed consideration shows that Re $= 17$ can be taken, and this bound also is not final at any rate).

§8. Asymptotic expansion of the solutions of the initial-value problem

Let $u(t, x)$, $t \geq 0$, $x \in \Omega$, be a solution of the equation (3.1) satisfying the initial condition
$$u|_{t=0} = u_0, \qquad u_0 \in H_1. \tag{8.1}$$
To formulate conditions on u and u_0, we introduce some notation. Let $v(t)$, $t \geq 0$, be a function with values in $H_{0,\gamma}$, then
$$F_{l,\gamma}^\infty = \sup\{\|v(t)\|_{l,\gamma}, \ t \geq 0\}, \tag{8.2}$$
$$F_{l,\gamma}^2 = \sup\left\{\left(\int_T^{T+1} \|v(t)\|_{l,\gamma}^2 \, dt\right)^{1/2}, \ T \geq 0\right\}. \tag{8.3}$$
Here $\|u\|_{l,\gamma}$ is defined by (1.11), where Φ is the function defined by (1.9) and conditions (1.5)–(1.10) are satisfied.

In this section we shall assume that
$$F_{1,0}^\infty(u) + F_{2,0}^2(u) \leq C, \tag{8.4}$$
$$\|u_0\|_{1,\gamma_1} \leq C, \qquad \gamma_1 > 0. \tag{8.5}$$
It is assumed also that (3.11) holds with the same $\gamma > 0$, $\gamma \leq \gamma_1$.

THEOREM 8.1. *Under the conditions imposed,*
$$F_{1,\gamma}^\infty(u) + F_{2,\gamma}^2(u) + F_{0,\gamma}^2(\partial_t u) \leq C. \tag{8.6}$$

PROOF. The argument is analogous to the proof of Theorem 3.1. The only difference is that all the functions are considered on the half-axis $t \geq 0$ instead of the whole axis. In particular, (3.80) holds with $T = 0$, and we use (8.5) to estimate $y(0)$. No more changes in the proof are needed, and Theorem 8.1 is proved.

Now we introduce the functions z_k, which describe the asymptotic behavior of $u(t, x)$ as $|x| \to \infty$.

Let z_1 be a solution of the equation (5.1) with initial condition
$$z_1|_{t=0} = g_1. \tag{8.7}$$

Such a solution exists by Lemma 5.1. Let z_k, $k = 2, 3, \ldots$, be solutions of equations (5.2) with initial conditions

$$z_k|_{t=0} = g_k. \tag{8.8}$$

(See Theorem 8.3 and Remark 8.1 on a possible choice of g_k.)

THEOREM 8.2. *Let* $g_i \in (H_{1,\gamma i})^3 \cap H_1$, $i = 1, \ldots, n$. *Then there exist solutions* $z_1, \ldots, z_n$ *of the problems* (5.1), (8.7) *and* (5.2), (8.8) *satisfying*

$$F_{1,i\gamma}^\infty(z_i) + F_{2,i\gamma}^2(z_i) + F_{0,i\gamma}^2(\partial_t z_i) \leqslant C_i, \tag{8.9}$$

where $i = 1, \ldots, n$.

PROOF. The argument is analogous to the one used in the proof of Theorem 5.1. Here we use $F_{j,\gamma k}$ instead of $J_{j,\gamma k}$. In place of Lemma 5.3 we use estimates for solutions of the equation (5.4) with initial condition (5.5), where $\tau = 0$. This estimate is of the form

$$F_{0,0}^\infty(\varphi \nabla v) + F_{0,0}^2(\varphi \Delta v) + F_{0,0}^2(\varphi \partial_t v) \leqslant C F_{0,0}^2(\varphi h) + C \|\varphi \nabla v_0\|. \tag{8.10}$$

The only difference with the deduction of (5.14) is that $t \geqslant 0$ everywhere and we consider (5.16) together with the initial condition

$$y(0) = \|\varphi v_0\|^2 + \eta \nu \|\varphi \nabla v_0\|^2.$$

There are no other significant differences in the proof, so applying the argument in the proof of Theorem 5.1 we obtain Theorem 8.2.

Now we give an estimate of the error of the approximation by $S_n = z_1 + \cdots + z_n$ in case of an appropriate choice of $g_1, \ldots, g_n$.

THEOREM 8.3. *Let*

$$u_0 - (g_1 + \cdots + g_n) \in H_{1,\gamma(n+1)}(\Omega)^3 \cap H_1. \tag{8.11}$$

Let $z_1, \ldots, z_n$ *be the same as in Theorem* 8.2. *Then the function*

$$w = u - S_n = u - (z_1 + \cdots + z_n) \tag{8.12}$$

satisfies the estimate

$$F_{1,(n+1)\gamma}^\infty(w) + F_{2,(n+1)\gamma}^2(w) + F_{0,\gamma(n+1)}^2(\partial_t w) \leqslant C. \tag{8.13}$$

PROOF. The function w satisfies the equation (6.3) with the initial condition

$$w|_{t=0} = u_0 - (g_1 + \cdots + g_n). \tag{8.14}$$

In the same way as in the proof of Theorem 6.1, we obtain the inequality (6.14). By (8.11), $y(0) \leqslant C$; applying Lemma 3.5, we see that (6.16) holds for any $T \geqslant 0$. Everywhere in the proof we take $T \geqslant 0$, $t \geqslant 0$. No more changes are needed, and applying the argument of the proof of Theorem 6.1 to our case we obtain the Theorem 8.3.

REMARK 8.1. It is possible to take $g_1 = u_0$, $g_i = 0$, $i = 2, 3, \ldots$. Obviously $u_0 - (g_1 + \cdots + g_n) = 0$ and (8.11) holds. If $u_0 \in H_{0,\gamma_1}(\Omega)^3$, $\gamma_1 \gg \gamma$, we can take $g_0 = 0$, $g_n = 0$ and (8.13) holds if $(n+1)\gamma \leqslant \gamma_1$. If $u_0 \in H_{0,\gamma}(\Omega)^3$ for any $\gamma > 0$, we can take $g_i = 0$, $i = 1, 2, \ldots$, and (8.13) holds for any n, $n = 1, 2, \ldots$.

Now we consider another generalization of the results of preceding sections. Namely, we shall consider a flow in a semitube Ω_+. Let

$$\Omega_+ = \omega \times (0, \infty), \tag{8.15}$$

where ω is the same as in (0.1). We consider a solution $u(t, x)$ that satisfies the Navier-Stokes system (I.1) for $-\infty < t < +\infty$, $x \in \Omega_+$. We suppose that the condition $v|_{\partial\Omega} = 0$ in (I.1) is replaced by the condition

$$v|_{\partial\omega \times (0, +\infty)} = 0. \tag{8.16}$$

It is assumed everywhere below in this section that the function v and $u = v - V$ satisfy conditions (3.11), (3.7), (3.8), and (3.15), where the $H_{l,\gamma}$-norm is defined by (1.11) with Ω replaced by Ω_+. It is also assumed that conditions (3.4), (3.5), (3.6) hold.

We shall investigate solutions defined in the half-tube by means of a reduction to the case of an entire tube. We shall use a cut-off function $y(x_3)$, $y \in C^\infty(\mathbb{R})$, such that

$$y(x_3) = 0 \quad \text{for } x_3 \leqslant 1/2, \tag{8.17}$$

$$y(x_3) = 1 \quad \text{for } x_3 \geqslant 1. \tag{8.18}$$

Let

$$w(t, x) = y(x_3)u(t, x). \tag{8.19}$$

This function is originally defined for $x_3 > 0$, but we extend it to $x_3 \leqslant 0$ setting

$$w = 0 \quad \text{for } x_3 \leqslant 0.$$

Obviously, w is defined in Ω. Now we write out a system to which w is a solution. Note that by (3.1) $u = v - V$ satisfies (in Ω_+) the system

$$\partial_t u - \nu \Delta u + B(V, u) + B(u, V) + \nabla p = f, \tag{8.20}$$

$$\operatorname{div} u = 0, \quad u|_{\omega \times (0, \infty)} = 0. \tag{8.21}$$

Since $\partial_t(yu) = y\partial_t u$, we deduce from (8.19) and (8.20) that w is a solution of the equation

$$\partial_t w - \nu \Delta w + B(V, w) + B(w, V) + B(w, w) + \nabla(py) = yf + f_1, \tag{8.22}$$

where

$$\begin{aligned}f_1 &= p\partial_3 y + \nu(y\Delta u - \Delta(yu)) \\ &\quad + B(V, yu) - yB(V, u) + B(yu, yu) - yB(u, u).\end{aligned} \tag{8.23}$$

Obviously,
$$\operatorname{div} w = u_3 \partial_3 y, \qquad w|_{\partial \Omega} = 0. \tag{8.24}$$
Let
$$W = G_3(u_3 \partial_3 y), \tag{8.25}$$
where the operator G_3 is defined by (0.33). Put
$$U = w - W. \tag{8.26}$$
By (0.34)
$$\operatorname{div} U = 0, \qquad U|_{\partial \Omega} = 0. \tag{8.27}$$
Substituting $w = W + U$ into (8.22), we obtain an equation for U:
$$\partial_t U - \nu \Delta U + B(V, U) + B(U, V) + B(U, U) + \nabla p_1 = fy + f_1 + f_2, \tag{8.28}$$
where f_1 is defined by (8.23) and
$$\begin{aligned} f_2 = &-\partial_t W + \nu \Delta W - B(V, W) - B(W, V) \\ &- B(W, W) - B(W, U) - B(U, W). \end{aligned} \tag{8.29}$$
Applying Π to (8.28), we obtain the equation
$$\partial_t U - \nu \Pi \Delta U + \Pi L_0 U + \Pi B(U, U) = \Pi(fy) + \Pi f_1 + \Pi f_2, \tag{8.30}$$
where L_0 is defined by (3.3). Obviously, this equation is of the form (3.1). By (8.26) and (8.19), we have
$$vy = Vy + W + U. \tag{8.31}$$
Since V is a known function and $y = 1$ for $x_3 \geqslant 1$, the behavior of v as $x_3 \to \infty$ may be described in terms of the behavior of W and U.

PROPOSITION 8.1. *Let W be defined by* (8.25). *Then*
$$W(x, t) = 0 \quad \text{when } x_3 \leqslant 0, \ x_3 \geqslant 1; \tag{8.32}$$
$$\int_T^{T+1} \|\Delta W(\cdot, t)\|^2 \, dt \leqslant C \qquad \forall T; \tag{8.33}$$
$$\|\nabla W(\cdot, t)\| \leqslant C \qquad \forall t; \tag{8.34}$$
$$\int_T^{T+1} \|\partial_t W(\cdot, t)\|^2 \, dt \leqslant C \qquad \forall T. \tag{8.35}$$

PROOF. Obviously $\partial_3 y = 0$ when $x_3 \leqslant 0$, $x_3 \geqslant 1$. Since the operator G_2 in (0.33) is linear and is independent of x_3 and t, we get (8.32) and
$$\partial_t W(x, t) = G(\partial_t u_3 \partial_3 y). \tag{8.36}$$
Using (3.15) and (0.35) we conclude that (8.35) holds. From (3.7) and (3.8), using (0.35) we deduce (8.33) and (8.34).

Since W equals zero for large x_3, the behavior of $u = v - V$ as $x_3 \to +\infty$ is the same as that of U. We shall show below that the function U and the right-hand side $fy + f_1 + f_2$ satisfy the conditions imposed in §3 on a solution u and on the right-hand side f.

PROPOSITION 8.2. *Let u be defined by* (8.26). *Then U satisfies* (3.7), (3.8), (3.15) *in* Ω.

PROOF. By (8.26) $U = uy - W$. Obviously, uy satisfies (3.7), (3.8), (3.15) in Ω, if u satisfies these conditions in Ω_+. Since W satisfies (3.7), (3.8), (3.15) in Ω by Proposition 8.1, U also satisfies these conditions.

PROPOSITION 8.3. *Let f_1 be defined by* (8.23). *Then*

$$f_1(x,t) = 0 \quad \text{when } |x_3| \geq 1 \tag{8.37}$$

and condition (3.11) *with f replaced by f_1 holds for any $\gamma > 0$.*

PROOF. Obviously,

$$y\Delta u - \Delta(yu) = -2\partial_3 y \partial_3 u - \partial_3^2 y u, \tag{8.38}$$
$$B(V, yu) - yB(V, u) = V_3 u \partial_3 y, \tag{8.39}$$
$$B(yu, yv) = yB(u, yu) = y^2 B(u, v) + yu_3 u \partial_3 y. \tag{8.40}$$

Since $y' = 0$, $y'' = 0$ and $y^2 - y = 0$ when $|x_3| \geq 1$, we see, using (8.38), (8.39), (8.40), that (8.37) holds. Since the function Φ in (1.11) is bounded when $|x_3| \leq 1$, it suffices to prove that condition (3.11) for f_1 holds for $\gamma = 0$. Using (3.7), (3.8), (3.15), we deduce from (8.38), (8.39), (8.40) the inequality

$$J_{0,0}^2(B(V, yu) - yB(V, u)) + J_{0,0}^2(y\Delta u - \Delta(yu)) \leq C. \tag{8.41}$$

Estimating $y^2 B(u, u)$ and $yu_3 u \partial_3 y$ as in Lemma 3.1, we can use (8.40) to get

$$J_{0,0}^2(B(yu, yu) - yB(u, u)) \leq C. \tag{8.42}$$

Choose p (by adding a constant) so that $\int_{\omega \times [0,1]} p\, dx = 0$. Then

$$\|p\partial_3 y\| \leq C \|\nabla p\|. \tag{8.43}$$

Expressing ∇p from (8.19) in terms of u and f, then using (3.7), (3.8), (3.15), (3.11), (3.18), we obtain:

$$J_{0,0}^2(p\partial_3 y) \leq C. \tag{8.44}$$

From (8.23), (8.44), (8.42), (8.41) it follows that (3.11) holds with f replaced by f_1. Since (8.37) is valid, any Φ and any γ may be taken in (3.11) and (1.11).

PROPOSITION 8.4. *Let f_2 be defined by* (8.28). *Then*

$$f_2(x,t) = 0 \quad \text{when } |x_3| \geq 1 \tag{8.45}$$

and (3.11) *holds with f replaced by f_2 for any $\gamma > 0$.*

PROOF. Using (8.32), we readily obtain (8.45). Using (8.33), (8.34), and (8.35), we obtain:

$$J_{0,0}^2(-\partial_t W + \nu \Delta W - B(V, W) - B(W, V)) \leq C. \tag{8.46}$$

Since B is bilinear and $U = yu - W$, we have
$$B(W, W) + B(W, U) + B(U, W)$$
$$= -B(W, W) + B(yu, W) + B(W, yu).$$
Using (3.18), (8.33), (8.34) and (3.7), (3.8), we obtain
$$J_{0,0}^2(B(W,W) + B(W,U) + B(U,W)) \leq C. \qquad (8.47)$$
Inequalities (8.46) and (8.47) yield (3.11) for f_2.

THEOREM 8.4. *The function u satisfies* (3.12), *where* $\|\cdot\|_{l,\gamma}$ *is defined by* (1.11) *with Ω replaced by $\omega \times (1, \infty)$.*

PROOF. The function $U = yu - W$ is a solution of (8.30). This equation is of the form of (3.1). By Propositions 8.2, 8.3, 8.4, all the conditions of Theorem 3.1 are fulfilled. Therefore U satisfies the estimate (3.12). By Proposition 8.1 W also satisfies this estimate. Hence so does $yu = U + W$ (with another C). Since $y(x_3) = 1$ when $x_3 \geq 1$, this implies the estimate for u on $\omega \times (1, \infty)$.

Now we give a generalization of Theorems 4.1 and 4.2. Let u_1 and u_2 be two solutions of (8.20), (8.21) in Ω_+ corresponding to the right-hand sides f_1 and f_2 respectively. It is assumed that both u_1, u_2 and both f_1, f_2 satisfy conditions imposed on u and f in this section. It is assumed also that the functions Φ and Φ_1 satisfy the conditions imposed in §4. As in §4, the norm (1.11) in condition (3.11) on f_1, f_2 includes the function $\Phi_f = \Phi$. It is assumed that f_1 and f_2 satisfy (4.4') with some $\beta > 0$ (Ω in (4.3) is replaced by $\omega \times (1, +\infty)$).

THEOREM 8.5. *There exists an $\varepsilon > 0$ such that inequality* (4.4) *holds.*

PROOF. Obviously, $yu_1 - yu_2 = U_1 - U_2 + W_1 - W_2$. By (8.32)–(8.35)
$$(J'^{\infty}_{1,\gamma} + J'^2_{2,\gamma})(W_1 - W_2) + J'^2_{0,\gamma}(\partial_t(W_1 - W_2)) \leq C \qquad (8.48)$$
for any γ. We apply Theorem 4.2 with f_1, f_2 replaced by $f_1 + f_{11} + f_{12}$ and $f_2 + f_{21} + f_{22}$ respectively. Obviously,
$$J'^2_{0,\beta}(f_1 + f_{11} + f_{12} - f_2 - f_{21} - f_{22})$$
$$\leq J'^2_{0,\beta}(f_1 - f_2) + J'^2_{0,\beta}(f_{11} + f_{12} - f_{21} - f_{22}). \qquad (8.49)$$
Using Propositions 8.3 and 8.4, we get
$$J'^2_{0,\beta}(f_{ij}) \leq C, \qquad i, j = 1, 2. \qquad (8.50)$$
Using this inequality and condition (4.4') imposed on f_1 and f_2, we see that all conditions of Theorem 4.2 are fulfilled.

Therefore
$$(J'^{\infty}_{1,\varepsilon} + J'^2_{2,\varepsilon})(U_1 - U_2) + J'^2_{0,\varepsilon}(\partial_t(U_1 - U_2)) \leq C. \qquad (8.51)$$

Combining (8.48) and (8.51), we obtain the estimate (4.4) for $yu_1 - yu_2$ in $\omega \times (-\infty, \infty)$. Since $y = 1$ when $x_3 \geq 1$, this estimate implies the estimate in $\omega \times (1, \infty)$ for $u_1 - u_2$.

Now we shall formulate and prove a generalization of Theorem 6.1 to asymptotic expansions of u. We suppose that φ is as in Lemma 1.0.

Let $z_1, z_2, \ldots$ be solutions of (5.1), (5.2) with f replaced by yf. These solutions exist by Theorem 5.1 and satisfy (5.3).

Let w_{n+1} be defined in $\omega \times (1, +\infty)$ by the formula (6.1), i.e.,

$$w_{n+1} = u - z_1 - \cdots - z_n.$$

THEOREM 8.6. *The error w_{n+1} satisfies the estimate (6.2), provided Ω in (1.11) is replaced by $\omega \times (1, +\infty)$.*

PROOF. Let U' be a solution of (8.30), where we set $f_1 = 0$, $f_2 = 0$. Note that by Propositions 8.3, 8.4, we have

$$J'^2_{0,\beta}(f_1 + f_2) \leq C. \tag{8.52}$$

Hence by Theorem 4.2

$$(J'^\infty_{1,\varepsilon} + J'^2_{2,\varepsilon})(U - U') + J'^2_{0,\varepsilon}(\partial_t(U - U')) \leq C. \tag{8.53}$$

Let

$$w'_{n+1} = U' - (z_1 + \cdots + z_n). \tag{8.54}$$

By Theorem 6.1 w'_{n+1} satisfies (6.2). Note that, since

$$(1 + |x|^2)^{\gamma n} \leq C e^{\varepsilon |x|},$$

(8.53) implies that $U - U'$ satisfies (6.2) for any n and γ. Further, W satisfies (6.2) for any γ and n by Proposition 8.1. Obviously, $w_{n+1} = W + U - U' + w'_{n+1}$ when $x_3 \geq 1$, since $u = qu$ for such x_3. Therefore w_{n+1} satisfies (6.2).

REMARK 8.2. Obviously, all the results hold if $\Omega_+ = \omega \times (l, +\infty)$, $l \in \mathbb{R}$. If a domain Ω_1 has several exits at infinity which are of the tube-shaped form of Ω_+, then Theorems 8.4–8.6 may be applied to any of these exits. It is supposed, of course, that the restriction of a solution u of (I.1) satisfies imposed conditions in these subdomains.

§9. Existence and properties of the attractor in the case of two-dimensional flows

In this section we shall consider the situation when all the functions do not depend on the variable x_1. In this case let

$$\Omega = \{(x_2, x_3) : 0 < x_2 < b, \ -\infty < x_3 < +\infty\}, \tag{9.1}$$

$$\omega = \{x_2 : 0 < x_2 < b\}, \tag{9.2}$$

$$\Delta u = \partial_2^2 + \partial_3^2, \quad B(u, v) = u_2 \partial_2 v + u_3 \partial_3 v, \quad u = (u_1, u_2). \tag{9.3}$$

Obviously, $\Omega \subset \mathbb{R}^2$, $\omega \subset \mathbb{R}$. The Poiseuille flow $V = (V_2, V_3)$, $V_2 = 0$, $V_3 = V_3(x_2)$, where

$$\partial_2^2 V_3 = \nu^{-1} p', \qquad V_3|_{\partial \omega} = 0, \tag{9.4}$$

p' is a constant. The space v is defined by (0.20), the spaces H_1, H_2 and the projection Π are defined in §0.

PROPOSITION 9.1. *The space H_1 coincides with the subspace of $H_1^0(\Omega)^2$ consisting of divergence-free vector fields.*

PROOF. The proof of this proposition coincides with the proof of Proposition 0.16. Proposition 0.14 used in this proof is valid in the case considered here. The operator G_2 in (0.33) acts in the case under consideration from $E_0(\omega)$ into $H_1^0(\omega)$,

$$G_2 h = v', \tag{9.5}$$

where $h \in H_l(\omega)$, $v' = v'(x_2)$ is the solution of the equation

$$\partial_2 v' = h, \qquad v'|_{\partial \omega} = 0. \tag{9.6}$$

In the case when v' does not depend on x_1, the condition (0.22) takes the form

$$\int_\omega h(x_2, x_3) \, dx_2 = 0, \tag{9.7}$$

for almost all $x_3 \in \mathbb{R}$. Obviously, the inequality (0.31) holds if (9.7) is fulfilled. The assertion of Proposition 0.14, where $H_l(\Omega)^3$ and $H_1^0(\omega)^3$ are replaced by $H_l(\Omega)^2$ and $H_1^0(\omega)^2$, follows from (0.31). The argument remains the same. Proposition 0.10 with $H_1(\Omega)^3$ replaced by $H_1(\Omega)^2$ is also valid. So, all the steps of the proof of Proposition 0.16 with $H_1^0(\Omega)^3$ replaced by $H_1^0(\Omega)^2$ remain the same, and we obtain the required statement.

PROPOSITION 9.2. *The Proposition 0.17 is valid with $H_{-1}(\Omega)^3$ replaced by $H_{-1}(\Omega)^2$ when Ω is defined by (9.1).*

The proof is the same as in Proposition 0.17.

PROPOSITION 9.3. *Let Ω be defined by (9.2). Then Propositions 0.21 and 0.22 are valid with $H_2(\Omega)^3$ replaced by $H_2(\Omega)^2$.*

PROOF. All arguments in the proofs of Propositions 0.18–0.22 in the case when Ω is defined by (9.2) can be repeated with obvious minor modifications and some simplifications. We leave this to the reader.

The weight functions φ and Φ are defined in §1.

PROPOSITION 9.4. *Let Ω be defined by (9.2). Then the statements of Lemmas 1.1 and 1.2 are valid.*

PROOF. The computations required to obtain (1.45) are the same as in the proof of Lemma 1.1. The equation (1.48), where Δ_2 is replaced by ∂_2^2, may be treated in the same way (with obvious simplifications) as the original equation (1.48). So (1.47) is valid.

In the case when Ω and ω are defined by (9.2), (9.3), we let S be defined by

$$Sh(x_3) = |\omega|^{-1} \int_\omega h(x_2, x_3)\, dx_2 \tag{9.8}$$

instead of (1.51), $|\omega| = b$. Inequality (1.51') obviously holds.

PROPOSITION 9.5. *Lemmas 1.3, 1.4 and 1.5 are valid when Ω and S are defined by (9.2) and (9.8).*

The proof is the same as in Lemma 1.3, with some simplifications due to the fact that all the functions are independent of x_1. In this case $\partial_1 g = 0$, $\partial_1 p_2 = 0$, $\Delta_2 = \partial_2^2$, $\nabla_2 = \partial_2$. In (1.71), $\partial_1^{\beta_1} \partial_2^{\beta_2} = \partial_2^{\beta_2}$, $\beta_1 = 0$.

PROPOSITION 9.6. *The operator π_0 defined by (1.42) may be written in the form (1.75), (1.75') where $e_3 = (0, 1) \in \mathbb{R}^2$ and the inequality (1.75'') holds.*

The proof is the same as that of Lemma 1.6.

THEOREM 9.1. *The inequality (1.43) is valid for any $h \in H$.*

The proof is the same as the proof of Theorem 1.1.

THEOREM 9.2. *Let Ω be defined by (9.2), K be defined by (2.1) for $h \in L_1(\Omega)^2 = H$. Then inequality (2.6) holds.*

PROOF. Lemmas 2.1–2.7 are valid in the case when Ω is defined by (9.2). The arguments remain the same with some simplifications, one can use results of §§0 and 1 as in Propositions 9.1–9.6.

THEOREM 9.3. *Let $u \in H_2$. Then inequality (2.65) is valid.*

PROOF. The argument is the same as in the proof of Theorem 2.2.

Let the operator L_0 be defined by (3.3), where $V = (V_2, V_3)$ is the Poiseuille flow, V_3 is a solution of (9.4). It is assumed that (3.4), (3.5), (3.6) hold. (Sufficient conditions will be given below in the final part of this section.)

The results on the behavior of the solutions of (3.1), which are similar to those obtained in preceding sections, are valid. The formulations of all theorems of §§3–6 remain the same; some of these results may be sharpened in the two-dimensional case. In particular, the following theorem is valid.

THEOREM 9.4. *Let Ω be defined by (9.2). Let f satisfy (3.11), u satisfy (3.7), (3.8). Then $u(t)$ satisfies (3.12).*

The proof is the same as in the three-dimensional case. All the results of §§0, 1, and 2 used in the arguments hold in two-dimensional case. Embedding theorems $H^l(\Omega) \subset L_p(\Omega)$ used in the 3-dimensional case hold in the two-dimensional case as well.

We shall consider in more detail the case when the function f in (3.1) does not depend on t,
$$f \in H_{0,\gamma}(\Omega)^2. \tag{9.9}$$
Here and below it is assumed that the norm in $H_{l,\gamma}$ is defined by (1.11), where Φ satisfies (4.2).

THEOREM 9.5. *Let $u_0 \in H_1$. Then there exists a unique solution $u(t)$ of the equation* (3.1) *satisfying the initial condition*
$$u|_{t=0} = u_0, \tag{9.10}$$
and belonging to
$$L_2([0,T], H_2) \cap L_\infty([0,T], H_1) \quad \forall T > 0 \tag{9.11}$$
(*the operators B and Δ are as in* (9.3)).
The equation (3.1) *generates the semigroup* $\{S_t\}$, $S_t: u_0 \to u(t)$ *for* $t \geqslant 0$.

PROOF. The existence and uniqueness theorems are proved in [13, 24]. Since f does not depend on time, by these theorems equation (3.1) generates the semigroup $\{S_t\}$; for more details see [6].

PROPOSITION 9.7. *The solution of* (3.1), (9.10) *satisfies the estimates*
$$\|u(t)\|^2 \leqslant \|u(0)\|^2 \exp(-\mu t) + \mu^{-2} \|f\|^2,$$
$$\mu = \nu'' \lambda_1 > 0 \quad \forall t \geqslant 0; \tag{9.12}$$
$$\nu'' \int_T^{T+1} \|\nabla u\|^2 \, dt \leqslant C(\|u(T)\|^2 + \mu^{-1} \|f\|^2), \tag{9.13}$$
where λ_1 is the same as in (0.7).

PROOF. Multiplying (3.1) by u and using (3.36), (3.4) and (3.5) with $\varepsilon = 0$, $\varphi = 1$, we obtain
$$(1/2)\partial_t \|u\|^2 + \nu'' \|\nabla u\|^2 \leqslant \|u\| \|f\|. \tag{9.14}$$
Using (0.7), we deduce
$$\partial_t \|u\|^2 + 2\lambda \nu'' \|u\|^2 \leqslant \delta \|u\|^2 + \delta^{-1} \|f\|^2. \tag{9.15}$$
Taking $\delta = \lambda \nu''$, we conclude that a solution of the differential inequality (9.15) satisfies the estimate (9.12). Integrating (9.14) over $[T, T+1]$ and using (0.7), we get (9.13).

PROPOSITION 9.8. *There exists a set $B_1 \subset H$ such that $S_t B_1 \subset B_1$ $\forall t \geqslant 0$ and for any $u_0 \in B_1$*
$$\|u_0\| \leqslant 4\mu^{-1} \|f\|. \tag{9.16}$$
For any $T \geqslant 0$, the function $u(t) = S_t u_0$, $u_0 \in B_1$, satisfies the inequality
$$\nu'' \int_T^{T+1} \|\nabla u(t)\|_1^2 \, dt \leqslant C\mu^{-2} \|f\|^2 \quad (u(t) = S_t u_0). \tag{9.17}$$

For any bounded set $B \in H$, there exists a $t_0 > 0$ such that $S_t B \subset B_1$ $\forall t \geq t_0$ (i.e., B_1 is an H-absorbing set).

PROOF. Let $B_0 = \{u : \|u\| \leq 2\mu^{-1} \|f\|\}$. If $B = \{u : \|u\| \leq R\}$, then by (9.12) we have $S_t B \subset B_0$ when $t \geq t_0$, $R^2 \exp(-t_0) < \mu^{-2} \|f\|^2$.
Therefore B_0 is an H-absorbing set. Let

$$B_1 = \bigcup \{S_t B_0, \ t \geq 0\}. \tag{9.18}$$

Obviously, $S_t B_1 \subset B_1$. By (9.12), inequality (9.16) holds for any $u_0 \in B_1$. It follows from (9.16) and (9.13) that (9.17) is valid.

PROPOSITION 9.8'. *There exists a set B_2 which is H-absorbing, $S_t B_2 \subset B_2$ $\forall t > 0$; moreover,*

$$\|u_0\| \leq C_1, \tag{9.19}$$

$$\|u(t)\|_2^2 \leq C_2 \tag{9.20}$$

for any $u_0 \in B_1$, $u(t) = S_t u_0$, where C_1, C_2 depend only on f.

PROOF. Let $B_2 = S_2 B_1$. Obviously, since $S_t B_1 \subset B_1$, we have $S_t B_2 \subset B_2$ $\forall t \geq 0$. The inequalities

$$\|S_1 u\|_1 \leq C(\|u_0\|), \qquad \|S_1 u_1\|_2 \leq C(\|u_1\|_1) \tag{9.21}$$

are valid for any $u_0 \in H$, $u_1 \in H_1$ (see, for example, [6]). From (9.16) and (9.21), we deduce that (9.19), (9.20) are valid.

By Proposition 9.8 and (9.19), the set

$$B_2 = \bigcup \{S_t B_0, \ t \geq 2\} \tag{9.22}$$

is invariant $(S_t B_2 \subset B_2)$, bounded in H_2 and H-absorbing.

Let z_1 be a solution of (5.1); obviously z_1 is independent of t. Therefore, by Theorem 5.1, we have $z_1 \in H_{2,\gamma}(\Omega)^2$. (Theorem 5.1 is valid in two-dimensional case, the argument is the same as in the three-dimensional case.)
Let

$$w = u(t) - z_1, \qquad u(t) = S_t u_0, \qquad u_0 \in B_2. \tag{9.23}$$

The function w satisfies the equation (6.3), where $u = 1$, $S_n = z_1$. Let

$$F_\tau = \bigcup \{w(t), \ t \geq \tau, \ u_0 \in B_2\}, \tag{9.24}$$

where $w(t)$ is a solution of (6.3) (depending on u_0).
Obviously, $F_\tau \subset F_t$ when $\tau > t$. Let

$$B_3 = \bigcap \{[F_\tau], \ \tau \geq 0\} \tag{9.25}$$

where [ ] denotes the closure in H. Since there exists time-independent solution z of (3.1) and $S_t z = z$ for any t, it follows that $z - z_1$ belongs to B_3. So, B_3 is not empty. Obviously, B_3 is closed in H.

PROPOSITION 9.9. *There exists an* $M_2 > 0$ *such that for any* $\rho > 0$ *there exists a* τ_0 *such that* $\tau \geqslant \tau_0$ *implies*

$$\|\varphi v\|^2 + \nu\eta\|\varphi\nabla v\|^2 \leqslant M_2, \qquad \forall v \in F_\tau. \tag{9.26}$$

PROOF. Let $u_0 \in B_2$. Let w be defined by (9.23). We obtain like in Theorem 6.1 that the inequality (6.15′) is valid. By (9.19), (9.20) and (5.3) with $k = 1$, the estimates (6.15), (6.15″) with constant C independent of $u_0 \in B_2$ hold for any $T \geqslant 0$. Applying Lemma 3.5, we obtain

$$\|\varphi w(t)\|^2 + \gamma\eta\|\varphi\nabla w(t)\|^2$$
$$\leqslant (\|\varphi w(0)\|^2 + \nu\eta\|\varphi\nabla w(0)\|^2)e^{-\mu t} + M, \tag{9.27}$$

where $\varphi = \varphi(x, \varepsilon, \rho, \gamma)$, M does not depend on $u_0 \in B_2$ and on ρ. Since $\varphi(x, \varepsilon, \rho, \gamma)$ is bounded when $\rho < +\infty$, we can take a τ_0 such that the right-hand side of (9.27) is bounded by $2M$ when $t \geqslant t_0$, $t_0 = t_0(\rho)$. So, (9.26) is proved.

PROPOSITION 9.10. *Let* B_3 *be defined by* (9.25). *Then* B_3 *is bounded in* H_2 *and in* $H_{1,\gamma}$.

PROOF. The function z_1 is bounded in H_2 by Theorem 5.1. Since $u_0 \in B_2$ and B_2 is invariant, $u(t) \in B_2$, $\forall t \geqslant 0$, therefore $u(t)$ is bounded in H_2 uniformly with respect to $t \geqslant 0$ and $u_0 \in B_2$. Since $w(t) = u(t) - z_1$, then the $w(t)$ are bounded in H_2. Hence F_τ is bounded in H_2. Since H_2 is a Hilbert space, the closure of F_τ in H is contained in the closure of F_τ in the weak topology of H_2 and, therefore, $[F_\tau]$ is bounded in H_2 for any τ. Hence B_3 is bounded in H_2.

Note now that (9.26) holds by Proposition 9.9 if $v \in F_\tau$. Since multiplication by φ_ρ is a bounded operator in $H_1(\Omega)^2$ when $\rho < \infty$, it follows that (9.26) holds with any $\rho > 0$, $\rho < +\infty$ when $v \in \bigcap F_\tau$. Using Fatou's lemma, we conclude that

$$\|\Phi v\|^2 + \eta\nu\|\Phi\nabla v\|^2 \leqslant M_2.$$

Hence v is bounded in $H_{1,\gamma}^2$.

PROPOSITION 9.11. *Let* $u_k(t) = S_t u_k$, $u_k \in B_2$, *and* $t_k \to +\infty$ *as* $k \to \infty$. *Then the sequence* $\{u_k(t_k)\}$ *has a subsequence converging in* H.

PROOF. The functions $u_k(t_k)$ are bounded in H_2 and, consequently (see Proposition 9.3), in $H_2(\Omega)^2$. Therefore the restrictions of the $u_k(t_k)$ to bounded domains $\Omega_j = \{x \in \Omega : |x_3| \leqslant j\}$ are bounded in $H_2(\Omega_j)^2$. The embedding $L_2(\Omega_j) \supset H_2(\Omega_j)$ is compact. Using this fact and a diagonal process, we can find a subsequence of $u_k(t_k)$ (which we denote by $u_l(t_l)$) such that the restrictions of $u_l(t_l)$ to Ω_j have the property

$$u_l(t_l) \to u \quad \text{in } L_2(\Omega_j)^2 \text{ as } l \to +\infty \tag{9.28}$$

for any j (obviously u does not depend on j since $\Omega_j \subset \Omega_{j+1}$). We shall see that $y(t_l) \to u$ in $L_2(\Omega)$. Since $t_l \to +\infty$, it follows that $u_l(t_l) = z_1 + v_l(t_l)$, $v_l(t_l) \in F_\tau$, $\tau = t_l$. By Proposition 9.9, inequality (9.26) holds with $v_l = v_l(t_l)$, if l is sufficiently large. By (4.2), (1.6) and (1.9), for any $N > 0$ there exist j_0 and ρ_0 such that for any $j \geq j_0$ and $\rho \geq \rho_0$

$$\varphi(x, \varepsilon, \rho, \gamma) \geq N \quad \text{when } x \in \Omega \setminus \Omega_j. \tag{9.29}$$

Note that since $u_l(t_l)$ are bounded in H_2 and in H, we may assume that $u_l(t_l) - z_1$ converge weakly in H_2 and in $L_2(\Omega)^2 = H$. Let $\delta > 0$ be a small number, let N be so large that $N^2 \geq 8M_2\delta^{-2}$, where M_2 is the same as in (9.26). By (9.29)

$$\int_{\Omega \setminus \Omega_j} |u_l(t_l, x) - z_1(x)|^2 \, dx \leq \delta^2/8 \tag{9.30}$$

if $j \geq j_0$, l is sufficiently large. Hence the same estimate holds for the weak limit $u(x)$ and

$$\int_{\Omega \setminus \Omega_j} |u_l(t_l, x) - u(x)|^2 \, dx \leq \delta^2/2, \tag{9.31}$$

if l is sufficiently large. Fixing j and using (9.28), we conclude that

$$\int_{\Omega_j} |u_l(t_l, x) - u(x)|^2 \, dx \leq \delta^2/2 \tag{9.32}$$

for sufficiently large l. Combining (9.31) and (9.32), we obtain

$$\|u_l(t_l) - u\| \leq \delta \quad \text{for } l \geq l_1(\delta).$$

Since δ is arbitrarily small, we see that $u_l(t_l) \to u$ in L_2 as $l \to \infty$, and the proposition is proved.

If the sets X, Y are bounded in H, let

$$\text{dist}(X, Y) = \sup_{x \in X} \inf_{y \in Y} \|x - y\|. \tag{9.33}$$

A set Y is called (H, H)-*attracting* for the semigroup $\{S_t\}$, $S_t: H \to H$, if for any set B bounded in H

$$\text{dist}(S_t B, Y) \to 0 \quad \text{as } t \to +\infty. \tag{9.34}$$

A set $\mathfrak{U}$ is called an (H, H)-*attractor* (or a *global attractor*) if $\mathfrak{U}$ is compact in H, $S_t\mathfrak{U} = \mathfrak{U}$ $\forall t \geq 0$ ($\mathfrak{U}$ is strictly invariant) and $\mathfrak{U}$ is (H, H)-attracting.

Note that since $S_t\mathfrak{U} = \mathfrak{U}$ $\forall t \geq 0$ it follows that any point u_0 lying on the attractor belongs to some trajectory $u(t) \in \mathfrak{U}$, $t \in \mathbb{R}$, $u(0) = u_0$. This trajectory is invariant, $S_t u(t) = u(t + \tau)$ $\forall t \in \mathbb{R}$, $\tau \geq 0$. Therefore the attractor is the union of invariant trajectories bounded in H.

THEOREM 9.6. *The semigroup $\{S_t\}$ corresponding to the equation* (3.1) *has an (H, H)-attractor $\mathfrak{U}$, $\mathfrak{U}$ is bounded in H_2 and in $H_{1,\gamma}(\Omega)^2$.*

PROOF. Note that S_t are continuous operators from H to H (the proof is the same as the one given in [6] for the case of a bounded domain). By the theorem on the existence of a global attractor (see [6] or [12]), it suffices to prove that there exists an (H, H)-attracting set B_4 compact in H. Let $B_4 = z_1 + B_3$, where B_3 is defined by (9.25). This set is closed in H and by Proposition 9.10 it is bounded in H_2 and in $H_{1,\gamma}$. This implies that B_4 is compact (see [2, 3]).

Now we shall prove that B_4 is (H, H)-attracting. Since B_2 is H-absorbing and invariant, then it suffices to prove that for any $B \in B_2$

$$\text{dist}(S_t B, B_4) \to 0 \quad \text{as } t \to \infty. \tag{9.35}$$

Suppose the contrary. In this case we can find an $\varepsilon > 0$, a sequence $u_{0k} \in B_2$ and a sequence $t_k \to +\infty$ such that $u_k(t) = S_t u_{0k}$ satisfy the estimate

$$\text{dist}(u_k(t_k), B_4) \geq \varepsilon. \tag{9.36}$$

By Proposition 9.11 $u_l(t_l) \to u = z_1 + v$ as $l \to +\infty$ and by (9.36)

$$\text{dist}(u, B_4) \geq \varepsilon > 0. \tag{9.37}$$

Obviously, $u_l(t_l) - z_k \in F_\tau$, $\tau \leq t_l$ and, therefore, $u - z_1 \in [F_\tau]$ for any τ and $u \in B_3 + z$. Since $B_4 = z_1 + B_3$, this contradicts (9.36) and this contradiction shows that (9.34) holds.

By the theorem on the existence of global attractors there exists an (H, H)-attractor $\mathfrak{U}$. Due to invariance, any point u_0 belongs to a trajectory $u(t)$, $t \in \mathbb{R}$, lying on the attractor, $u_0 = u(0)$. Since $u(t) \in \mathfrak{U}$ $\forall t$ and $\mathfrak{U}$ is bounded in H_2, it follows that $u(t)$ satisfies (3.7), (3.8). By Theorem 9.4, u satisfies (3.12), and, therefore, $\|u(t)\|_{1,\gamma} \leq C$ $\forall t$, where C depends on bounds of H_2-norms of $u \in H_2$. Therefore $\mathfrak{U}$ is bounded in $H_{1,\gamma}$.

THEOREM 9.7. *Any trajectory $u(t) = S_t u_0$, $t \in \mathbb{R}$, lying on the attractor $\mathfrak{U}$, satisfies* (3.12).

PROOF. Since $\mathfrak{U}$ is bounded in H_2, it follows that any trajectory $u(t)$ satisfies (3.7), (3.8). Hence by Theorem 9.4 $u(t)$ satisfies (3.12).

THEOREM 9.8. *Let z be a steady-state solution of* (4.32). *Then there exist γ_1 and $C > 0$ such that for any trajectory $u(t) \in \mathfrak{U}$ we have*

$$\int_\Omega e^{\gamma|x_3|} |\nabla(z - u(t))|^2 dx \leq C \quad \forall t, \tag{9.38}$$

$$\int_T^{T+1} \int_\Omega e^{\gamma|x_3|} (|\Delta(z - u(t))| + |\partial_t u(t)|^2) dx\, dt \leq C \quad \forall T. \tag{9.39}$$

PROOF. Theorem 4.2 holds in the two-dimensional as well as in the three-dimensional case. The argument is the same. So (4.4) is valid, and taking into account (4.1), we conclude that (9.38) and (9.39) are valid.

THEOREM 9.9. *Let* $z_1, z_2, \ldots$ *be solutions of* (5.1), (5.2), *where* f *and* z_k *are independent of* t, $\partial_t z_k = 0$. *Then*

$$\|z_k\|_{2,k\gamma} \leq C_k. \tag{9.40}$$

Let $u \in \mathfrak{U}$ *and* $u - (z_1 + \cdots + z_n) = w_{n+1}$. *Then the function* w_{n+1} *satisfies* (6.2) *where* C_{n+1} *does not depend on* $u \in \mathfrak{U}$.

PROOF. The estimate (9.40) follows from (5.3), which is valid in the two-dimensional case (the argument is the same as in the three-dimensional case). The estimate (6.2) is also valid. The constant C_{n+1} does not depend on $u \in \mathfrak{U}$, since $\mathfrak{U}$ is bounded in H_2, and the constants M_0 and M_1 in (3.7) and (3.8) do not depend on $u \in \mathfrak{U}$.

THEOREM 9.10. *The attractor* $\mathfrak{U}$ *has finite Hausdorff dimension*:

$$\dim \mathfrak{U} \leq C(\nu'')^{-4} \lambda_1^{-2} \|f\|^2.$$

PROOF. The computations are the same as in [2], with ν replaced by $\nu''/2$, since by (3.4), (3.5), (3.6)

$$-\nu'(\Delta u, u) + (L_0 u, u) \geq (\nu''/2)(\Delta u, u) \qquad \forall u \in H_1.$$

Now we shall give some sufficient conditions on V for (3.4), (3.5) to hold. These conditions are quite similar to those given in §7 in the three-dimensional case.

PROPOSITION 9.12. *Let* $V = (0, V_3)$, $V_3 = V_3(x_2)$, *where* V_3 *is a solution of* (9.4). *Then condition* (3.5) *holds with some* $C > 0$ *and condition* (3.4) *holds with* $\nu' = \lambda_1^0$, *where* λ_1^0 *is defined by* (7.3).

PROOF. The argument is the same as in the three-dimensional case. The validity of (3.5) is proved in Lemma 7.1. In the proof of Lemma 7.2 concerning (3.4) some minor modifications must be made. In (7.3), $\partial_1 V_3 = 0$, in (7.10) the operator G_3 defined by (0.33) is expressed in terms of the operator G_2 defined by (9.5), (9.6). In (7.11) we take $H_1^0(\Omega)^2$ instead of $H_1^0(\Omega)^3$. In (7.9) $dx_1 dx_2$ is replaced by dx_2. Everything else is the same as in the proof of Lemma 7.2.

REMARK 9.1. In the same way as in the final part of §7, one can easily see that (3.5) is fulfilled; we can take $\nu' = V_m l/\pi$ and all the results are valid if $V_m l/\nu < \pi$. Of course, this condition may be improved.

REFERENCES

1. F. Abergel, *Attractor for a Navier-Stokes flow in an unbounded domain*, RAIRO Modél. Math. Anal. Numér. **23** (1989), no. 3, 359–370.
2. A. V. Babin, *Attractor of Navier-Stokes system in an unbounded channel-like domain*, J. Dynamics Differential Equations (to appear).
3. _____, *Asymptotic behavior as* $|x| \to \infty$ *of functions lying on the attractor of two-dimensional Navier-Stokes system in an unbounded planar domain*, Mat. Sb. **182** (1991), no. 12, 1683–1709; English transl. in Math. USSR-Sb. **74** (to appear).

4. _____, *Asymptotic behaviour as* $|x| \to \infty$ *of strongly perturbed Poiseuille flows*, Dokl. Akad. Nauk SSSR **316** (1990), no. 4; English transl. in Soviet Math. Dokl. **43** (1991).

5. _____, *Asymptotic behaviour as* $|x| \to \infty$ *of settled flows in a tube*, Mat. Zametki (to appear). (Russian)

6. A. V. Babin and M. I. Vishik, *Attractors of evolution equation*, "Nauka", Moscow, 1989. (Russian)

7. M. E. Bogovskiĭ, *On L_p-theory for the Navier-Stokes systems in unbounded domains with noncompact boundaries*, Dokl. Akad. Nauk SSSR **255** (1980), 1296–1300; English transl. in Soviet Math. Dokl. **22** (1980).

8. L. Caffarelli, R. Kohn, and L. Nirenberg, *Partial regularity of suitable weak solutions of the Navier-Stokes equations*, Comm. Pure Appl. Math. **35** (1982), 771–831.

9. P. Constantin and C. Foiaş, *Navier-Stokes equations*, The University of Chicago Press, Chicago and London, 1988.

10. P. Constantin, C. Foiaş, and R. Temam, *Attractors representing turbulent flows*, Mem. Amer. Math. Soc. **53** (1985), no. 314.

11. G. P. Galdi and S. Rionero, *Weighted energy methods in fluid dynamics and elasticity*, Lecture Notes in Math., vol. 1134, Springer-Verlag, Berlin and Heidelberg, 1985.

12. J. K. Hale, *Asymptotic behaviour of dissipative systems*, Math. Surveys and Monographs, vol. 25, American Mathematical Society, Providence, RI, 1988.

13. O. A. Ladyzhenskaya, *The mathematical theory of viscous incompressible flow*, Gordon and Breach, New York and London, 1963.

14. _____, *On a dynamical system generated by Navier-Stokes equations*, Zap. Nauchn. Sem. Leningrad. Otdel. Mat. Inst. Steklov. (LOMI) **27** (1972), 91–115; English transl. in J. Soviet Math. **3** (1975), 458–479.

15. _____, *On the determination of minimal global attractors for the Navier-Stokes equations and other partial differential equations*, Uspekhi Mat. Nauk **42** (1987), no. 6, 25–60; English transl. in Russian Math. Surveys **42** (1987), no. 6, 27–73.

16. O. A. Ladyzhenskaya and N. N. Uraltseva, *Linear and quasilinear elliptic equations*, "Nauka", Moscow, 1973; English transl. of the 1st ed., Academic Press, New York, 1968.

17. L. D. Landau and E. M. Lifshits, *Fluid mechanics*, "Nauka", Moscow, 1988; English transl., Pergamon Press, New York; Addison-Wesley, Reading, MA, 1959.

18. J. L. Lions and E. Magenes, *Problèmes aux limites non homogenes et applications*, 1, Dunod, Paris, 1968.

19. V. N. Maslennikova and M. E. Bogovskiĭ, *Approximation of potential and solenoidal vector fields*, Sibirsk. Mat. Zh. **24** (1983), no. 5, 149–171; English transl. in Siberian Math. J. **24** (1983), no. 5.

20. V. P. Maslov and P. P. Mosolov, *Equations of one-dimensional barotropic gas*, "Nauka", Moscow, 1990. (Russian)

21. M. Miklavčič, *Nonlinear stability of asymptotic suction*, Trans. Amer. Math. Soc. **281** (1984), no. 1, 215–231.

22. D. Ruelle and R. Takens, *On the nature of turbulence*, Comm. Math. Phys. **20** (1971), 167–192.

23. V. A. Solonnikov, *Stokes and Navier-Stokes equations in domains with noncompact boundaries*, Nonlinear partial differential equations and their applications, Res. Notes in Math., vol. 84, Pitman, Boston and London, 1983, pp. 240–349.

24. R. Temam, *Navier-Stokes equations: theory and numerical analysis*, North Holland, Amsterdam and New York, 1977.

25. _____, *Infinite-dimensional systems in mechanics and physics*, Springer-Verlag, Berlin, Heidelberg, and New York, 1988.

Translated by THE AUTHOR

Unbounded Attractors of Evolution Equations

V. V. CHEPYZHOV AND A. YU. GORITSKIĬ

Introduction

In the theory of evolution partial differential equations great attention is devoted to studying the limiting behavior of solutions as time tends to infinity.

To describe this behavior, we can use the ideas, notions and methods of finite-dimensional theory of dynamical systems [19], [23]. With the system of evolution equations

$$\partial_t u = Au, \qquad u|_{t=0} = u_0 \qquad (1)$$

we associate the semigroup of operators $\{S_t\}$, $t \geq 0$, acting in the Banach space E of initial conditions of problem (1) and assigning at the moment of time t to the function u_0 the value of the corresponding solution $u(t)$: $S_t u_0 = u(t)$. O. A. Ladyzhenskaya [25–28], A. V. Babin, M. I. Vishik [1–7], C. Foias [13–16], J.-M. Chidaglia [11], R. Temam [11, 13, 15, 16, 34], A. Haraux [20], J. K. Hale [21, 22] and other authors studied the existence, structure and dimension of bounded attractors of the semigroups corresponding to the evolution equations, i.e., bounded strictly invariant sets to which all the trajectories of this semigroup are attracted as $t \to +\infty$. Questions concerning the character of this attraction and the construction of finite-dimensional asymptotics of solutions were also studied. These works involve such equations of mathematical physics as Navier-Stokes systems, magnetohydrodynamics equations, reaction-diffusion equations, wave equations with dissipation and nonlinear terms of interaction, series of hyperbolic systems of equations. The book [7] systematically states the results of study of the bounded attractors of partial differential evolution equations. An extensive bibliography devoted to these questions is given there.

In all the works enumerated, the semigroup considered has a bounded absorbing set, i.e., all the solutions of the dynamical systems are bounded when $t \geq 0$. Evolution equations possessing solutions unbounded as $t \to +\infty$ are also of great interest. Such equations certainly have no bounded attractors.

1991 *Mathematics Subject Classification.* Primary 58F12, 58F39; Secondary 35G25.

For example, if an equation is linear, and its right-hand side contains a linear selfadjoint semibounded elliptic operator that possesses a finite number of positive eigenvalues, then, as we can see, any solution $u(t)$ converges to zero or goes to infinity as $t \to +\infty$, being attracted to the finite-dimensional subspace E_+, whose basis consists of the eigenfunctions of the operator with positive eigenvalues. So, in the linear case, it is natural to define the attractor as the invariant subspace E_+, i.e., an unbounded set. It is necessary to generalize the notion of maximal attractor $\mathfrak{A}$, replacing the boundedness condition by the following minimality property: there does not exist a closed set $\mathfrak{A}' \subset \mathfrak{A}$ ($\mathfrak{A}' \neq \mathfrak{A}$) that also has the strict invariance property and the attraction property. This definition implies that the set $\mathfrak{A}$, generally speaking, is unbounded and may not be unique, which is also impossible in the bounded case.

An important role in the study of the maximal attractors of semigroups is played by maximal invariant sets. The set-theoretical union of all of the semigroup bounded in the past trajectories is said to be the maximal invariant set $\mathfrak{J}$. A trajectory of the semigroup is a continuous curve $\gamma(s)$, $s \in \mathbb{R}$, for which $S_t \gamma(s) = \gamma(t+s)$ when $t \geqslant 0$, $s \in \mathbb{R}$. The trajectory $\gamma(s)$ is called bounded in the past, if the set $\{\gamma(s) : s \leqslant 0\}$ is bounded in E. It is clear that the maximal invariant set $\mathfrak{J}$ is defined uniquely by the semigroup, is strictly invariant, contains all the bounded strictly invariant sets and lies in any maximal attractor of the semigroup (if they exist). The set $\mathfrak{J}$ itself may not be a maximal attractor.

Unbounded invariant sets and unbounded maximal attractors for certain semilinear equations and systems of parabolic type were first studied in [8–10].

The asymptotic behavior of solutions of semilinear hyperbolic equations with dissipation, for which no bounded absorbing set exists either, was studied in [17, 18].

The present paper is devoted to constructing the maximal invariant sets and the maximal attractors of the semigroups corresponding to abstract evolution equations in Hilbert space, and also to studying the structure of these sets and the way of approaching the attractor. The results obtained are applied to studying partial differential evolution equations and systems of the second order of parabolic and hyperbolic types. Thus we succeed in studying parabolic and hyperbolic equations from a unified point of view, avoiding the huge technical specifics of each of these types of equations.

The authors express their deep gratitude to professor M. I. Vishik for useful discussions of this paper.

§1. Formulation of the main results

Let E be a Banach space supplied with an action of a nonlinear semigroup of operators $\{S_t, t \geqslant 0\}$, $S_t: E \to E$, $S_t \cdot S_\tau = S_{t+\tau}$, where $S_0 = \mathrm{Id}$ is the

identity. For any sets X and Y from E we define
$$\operatorname{dist}(X, Y) = \sup_{x \in X} \inf_{y \in Y} \|x - y\|_E.$$
A continuous curve $\gamma(s)$ in E, $s \in \mathbb{R}$, is called a *trajectory* of the semigroup $\{S_t\}$, if $S_t(\gamma(s)) = \gamma(s+t)$ for all $t \geqslant 0$, $s \in \mathbb{R}$. A trajectory $\gamma(s)$ is called *bounded in the past*, if the set $\{\gamma(s) : s \leqslant 0\}$ is bounded in E, i.e., $\|\gamma(s)\|_E \leqslant \mathrm{const}$ when $s \leqslant 0$.

DEFINITION 1.1. The *maximal invariant set* $\mathfrak{J}$ of the semigroup $\{S_t\}$ is the set-theoretic union of all trajectories bounded in the past of the semigroup $\{S_t\}$.

Let us note that the set $\mathfrak{J}$ is strictly invariant with respect to the semigroup $\{S_t\}$, i.e., $S_t(\mathfrak{J}) = \mathfrak{J}$ for all $t \geqslant 0$. Also the set $\mathfrak{J}$ contains all the bounded strictly invariant sets of the semigroup, i.e., if $A \subset E$, $S_t(A) = A$ for all $t \geqslant 0$, then $A \subseteq \mathfrak{J}$. We understand the maximality property of the set $\mathfrak{J}$ in this sense. We also note that the set $\mathfrak{J}$ can be unbounded, because a trajectory $\gamma(s)$ can increase unboundedly as $s \to +\infty$.

DEFINITION 1.2. A closed set $\mathfrak{A}$ from E is said to be a *maximal attractor* of the semigroup $\{S_t\}$ if the following properties hold:

1) $S_t(\mathfrak{A}) = \mathfrak{A}$ for all $t \geqslant 0$ (strict invariance property);
2) for any bounded set K from E,
$$\operatorname{dist}(S_t(K), \mathfrak{A}) \to 0 \quad (t \to +\infty) \quad \text{(attraction property)};$$
3) there is no proper closed subset $\mathfrak{A}' \subset \mathfrak{A}$ that also satisfies the strict invariance and attraction properties (minimality property).

From Definition 1.2 we see that a maximal attractor may be an unbounded set in E and may not be defined uniquely. But the maximal attractor $\mathfrak{A}$ always contains any maximal invariant set $\mathfrak{J}$. Indeed, if $y \in \mathfrak{J}$, then $\gamma(0) = y$ for some bounded in the past trajectory $\gamma(s)$. Since the set $\{\gamma(s) : s \leqslant 0\}$ is bounded in E, the attraction property implies
$$\operatorname{dist}\left(S_t\{\gamma(s) : s \leqslant 0\}, \mathfrak{A}\right) \to 0 \quad (t \to +\infty).$$
We note that
$$y \in \{\gamma(s) : s \leqslant 0\} \subseteq \{\gamma(s) : s \leqslant t\} = S_t\{\gamma(s) : s \leqslant 0\};$$
then $\operatorname{dist}(\{y\}, \mathfrak{A}) \to 0$ $(t \to +\infty)$, i.e., $\operatorname{dist}(\{y\}, \mathfrak{A}) = 0$. The set $\mathfrak{A}$ is closed, so $y \in \mathfrak{A}$.

We should also note that the set $\mathfrak{J}$ itself may not be a maximal attractor. Below we are interested in the following question: under what conditions is the maximal invariant set of the semigroup a maximal attractor.

Now let us consider semigroups of evolution equations.

Let H be a Hilbert space with scalar product $(\cdot, \cdot)$. Consider the abstract differential equation in the space H:
$$\frac{d}{dt} y(t) = A y(t) + F(y(t)) \tag{1.1}$$

with initial condition
$$y|_{t=0} = y_0 \in H. \tag{1.2}$$
Here A is a linear operator with domain $\mathscr{D}(A)$, F is a nonlinear operator with domain H.

The solution of problem (1.1), (1.2) is a function $y(t)$, $t \in [0, T]$ with values in $\mathscr{D}(A)$ when $t > 0$, weakly continuous in H for $t \geq 0$, for which we have:
$$\frac{d}{dt}(y(t), v) = (Ay(t), v) + (F(y(t)), v)$$
for any $v \in H$. The last equation should be regarded as an equality of distributions on $\mathbb{R}$. The initial condition $y(0) = y_0$ is understood in the weak sense.

In this section we shall not give complete formulations of conditions under which the abstract Cauchy problem (1.1), (1.2) is solved uniquely and possesses the properties that we require. We shall state these properties as assumptions in this section. In the next sections we shall give examples of partial differential evolution equations of parabolic and hyperbolic types that satisfy these conditions, and the conclusions of the abstract approach will be applied to them.

So, let us formulate the properties that the problem (1.1), (1.2) must satisfy.

PROPERTY I. The problem (1.1), (1.2) has a unique solution for any $y_0 \in H$ and for any interval of time $[0, T]$. The corresponding semigroup $\{S_t\}_{t \geq 0}$ of nonlinear operators is continuous in the arguments (y_0, t), $y_0 \in H$, $t \in \mathbb{R}_+$.

PROPERTY II. For any solution $y(t)$, the real-valued function
$$\|y(t)\|^2 = (y(t), y(t))$$
is absolutely continuous and
$$\frac{d}{dt}\|y(t)\|^2 = 2\left(\frac{d}{dt}y(t), y(t)\right). \tag{1.3}$$

PROPERTY III. The spectrum σ of the linear operator A does not intersect the imaginary axis. Let us denote the spectral sets:
$$\sigma_+ = \sigma \cap \{\operatorname{Re} \zeta > 0\} \quad \text{and} \quad \sigma_- = \sigma \cap \{\operatorname{Re} \zeta < 0\}, \quad \sigma = \sigma_+ \cup \sigma_-.$$

Let E_+ and E_- be the invariant subspaces of the operator A corresponding to the spectral sets σ_+ and σ_-. We assume that the space H can be represented as the sum of the subspaces E_+ and E_-: $H = E_+ \oplus E_-$, and the spaces E_+ and E_- themselves are orthogonal. Also we assume that the subspace E_+ is finite-dimensional, and, finally, that there exists a positive constant $\varkappa$ such that
$$\forall p \in E_+ \quad (Ap, p) \geq +\varkappa \|p\|^2, \tag{1.4}$$
$$\forall q \in E_- \quad (Aq, q) \leq -\varkappa \|q\|^2. \tag{1.5}$$

PROPERTY IV. The nonlinear operator $F(y)$ satisfies the estimate

$$\|F(y)\| \leqslant \varepsilon\|y\| + C, \tag{1.6}$$

where ε and C are positive constants.

PROPERTY V. The semigroup $\{S_t\}$ satisfies the following condition of asymptotic compactness. For any bounded set $B \in H$ and for any $t > 0$, there exist a compact set $K = K(B, t)$ from H and a function $\varepsilon = \varepsilon(B, t) > 0$ such that $S_t(B) \subset \mathscr{O}_{\varepsilon(B, t)}(K)$ and $\varepsilon(B, t) \to 0$ $(t \to \infty)$. (Here and later $\mathscr{O}_\varepsilon(P)$ denotes the ε-neighborhood of a set P from H.)

Let us formulate the main results of this paper.

THEOREM 1.1. *Let the semigroup* $\{S_t\}$ *acting in the space H possess Properties I–V and let* $\varepsilon < \varkappa$. *Then this semigroup has the maximal invariant set* $\mathfrak{I}$, *and the following properties hold*:

a) $\mathfrak{I}$ *is a bounded compact set in H*;
b) *the projection of* $\mathfrak{I}$ *onto E_+ parallel to E_- coincides with E_+*:

$$\Pi_{E_+}(\mathfrak{I}) = E_+;$$

c) *if* $\varepsilon = 0$, *then the projection of* $\mathfrak{I}$ *onto E_- is bounded in H*.

THEOREM 1.2. *If Properties I–V hold,* $\varepsilon = 0$, *and we have $F(p+q) \to 0$ as $\|p\| \to +\infty$ uniformly on any set $B_R^- = \{q \in E_- : \|q\| \leqslant R\}$, then the maximal invariant set $\mathfrak{I}$ is the maximal attractor of the semigroup $\{S_t\}$*: $\mathfrak{I} = \mathfrak{A}$. *Also*:

$$\operatorname{dist}(\mathfrak{A} \setminus B_R, E_+) \to 0 \quad (R \to +\infty); \tag{1.7}$$

here and below B_R denotes the ball of radius R in H centered at zero.

Theorems 1.1 and 1.2 will be proved in the next sections.

In conclusion let us note that in the linear case, when $F(y) \equiv 0$ in equation (1.1), the maximal invariant set and the maximal attractor of the linear semigroup is the invariant subspace E_+. This may be easily established by using Property III.

§2. Proof of Theorem 1.1

Let us project the solution $y(t)$ of problem (1.1), (1.2) onto E_+ and E_-. We denote by $p(t)$ the projection onto E_+ and by $q(t)$ the projection onto E_-: $y(t) = p(t) + q(t)$, $y_0 = p_0 + q_0$. The functions $p(t)$ and $q(t)$ satisfy the equations:

$$\frac{d}{dt}p(t) = Ap(t) + F_1(y(t)), \quad F_1(y) = \Pi_{E_+}(F(y)), \tag{2.1}$$

$$\frac{d}{dt}q(t) = Aq(t) + F_2(y(t)), \quad F_2(y) = \Pi_{E_-}(F(y)). \tag{2.2}$$

PROPOSITION 2.1. *For any function* $y(t) = S_t(y_0) = p(t) + q(t)$, *the following inequalities hold*:

$$\frac{1}{2}\frac{d}{dt}\|p(t)\|^2 \geq +\varkappa\|p(t)\|^2 + (F(y(t)), p(t)), \qquad (2.3)$$

$$\frac{1}{2}\frac{d}{dt}\|q(t)\|^2 \leq -\varkappa\|q(t)\|^2 + (F(y(t)), q(t)). \qquad (2.4)$$

PROOF. Take the scalar product in H of (2.1) with $p(t)$ and use Properties II and III:

$$\frac{1}{2}\frac{d}{dt}\|p(t)\|^2 = (p', p) = (Ap, p) + (F_1(y), p)$$

$$\geq \varkappa\|p(t)\|^2 + (F_1(y(t)), p(t)).$$

By the orthogonality of the subspaces E_+ and E_-, we have the equality $(F_1(y(t)), p(t)) = (F(y(t)), p(t))$. This proves inequality (2.3). Inequality (2.4) is proved similarly. □

DEFINITION 2.1. A *pseudoball* in H is a set of the form

$$G_R^+ = \{y = p + q : p \in E_+, q \in E_-, \|q\|^2 - \|p\|^2 \leq R^2\}.$$

We shall say that a set B from H is *pseudobounded*, if $B \subseteq G_R^+$ for some R.

PROPOSITION 2.2. *Let* $R_0 = 2C/(\varkappa - \varepsilon)$. *If* $R \geq R_0$, *then*
  a) $S_t(G_R^+) \subseteq G_R^+$ *when* $t \geq 0$ (*semi-invariance property*);
  b) *if a set* B *is pseudobounded in* H, *then* $S_t(B) \subseteq G_{R_0}^+$ *if* $t \geq T$ *for some* $T = T(B) \geq 0$ (*absorbing property*).

PROOF. Subtract inequality (2.3) from inequality (2.4):

$$\frac{1}{2}\frac{d}{dt}(\|q(t)\|^2 - \|p(t)\|^2) \leq -\varkappa(\|q\|^2 + \|p\|^2) + (F(y), q - p)$$

$$\leq -\varkappa\|y\|^2 + \|F(y)\|\,\|p - q\|$$

$$= -\varkappa\|y\|^2 + \|F(y)\|\,\|p + q\|$$

$$= -\varkappa\|y\|^2 + \|F(y)\|\,\|y\|.$$

Using Property IV:

$$\frac{1}{2}\frac{d}{dt}(\|q(t)\|^2 - \|p(t)\|^2) \leq -\varkappa\|y\|^2 + (\varepsilon\|y\| + C)\|y\|$$

$$= -((\varkappa - \varepsilon)\|y\| - C)\|y\|.$$

If $\|q\|^2 - \|p\|^2 \geq R_0^2$, then

$$\|y\| = (\|q\|^2 + \|p\|^2)^{1/2} \geq R_0 = 2C/(\varkappa - \varepsilon)$$

and so

$$-((\varkappa - \varepsilon)\|y\| - C)\|y\| \leq -CR_0.$$

Hence, if $\|q(t)\|^2 - \|p(t)\|^2 \geq R^2 \geq R_0^2$ for some $t \geq 0$, then

$$\frac{1}{2}\frac{d}{dt}(\|q(t)\|^2 - \|p(t)\|^2) \leq -CR_0. \tag{2.5}$$

This means that if $\|q_0\|^2 - \|p_0\|^2 \leq R^2$, where $R \geq R_0$, then $\|q(t)\|^2 - \|p(t)\|^2 \leq R^2$ for all $t \geq 0$. The semi-invariance property is proved.

To prove the absorbing property, let us note that if a set B is pseudobounded, then $B \subset G_{R_1}^+$ for some R_1. If $R_1 \leq R_0$, then by semi-invariance, we can take $T = 0$. If $R_1 > R_0$, then according to (2.5), we can take $T = (R_1 - R_0)/(2CR_0)$. $\square$

Choose a positive number α and consider the set

$$G_{R,\alpha}^- = \{y = p + q : p \in E_+, q \in E_-, \|q\|^2 - (1+\alpha)\|p\|^2 < -R^2\}.$$

PROPOSITION 2.3. *There exist constants $\alpha > 0$ and $R' > 0$ such that the set $G_{R,\alpha}^-$ is semi-invariant when $R \geq R'$.*

PROOF. Let us multiply inequality (2.3) by $(1+\alpha)$ and subtract the product from inequality (2.4):

$$\frac{1}{2}\frac{d}{dt}(\|q(t)\|^2 - (1+\alpha)\|p(t)\|^2)$$
$$\leq -\varkappa(\|q\|^2 + (1+\alpha)\|p\|^2) + (F(y), q - (1+\alpha)p)$$
$$\leq -\varkappa(\|q\|^2 + \|p\|^2) - \varkappa\alpha\|p\|^2 + \|F(y)\|(\|p-q\| + \alpha\|p\|)$$
$$\leq -\varkappa\|y\|^2 + \|F(y)\|(\|y\| + \alpha\|p\|)$$
$$\leq -\varkappa\|y\|^2 + \|F(y)\|(1+\alpha)\|y\|.$$

Using Property IV again,

$$\frac{1}{2}\frac{d}{dt}(\|q(t)\|^2 - (1+\alpha)\|p(t)\|^2)$$
$$\leq -\varkappa\|y\|^2 + (\varepsilon\|y\| + C)(1+\alpha)\|y\|$$
$$= -((\varkappa - \varepsilon - \varepsilon\alpha)\|y\| - C(1+\alpha))\|y\|. \tag{2.6}$$

Now choose α so as to have $\varkappa - \varepsilon - \varepsilon\alpha > 0$. Define

$$R' = C(1+\alpha)^{3/2}(\varkappa - \varepsilon - \varepsilon\alpha)^{-1}.$$

If $\|q\|^2 - (1+\alpha)\|p\|^2 < -R^2$, where $R \geq R'$, then $\|q\|^2 + (1+\alpha)\|p\|^2 > R^2$, and

$$\|y\|^2 = \|q\|^2 + \|p\|^2 \geq \frac{\|q\|^2 + (1+\alpha)\|p\|^2}{1+\alpha} > \frac{R^2}{1+\alpha} \geq \left(\frac{C(1+\alpha)}{\varkappa - \varepsilon - \varepsilon\alpha}\right)^2.$$

Thus, $\|y\| > C(1+\alpha)/(\varkappa - \varepsilon - \varepsilon\alpha)$, i.e.,

$$-((\varkappa - \varepsilon - \varepsilon\alpha)\|y\| - C(1+\alpha))\|y\| < 0.$$

Now using inequality (2.6), we obtain

$$\frac{1}{2}\frac{d}{dt}(\|q\|^2 - (1+\alpha)\|p\|^2) < 0 \quad \text{when } \|q\|^2 - (1+\alpha)\|p\|^2 \leq -R'^2.$$

So, if $y_0 = p_0 + q_0 \in G_{R,\alpha}^-$, $R > R'$, then

$$\|q(t)\|^2 - (1+\alpha)\|p(t)\|^2 \leq \|q_0\|^2 - (1+\alpha)\|p_0\|^2 < -R^2$$

when $t \geq 0$, and $y \in G_{R,\alpha}^-$. $\square$

COROLLARY 2.1. *If $y_0 \in G_{R_0}^+ \cap G_{R,\alpha}^-$, where $R > R'$, then $y(t) = S_t y(0) \in G_{R_0}^+ \cap G_{R,\alpha}^-$ for all $t > 0$.*

We define the sets $H_R = G_{R_0}^+ \setminus G_{R,\alpha}^-$, $R > R'$. These sets possess the following properties:

a) The sets H_R are bounded. Indeed, if $y = p + q \in H_R$, then $\|q\|^2 - \|p\|^2 \leq R_0^2$ and $\|q\|^2 - (1+\alpha)\|p\|^2 \geq -R^2$. We subtract the second inequality from the first, obtaining $\alpha\|p\|^2 \leq R_0^2 + R^2$, i.e., $\|p\|^2 \leq (R_0^2 + R^2)/\alpha$, and so

$$\|q\|^2 \leq R_0^2 + \|p\|^2, \qquad \|y\|^2 = \|p\|^2 + \|q\|^2 \leq 2(R_0^2 + R^2)/\alpha + R_0^2.$$

b) If B is a bounded set from $G_{R_0}^+$, then B is contained in some set H_R. To see this, it is sufficient to show that for any bounded set B in H there exists an $R > R'$ such that $B \cap G_{R,\alpha}^- = \emptyset$. If $y = p + q \in G_{R,\alpha}^-$, then $\|p\|^2 - (1+\alpha)\|q\|^2 < -R^2$, hence $\|y\|^2 \geq \|q\|^2 > R^2/(1+\alpha)$, i.e., $y \notin B$ if R is sufficiently large.

c) The sets H_R are closed, because $G_{R_0}^+$ is closed and $G_{R,\alpha}^-$ is open.

PROPOSITION 2.4. *If $y(0) \in G_{R_0}^+$, $y(t) = S_t y(0) \in H_R$, then $y(\tau) \in H_R$ when $\tau \in [0, t]$.*

PROOF. If $y(0) \in G_{R_0}^+$, then $y(\tau) \in G_{R_0}^+$ $\forall \tau \geq 0$. If $y(\tau) \in G_{R,\alpha}^-$ when $\tau \leq t$, then $y(t) \in S_{t-\tau} G_{R,\alpha}^- \subset G_{R,\alpha}^-$ and $y(t) \notin H_R$. Therefore, $y(\tau) \in G_{R_0}^+ \setminus G_{R,\alpha}^- = H_R$. $\square$

For our further arguments we need the following lemma.

LEMMA 2.1. *Let $\{L_n\}$ be a sequence of nested sets in a Banach space E: $L_1 \supset L_2 \supset L_3 \supset \cdots$, every set L_n lies in the ε_n-neighborhood of some compact subset K_n: $L_n \subseteq \mathscr{O}_{\varepsilon_n}(K_n)$, and $\varepsilon_n \to 0$ $(n \to +\infty)$. Then from any sequence of points $\{y_n\}$, where $y_n \in L_n$, we can choose a convergent subsequence.*

PROOF. Let $y_n \in L_n \subset L_1 \subset \mathscr{O}_{\varepsilon_1}(K_1)$ for any $n \in \mathbb{N}$. From the sequence $\{\bar{y}^n\} \subset K_1$, where $\|y_n - \bar{y}^n\| \leq 2\varepsilon_1$, we choose a convergent subsequence (keeping its old notation) $\bar{y}^n \to \bar{y}_1 \in K_1$. Then, choosing a subsequence again, we see that $\mathscr{O}_{\varepsilon_1}(\bar{y}_1)$ contains all the $\bar{y}^n$, and so

$$\|y_n - \bar{y}_1\| \le \|y_n - \bar{y}^n\| + \|\bar{y}^n - \bar{y}_1\| \le 3\varepsilon_1.$$

Now we fix y_1. Then $y_n \in L_n \subset L_2 \subset \mathscr{O}_{\varepsilon_2}(K_2)$ when $n \ge 2$. Choosing a subsequence in $\{y_n\}_{n \ge 2}$ similarly, we see that there exists a point $\bar{y}_2$ for which $\|y_n - \bar{y}_2\| \le 3\varepsilon_2$ when $n \ge 2$. Now we fix y_2 and so on.

As the result, we obtain two sequences $\{y_n\}$ and $\{\bar{y}_n\}$, where $\{y_n\}$ is a subsequence of the initial sequence, for which the inequality $\|y_n - \bar{y}_k\| \le 3\varepsilon_k$ holds when $n \ge k$. Then

$$\|\bar{y}_{k+1} - \bar{y}_k\| \le \|y_{k+1} - \bar{y}_{k+1}\| + \|y_{k+1} - \bar{y}_k\| \le 3\varepsilon_{k+1} + 3\varepsilon_k.$$

Choosing a subsequence again so that the series $\sum \varepsilon_k$ converges, we see that the sequence $\{\bar{y}_k\}$ is Cauchy, and so $\bar{y}_k \to \bar{y}$ $(k \to \infty)$. Since $\|y_k - \bar{y}_k\| \le \varepsilon_k \to 0$ as $k \to \infty$, we have $y_k \to \bar{y}$. The lemma is proved. $\square$

REMARK 2.1. Under the conditions of the lemma, the set $L = \bigcap_{n=1}^{\infty} L_n$ is compact.

PROOF. L is closed as the intersection of closed sets and for any n there exists a finite $2\varepsilon_n$-net for the set $L \subset L_n \subset \mathscr{O}_{\varepsilon_n}(K_n)$ (namely the ε_n-net for K_n), and $\varepsilon_n \to 0$. So L is compact. $\square$

Let us apply the statements proved above to the study of the semigroup.

PROPOSITION 2.5. *Let* $\{S_{t_n} y_n\} \in G_{R_0}^+$, $\{S_{t_n} y_n\}$ *be a bounded sequence,* $y_n \in G_{R_0}^+$, $t_n \to +\infty$. *Then we can choose a convergent subsequence from* $\{S_{t_n} y_n\}$.

PROOF. $\{S_{t_n} y_n\} \subset H_R$ for some R, by virtue of property b) of the sets H_R. Then Proposition 2.4 implies that $\{y_n\} \subset H_R$. Without loss of generality, we can assume that t_n is an increasing sequence. Then the sequence of sets $L_n = S_{t_n}(G_{R_0}^+) \cap H_R = S_{t_n}(H_R) \cap H_R$ is nested and by Property V we have $L_n \subset \mathscr{O}_{\varepsilon(H_R, t_n)}(K(H_R, t_n))$, where $K(H_R, t_n)$ is compact and $\varepsilon(H_R, t_n) \to 0$ when $n \to \infty$. Now we can apply Lemma 2.1 to the sequence of points $S_{t_n} y_n \subset L_n$. The proposition is proved. $\square$

Let us define a set $\mathfrak{J}$ by setting:

$$\mathfrak{J} = \bigcap_{t \ge 0} \overline{S_t(G_{R_0}^+)}.$$

(The bar means closure in the space H.) We shall prove below that the set $\mathfrak{J}$ is the maximal invariant set of the semigroup.

PROPOSITION 2.6. $\mathfrak{J}$ *is a bounded-compact set (i.e., its intersection with any closed bounded set is compact).*

PROOF. Since $\mathfrak{J} \subset G_{R_0}^+$, the intersection of $\mathfrak{J}$ with any ball from H is contained in some H_R. So, to prove the statement, it is sufficient to show that $\mathfrak{I} \cap H_R$ is compact. We have:

$$\mathfrak{I} \cap H_R = \bigcap_{t \geq 0} (\overline{S_t(G_{R_0}^+)}) \cap H_R = \bigcap_{t \geq 0} (\overline{S_t(H_R)}) \cap H_R.$$

As in the proof of Proposition 2.5, we can show that the sets $S_t(H_R) \cap H_R$ satisfy the conditions of Lemma 2.1, and then $\mathfrak{I} \cap H_R$ is compact by Remark 2.1. □

PROPOSITION 2.7. *The set $\mathfrak{I}$ is strictly invariant for the semigroup $\{S_t\}$, i.e., $S_t(\mathfrak{I}) = \mathfrak{I}$ for all $t \geq 0$.*

PROOF. By the definition of the set $\mathfrak{I}$, we have $y \in \mathfrak{I}$ iff there exists a sequence $y_n \in G_{R_0}^+$, $t_n \to +\infty$, such that $S_{t_n} y_n \to y$. Then $S_{t_n+t} y_n \to S_t y$ ($t_n \to +\infty$) since the map S_t is continuous, and then $S_t(\mathfrak{I}) \subseteq \mathfrak{I}$.

Let us prove the opposite inclusion. Let $y \in \mathfrak{I}$ and

$$S_{t_n} y_n \to y, \qquad y_n \in G_{R_0}^+, \quad t_n \to \infty.$$

Note that $\{S_{t_n} y_n\} \subset H_R$ for some $R > R'$ as a bounded sequence from $G_{R_0}^+$. By Proposition 2.4, $\{S_{t_n-t} y_n\} \subset H_R$ and the sequence $\{S_{t_n-t} y_n\}$ is bounded. From this sequence, by Proposition 2.5, we can choose a convergent subsequence $S_{t_{n(k)}-t} y_{n(k)} \to \bar{y} \in \mathfrak{I}$. We have

$$S_t \bar{y} = \lim_{n(k) \to \infty} S_t(S_{t_{n(k)}-t} y_{n(k)}) = \lim_{n(k) \to \infty} S_{t_{n(k)}} y_{n(k)} = y \in \mathfrak{I},$$

where $\bar{y} \in \mathfrak{I}$. The inclusion $S_t(\mathfrak{I}) \supseteq \mathfrak{I}$ is proved. □

Let us show that $\mathfrak{I}$ is not empty. For this we need the following topological lemma, proved in [24].

LEMMA 2.2. *Let B_R be a ball in $\mathbb{R}^N$ centered at zero, suppose $x_0 \in B_R$, $\rho: [0, T] \times B_R \to \mathbb{R}^N$ is a continuous map such that*
  1) $\rho(0, x) = x$ *for all* $x \in B_R$;
  2) $\rho(t, \partial B_R)$ *does not contain the point x_0 for all $t \in [0, T]$.*
Then $x_0 \in \rho(t, B_R)$ for all $t \in [0, T]$.

Let us define a plane in H by putting $L_{p_0} = p_0 + E_-$, $p_0 \in E_+$.

PROPOSITION 2.8. *For any $p_0 \in E_+$ we have $L_{p_0} \cap \mathfrak{I} \neq \varnothing$ (i.e., the projection of $\mathfrak{I}$ onto E_+ coincides with E_+).*

PROOF. Let us consider the sets $L_{p_0} \cap S_n(G_{R_0}^+)$ ($n = 1, 2, \ldots$). We shall show that these sets are not empty. If B_R is any ball in E_+, then $B_R \times \{0\} \subset G_{R_0}^+$. We define the map

$$\rho: [0, T] \times B_R \to E_+: \quad \rho(t, p) = \Pi_{E_+}(S_t(p + 0)),$$

where $p \in B_R \subset E_+$, $0 \in E_-$, Π_{E_+} is the projection onto E_+. Since $\partial B_R \times \{0\} \subset G_{R,\alpha}^-$, by Proposition 2.3 we have $S_t(\partial B_R \times \{0\}) \subset G_{R,\alpha}^-$ when

$t \geqslant 0$. So $\|\Pi_{E_+} S_t(\partial B_R \times \{0\})\| \geqslant R(1+\alpha)^{-1/2}$, and $\rho(t, \partial B_R)$ does not contain p_0 if R is sufficiently large. From Lemma 2.2 we see that $\rho(n, B_R)$ contains p_0, and so $L_{p_0} \cap S_n(G_{R_0}^+) \neq \varnothing$.

Let us choose a sequence of points $y_n^* \in L_{p_0} \cap S_n(G_{R_0}^+)$. Then $y_n^* = S_n y_n$, where $y_n \in G_{R_0}^+$. Let $L_{p_0} \cap S_n(G_{R_0}^+) \subset L_{p_0} \cap G_{R_0}^+$ be bounded. By Proposition 2.5, we can choose a convergent subsequence $y_{n(k)}^* = S_{n(k)} y_{n(k)} \to y^*$. Since $n(k) \to \infty$, $y_{n(k)} \in G_{R_0}^+$, we have $y^* \in \mathfrak{I}$. Taking into consideration $\Pi_{E_+}(y_{n(k)}^*) = p_0$, we obtain $\Pi_{E_+}(y^*) = p_0$. This means that $y^* \in L_{p_0} \cap \mathfrak{I}$, and the proposition is proved. $\square$

Now let us verify that in fact $\mathfrak{I}$ is the maximal invariant set of the semigroup $\{S_t\}$.

If $y_0 \in \mathfrak{I}$, then by the strict invariance of the set $\mathfrak{I}$ (Proposition 2.7), there exists a trajectory $\{\gamma(\tau), \tau \in \mathbb{R}\} \subseteq \mathfrak{I} \subseteq G_{R_0}^+$, $\gamma(0) = y_0$. Let us also note that by property b) of the family of sets H_R, there exists a number R such that $y_0 \in H_R$. So, from Proposition 2.4, we have $\{\gamma(\tau), \tau \leqslant 0\} \subseteq H_R$ and then $\gamma(\tau)$ is a trajectory bounded in the past, i.e., y_0 is a point of the maximal invariant set.

Conversely, let y_0 lie in the maximal invariant set; then there exists a trajectory $\gamma(t)$ bounded in the past for which $\gamma(t) = y_0$. Then, the set $\{\gamma(\tau), \tau \leqslant 0\}$ is bounded, and by the absorbing property (Proposition 2.2b), there exists a number $T \geqslant 0$ such that

$$S_T\{\gamma(\tau), \tau \leqslant 0\} = \{\gamma(\tau), \tau \leqslant T\} \subseteq G_{R_0}^+.$$

Hence

$$y_0 = \gamma(0) \in \{\gamma(\tau), \tau \leqslant T+t\} = S_t\{\gamma(\tau), \tau \leqslant T\} \subseteq S_t(G_{R_0}^+)$$

for all $t \geqslant 0$, and so $y_0 \in \mathfrak{I}$ by the definition of $\mathfrak{I}$.

Thus the items a) and b) of Theorem 1.1 follow from Propositions 2.6 and 2.8. Let us prove item c). Let $\varepsilon = 0$, i.e., $\|F(y)\| \leqslant C$.

PROPOSITION 2.9. *If $\varepsilon = 0$, then for any function $y(t) = S_t(y_0) = p(t) + q(t)$ one has:*

$$\frac{d}{dt}\|p(t)\|^2 \geqslant \varkappa \|p(t)\|^2 - C_1, \tag{2.7}$$

$$\frac{d}{dt}\|q(t)\|^2 \leqslant -\varkappa \|q(t)\|^2 + C_1, \tag{2.8}$$

where $C_1 = C^2/\varkappa$.

PROOF. From the inequalities (2.3), we have:

$$\frac{d}{dt}\|p(t)\|^2 \geqslant 2\varkappa\|p\|^2 + 2(F(y), p) \geqslant 2\varkappa\|p\|^2 - \varkappa\|p\|^2 - (1/\varkappa)\|F(y)\|^2$$

$$\geqslant \varkappa\|p\|^2 - C^2/\varkappa = \varkappa\|p\|^2 - C_1.$$

Similarly, from (2.4):

$$\frac{d}{dt}\|q(t)\|^2 \leq -2\varkappa\|q\|^2 + 2(F(y), q) \leq -2\varkappa\|q\|^2 + \varkappa\|q\|^2 + (1/\varkappa)\|F(y)\|^2$$
$$\leq -\varkappa\|q\|^2 + C^2/\varkappa = -\varkappa\|q\|^2 + C_1.$$

The proposition is proved. □

For further arguments we need the following elementary differential inequalities.

LEMMA 2.3. *Let $z(t)$ be an absolutely continuous function on the segment $[0, T]$, α and β be arbitrary real numbers, $\alpha \neq 0$.*

$$\text{If } z'(t) \geq \alpha z(t) + \beta, \quad \text{then } z(t) \geq (z(0) + \beta/\alpha)e^{\alpha t} - \beta/\alpha. \quad (2.9)$$

$$\text{If } z'(t) \leq \alpha z(t) + \beta, \quad \text{then } z(t) \leq (z(0) + \beta/\alpha)e^{\alpha t} - \beta/\alpha. \quad (2.10)$$

These inequalities can be proved by integration.

COROLLARY 2.2. *There exist numbers $D \geq 0$ and $\delta > 0$ such that*

$$\|p(t)\|^2 \geq \|p(0)\|^2 e^{\delta t}, \quad \text{if only } \|p(0)\| \geq D.$$

PROOF. If $\|p\|^2 \geq 2C_1/\varkappa = 2(C/\varkappa)^2 = D^2$, then inequality (2.7) implies $(d/dt)\|p(t)\|^2 \geq (\varkappa/2)\|p(t)\|^2$. Now we use the differential inequality (2.9) in which $z(t) = \|p(t)\|^2$, $\alpha = \varkappa/2$, $\beta = 0$:

$$\|p(t)\|^2 \geq \|p(0)\|^2 e^{\varkappa t/2} = \|p(0)\|^2 e^{\delta t},$$

where $\delta = \varkappa/2$. □

Define the set $Q = \{y = p + q, \ p \in E_+, \ q \in E_-, \ \|q\| \leq D\}$. Let us prove an analog of Proposition 2.2:

PROPOSITION 2.10. *If $\varepsilon = 0$, then*

a) $S_t(Q) \subseteq Q$ *when $t \geq 0$ (semi-invariance property);*
b) *if a set B is bounded in H, then $S_t(B) \subseteq Q$ when $t \geq T$ for some $T = T(B) \geq 0$ (absorbing property);*
c) $\mathfrak{J} = \bigcap_{t \geq 0} \overline{S_t(Q)}$.

PROOF. We apply the differential inequality (2.10) to the inequality (2.8):

$$\|q(t)\|^2 \leq (\|q(0)\|^2 - (C/\varkappa)^2)e^{-\varkappa t} + (C/\varkappa)^2. \quad (2.11)$$

If $\|q(0)\|^2 \leq D^2 = 2(C/\varkappa)^2$, then by (2.11) $\|q(t)\|^2 \leq 2(C/\varkappa)^2$, and so $S_t(Q) \subseteq Q$ when $t \geq 0$.

The absorbing property immediately follows from (2.11).

To prove item c), we note that $Q \subseteq G_{R_0}^+$, and so $S_t(Q) \subseteq S_t(G_{R_0}^+)$ for all $t \geq 0$, i.e.,

$$\bigcap_{t \geq 0} \overline{S_t(Q)} \subseteq \bigcap_{t \geq 0} \overline{S_t(G_{R_0}^+)} = \mathfrak{J}.$$

If $\gamma(\tau)$ is a trajectory bounded in the past of the semigroup, lying on the maximal invariant set $\mathfrak{I}$, then by the property b) of the set Q from Proposition 2.10, we can find a number $T \geq 0$ for which

$$S_t\{\gamma(\tau),\ \tau \leq 0\} = \{\gamma(\tau),\ \tau \leq t\} \subseteq Q \quad \text{when } t \geq T.$$

Then $\gamma(\tau) \in Q$, and so $\gamma(t+\tau) \in S_t(Q)$ for all $\tau \in \mathbb{R}$, $t \geq 0$, i.e.,

$$\mathfrak{I} \subseteq \bigcap_{t \geq 0} \overline{S_t(Q)} \subseteq Q.$$

The proposition is proved. □

It remains to notice that item c) of Theorem 1.1 follows from the fact that $\mathfrak{I} \subseteq Q$. Theorem 1.1 is proved completely. □

§3. Proof of Theorem 1.2

As it was shown in Proposition 2.10, when $\varepsilon = 0$, the maximal invariant set satisfies

$$\mathfrak{I} = \bigcap_{t \geq 0} \overline{S_t(Q)}, \quad \text{where } Q = \{y = p + q,\ p \in E_+,\ q \in E_-,\ \|q\| \leq D\}.$$

Let us show that the maximal attractor of the semigroup is $\mathfrak{A} = \mathfrak{I}$. To do this, it is necessary to check the attraction property.

PROPOSITION 3.1. *There exist constants $a > 0$ and $c > 0$ such that for any solution $y(t) = p(t) + q(t)$, we have*

$$\|p(t)\|^2 \leq e^{a(t-s)}(\|p(s)\|^2 + c), \quad \text{when } t \geq s.$$

PROOF. Let us take the scalar product of (2.1) with p:

$$\frac{1}{2}\frac{d}{dt}\|p(t)\|^2 \leq \|Ap\|\,\|p\| + \|F(y)\|\,\|p\|.$$

Note that E_+ is a finite-dimensional subspace, and so the operator A is bounded on it; hence

$$\frac{d}{dt}\|p(t)\|^2 \leq \eta\|p\|^2 + 2C\|p\| \leq (\eta+1)\|p\|^2 + C^2 = a\|p\|^2 + ca.$$

We denote $\eta + 1 = a$, $c = C^2/a$. Using Lemma 2.3 on differential inequalities, we obtain the estimate claimed. □

PROPOSITION 3.2. *For any $\varepsilon > 0$ there exist numbers $R > 0$ and $T > 0$ such that $S_t(Q) \cap \{y = p + q\mid \|p\| \geq R\} \subseteq \mathscr{O}_\varepsilon(E_+)$ when $t \geq T$.*

PROOF. By the assumption of Theorem 1.2, the function

$$F(y) = F(p+q)$$

converges to zero when $\|p\| \to \infty$ uniformly on $y \in Q$. Let us fix some number $\varepsilon_1 > 0$ and choose $R_1 > D$ so as to obtain the inequality

$$\|F(p+q)\| \leq \varepsilon_1 \quad \text{if } \|p\| \geq R_1,\ y \in Q. \tag{3.1}$$

Let us assume that the statement is wrong. This means that there exist $\varepsilon > 0$, $t_n \to \infty$, $y_n(0) \in Q$ for which
$$S_{t_n}(y_n(0)) \notin \mathcal{O}_\varepsilon(E_+), \qquad \|\Pi_{E_+} S_{t_n}(y_n(0))\| \to \infty \quad (n \to \infty).$$
We denote
$$y_n(t) = S_t(y_n(0)) = p_n(t) + q_n(t).$$
For this notation
$$\|q_n(0)\| \leq D \quad (\text{as } y_n(0) \in Q), \qquad \|q_n(t_n)\| \geq \varepsilon, \qquad \|p_n(t_n)\| \to \infty.$$
We can assume that $\|p_n(t_n)\| \geq R_1$ for all n. Let us denote by s_n the time of exit of the solution $y_n(t)$ from the set $H_{R_1} = Q \cap \{\|p\| < R_1\}$, i.e., $\|p_n(s_n)\| \geq R_1$, $\|p_n(\tau)\| < R_1$ when $0 \leq \tau < s_n$.

Let us show that the sequence $r_n = t_n - s_n$ unboundedly increases when n increases. In the converse case, $r_n \leq r$, $s_n = t_n - r_n \geq t_n - r \to +\infty$ and, choosing a subsequence, we can obtain $s_n > 0$ for all n, i.e., $q_n(0) \in H_{R_1}$ and $p_n(s_n) = R_1$. Then by Proposition 3.1,
$$\|p_n(t_n)\|^2 \leq \exp(a(t_n - s_n))(\|p_n(s_n)\|^2 + c) \leq (R_1^2 + c)e^a,$$
which contradicts the assumption $\|p_n(t_n)\| \to \infty \; (n \to \infty)$.

So the sequence r_n is unbounded, and choosing a subsequence, we have: $r_n \to \infty \; (n \to \infty)$. Now if we take the sequence $\{r_n\}$ instead of $\{t_n\}$, and $\{y_n(s_n)\}$ instead of $\{y_n(0)\}$, then these new sequences satisfy the same properties as the previous ones, i.e.,
$$\|q_n(0)\| \leq D, \qquad \|q_n(t_n)\| \geq \varepsilon, \qquad \|p_n(t_n)\| \to \infty \quad (t_n \to +\infty),$$
and also $\|p_n(0)\| \geq R_1$. From Corollary 2.2 we obtain $\|p_n(t)\| \geq R_1$ when $t \geq 0$ (recall that $R_1 > D$). So, by inequalities (3.1),
$$\|F(y_n(t))\| = \|F(p_n(t) + q_n(t))\| \leq \varepsilon_1 \quad \text{for all } t \geq 0, \; n \in \mathbb{N}.$$
By inequality (2.4),
$$\frac{d}{dt}\|q_n(t)\|^2 \leq -2\varkappa\|q_n(t)\|^2 + 2(F(y_n(t)), q_n(t))$$
$$\leq -2\varkappa\|q_n(t)\|^2 + \varkappa\|q_n(t)\|^2 + \|F(y_n(t))\|^2/\varkappa$$
$$\leq -\varkappa\|q_n(t)\|^2 + \varepsilon_1^2/\varkappa.$$
Now we use the lemma on differential inequalities:
$$\|q_n(t_n)\|^2 \leq \|q_n(0)\|^2 \exp(-\varkappa t_n) + \varepsilon_1^2/\varkappa^2 \leq D^2 \exp(-\varkappa t_n) + \varepsilon_1^2/\varkappa^2.$$
If from the very beginning we choose ε_1 (and correspondingly R_1) so that $\varepsilon_1 < \varepsilon\varkappa$, then by the inequalities $\|q_n(t_n)\|^2 \geq \varepsilon^2$ we obtain
$$D^2 \exp(-\varkappa t_n) + \varepsilon_1^2/\varkappa^2 \geq \varepsilon^2,$$
or
$$\exp(-\varkappa t_n) \geq (\varepsilon^2 - \varepsilon_1^2/\varkappa^2)/D^2 = \omega > 0,$$
i.e., $t_n \leq -\ln\omega/\varkappa$, where $\ln$ means natural logarithm. The last inequality contradicts the initial assumption $t_n \to +\infty \; (n \to +\infty)$. $\square$

PROPOSITION 3.3. *For any $\varepsilon > 0$ there exists a number $R > 0$, such that* $\mathfrak{A} \cap \{y = p + q \mid \|p\| \geq R\} \subseteq \mathcal{O}_\varepsilon(E_+)$.

PROOF. It is sufficient to notice that $\mathfrak{A} \subseteq S_T(Q)$ (Proposition 2.10) for any $T \geq 0$, and to use Proposition 3.2. □

PROPOSITION 3.4. *For any $\varepsilon > 0$ there exists a $T > 0$ such that*

$$S_t(Q) \subseteq \mathcal{O}_\varepsilon(\mathfrak{A}) \quad \text{when } t \geq T.$$

PROOF. From Propositions 3.2 and 3.3 we have

$$\forall \varepsilon > 0 \quad \exists R > 0, \ T_0 \geq 0 \quad \forall t \geq T_0$$
$$S_t(Q) \cap \{y = p + q \mid \|p\| \geq R\} \subseteq \mathcal{O}_{\varepsilon/2}(E_+),$$
$$\mathfrak{A} \cap \{y = p + q \mid \|p\| \geq R\} \subseteq \mathcal{O}_{\varepsilon/2}(E_+).$$

The projection of the set $\mathfrak{A}$ onto E_+ coincides with E_+ (Proposition 2.8), so we have

$$S_t(Q) \cap \{y = p + q \mid \|p\| \geq R\} \subseteq \mathcal{O}_\varepsilon(\mathfrak{A}) \quad \text{when } t \geq T_0. \tag{3.2}$$

We shall prove the proposition by *reductio ad absurdum*. Let the statement be wrong. This means that for some number $\varepsilon > 0$ there exist sequences $t_n \to +\infty$, $y_n(0) \in Q$, for which

$$\text{dist}_E(y_n(t_n), \mathfrak{A}) \geq \varepsilon. \tag{3.3}$$

By (3.2), $\{y_n(t_n)\} \subseteq \{y = p + q \mid \|p\| \leq R\}$. Also $y_n(t_n) \subseteq Q$ (since $y_n(0) \subseteq Q$ and Q is semi-invariant for $\{S_t\}$). So, the sequence $\{y_n(t_n)\}$ is bounded. Then Proposition 2.5 allows us to choose from it a convergent subsequence

$$y_{n(k)}(t_{n(k)}) = S_{t_{n(k)}}(y_{n(k)}(0)) \to y^* \quad (n \to \infty).$$

Since $y_{n(k)}(0) \in Q$, $t_{n(k)} \to +\infty$ $(n \to \infty)$, we have $y^* \in \mathfrak{A}$ and

$$\text{dist}_E(y_{n(k)}(t_{n(k)}), \mathfrak{A}) \leq \|y_{n(k)}(t_{n(k)}) - y^*\| \to 0,$$

which contradicts inequality (3.3). The proposition is proved. □

Finally let us prove the attraction property of $\mathfrak{A}$. If B is a bounded set, then by Proposition 2.10 b) there exists a moment t_1 of time such that $S_{t_1}(B) \subseteq Q$. Then from Proposition 3.4 we see that for all $\varepsilon > 0$ there exists a $T > 0$ such that $S_{t+t_1}(B) = S_t(S_{t_1}(B)) \subseteq S_t(Q) \subseteq \mathcal{O}_\varepsilon(\mathfrak{A})$ when $t \geq T$, i.e., $S_t(B) \subseteq \mathcal{O}_\varepsilon(\mathfrak{A})$ when $t \geq T + t_1$. The attraction property is proved.

We must check the minimality property. It follows from the remark in §1 saying that any maximal attractor contains the maximal invariant set $\mathfrak{I}$.

At last let us note that (1.7) follows from Proposition 3.3 and the boundedness of the projection of $\mathfrak{A}$ onto E_-. Theorem 1.2 is proved completely. □

§4. Examples of parabolic and hyperbolic equations possessing unbounded attractors

In this section for some families of semilinear partial differential equations of the parabolic and hyperbolic types the results of §§1–3 are used to prove existence theorems of unbounded maximal invariant sets and maximal attractors of the semigroups corresponding to these equations.

Below we shall use the following notation. Ω is a bounded domain (open and connected set) in $\mathbb{R}^n$ with smooth boundary $\partial\Omega$, $H^s(\Omega)$ are Sobolev spaces of order s. The norm in $H^s(\Omega)$ is denoted by $\|\cdot\|_s$; $\|\cdot\|_0$ means the norm in the space $L^2(\Omega)$. $H_0^s(\Omega)$ is the subspace of $H^s(\Omega)$ of functions with zero boundary conditions on $\partial\Omega$. Δ is the Laplace operator in $\mathbb{R}^n$, ∇ is the gradient in $\mathbb{R}^n$, $\mu(\Sigma)$ denotes the Lebesgue measure in $\mathbb{R}^n$ of the set $\Sigma \subset \mathbb{R}^n$.

EXAMPLE 4.1. *The parabolic equation.*

In Ω consider the problem:

$$\partial_t u = \Delta u + \lambda u + f(u), \qquad u|_{\partial\Omega} = 0, \qquad u|_{t=0} = u_0(x). \qquad (4.1)$$

Here $u = u(x, t)$, $x \in \Omega$, $t \geq 0$, $f: \mathbb{R} \to \mathbb{R}$, $f \in C^2(\mathbb{R})$, $u_0(x) \in L^2(\Omega)$, λ is a positive number. As for the function f, we assume:

$$|f(u)| \leq \varepsilon|u| + C, \qquad |f'(u)| \leq C_0. \qquad (4.2)$$

Under these conditions, to the problem (4.1) corresponds the semigroup $\{S_t\}$ acting in the space $L^2(\Omega)$ which maps at each moment of time $t \geq 0$ the function $u_0(\cdot)$ to the function $u(x, t)$: $S_t(u_0(\cdot)) = u(x, t)$, $t \geq 0$. The semigroup has Properties I and II. The corresponding theorems on existence, uniqueness and continuous dependence may be proved by the standard method of Galerkin approximations (see [7, 29, 30]).

To construct invariant subspaces of the operator $\Delta + \lambda$, we consider the sequence $\{X_i(x)\}$ of eigenfunctions of the Dirichlet problem with zero boundary conditions:

$$-\Delta X_i(x) = \lambda_i X_i(x), \qquad X_i|_{\partial\Omega} = 0,$$
$$i = 1, 2, \ldots, \quad 0 < \lambda_1 < \lambda_2 \leq \cdots, \quad \lambda_i \to +\infty.$$

We assume that for some integer N

$$\lambda_N < \lambda < \lambda_{N+1}. \qquad (4.3)$$

So the spectrum σ of the operator $\Delta + \lambda$ does not intersect the imaginary axis. Under the notation of §1 we have

$$\sigma_+ = \{\lambda - \lambda_1, \lambda - \lambda_2, \ldots, \lambda - \lambda_N\}, \qquad \sigma_- = \{\lambda - \lambda_{N+1}, \lambda - \lambda_{N+2}, \ldots\},$$

where E_+ is the linear hull of the functions $X_1, X_2, \ldots, X_N$, $E_- = E_+^\perp$. The operator Δ is selfadjoint, so inequalities (1.4) and (1.5) in which we can put $\varkappa = \min\{\lambda - \lambda_N, \lambda_{N+1} - \lambda\}$ hold. So, Property III is also fulfilled. Property IV follows from the next

PROPOSITION 4.1. *For any* $u(x) \in L^2(\Omega)$
$$\|f(u(\cdot))\|_0 \leqslant \varepsilon \|u\|_0 + C(\mu(\Omega))^{1/2}.$$

PROOF.
$$\|f(u)\|_0^2 = \int_\Omega f(u(x))^2 \, dx \leqslant \int_\Omega (\varepsilon |u(x)| + C)^2 \, dx$$
$$= \varepsilon^2 \|u\|_0^2 + 2C\varepsilon \int_\Omega |u(x)| \, dx + C^2 \mu(\Omega)$$
$$\leqslant \varepsilon^2 \|u\|_0^2 + 2C\varepsilon \|u\|_0 (\mu(\Omega))^{1/2} + C^2 \mu(\Omega)$$
$$= (\varepsilon \|u\|_0 + C(\mu(\Omega))^{1/2})^2.$$

Here the Cauchy-Bunyakovskii inequality was used. □

Property V follows from the smoothing properties of parabolic equations: if B is a bounded set in $L^2(\Omega)$, then $S_t(B)$ is bounded in $H^1(\Omega)$ when $t > 0$. So, for the compact set $K(B, t)$ we can take the set $\overline{S_t(B)}$. Then we can formulate Theorem 1.1 for the problem (4.1) as follows.

THEOREM 4.1. *Let conditions* (4.2) *and* (4.3) *hold. If* $\varepsilon < \varkappa$, *then the semigroup* $\{S_t\}$ *of the problem* (4.1) *acting in the space* $L^2(\Omega)$, *possesses the maximal invariant set* $\mathfrak{J}$ *which is bounded-compact in* $L^2(\Omega)$, *its projection onto* E_+ *coincides with* E_+, *and lies in the pseudoball*
$$G_R^+ = \{u = p + q : p \in E_+, q \in E_-, \|p\|_0^2 - \|q\|_0^2 \leqslant R^2\},$$
where $R = 2C(\mu(\Omega))^{1/2}(\varkappa - \varepsilon)^{-1}$. *If* $\varepsilon = 0$, *then the projection of* $\mathfrak{J}$ *onto* E_- *is bounded.*

Let us note that by the smoothing properties $\mathfrak{J} \in H^2(\Omega) \cap H_0^1(\Omega)$.
Let us formulate the existence theorem of the maximal attractor.

THEOREM 4.2. *If the conditions of Theorem* 4.1 *are satisfied and also* $f(u) \to 0$ ($|u| \to +\infty$), *then the maximal invariant set is the maximal attractor of the semigroup* $\{S_t\}$, $\mathfrak{A} = \mathfrak{J}$, *and*
$$\mathrm{dist}(\mathfrak{A} \setminus B_R, E_+) \to 0 \quad (R \to \infty).$$

To use Theorem 1.2, we need the following proposition.

PROPOSITION 4.2. *Let* D *be any positive number, then for any* $\varepsilon \geqslant 0$ *there exists such a number* $R > 0$ *that for* $p(x) \in E_+$, $q(x) \in E_-$, $\|p\|_0 \geqslant R$, $\|q\|_0 \leqslant D$ *inequality* $\|f(p+q)\|_0 \leqslant \varepsilon$ *holds.*

Now we need the following lemma.

LEMMA 4.1. *Let* $e_1(x), e_2(x), \ldots, e_N(x)$ *be functions continuous on* $\overline{\Omega}$, *real analytic inside* Ω, *and linearly independent in* Ω. *Then for any number* $M > 0$
$$\mu\left(x \in \Omega : \left|\sum_{i=1}^N \gamma_i e_i(x)\right| \leqslant M\right) \to 0 \quad (|\gamma| \to +\infty).$$
Here $|\gamma|$ *means the norm in* $\mathbb{R}^N$ *of a vector* $\gamma = (\gamma_1, \gamma_2, \ldots, \gamma_N)$.

The lemma is proved in the Appendix.

COROLLARY 4.1. *If $p(x) \in E_+$, then*

$$\mu(|p(x)| \leq M) \to 0 \quad \text{when } \|p\|_0 \to +\infty.$$

Indeed, if $p(x) \in E_+$, then

$$p(x) = \sum_{i=1}^{N} \gamma_i e_i(x), \quad \text{where } \gamma = (\gamma_1, \gamma_2, \ldots, \gamma_N) \in \mathbb{R}^N.$$

Eigenfunctions of the Laplace operator are continuous in $\overline{\Omega}$, analytic inside Ω and linearly independent. Now we note that $|\gamma|^2 = \sum_{i=1}^{N} \gamma_i^2 = \|p\|_0^2$ and use Lemma 4.1.

PROOF OF PROPOSITION 4.2. Let us fix any number $\varepsilon > 0$. Since $f(u) \to 0$ ($|u| \to \infty$), there exists a number R_1 such that $|u| \geq R_1$ implies $|f(u)| < \varepsilon$. Let $\|q(\cdot)\|_0 \leq D$. We write the following Chebyshev inequality:

$$\mu(|q(x)| \geq R_2) \leq D^2/R_2^2.$$

Consider any function $u(x) = p(x) + q(x)$ for which $\|q\| \leq D$. We have the following chain of inequalities:

$$\begin{aligned}
\mu(|u(x)| \leq R_1) &= \mu(|u(x)| \leq R_1, |q(x)| \geq R_2) \\
&\quad + \mu(|u(x)| \leq R_1, |q(x)| < R_2) \\
&\leq \mu(|q(x)| \geq R_2) + \mu(|u-q| \leq R_1 + R_2) \\
&= \mu(|q(x)| \geq R_2) + \mu(|p(x)| \leq R_1 + R_2) \\
&\leq \mu(|p(x)| \leq R_1 + R_2) + D^2/R_2^2.
\end{aligned}$$

We have obtained:

$$\mu(|u(x)| \leq R_1) \leq \mu(|p(x)| \leq R_1 + R_2) + D^2/R_2^2. \tag{4.4}$$

Choose the number R_2 from the condition: $D^2/R_2^2 \leq \varepsilon/2$. Now we use Corollary 4.1. There exists a number R such that $\|p\|_0 \geq R$ implies $\mu(|p(x)| \leq R_1 + R_2) \leq \varepsilon/2$, and by (4.4) $\mu(|u(x)| \leq R_1) < \varepsilon$. Then

$$\begin{aligned}
\|f(u)\|_0^2 &= \|f(p+q)\|_0^2 = \int_\Omega |f(u(x))|^2 dx \\
&= \int_{|u(x)| \leq R_1} |f|^2 dx + \int_{|u(x)| > R_1} |f|^2 dx \\
&\leq C^2 \mu(|u(x)| \leq R_1) + \varepsilon^2 \mu(\Omega) \leq C^2 \varepsilon + \varepsilon^2 \mu(\Omega),
\end{aligned}$$

if only $\|q\|_0 \leq D$, $\|p\|_0 > R$. The proposition is proved. $\square$

Now we consider a generalization of problem (4.1).

EXAMPLE 4.2. *The parabolic system.*
Let us consider the system of equations:

$$\partial_t u = A\Delta u + Bu + f(x, u, \nabla u) + g(x), \quad u|_{t=0} = u_0(x),$$
$$u|_{\partial\Omega} = 0 \quad \text{or} \quad \left.\frac{\partial u}{\partial \nu}\right|_{\partial\Omega} = 0. \tag{4.5}$$

Here

$$u = (u_1, u_2, \ldots, u_m), \quad u = u(x, t),$$
$$f = (f_1, f_2, \ldots, f_m), \quad f: \Omega \times \mathbb{R}^m \times \mathbb{R}^{n \times m} \to \mathbb{R}^m,$$
$$g = (g_1, g_2, \ldots, g_m), \quad g(x) \in (L^2(\Omega))^m, \quad u_0 \in (H_0^1(\Omega))^m$$

for the Dirichlet problem and $u_0 \in (H^1(\Omega))^m$ for the Neumann problem. A and B are matrices with constant coefficients and their dimension is $m \times m$, the matrix $A+A^*$ is positive. We assume that the vector-function $f(x, u, \xi)$ is twice continuously differentiable with respect to all the arguments and satisfies the Lipschitz condition:

$$|f(x_1, u_1, \xi_1) - f(x_2, u_2, \xi_2)| \leq c_0(|x_1 - x_2| + |u_1 - u_2| + |\xi_1 - \xi_2|),$$

for some number c_0, and for all $x_1, x_2 \in \Omega$, $u_1, u_2 \in \mathbb{R}^m$, $\xi_1, \xi_2 \in \mathbb{R}^{n \times m}$. Also let the following condition hold

$$|f(x, u, \xi)| \leq \varepsilon(|u| + |\xi|) + C. \tag{4.6}$$

We shall be searching for the solution of the problem (4.5) in the space $L^2(0, T; (H_0^1(\Omega))^m)$ for the Dirichlet problem and, and for the Neumann problem, in the space $L^2(0, T; (H^1(\Omega))^m)$. Equation (4.5) is understood as the corresponding integral identity.

Under the above conditions problem (4.5) possesses a unique solution (see [7]). The semigroup $\{S_t\}$ acting in the space $(H_0^1(\Omega))^m$ for the Dirichlet problem and in the space $(H^1(\Omega))^m$ for the Neumann problem is defined. (Below we shall omit the mention of the Dirichlet or Neumann problems, keeping in mind one of them and the semigroup corresponding to it.)

We consider the operator $A\Delta + B$ with boundary conditions acting in the space $(L^2(\Omega))^m$. It is well known that the spectrum σ of this operator is discrete and contains eigenvalues of finite multiplicity. For all $\alpha \leq 0$ the set $\{\zeta \in \sigma : \operatorname{Re}\zeta \geq \alpha\}$ is finite.

We shall assume that

$$\operatorname{Re}\sigma \neq 0. \tag{4.7}$$

We denote by $\mathscr{E}_+$ the invariant subspace of operator $A\Delta + B$ corresponding to the spectrum set σ_+, by $\mathscr{E}_-$ the invariant subspace corresponding to σ_-. Let us note that $\mathscr{E}_+$ is finite-dimensional.

We have the following theorems.

THEOREM 4.3. *If condition* (4.6) *and condition* (4.7) *are satisfied, where the number ε is sufficiently small, then the semigroup $\{S_t\}$ of problem* (4.5) *possesses the maximal invariant set $\mathfrak{I}$ with the following properties*:

   a) *the set $\mathfrak{I}$ is a bounded-compact set in $(H^1(\Omega))^m$*;
   b) *the projection of $\mathfrak{I}$ onto $\mathscr{E}_+$ parallel to $\mathscr{E}_-$ coincides with $\mathscr{E}_+$*;
   c) *if $\varepsilon = 0$, then the projection of $\mathfrak{I}$ onto $\mathscr{E}_-$ is bounded*.

THEOREM 4.4. *If the conditions of Theorem* 4.3 *are satisfied and also $|f(x, u, \xi)| \to 0$ when $|u| \to +\infty$ uniformly on $x \in \Omega$, $\xi \in \mathbb{R}^{n \times m}$, then the maximal invariant set is the maximal attractor of the semigroup $\{S_t\}$: $\mathfrak{A} = \mathfrak{I}$, and*

$$\operatorname{dist}(\mathfrak{A} \setminus B_R, h + \mathscr{E}_+) \to 0 \quad (R \to \infty),$$

where $h = -(A\Delta + B)^{-1} g$.

To prove these theorems, it is necessary to check the corresponding properties of the semigroup. One can do this as in the scalar case of Example 1. We shall only make some remarks. To obtain the inequalities (1.4), (1.5), and also orthogonal complements to the subspaces $\mathscr{E}_+$ and $\mathscr{E}_-$, it is necessary to consider a certain scalar product in $(L^2(\Omega))^m$ (equivalent to the initial one) whose existence is not difficult to prove by using the expansion of $(L^2(\Omega))^m$ in the basis of eigenfunctions of the Laplace operator. (A detailed proof is given in [10].) Property IV is obtained from (4.6) (see Proposition 4.1). Property V follows from the smoothing properties of systems of parabolic equations.

Proving Theorem 4.4, at first we must reduce the nonhomogeneous problem (4.5) to a homogeneous one, making the substitution $u = u' + h$, where $h = -(A\Delta + B)^{-1} g$. The analog of Proposition 4.2 is proved in the same way by using Lemma 4.1.

EXAMPLE 4.3. *The hyperbolic semilinear equation with dissipation*.

We consider the equation

$$\frac{\partial^2 u}{\partial t^2} + \gamma \frac{\partial u}{\partial t} = \Delta u + \lambda u + f(u), \tag{4.7}$$

where $\gamma > 0$, in a bounded domain $\Omega \subset \mathbb{R}^n$ with Dirichlet boundary conditions $u|_{\partial \Omega} = 0$, and initial conditions

$$u|_{t=0} = u_0 \in H_0^1(\Omega), \quad \left.\frac{\partial u}{\partial t}\right|_{t=0} = p|_{t=0} = p_0 \in L_2(\Omega). \tag{4.8}$$

The function $f(u) \in C^1(\mathbb{R})$ satisfies (4.2).

Equation (4.7) can be rewritten as the system

$$\begin{cases} \partial_t u = p, \\ \partial_t p = -\gamma p + \Delta u + \lambda u + f(u) \end{cases} \tag{4.9}$$

that corresponds to the equation (1.1), where

$$y = \begin{pmatrix} u \\ p \end{pmatrix}, \quad A = \begin{pmatrix} 0 & 1 \\ \Delta + \lambda & -\gamma \end{pmatrix}, \quad F = F\begin{pmatrix} u \\ p \end{pmatrix} = \begin{pmatrix} 0 \\ f(u) \end{pmatrix}.$$

In the space $E = H_0^1(\Omega) \times L_2(\Omega)$, to problem (4.7)–(4.8) corresponds the nonlinear semigroup $\{S_t\}$ which maps the initial conditions $y_0 = (u_0, p_0)$ to the pair $(u(x, t), p(x, t))$, where $u(x, t)$ is the solution of problem (4.7)–(4.8) at the moment of time t, $p(x, t) = (\partial u/\partial t)(x, t)$. The existence, uniqueness and continuous dependence (Property I) of this solution in the space E are proved by the standard method of Galerkin approximations (see [29]).

It is necessary to note that Property II for the hyperbolic equation is not satisfied exactly, because

$$u \in H_0^1(\Omega), \quad \partial_t u = p \in L_2(\Omega), \quad \partial_t p \in H^{-1}(\Omega),$$

and the scalar products $(u, \partial_t u)_1 = (\nabla u, \nabla p)$ and $(\partial_t p, p)$ may not be defined. But when we prove the theorems of §1 we use (1.3), and also inequalities (1.4) and (1.5) after integration and all the results can be generalized to the hyperbolic case in the following way. If instead of initial condition (4.8) we consider the smoother ones

$$u|_{t=0} = u_0 \in H^2(\Omega) \cap H_0^1(\Omega), \quad \left.\frac{\partial u}{\partial t}\right|_{t=0} = p|_{t=0} = p_0 \in H_0^1(\Omega), \quad (4.10)$$

then the solution exists in the spaces

$$u \in H^2(\Omega) \cap H_0^1(\Omega), \quad p \in H_0^1(\Omega), \quad \partial_t p \in L_2(\Omega), \quad (4.11)$$

and (1.3)–(1.5) hold for these smoother solutions (we understand $\|y(t)\|$ as the norm in the space $E = H_0^1(\Omega) \times L_2(\Omega)$). So, all the necessary estimations are proved by integration for conditions (4.10), and can be carried over to conditions (4.8) by using the uniform continuity of $\{S_t\}$ on E when $t \in [0, T]$ and by approximating $u_0 \in H_0^1(\Omega)$ and $p \in L_2(\Omega)$ by the smoother initial conditions $u_0^n \in H^2(\Omega) \cap H_0^1(\Omega)$ and $p_0^n \in H_0^1(\Omega)$:

$$u_0^n \to u_0 \text{ in } H_0^1(\Omega), \quad p_0^n \to p_0 \text{ in } L_2(\Omega) \text{ when } n \to +\infty.$$

Let us construct the invariant spaces E_+ and E_-.

As in the parabolic case we shall assume that (4.3) holds. The spectrum of the operator A under these conditions contains N positive eigenvalues (multiplicity taken into account), a finite number of negative ones, and all other points of the spectrum lies on the line $\{\operatorname{Re}\zeta = -\gamma/2\}$. So, the spectrum A does not intersect the imaginary axis. Let us show that for a certain scalar product equivalent to the initial one, the inequalities (1.4), (1.5) are satisfied. As above, we shall assume that the solutions are smooth enough to define all the scalar products below, i.e., (4.11) holds. We denote by $H_{0(-N)}^1$ and $L_{2(-N)}$ the subspaces of $H_0^1(\Omega)$ and $L_2(\Omega)$ respectively orthogonal to the first N eigenvectors $X_1, X_2, \ldots, X_N$ of the operator Δ in $H_0^1(\Omega)$. Then $E_1 = H_{0(-N)}^1 \times L_{2(-N)} \subset E$ is an invariant subspace of codimension $2N$.

We consider the function:

$$\Phi_\delta(y) = \Phi_\delta(u, p) = \|u\|_1^2 - \lambda\|u\|^2 + \|p\|^2 + \delta(u, p), \qquad \delta > 0.$$

PROPOSITION 4.3. $\Phi_\delta(y)$ on E_1 is equivalent to the norm $\|y\|^2 = \|u\|_1^2 + \|p\|^2$ when $\delta > 0$ is sufficiently small.

PROOF. We define $\alpha = 1 - \lambda/\lambda_{N+1}$, $0 < \alpha < 1$. Then, since $\|u\|_1^2 \geq \lambda_{N+1}\|u\|^2$ when $u \in H_{0(-N)}^1$, we have

$$\alpha\|u\|_1^2 = \|u\|_1^2 - \lambda\lambda_{N+1}^{-1}\|u\|_1^2 \leq \|u\|_1^2 - \lambda\|u\|^2 \quad \text{when } u \in H_{0(-N)}^1. \qquad (4.12)$$

By (4.12), for $(u, p) \in E_1$ we have:

$$\Phi_\delta(u, p) = \|u\|_1^2 - \lambda\|u\|^2 + \|p\|^2 + \delta(u, p)$$
$$\geq \alpha\|u\|_1^2 + \|p\|^2 - (\delta/2)\|u\|^2 - (\delta/2)\|p\|^2$$
$$\geq (\alpha - \delta/(2\lambda_{N+1}))\|u\|_1^2 + (1 - \delta/2)\|p\|^2 \geq c_1^2\|y\|^2,$$

if $\delta < 2\alpha\lambda_{N+1}$, $\delta < 2$. On the other hand

$$\Phi_\delta(u, p) = \|u\|_1^2 - \lambda\|u\|^2 + \|p\|^2 + \delta(u, p)$$
$$\leq (1 + \delta/(2\lambda_{N+1}))\|u\|_1^2 + (1 + \delta/2)\|p\|^2 \leq c_2^2\|y\|^2. \quad \square$$

Let us define a new norm $(\Phi_\delta(y))^{1/2}$ on E_1, equivalent to the initial one, and the corresponding scalar product:

$$2[y_1, y_2] = [y_1 + y_2, y_1 + y_2] - [y_1, y_1] - [y_2, y_2]$$
$$= \Phi_\delta(y_1 + y_2) - \Phi_\delta(y_1) - \Phi_\delta(y_2).$$

If $y_1 = (u_1, p_1)$, $y_2 = (u_2, p_2)$, then

$$[y_1, y_2] = (\nabla u_1, \nabla u_2) - \lambda(u_1, u_2) + (p_1, p_2) + (\delta/2)((u_1, p_2) + (u_2, p_1)).$$

PROPOSITION 4.4. There exists a $\varkappa > 0$ such that

$$[Ay, y] \leq -\varkappa[y, y] \quad \text{if } y \in E_1. \qquad (4.13)$$

PROOF. If $y = (u, p)$, then $Ay = (p, \Delta u + \lambda u - \gamma p)$ and

$$[Ay, y] = (\nabla u, \nabla p) - \lambda(u, p) + (\Delta u + \lambda u - \gamma p, p)$$
$$+ (\delta/2)(p, p) + (\delta/2)(u, \Delta u + \lambda u - \gamma p)$$
$$= -(\gamma - \delta/2)\|p\|^2 - (\delta/2)(\|u\|_1^2 - \lambda\|u\|^2) - (\gamma\delta/2)(u, p).$$

Therefore,

$$[Ay, y] + \varkappa[y, y] = -(\gamma - \delta/2 - \varkappa)\|p\|^2$$
$$- (\delta/2 - \varkappa)(\|u\|_1^2 - \lambda\|u\|^2) + (\varkappa\delta - \gamma\delta/2)(u, p).$$

By $\|u\|_1^2 - \lambda\|u\|^2 \geq 0$ when $y \in E_1$, if $\delta/2 < \gamma$ and $\varkappa < \delta/2$, the first two terms on the right-hand side of the last inequality are negative, and the third is "subordinate" to the first two because

$$(u, p) \leq \varepsilon\|u\|^2 + \frac{1}{4\varepsilon}\|p\|^2 \leq \varepsilon\frac{\|u\|_1^2}{\lambda_{N+1}} + \frac{1}{4\varepsilon}\|p\|^2$$

$$\leq \frac{\varepsilon}{\alpha\lambda_{N+1}}(\|u\|_1^2 - \lambda\|u\|^2) + \frac{1}{4\varepsilon}\|p\|^2,$$

and choosing small $\delta/2 < \gamma$, $\varkappa < \delta/2$ and $\varepsilon > 0$ we can obtain $[Ay, y] + \varkappa[y, y] \leq 0$. The proposition is proved. □

Now we consider the space $E_1^\perp$. It spans the first N basis vectors in u and the first N basis vectors in p. Let us take the scalar product of the linear part of equations (4.9) with X_k. If we denote $(u, X_k) = u_k$, $(p, X_k) = p_k$ and recall that $(\Delta u, X_k) = -\lambda_k(u, X_k) = \lambda_k u_k$, we obtain

$$\begin{cases} u'_k = p_k, \\ p'_k = -\gamma p_k + (\lambda - \lambda_k)u_k. \end{cases}$$

When $k \leq N$, i.e., $\lambda - \lambda_k > 0$ the matrix $\begin{pmatrix} 0 & 1 \\ \lambda - \lambda_k & -\gamma \end{pmatrix}$ has one positive (α_k) and one negative $(-\beta_k)$ eigenvalue. The invariant subspace of the operator $A|_{E_1^\perp}$ corresponding to the negative eigenvalue is denoted by E_2, to the positive one by E_3. Then

$$(Ay, y) \leq -\varkappa_1\|y\|^2 \quad \text{when } y \in E_2, \ \varkappa_1 = \min(\beta_1, \ldots, \beta_N), \quad (4.14)$$

$$(Ay, y) \geq +\varkappa_2\|y\|^2 \quad \text{when } y \in E_3, \ \varkappa_2 = \min(\alpha_1, \ldots, \alpha_N). \quad (4.15)$$

Let us define $E_- = E_1 \oplus E_2$, $E_+ = E_3$. Then (1.4) follows from (4.15), and (1.5) follows from (4.13) and (4.14). Let us note that the spaces E_2 and E_3 are not orthogonal, but we can achieve this by defining a new scalar product, equivalent to the initial one in the finite-dimensional space $E_2 \oplus E_3$. So Property III is also checked.

Property IV is a consequence of Proposition 4.1. Indeed,

$$\|F(y)\|_E = \|f(u)\|_0 \leq \varepsilon\|u\|_0 + C_1 \leq (\varepsilon/\lambda_1)\|u\|_1 + C_1 \leq (\varepsilon/\lambda_1)\|y\|_E + C_1.$$

Finally let us check Property V. For this we define the linear semigroup $\{T_t\}$ corresponding to the problem (4.7)–(4.8) with $f \equiv 0$. Then

$$y(t) = S_t y(0) = T_t y(0) + \int_0^t T_{t-\tau} g(u(\tau))\, d\tau, \quad (4.16)$$

where $g(u(\tau)) = (0, f(u(\tau))) \in H_0^1(\Omega) \times L_2(\Omega) = E$. If the initial conditions $y(0) = (u(0), p(0))$ were taken from some bounded set $B \subset E$, then $\|y(\tau)\|_E \leq C_1(B, t)$ when $0 \leq \tau \leq t$. So, $\|u(\tau)\|_1 \leq C_1(B, t)$ and by (4.2) $\|f(u(\tau))\|_1 \leq C_2(B, t)$ when $0 \leq \tau \leq t$.

The operators T_τ are bounded uniformly on $\tau \in [0, t]$ not only in the space E, but also in the smoother space $E' = H^2(\Omega) \times H^1(\Omega)$. Since the vector $g(u(\tau)) = (0, f(u(\tau)))$ is also bounded in this space, we have

$$\left\| \int_0^t T_{t-\tau} g(u(\tau)) \, d\tau \right\|_{E'} \leqslant C_3(B, t). \qquad (4.17)$$

We rewrite (4.16) as:

$$y(t) = T_t|_{E_-} \Pi|_{E_-} y(0) + T_t|_{E_+} \Pi|_{E_+} y(0) + \int_0^t T_{t-\tau} g(u(\tau)) \, d\tau. \qquad (4.18)$$

The second term is finite-dimensional (since E_+ is finite-dimensional) and bounded (since the operator T_t is bounded in E), the third term by (4.17) is bounded in E' and so is compact in E. Then we can claim that

$$T_t|_{E_+} \Pi|_{E_+} y(0) + \int_0^t T_{t-\tau} g(u(\tau)) \, d\tau \in K(B, t),$$

where $K(B, t)$ is a compact set in E.

As for the first term in (4.18), by (1.5) it is exponentially small in t:

$$\| T_t|_{E_-} \Pi|_{E_-} y(0) \|_E \leqslant \| y(0) \|_E \exp(-\varkappa t) \leqslant C_4 \exp(-\varkappa t), \quad \text{if } y(0) \in B.$$

If we put $\varepsilon(B, t) = C_4 \exp(-\varkappa t)$, we obtain Property V.

So, for the semigroup $\{S_t\}$ corresponding to the hyperbolic equation, all the conditions of Theorem 1.1 are satisfied, and it can be restated as follows

THEOREM 4.5. *Let conditions (4.2) and (4.3) hold. Then for small $\varepsilon > 0$ the semigroup $\{S_t\}$ corresponding to the problem (4.7)-(4.8) and acting in the space $E = H_0^1(\Omega) \times L_2(\Omega)$ has the maximal invariant set $\mathfrak{I}$ which is bounded-compact in E, its projection onto E_+ coincides with E_+. If $\varepsilon = 0$, then the projection of $\mathfrak{I}$ onto E_- is bounded.*

Let us formulate the existence theorem of the maximal attractor.

THEOREM 4.6. *Assume that the conditions of Theorem 4.5 are satisfied and also $f(u) \to 0$ ($|u| \to +\infty$); then the maximal invariant set is the maximal attractor of the semigroup $\{S_t\}$: $\mathfrak{A} = \mathfrak{I}$, and*

$$\text{dist}(\mathfrak{A} \setminus B_R, E_+) \to 0 \quad (R \to \infty).$$

Here we must also use Proposition 4.2.

§5. Structure of the attractor when a Lyapunov function exists

In this section we return to the general outline of §§1–3. We study the structure of the maximal invariant set and the attractor from Theorems 1.1 and 1.2 when the semigroup possesses a global Lyapunov function. Under this assumption, we prove that the maximal invariant set is an unstable manifold issuing from the set of equilibrium points of the semigroup.

Let a semigroup $\{S_t\}$ acting in a Banach space E be defined.

DEFINITION 5.1. An *equilibrium point* of the semigroup $\{S_t\}$ is a point $z \in E$ such that $S_t z = z$ when $t \geq 0$.

We shall denote by $\mathfrak{N}$ the set of all equilibrium points of the semigroup.

DEFINITION 5.2. A continuous functional $\Phi(y)$ in E is said to be a *Lyapunov function* of the semigroup $\{S_t\}$, if for any $y \in E$ the function $\Phi(S_t y)$ is nonincreasing in the variable t, and $\Phi(y) = \Phi(S_t y)$ for some $t > 0$ implies that $y = z$ is an equilibrium point of the semigroup.

DEFINITION 5.3. The *unstable set* $M^+(Y)$ issuing from the set Y is the set-theoretic union of all the trajectories $\gamma(\tau)$ which converge to Y when $\tau \to -\infty$:
$$\text{dist}_E(\gamma(\tau), Y) \to 0 \quad (\tau \to -\infty).$$

Let us consider the semigroup corresponding to the problem (1.1), (1.2) and acting in the Hilbert space H.

THEOREM 5.1. *Let the conditions of Theorem 1.1 hold and, moreover, the semigroup $\{S_t\}$ possess a Lyapunov function. Then the maximal invariant set of this semigroup is the unstable set issuing from the set of equilibrium points of the semigroup:* $\mathfrak{I} = M^+(\mathfrak{N})$.

PROOF. Note that $\mathfrak{N} \subseteq \mathfrak{I}$, because the trajectory $\gamma(\tau) \equiv z$ is bounded for any $z \in \mathfrak{N}$. Further, the set $\mathfrak{N}$ is bounded in H. This follows, for example, from the inequality (2.6). Then the set $M^+(\mathfrak{N})$ contains trajectories $\gamma(\tau)$ that converge to the bounded set $\mathfrak{N}$ when $\tau \to -\infty$, i.e., are bounded in the past and so we have $\{\gamma(\tau)\} \subseteq \mathfrak{I}$ and $M^+(\mathfrak{N}) \subseteq \mathfrak{I}$.

Let us prove the opposite inclusion. Let $y_0 \in \mathfrak{I}$. Then $y_0 = \gamma(0)$ for some trajectory $\gamma(\tau)$, $\tau \in \mathbb{R}$ and the set $\{\gamma(\tau), \tau \leq 0\}$ is bounded. We denote
$$\mathfrak{N}^{y_0} = \bigcap_{T \leq 0} \overline{\{\gamma(\tau), \tau \leq T\}}.$$

This set is not empty as the intersection of nested compact sets
$$\overline{\{\gamma(\tau), \tau \leq T\}} \subseteq \mathfrak{I}.$$

Let $y^* \in \mathfrak{N}^{y_0}$. Then there exists a sequence $\tau_j \to -\infty$ $(j \to \infty)$ such that $\gamma(\tau_j) \to y^*$. By continuity of the mapping S_t when $t \geq 0$, we have: $\gamma(\tau_j + t) = S_t \gamma(\tau_j) \to S_t y^*$ $(\tau_j \to -\infty)$. By the definition of a Lyapunov function
$$\Phi(y^*) = \lim_{\tau_j \to -\infty} \Phi(\gamma(\tau_j)) = \sup_{\tau \in \mathbb{R}} \Phi(\gamma(\tau)),$$
$$\Phi(S_t y^*) = \lim_{\tau_j \to -\infty} \Phi(\gamma(t + \tau_j)) = \sup_{\tau \in \mathbb{R}} \Phi(\gamma(\tau)).$$

So, $\Phi(y^*) = \Phi(S_t y^*)$ when $t \geq 0$, and y^* is an equilibrium point of the semigroup $\{S_t\}$, i.e., $\mathfrak{N}^{y_0} \subseteq \mathfrak{N}$.

Let us show that $\text{dist}_E(\gamma(\tau), \mathfrak{N}^{y_0}) \to 0$ $(\tau \to -\infty)$. If this is false, then for some number $\varepsilon > 0$ there exists a sequence $\tau_j \to -\infty$ $(j \to \infty)$ such

that
$$\operatorname{dist}_E(\gamma(\tau_j), \mathfrak{N}^{y_0}) \geq \varepsilon. \qquad (5.1)$$

This sequence is bounded and lies in the bounded-compact set $\mathfrak{I}$. Choosing an appropriate subsequence, we can assume (without changing the notation) that $\gamma(\tau_j) \to y^*$ ($\tau_j \to -\infty$). So $y^* \in \mathfrak{N}^{y_0} \subseteq \mathfrak{N}$ which contradicts inequality (5.1). The theorem is proved. □

REMARK 5.1. If the set of equilibrium points is finite, i.e.,
$$\mathfrak{N} = \{z_1, z_2, \ldots, z_k\},$$
then
$$\mathfrak{I} = M^+(\mathfrak{N}) = \bigcup_{j=1}^k M^+(z_j).$$

DEFINITION 5.4. A semigroup $\{S'_t\}$ of linear operators is called *semistable*, if there exists a number $r_0 < 1$ such that there exist only a finite number of points of the spectrum $\sigma(S'_t)$ of the operator S'_t, $t > 0$, outside the circle $\{|\zeta| < r_0^t, \zeta \in \mathbb{C}\}$ and the invariant subspace of the operator S'_t corresponding to these points of the spectrum has finite dimension; also it is assumed that $S'_t y$ continuously depends on t when $t > 0$, $y \in E$.

DEFINITION 5.5. Suppose z is an equilibrium point of the semigroup $\{S_t\}$, the linear semigroup $\{S'_t\}$ is semistable, and the spectrum of the operator $S'_t(z)$ does not contain points of the circumference $\{|\zeta| = 1\}$ $\forall t > 0$. We assume that the operator $S_t y$ on y belongs to $C^{1+\alpha}$ in a neighborhood of the point z. Then the point z is called *hyperbolic*.

REMARK 5.2 (see [7]). If the point z is hyperbolic, then the unstable invariant set $M^+(z)$ issuing from the point z is a differential manifold.

Now let us consider examples of partial differential equations to which the obtained results may be applied.

EXAMPLE 5.1. *The parabolic equation (problem (4.1))*.

The semigroup corresponding to this equation possesses the following Lyapunov function:
$$\Phi(u(\cdot)) = \int_\Omega \left[\frac{1}{2} \sum_{i=1}^n \left(\frac{\partial u}{\partial x}(x) \right)^2 - \frac{\lambda}{2} u(x)^2 - F(u(x)) \right] dx.$$

Here $F(u)$ is the primitive of the function $f(u)$. We can show that for any solution $u(x, t)$ of equation (4.1) the following relation holds
$$\Phi(u(\cdot, t_2)) - \Phi(u(\cdot, t_1)) = -\int_{t_1}^{t_2} \int_\Omega \left| \frac{\partial u}{\partial t}(x, t) \right|^2 dx dt, \quad \text{for } t_1, t_2 > 0.$$

So, we can use Theorem 5.1 and Remarks 5.1, 5.2.

EXAMPLE 5.2. *The parabolic system (problem (4.5))*.

This problem possesses a Lyapunov function in the case when the right-hand side of system (5.1) has gradient form.

Let us assume that the matrices A and B are symmetric, the vector-function f does not depend on ∇u and satisfies the following condition: there exists a scalar function $F(x, u)$ such that

$$f^i(x, u) = \frac{\partial}{\partial u_i} F(x, u), \qquad i = 1, 2, \dots, n.$$

Under these assumptions, the semigroup of our problem possesses the following Lyapunov function:

$$\Phi(u(\cdot)) = \int_\Omega \left[\frac{1}{2}(A\nabla u, \nabla u) - \frac{1}{2}(Bu, u) - F(x, u(x)) - (g(x), u(x)) \right] dx.$$

So we are under the conditions of Theorem 5.1.

Some words about Remark 5.2. To use the statement formulated there, it is necessary to verify that all the equilibrium points of the semigroup are hyperbolic. But in the general case for a concrete functions $g(x)$ when the operator $A\triangle u + Bu + f(x, u, \nabla u)$ is fixed, the problem seems hopeless. Nevertheless if $g(x)$ is a generic function, then all the equilibrium points of the semigroup are hyperbolic. This result, founded on the generalization of the Sard-Smale theorem, appears in [7], where it is proved that for any operator $A\triangle u + Bu + f(x, u, \nabla u)$ there exists an open and dense set in $(L^2(\Omega))^m$ such that if the function $g(x)$ belongs to this set, then all the equilibrium points of the corresponding semigroup possess the hyperbolic property.

If the right-hand side of system (4.5) is not in gradient form, then the structure of the maximal invariant set and the attractor of the semigroup may be very irregular. In [9], lower and upper bounds for the Hausdorff dimension of the unbounded maximal invariant set in this case are established. The estimates obtained are of the same kind as the estimates for dimensions of bounded attractors of evolution equations of such type (see [7]).

EXAMPLE 5.3. *The hyperbolic equation (problem (4.7), (4.8)).*

The Lyapunov function for this equation is:

$$\Phi(y) = \Phi(u, p) = \frac{1}{2}\|\nabla u\|^2 + \frac{1}{2}\|p\|^2 - \frac{\lambda}{2}\|u\|^2 + (F(u), 1),$$

where $F(u)$ is the primitive of $f(u)$, and Theorem 5.1 may also be applied to this equation.

§6. Spectral asymptotics of solutions

From the results of the previous sections, we see that under the conditions of Theorem 1.2 for any $y_0 \in H$, the solution of problem (1.1), (1.2) $y(t) = S_t y_0$ converges when $t \to +\infty$ to the maximal attractor $\mathfrak{A}$. In this section we shall study the rate and character of this convergence. We shall construct spectral asymptotics of solutions lying on the attractor. Solutions approach these asymptotics with exponential rate uniformly on any bounded set of initial conditions.

We assume that the conditions of Theorems 1.2 and 5.1 are satisfied, and also that the set $\mathfrak{N}$ of equilibrium points of the semigroup is finite and all the equilibrium points are hyperbolic. Then the maximal attractor is the union of smooth manifolds:

$$\mathfrak{A} = M^+(\mathfrak{N}) = \bigcup_{j=1}^{k} M^+(z_j).$$

DEFINITION 6.1. Let $z_1, z_2, \ldots, z_k \in \mathfrak{N}$ be hyperbolic equilibrium points of a semigroup $\{S_t\}$. A *finite-dimensional composite trajectory* is a function $\tilde{y}(t)$, $t \in [0, +\infty)$ with values in E possessing the following properties:

1) there exist moments of time $0 = t_0 < \cdots < t_m < t_{m+1} = +\infty$, such that $\tilde{y}(t)$ is a continuous function on $[t_i, t_{i+1})$;
2) $\tilde{y}(t_j) = \tilde{y}(t_j + 0) \in M^+(z_j)$, $j = 1, 2, \ldots, m$.

Let us note that since $M^+(z_j)$ is invariant, we have the inclusion: $\tilde{y}(t) = S_{t-t_j}\tilde{y}(t_j) \in M^+(z_j)$ when $t \in [t_j, t_{j+1})$. So $\tilde{y}(t)$ lies on the attractor.

REMARK 6.1. Each solution $\{y(t), t \geq 0\}$ lying in $M^+(z_j)$ is uniquely determined by its value $y(0)$ when $t = 0$. So, solutions lying on $M^+(z_j)$ form an n_j-parametric family, where $n_j = \dim(M^+(z_j)) < +\infty$.

THEOREM 6.1. *Let Properties* I, II, III, IV, V *be satisfied and also suppose that the following properties hold*:

1) *there exists a Lyapunov function* $\Phi(y)$;
2) *the set* $\mathfrak{N}$ *of equilibrium points of the semigroup* $\{S_t\}$ *is finite*,

$$\mathfrak{N} = \{z_1, z_2, \ldots, z_k\};$$

3) *the semigroup* $\{S_t\}$ *belongs to* $C^{1+\alpha}$ *in a neighborhood of any point* $z_j \in \mathfrak{N}$ *and all the points* z_j *are hyperbolic*;
4) *there exist constants* C', $a > 0$, *such that for any two solutions* $y_1(t) = S_t y_1(0)$ *and* $y_2(t) = S_t y_2(0)$ *the following inequality holds*:

$$\|y_1(t_2) - y_2(t_2)\| \leq C' \exp(a(t_2 - t_1)) \|y_1(t_1) - y_2(t_1)\|$$

when $t_1 \geq t_2 \geq 0$;
5) *we have the following inequality in the set* $\{\|q\| \leq R\}$

$$\|F(y)\|_E \leq \frac{C'(R)}{1 + \|p\|^\vartheta}, \quad \text{where } y = p + q.$$

Then there exists a number $\eta > 0$ *such that for any initial value* y_0 *there exists a finite-dimensional composite trajectory* $\tilde{y}(t) \in \mathfrak{A}$ *for which*

$$\|y(t) - \tilde{y}(t)\| = \|S_t y_0 - \tilde{y}(t)\| \leq C(\|y_0\|) \exp(-\eta t).$$

The number m *of jump points of* $\tilde{y}(t)$ *is not more than* $k + 1$ (k *is the number of equilibrium points of the semigroup*).

To prove the theorem, we shall first construct the asymptotics of unbounded solutions. Define the set

$$Q_R = Q \cap \{y = p + q \mid \|p\| \geqslant R\} = \{y = p + q \mid \|q\| \leqslant D, \|p\| \geqslant R\}.$$

If $y(0) \in Q_R$, then by Corollary 2.2 and Proposition 2.10 we have $y(t) = S_t y(0) \in Q_R$ and the solution $y(t)$ is unbounded. On the other hand if $y(t)$ is an unbounded solution, then starting from some moment of time we have $y(t) \in Q_R$, because the set Q is absorbing and $Q \setminus Q_R$ is bounded. So, for the study of unbounded solutions of problem (1.1), (1.2), it is sufficient to consider solutions with initial values from Q_R, where $R > D$ is large enough.

THEOREM 6.2. *Let Properties I–V be satisfied, and also suppose that whenever $y \in Q_D$ we have*

$$\|F(y)\| \leqslant C_1 \|p\|^{-\vartheta}, \qquad \vartheta > 0. \tag{6.1}$$

Then we can find a number $R > D$ such that for $y(t) = S_t y(0)$, where $y(0) \in Q_R$, there exists a trajectory $\tilde{y}(t)$, lying in the attractor $\mathfrak{A}$, that satisfies

$$\|y(t) - \tilde{y}(t)\| \leqslant C \exp(-\eta t),$$

where C and η do not depend on the initial conditions $y(0) \in Q_R$.

Note that inequality (6.1) follows from condition 5) of Theorem 6.1.

PROPOSITION 6.1. *If under the conditions of Theorem 6.2, $y(0) \in Q_D$, then*

$$\|F(y(t))\| \leqslant C_0 \exp(-\gamma_0 t), \tag{6.2}$$

where C_0 and γ_0 do not depend on the initial condition $y(0)$.

PROOF. From Corollary 2.2 and (6.1) we obtain:

$$\|F(y(t))\| \leqslant C_1 \|p(t)\|^{-\vartheta} \leqslant C_1 (D \exp(\delta t/2))^{-\vartheta} = C_0 \exp(-\gamma_0 t),$$

where $C_0 = C_1(D)^{-\vartheta}$, $\gamma_0 = \vartheta \delta / 2$. □

PROPOSITION 6.2. *There exist C_1 and $\eta_1 > 0$ such that $y(0) \in Q_D$ implies that $q(t) = \Pi_{E_-} y(t)$ satisfies the inequality:*

$$\|q(t)\| \leqslant C_1 \exp(-\eta_1 t), \qquad t \geqslant 0.$$

PROOF. We use (2.4) and (6.2):

$$\frac{d}{dt}\|q(t)\|^2 \leqslant -\varkappa \|q\|^2 + \frac{1}{\varkappa}\|F(y(t))\|^2 \leqslant -\varkappa \|q\|^2 + \frac{C_0^2}{\varkappa} \exp(-2\gamma_0 t).$$

Therefore,

$$\frac{d}{dt}(\|q(t)\|^2 \exp(\varkappa t)) \leqslant C \exp((\varkappa - 2\gamma_0)t).$$

We integrate the last inequality and obtain

$$\|q(t)\|^2 \exp(\varkappa t) - \|q(0)\|^2 \leqslant C \int_0^t \exp((\varkappa - 2\gamma_0)\tau) \, d\tau.$$

Since $\|q(0)\| \leq D$ when $y(0) \in Q$, we have:

$$\|q(t)\|^2 \leq \|q(0)\|^2 \exp(-\varkappa t) + C \exp(-\varkappa t) \int_0^t \exp\left((\varkappa - 2\gamma_0)(t - \tau)\right) d\tau$$

$$\leq D^2 \exp(-\varkappa t) + C \exp(-2\gamma_0 t) \int_0^t \exp\left(-(\varkappa - 2\gamma_0)\tau\right) d\tau.$$

If $\varkappa > 2\gamma_0$, then

$$\|q(t)\|^2 \leq D^2 \exp(-\varkappa t) + C(\varkappa - 2\gamma_0)^{-1} \exp(-2\gamma_0 t) \leq C_1^2 \exp(-2\eta_1 t),$$

where $2\eta_1 = 2\gamma_0$.

If $\varkappa < 2\gamma_0$, then

$$\|q(t)\|^2 \leq D^2 \exp(-\varkappa t) + C(2\gamma_0 - \varkappa)^{-1} \exp(-2\gamma_0 t) \left[\exp((2\gamma_0 - \varkappa)t) - 1\right]$$

$$\leq D^2 \exp(-\varkappa t) + C(2\gamma_0 - \varkappa)^{-1} \exp(-\varkappa t) \leq C_1^2 \exp(-2\eta_1 t),$$

where $2\eta_1 = \varkappa$.

If $\varkappa = 2\gamma_0$, then

$$\|q(t)\|^2 \leq D^2 \exp(-\varkappa t) + Ct \exp(-2\gamma_0 t) \leq C_1^2 \exp(-2\eta_1 t),$$

where $2\eta_1 = \varkappa - \varepsilon$, $\varepsilon > 0$.

The proposition is proved. $\square$

To prove Theorem 6.2, we need the following lemma.

LEMMA 6.1. *Let* $A: \mathbb{R}^N \to \mathbb{R}^N$ *be a linear operator,* $(Ax, x) \geq \varkappa(x, x)$, $\varkappa > 0$ *for all* $x \in \mathbb{R}^N$. *Let* $x_1(t)$ *and* $x_2(t)$ *be solutions of the differential equations*:

$$\frac{d}{dt}x_1 = Ax_1 + \beta_1(t), \qquad \frac{d}{dt}x_2 = Ax_2 + \beta_2(t)$$

and $x_1(T) = x_2(T)$. *Let* $\|\beta_1(\tau)\| \leq \delta$, $\|\beta_2(\tau)\| \leq \delta$ *when* $\tau \in [t, T]$. *Then*

$$\|x_1(t) - x_2(t)\| \leq 2\delta/\varkappa.$$

PROOF. We shall prove the statement for $t = 0$. The difference $u(t) = x_1(t) - x_2(t)$ satisfies the equation

$$\frac{d}{dt}u = Au + (\beta_1(t) - \beta_2(t)), \qquad u(T) = 0.$$

Hence

$$\frac{d}{dt}(\exp(-At)u) = \exp(-At)(\beta_1(t) - \beta_2(t)),$$

and

$$\frac{d}{dt}\|\exp(-At)u\| \geq -\left\|\frac{d}{dt}\exp(-At)u\right\| = -\|\exp(-At)(\beta_1(t) - \beta_2(t))\|$$

$$\geq -\|\exp(-At)\|\|\beta_1(t) - \beta_2(t)\| \geq -2\delta \exp(-\varkappa t).$$

We integrate the last inequality from 0 to T, obtaining

$$\|\exp(-AT)u(T)\| - \|u(0)\| \geq -2\delta/\varkappa.$$

Taking into consideration the fact that $u(T) = 0$, we obtain $\|u(0)\| \leq 2\delta/\varkappa$. The lemma is proved. □

PROOF OF THEOREM 6.2. For any integer n, we find a trajectory $\tilde{y}_n(t)$ on the attractor such that $\tilde{p}_n(n) = p(n)$, i.e., $\tilde{y}_n(t)$ and $y(t)$ have the same projection onto E_+ when $t = n$. We can do this because the projection of $\mathfrak{A}$ onto E_+ is the entire space E_+, and trajectories on the attractor may be continued also in the past since $\mathfrak{A}$ is invariant. The projections onto E_+ of the trajectories $\tilde{y}_n(t)$ and $y(t) - \tilde{p}_n(t)$ and $p(t)$ satisfy the equations:

$$\frac{d}{dt}p(t) = A|_{E_+} p(t) + F_1(y(t)),$$

$$\frac{d}{dt}\tilde{p}_n(t) = A|_{E_+} \tilde{p}_n(t) + F_1(\tilde{y}_n(t)),$$

where $A|_{E_+}$ is a positive operator in N-dimensional space E_+,

$$\|F_1(y)\|_{E_+} \leq \|F(y)\| \leq C.$$

Hence by Lemma 6.1, $\|p(0) - \tilde{p}_n(0)\| \leq 2C/\varkappa$, and the projection of the set of initial conditions of the constructed trajectories $\{\tilde{y}_n(0)\}$ onto E_+ is bounded. Since $\{\tilde{y}_n(0)\} \in \mathfrak{A}$, and $\Pi_{E_-}\mathfrak{A}$ is bounded, the sequence $\{\tilde{y}_n(0)\}$ is bounded in H. Since $\mathfrak{A}$ is bounded-compact, then from the bounded sequence $\{\tilde{y}_n(0)\} \subset \mathfrak{A}$ we can choose a convergent subsequence $\tilde{y}_{n_k}(0) \to \tilde{y}(0) \in \mathfrak{A}$ ($n_k \to \infty$). Now we consider the trajectory $\tilde{y}(t) = S_t \tilde{y}(0)$. Note that $y(0) \in Q_R$, and since

$$\|p_{n_k}(0)\| \geq \|p(0)\| - 2C/\varkappa \geq R - 2C/\varkappa \geq D,$$

as soon as R is sufficiently large, we have

$$\tilde{y}_{n_k}(0) \in Q \cap \{y = p + q \mid \|p\| \geq D\} = Q_D.$$

So by Proposition 6.1

$$\|F_1(y(t))\| \leq \|F(y(t))\| \leq C_0 \exp(-\gamma_0 t),$$
$$\|F_1(\tilde{y}_{n_k}(t))\| \leq C_0 \exp(-\gamma_0 t) \quad \text{for all } n_k.$$

If $t < n_k$, then whenever $\tau \in [t, n_k]$, we have

$$\|F_1(y(\tau))\| \leq C_0 \exp(-\gamma_0 t), \qquad \|F_1(\tilde{y}_{n_k}(\tau))\| \leq C_0 \exp(-\gamma_0 t),$$

and by Lemma 6.1

$$\|p(t) - \tilde{p}_{n_k}(t)\| \leq 2(C_0/\varkappa)\exp(-\gamma_0 t) \quad \text{when } 0 \leq t \leq n_k.$$

Taking the limit as $n_k \to +\infty$ when $t \geq 0$ is fixed, we obtain

$$\|p(t) - \tilde{p}(t)\|_{E_+} \leq 2(C_0/\varkappa)\exp(-\gamma_0 t),$$

because $\tilde{y}_{n_k}(0) \to \tilde{y}(0)$ implies $\tilde{y}_{n_k}(t) \to \tilde{y}(t)$ ($n_k \to \infty$) (by the continuity of the semigroup). As to the projections of the solutions $y(t)$ and $\tilde{y}(t)$ onto E_-, by Proposition 6.2

$$\|q(t) - \tilde{q}(t)\| \leq \|q(t)\| + \|\tilde{q}(t)\| \leq 2C_1 \exp(-\eta_1 t).$$

Now taking $\eta = \min(\gamma_0, \eta_1)$, we obtain the necessary statement. □

DEFINITION 6.2. We call the number T the *travelling time* for $\{S_t\}$ from a set B_0 to an open set O, if for any $y_0 \in B_0$ there exists a $t \in [0, T]$ such that $S_t y_0 \in O$.

PROPOSITION 6.3. *For any bounded set B in H, the travelling time from $B_0 = \bigcup_{t \geq 0} S_t(B)$ to $\mathscr{O}_\delta(\mathfrak{N}) \cup Q_R^0$ is finite. Here the set*
$$Q_R^0 = Q_R \setminus \partial Q_R = \{y = p + q \mid \|q\| < D, \|p\| > R\},$$
where R is defined in Theorem 6.2, plays the role of a neighborhood of infinity.

To prove this proposition we need the following lemma.

LEMMA 6.2. *For any compact set K in H there exist an $\varepsilon > 0$ and a $T \geq 0$ such that*
$$y(t) = S_t y(0) \in \mathscr{O}_\delta(\mathfrak{N}) \cup Q_R^0$$
for some $t \leq T$, if only $y(0)$ lies in $\mathscr{O}_\varepsilon(K)$, a neighborhood of the set K.

PROOF. We fix $y_0 \in K$. If a trajectory $y(t) = S_t y(0)$ is unbounded when $t \to +\infty$, then $y(t) \in Q_R^0$ for some t. If $y(t)$ is bounded, then by the existence of a Lyapunov function of the semigroup $\{S_t\}$, we have $y(t) \to \mathfrak{N}$ when $t \to +\infty$, and then $y(t) \in \mathscr{O}_\delta(\mathfrak{N}) \cup Q_R^0$ for some $t(y_0)$. The proof of this statement is similar to the proof of Theorem 5.1, except that we must consider the behavior of trajectories not as $t \to -\infty$, but as $t \to +\infty$.

Hence, $S_t y(0) \subseteq \mathscr{O}_\delta(\mathfrak{N}) \cup Q_R^0$ for some $t = t(y_0)$. Since the mapping S_t is continuous and the set $\mathscr{O}_\delta(\mathfrak{N}) \cup Q_R^0$ is open, there exists a neighborhood $\mathscr{U}(y_0)$ for which $S_t(\mathscr{U}(y_0)) \subseteq \mathscr{O}_\delta(\mathfrak{N}) \cup Q_R^0$ for the same t. Let us choose from the covering of the compact set K by the neighborhoods $\mathscr{U}(y_0)$ a finite subcover: $K \subseteq \bigcup_{i=1}^s \mathscr{U}(y_i)$. Then by the compactness of K, there exists an $\varepsilon > 0$ such that $\mathscr{O}_\varepsilon(K) \subseteq \bigcup_{i=1}^s \mathscr{U}(y_i)$. Denoting $T = \max\{t(y_1), t(y_2), \ldots, t(y_s)\}$, we see that the travelling time from $\mathscr{O}_\varepsilon(K)$ to $\mathscr{O}_\delta(\mathfrak{N}) \cup Q_R^0$ does not exceed T. The lemma is proved. □

PROOF OF PROPOSITION 6.3. Let us consider the set:
$$Q_{R+1}^0 = Q_{R+1} / \partial Q_{R+1} = \{y = p + q \mid \|q\| < D, \|p\| > R + 1\}.$$
The set $K = \mathfrak{A} \setminus Q_{R+1}^0$ is compact, because $\mathfrak{A}$ is bounded-compact, and the part of $\mathfrak{A}$ lying outside of Q_{R+1}^0 is bounded. Then by Lemma 6.2 the travelling time from $\mathscr{O}_\varepsilon(K)$ to $\mathscr{O}_\delta(\mathfrak{N}) \cup Q_R^0$ is finite.

Since
$$\operatorname{dist}_E(S_t(B), \mathfrak{A}) \to 0 \quad \text{when } t \to +\infty,$$
we have $S_t(B) \subseteq \mathscr{O}_\varepsilon(\mathfrak{A}) \subseteq [\mathscr{O}_\varepsilon(\mathfrak{A}) \setminus Q_R^0] \cup Q_R^0$ when $t \geq T(B)$ ($\varepsilon > 0$ is taken from Lemma 6.2).

Let us show that $\mathscr{O}_\varepsilon(\mathfrak{A}) \setminus Q_R^0 \subseteq \mathscr{O}_\varepsilon(\mathfrak{A} \setminus Q_{R+1}^0)$ if $\varepsilon < 1$. Indeed, if $y = p + q \in \mathscr{O}_\varepsilon(\mathfrak{A}) \setminus Q_R^0$, then $\|p\| \leq R$ and there exists $y_1 = p_1 + q_1 \in \mathfrak{A}$ such that $\|y_1 - y\| \leq \varepsilon$. Then $\|p_1\| \leq \|p\| + \varepsilon \leq R+1$ and $y_1 \in \mathfrak{A} \setminus Q_{R+1}^0$, i.e., $y \in \mathscr{O}_\varepsilon(\mathfrak{A} \setminus Q_{R+1}^0) = \mathscr{O}_\varepsilon(K)$.

So $S_t(B) \subseteq \mathscr{O}_\varepsilon(K) \cup Q_R^0$ when $t \geq T(B)$. Then

$$S_{T(B)}(B_0) = S_{T(B)}\left(\bigcup_{t \geq 0} S_t(B)\right) = \bigcup_{t \geq T(B)} S_t(B) \subseteq \mathscr{O}_\varepsilon(K) \cup Q_R^0.$$

Since by Lemma 6.2 the travelling time from $\mathscr{O}_\varepsilon(K)$ to $\mathscr{O}_\delta(\mathfrak{N}) \cup Q_R^0$ is finite, and the travelling time from Q_R^0 to the same set equals zero, then the travelling time from $B_0 = \bigcup_{t \geq 0} S_t(B)$ to $\mathscr{O}_\delta(\mathfrak{N}) \cup Q_R^0$ is finite. The proposition is proved. □

PROOF OF THEOREM 6.1. In the works of Babin, Vishik [6, 7] it is shown that if a solution $y(t)$ is contained in a small neighborhood $\mathscr{O}_\delta(z_i)$ of a hyperbolic equilibrium point $z_i \in \mathfrak{N}$, then on $M_+(z_i)$ there exists a trajectory $\tilde{y}_i(t)$ which approaches $y(t)$ at an exponential rate while $y(t) \in \mathscr{O}_\delta(z_i)$. Theorem 6.2 states that a similar result is also correct for Q, "a neighborhood of infinity".

Suppose the solution $y(t)$ successively goes through the neighborhoods $\mathscr{O}_\delta(z_1), \mathscr{O}_\delta(z_2), \ldots, \mathscr{O}_\delta(z_l)$ and possibly Q (if the solution $y(t)$ is unbounded when $t \to +\infty$). In [7] it is also shown that in the case of the existence of Lyapunov function of the semigroup $\{S_t\}$, we can choose δ so small that any solution $y(t)$ issuing from $\mathscr{O}_\delta(z_i)$ will never come back to this neighborhood, i.e., all the points $z_1, z_2, \ldots, z_l$ are different and $l \leq k$. In the neighborhood $\mathscr{O}_\delta(z_i)$ and Q we have constructed asymptotics $\tilde{y}_i(t)$ ($i = 1, 2, \ldots, l, \infty$). Uniting this asymptotics into a piecewise-continuous function $\tilde{y}(t)$, as it is done in [7], we obtain a finite-dimensional composite trajectory which approaches $y(t)$ at an exponential rate in any $\mathscr{O}_\delta(z_i)$ and in Q. We can have jumps of $\tilde{y}(t)$ only when the solution $y(t)$ comes into $\mathscr{O}_\delta(z_i)$ or Q, i.e., the number of jumps of $\tilde{y}(t)$ is not more than $l+1 \leq k+1$, where k is the number of equilibrium points of the semigroup $\{S_t\}$.

To finish the proof, we note that $y(t)$ and $\tilde{y}(t)$ going from $\mathscr{O}_\delta(z_i)$ to $\mathscr{O}_\delta(z_{i+1})$ (or Q) cannot move away from each other by more than $C'\exp(aT) = C_1$ times their original distance by Proposition 6.3 and condition 4) of Theorem 6.1. This only influences the constant C in the last estimate. The theorem is proved. □

Let us apply the obtained results to concrete examples of partial differential equations.

EXAMPLE 6.1. *The parabolic equation (problem* (4.1)).

THEOREM 6.3. *Let* (4.1) *hold, and assume that*

$$|f(u)| \leq \frac{C_1}{1 + |u|^\vartheta}, \qquad \vartheta > 0, \tag{6.3}$$

and

$$|f'(u+w) - f'(u)| \leq C|w|^\alpha, \qquad \alpha > 0. \tag{6.4}$$

Let the semigroup $\{S_t\}$ corresponding to problem (4.1) possess a finite number of equilibrium points, all of them being hyperbolic. We also assume that the eigenfunctions of Laplace operator are analytic up to the boundary of the domain Ω (this will hold if the boundary of the domain is an analytic manifold). Then we can find a number $\eta > 0$ such that for any solution $u(t) = S_t u_0$ there exists a finite-dimensional composite trajectory $\tilde{y}(t) \in \mathfrak{A}$ for which $\|u(t) - \tilde{y}(t)\| \leq C \exp(-\eta t)$, and C depend only on $\|u_0\|$.

To prove theorem 6.3, let us check the conditions of Theorem 6.1 for the semigroup $\{S_t\}$.

Indeed, the existence of a Lyapunov function for this equation is established in the previous sections, the smoothness of the semigroup follows from (6.4) (see [7]), the finiteness and hyperbolicity of the equilibrium points is one of the conditions of Theorem 6.3. Condition 4) of Theorem 6.1 is proved just like the uniqueness of the solution of the problem (4.1). We must check condition 5) of the theorem.

PROPOSITION 6.4. *Suppose* (6.3) *holds*, $u = p + q$, $p \in E_+$, $q \in E_-$. *Then there exist numbers* C_2, R_1, $\eta > 0$ *such that*

$$\|f(u)\|_0 \leq C_2(R)\|p\|^{-\eta} \quad \text{when } \|p\| \geq R_1, \|q\| \leq R.$$

To prove this, we need the following lemma.

LEMMA 6.3. *Let* $e_1(x), \ldots, e_N(x)$ *be functions defined in a domain* Ω, *which are real analytic up to the boundary* $\partial\Omega$ *and linearly independent in* Ω. *Then there exist numbers* $L > 0$ *and* $P > 0$ *such that*

$$\mu\left(x \in \Omega : \left|\sum_{i=1}^{N} \gamma_i e_i(x)\right| \leq \varepsilon\right) \leq L\varepsilon^{1/P}$$

for all $\varepsilon \in [0, 1]$ *and all* $\gamma = (\gamma_1, \gamma_2, \ldots, \gamma_N) \in S^{N-1}$. *Here* S^{N-1} *is a sphere of radius* 1 *in* $\mathbb{R}^N$.

Lemma 6.3 is proved in the Appendix.

PROOF OF PROPOSITION 6.4. By the Chebyshev inequality

$$\mu(|q(x)| \leq D) \leq \|q\|^2/D^2 \leq R^2/D^2.$$

Then

$$\mu(|u(x)| \leq K) \leq \mu(|p(x)| \leq K + D) + \mu(|q(x)| \geq D)$$
$$\leq \mu(|p(x)|/\|p(x)\| < (K + D)/\|p(x)\|) + R^2/D^2.$$

Note that

$$\frac{|p(x)|}{\|p(x)\|} = \sum_{i=1}^{N} \gamma_i X_i(x),$$

where $\gamma = (\gamma_1, \gamma_2, \ldots, \gamma_N) \in S^N$, and the $X_i(x)$ are analytic functions up to the boundary. Then, estimating the first term by Lemma 6.3, we obtain

$$\mu(|u(x)| \leqslant K) \leqslant L((K+D)/\|p\|)^{1/P} + R^2/D^2.$$

So, for any $K, D > 0$

$$\|f(u)\|_0^2 = \int_{|u(x)|\leqslant K} |f(u(x))|^2 dx + \int_{|u(x)|>K} |f(u(x))|^2 dx$$

$$\leqslant C_1^2 \mu(|u(x)| \leqslant K) + |\Omega| C_1^2 /(1+K^\vartheta)^2$$

$$\leqslant C_1^2 L((K+D)/\|p\|)^{1/P} + C_1^2 R^2/D^2 + |\Omega| C_1^2/(1+K^\vartheta)^2.$$

To obtain the estimate $\|f(u)\|_0^2 \leqslant C_2^2 \|p\|^{-2\eta}$, we choose K and D depending on $\|p\|$: $K = \|p\|^{\varepsilon_1}$, $D = \|p\|^{\varepsilon_2}$. Then when $\|p\|$ is large, the first term on the right-hand side of the last inequality decreases as $\|p\|^{-(1-\max(\varepsilon_1, \varepsilon_2))/P}$, the second, as $\|p\|^{-2\varepsilon_2}$, the third, as $\|p\|^{-2\varepsilon_1 \vartheta}$. So, it suffices to put

$$2\eta = \min((1-\max(\varepsilon_1, \varepsilon_2))/P, 2\varepsilon_2, 2\varepsilon_1 \vartheta) > 0$$

for any $\varepsilon_1, \varepsilon_2 \in (0, 1)$. □

Condition 5) of Theorem 6.1 follows from Proposition 6.4. Now we can apply this theorem to the equation under study.

EXAMPLE 6.2. *The hyperbolic equation (problem (4.7), (4.8))*.

If we impose conditions (6.3) and (6.4) on the function f and also assume that the semigroup of this problem possesses a finite number of hyperbolic equilibrium points, then Theorem 6.1 is applicable to the hyperbolic equation.

Appendix

I) PROOF OF LEMMA 4.1.

Let $\psi(x)$ be a real analytic function in Ω (Ω is a connected domain in $\mathbb{R}^n$).

PROPOSITION A.1. *If $\psi(x) \not\equiv 0$ in Ω, then the set of roots of the function $\psi(x)$ has zero Lebesgue measure in $\mathbb{R}^n$.*

PROOF. In the one-dimensional case ($n = 1$) the fact is evident. The multi-dimensional cases are obtained by induction on n, the number of variables of the function $\psi(x)$. Here we use the following corollary of the Fubini theorem: the set $G \subset \mathbb{R}^n$ has measure zero if for almost all points $x' \in \mathbb{R}^{n-1}$ the measure of the projection of the set $\{x'\} \times \mathbb{R} \cap G$ onto $\mathbb{R}$ equals zero. □

Recall that $\mu(\psi(x) = M)$ denotes the Lebesgue measure (in $\mathbb{R}^n$) of the set of points $x \in \Omega$ for which $\psi(x) = M$.

Let $e_1(x), \ldots, e_N(x)$ be certain analytic linearly independent functions in Ω which are continuous in $\overline{\Omega}$.

COROLLARY A.1. *For any numbers* $\gamma_1, \gamma_2, \ldots, \gamma_N$ *that are not equal to zero simultaneously,*

$$\mu\left(\sum_{i=1}^{N} \gamma_i e_i(x) = 0\right) = 0.$$

We denote by γ the vector in $\mathbb{R}^N$ with coordinates $(\gamma_1, \ldots, \gamma_N)$, $|\gamma|$ is the norm of the vector γ in $\mathbb{R}^N$.

LEMMA 4.1. *For any number* $M > 0$,

$$\mu\left(x \in \Omega : \left|\sum_{i=1}^{N} \gamma_i e_i(x)\right| \leq M\right) \to 0 \qquad (|\gamma| \to +\infty).$$

PROOF. Let us fix $M > 0$. We consider the family of functions $\{e_s(\gamma)\}$, $\gamma \in \mathbb{S}_R^{N-1}$,

$$e_s(\gamma) = \mu\left(s\left|\sum_{i=1}^{N} \gamma_i e_i(x)\right| \leq M\right), \qquad s \geq 1,$$

where $\mathbb{S}_R^{N-1}$ is the sphere of radius R in $\mathbb{R}^N$ centered at 0. Here R is some fixed number, chosen so that if the function $\mathrm{Id}(x) \equiv 1$, $x \in \Omega$ does not belong to the linear hull of the functions $e_1(x), e_2(x), \ldots, e_N(x)$, then $R = 1$, in the opposite case there exists a unique vector $\gamma^1 \in \mathbb{R}^{N-1}$ for which $\mathrm{Id}(x) = \sum_{i=1}^{N} \gamma_i^1 e_i(x)$, and $R = 2M|\gamma^1|$.

Let us note that for any fixed $\gamma \in \mathbb{S}_R^{N-1}$ the function $e_s(\gamma)$ on s decreases when s increases and $e_s(\gamma) \to 0$ $(s \to +\infty)$. Indeed

$$e_s(\gamma) = \mu\left(\left|\sum_{i=1}^{N} \gamma_i e_i(x)\right| \leq \frac{M}{s}\right).$$

Also

$$\left\{x : \left|\sum_{i=1}^{N} \gamma_i e_i(x)\right| \leq 0\right\} = \bigcap_{s \geq 1}\left\{x : \left|\sum_{i=1}^{N} \gamma_i e_i(x)\right| \leq \frac{M}{s}\right\}.$$

Now we use Proposition A.1 and the continuity of Lebesgue measure

$$\mu\left(\left|\sum_{i=1}^{N} \gamma_i e_i(x)\right| \leq \frac{M}{s}\right) \to \mu\left(\left|\sum_{i=1}^{N} \gamma_i e_i(x)\right| \leq 0\right) = 0 \qquad (s \to +\infty).$$

Let us show now that for any fixed $s \geq 1$ the function $e_s(\gamma)$ is continuous on $\gamma \in \mathbb{S}_R^{N-1}$. We fix any vector $\gamma^0 \in \mathbb{S}_R^{N-1}$. First of all let us note that

$$\mu\left(s\left|\sum_{i=1}^{N} \gamma_i^0 e_i(x)\right| \leq M + \delta\right) \to e_s(\gamma^0) \qquad (\delta \to 0). \tag{A.1}$$

Indeed, the expression

$$\mu\left(s\left|\sum_{i=1}^{N} \gamma_i^0 e_i(x)\right| \leq M + \delta\right)$$

as a function of δ increases and is continuous at $\delta = 0$, because

$$\mu\left(s\left|\sum_{i=1}^{N}\gamma_i^0 e_i(x)\right| = M\right) = 0.$$

The last equality follows from Corollary A.1, since in the opposite case we would have

$$s\sum_{i=1}^{N}\gamma_i^0 e_i(x) \equiv \pm M \operatorname{Id}(x).$$

The last identity is excluded in the case when the function $\operatorname{Id}(x)$ belongs the linear hull of the functions $e_1(x), e_2(x), \ldots, e_N(x)$. If

$$\operatorname{Id}(x) = \sum_{i=1}^{N}\gamma_i^1 e_i(x),$$

then $s\gamma^0 = \pm M\gamma^1$, i.e., $|\gamma^0| = (M/s)|\gamma^1| \leqslant M|\gamma^1| < 2M|\gamma^1| = R$, which contradicts the condition $\gamma^0 \in \mathbb{S}_R^{N-1}$.

The functions $e_i(x)$ are bounded in Ω. Thus for any $\delta > 0$ we can find a neighborhood $\mathscr{O}(\gamma^0)$ on the sphere $\mathbb{S}_R^{N-1}$ such that

$$s\sum_{i=1}^{N}|\gamma_i^0 - \gamma_i||e_i(x)| \leqslant \delta \quad \text{for all } \gamma \in \mathscr{O}(\gamma^0),\ x \in \Omega.$$

So, for any $\gamma \in \mathscr{O}(\gamma^0)$ we have

$$e_s(\gamma) = e_s(\gamma - \gamma^0 + \gamma^0)$$

$$= \mu\left(s\left|\sum_{i=1}^{N}(\gamma_i - \gamma_i^0)e_i(x) + \sum_{i=1}^{N}\gamma_i^0 e_i(x)\right| \leqslant M\right)$$

$$= \mu\left(-M - s\sum_{i=1}^{N}(\gamma_i - \gamma_i^0)e_i(x) \leqslant s\sum_{i=1}^{N}\gamma_i^0 e_i(x)\right.$$

$$\left. \leqslant M - s\sum_{i=1}^{N}(\gamma_i - \gamma_i^0)e_i(x)\right)$$

$$\leqslant \mu\left(-M - \delta \leqslant s\sum_{i=1}^{N}\gamma_i^0 e_i(x) \leqslant M + \delta\right)$$

$$= \mu\left(s\left|\sum_{i=1}^{N}\gamma_i^0 e_i(x)\right| \leqslant M + \delta\right).$$

Therefore

$$e_s(\gamma) \leqslant \mu\left(s\left|\sum_{i=1}^{N}\gamma_i^0 e_i(x)\right| \leqslant M + \delta\right), \quad \text{if } \gamma \in \mathscr{O}(\gamma^0).$$

Similarly we can prove that
$$e_s(\gamma) \geq \mu\left(s\left|\sum_{i=1}^{N} \gamma_i^0 e_i(x)\right| \leq M - \delta\right).$$

Let us apply the property (A.1). For any $\varepsilon > 0$ there exists a $\delta > 0$ such that
$$\mu\left(s\left|\sum_{i=1}^{N} \gamma_i^0 e_i(x)\right| \leq M + \delta\right) \leq e_s(\gamma^0) + \varepsilon,$$
$$\mu\left(s\left|\sum_{i=1}^{N} \gamma_i^0 e_i(x)\right| \leq M - \delta\right) \geq e_s(\gamma^0) - \varepsilon.$$

Hence $|e_s(\gamma) - e_s(\gamma^0)| \leq \varepsilon$ for any $\gamma \in \mathcal{O}(\gamma^0)$ (the neighborhood $\mathcal{O}(\gamma^0)$ is determined by the number δ).

So we have a family of continuous functions $\{e_s(\gamma)\}_{s \geq 1}$ on the compact set $\mathbb{S}_R^{N-1}$ monotonically converging to zero when $s \to +\infty$. By the Dini theorem about monotone convergence, we have $e_s(\gamma) \to 0$ as $s \to +\infty$ uniformly on $\gamma \in \mathbb{S}_R^{N-1}$, which was to be proved. □

II) PROOF OF LEMMA 6.3.

Let $\Omega \Subset \mathbb{R}^n$, $\partial \Omega$ be smooth, Ω connected, $e_1, \ldots, e_N : \Omega \to \mathbb{R}$ be real-analytic functions, analytic up to the boundary (i.e., analytic in some larger domain Ω').

Denote by $\gamma = (\gamma_1, \gamma_2, \ldots, \gamma_N) \in \mathbb{S}^{N-1}$ an element of the sphere in $\mathbb{R}^N$,
$$|\gamma|^2 = \sum_{i=1}^{N} \gamma_i^2 = 1.$$

Also we define the function
$$e_\gamma(x) = \sum_{i=1}^{N} \gamma_i e_i(x).$$

LEMMA 6.3. *Let $e_1, e_2, \ldots, e_N$ be fixed functions, real-analytic up to the boundary and linearly independent in Ω. Then there exist positive numbers L, p, such that*
$$\mu(|e_\gamma(x)| \leq \varepsilon) \leq L\varepsilon^{1/p} \quad \forall \varepsilon \in [0, \varepsilon_0], \ \varepsilon_0 > 0, \ \forall \gamma \in \mathbb{S}^{N-1}.$$

Note that the number L is large and the number $1/p$ is small.

DEFINITION A.1. Let $e_\gamma(x)$ be an analytic function in $\overline{\Omega}$. The *order* of the root of the function $e_\gamma(x)$ at the point $x \in \overline{\Omega}$ is a natural number m such that:

1) for any $\alpha \in \mathbb{Z}_+^n$, $|\alpha| < m$, we have $|\partial_x^\alpha e_\gamma(x)| = 0$;

2) there exists an α' such that $|\alpha'| = m$ and $|\partial_x^{\alpha'} e_\gamma(x)| \neq 0$.

Notation: $P_x(e_\gamma) = m$.

PROPOSITION A.2. *There exists a* $p_0 \in \mathbb{Z}_+$ *such that* $P_x(e_\gamma) \leqslant p_0$ *for all* $x \in \overline{\Omega}$, $\gamma \in \mathbb{S}^{N-1}$.

PROOF. Let us assume the converse, i.e., that there exist sequences $\{x_n\} \in \overline{\Omega}$ and $\{\gamma_n\} \in \mathbb{S}^{N-1}$ such that $P_{x_n}(e_{\gamma_n}) \geqslant n$ for all n. We choose converging subsequences from these sequences (we also denote them as $\{x_n\}$ and $\{\gamma_n\}$): $x_n \to x_0$, $\gamma_n \to \gamma_0$ $(n \to \infty)$. Then by the continuity of the functions $e_\gamma(x)$ and all their derivatives with respect to x and γ, we obtain $\partial_x^\alpha e_{\gamma_n}(x_n) \to \partial_x^\alpha e_{\gamma_0}(x_0)$ $(n \to \infty)$ for any α.

Let us fix an α. If $n > |\alpha|$, then by the choice of $\{x_n\}$ and $\{\gamma_n\}$, we have $\partial_x^\alpha e_{\gamma_n}(x_n) = 0$, and so $\partial_x^\alpha e_{\gamma_0}(x_0) = 0$ for all $\alpha \in \mathbb{Z}_+^n$.

Hence all the coefficients of the Taylor series for the function $e_{\gamma_0}(x)$ at the point x_0 equal zero and we have $e_{\gamma_0}(x) \equiv 0$ in $\overline{\Omega}$, which contradicts the linear independence of the functions $e_1, \ldots, e_N$. □

From the proposition proved above, it follows that we can define the order for any system of functions in a domain.

DEFINITION A.2.

$$P(e_1, \ldots, e_N) = \max\{P_x(e_\gamma) : x \in \overline{\Omega}, \gamma \in \mathbb{S}^{N-1}\}$$

is the *order* of the system of functions $e_1, \ldots, e_N$ in $\overline{\Omega}$.

We denote $x = (x_1, \ldots, x_{n-1}, x_n) = (x', x_n)$, where we have put $x' = (x_1, \ldots, x_{n-1}) \in \mathbb{R}^{n-1}$. Let $G = G' \times I$, where G' is a domain in $\mathbb{R}^{n-1}$, $I = (a, b) \subset \mathbb{R}$.

In the domain G, we consider the continuous function analytic in x_n

$$Q(x) = (x_n - u_1(x'))(x_n - u_2(x')) \cdots (x_n - u_m(x')),$$

where $u_1(x'), \ldots, u_m(x')$ are continuous functions in G'.

PROPOSITION A.3. *For any* $\varepsilon \geqslant 0$,

$$\mu(|Q(x)| \leqslant \varepsilon) \leqslant 2m\varepsilon^{1/m}\mu(G').$$

PROOF. We fix a point $x \in G$. If $|Q(x)| \leqslant \varepsilon$, then there exists an i, $1 \leqslant i \leqslant m$, such that $|x_n - u_i(x')| \leqslant \varepsilon^{1/m}$. So,

$$\{x \in \mathbb{R}^n : |Q(x)| \leqslant \varepsilon\} \subset \bigcup_{i=1}^m \{x \in \mathbb{R}^n : |x_n - u_i(x')| \leqslant \varepsilon^{1/m}\}.$$

Thus,

$$\mu\{x \in \mathbb{R}^n : |Q(x)| \leqslant \varepsilon\} \leqslant \sum_{i=1}^m \mu\{x \in \mathbb{R}^n : |x_n - u_i(x')| \leqslant \varepsilon^{1/m}\}.$$

Let us estimate the terms of this sum. We have

$$\mu\{x \in \mathbb{R}^n : |x_n - u(x')| \leqslant \varepsilon^{1/m}\} = \int_{G'} \mu\{x_n \in \mathbb{R} : |x_n - u(x')| \leqslant \varepsilon^{1/m}\} dx'.$$

Note that
$$\mu\{x_n \in \mathbb{R} : |x_n - u(x')| \leq \varepsilon^{1/m}\} \leq 2\varepsilon^{1/m}.$$
Then
$$\mu\{x \in \mathbb{R}^n : |x_n - u(x')| \leq \varepsilon^{1/m}\} \leq 2\varepsilon^{1/m}\mu(G').$$
And so
$$\mu(|Q(x)| \leq \varepsilon) \leq 2m\varepsilon^{1/m}\mu(G').$$
The proposition is proved. □

PROPOSITION A.4. *Let us consider any pair* $x_0 \in \overline{\Omega}$, $\gamma_0 \in \mathbb{S}^{N-1}$. *We denote* $m_0 = P_{x_0}(e_{\gamma_0})$. *Then there exist neighborhoods* $\mathcal{O}(x_0)$ *and* $\mathcal{O}(\gamma_0) \subset \mathbb{S}^{N-1}$ *such that* $\gamma \in \mathcal{O}(\gamma_0)$ *implies*

a) $\mu(x \in \mathcal{O}(x_0) : |e_\gamma(x)| \leq \varepsilon) \leq L_0 \varepsilon$ *if* $m_0 = 0$,

b) $\mu(x \in \mathcal{O}(x_0) : |e_\gamma(x)| \leq \varepsilon) \leq L_0 \varepsilon^{1/m_0}$ *if* $m_0 > 0$,

where $\varepsilon \in [0, 1]$.

PROOF. First we consider item a), i.e., $e_{\gamma_0}(x_0) \neq 0$. Then there exist a $\delta_0 > 0$ and neighborhoods $\mathcal{O}(\gamma_0)$, $\mathcal{O}(x_0)$ of the points $\gamma_0 \in \mathbb{S}^{N-1}$ and $x_0 \in \overline{\Omega}$ such that $|e_\gamma(x)| \geq \delta_0$ for all $\gamma \in \mathcal{O}(\gamma_0)$, $x \in \mathcal{O}(x_0)$. Then for all $\gamma \in \mathcal{O}(\gamma_0)$

$$\mu(x \in \mathcal{O}(x_0) : |e_\gamma(x)| \leq \varepsilon) \leq \begin{cases} 0, & 0 \leq \varepsilon < \delta_0, \\ \mu(\mathcal{O}(x_0)), & \delta_0 \leq \varepsilon < 1, \end{cases}$$

i.e.,
$$\mu(x \in \mathcal{O}(x_0) : |e_\gamma(x)| \leq \varepsilon) \leq \mu(\mathcal{O}(x_0))\delta_0^{-1}\varepsilon$$
when $\varepsilon \in [0, 1]$, and we can put $L_0 = \mu(\mathcal{O}(x_0))/\delta_0$.

Now we consider item b). Since the order of the function $e_{\gamma_0}(x)$ at the point x_0 equals m_0, there exists some direction such that the derivative of order m_0 in this direction at the point x_0 is not zero. If we now choose an orthogonal substitution of coordinates under which the nth axis of coordinates (x_n) coincides with this direction, then, assuming for simplicity $x_0 = 0$, we see that $e_{\gamma_0}(x)$ in the new coordinates is

$$e_{\gamma_0}(x) = ax_n^{m_0} + \sum_{\substack{|\alpha| \geq m_0, \\ \alpha \neq (0,\ldots,0,m_0)}} a_\alpha x^\alpha$$

$$= ax_n^{m_0} + \sum_{\substack{|\alpha| \geq m_0, \\ \alpha \neq (0,\ldots,0,m_0)}} a_{\alpha_1,\ldots,\alpha_n} x_1^{\alpha_1} x_2^{\alpha_2} \cdots x_n^{\alpha_n},$$

($a \neq 0$), because all the derivatives of the function $e_{\gamma_0}(x)$ up to the order $m_0 - 1$ equal zero.

Note that all the $e_i(x)$ can be uniquely extended to the complex domain $\mathcal{O}(\overline{\Omega}) \subset \mathbb{C}^n$; consider e_γ as a function of the complex variable z analytic in the domain $\mathcal{O}(\overline{\Omega})$ containing $\overline{\Omega}$.

Thus, after the substitution we can assume that $z_0 = (0, 0, \ldots, 0)$ and the function $e_{\gamma_0}(0', z_n)$ of one variable z_n has a root of order m_0 at the point $z_n = 0$. Then by the theorem on the roots of an analytic function of one variable, there exists an $a > 0$ such that $e_{\gamma_0}(0', z_n) \neq 0$ when $0 < |z_n| \leq a$. Since the function $e_{\gamma}(z)$ is continuous with respect to z and γ_0, there exist a neighborhood of $0'$, $V' \subset \mathbb{C}^{n-1}$, and $\mathscr{O}(\gamma_0) \subset \mathbb{S}^{N-1}$ such that $e_{\gamma_0}(z', z_n) \neq 0$ when $z' \in V'$, $\gamma \in \mathscr{O}(\gamma_0)$, $|z_n| = a$.

By the argument principle, for all $z' \in V'$, $\gamma \in \mathscr{O}(\gamma_0)$, the number of roots of the function $e_{\gamma_0}(z', z_n)$ of one variable z_n is given by the formula

$$\frac{1}{2\pi i} \int_{|z_n|=a} \frac{(\partial/\partial z_n) e_{\gamma}(z', z_n)}{e_{\gamma}(z', z_n)} dz_n.$$

At the point $z' = 0$, $\gamma = \gamma_0$, we know the value of this integral: it equals m_0. The integral is continuous on z' and γ, because the denominator does not equal zero in the set considered. So, for all $z' \in V'$, $\gamma \in \mathscr{O}(\gamma_0)$, the function $e_{\gamma}(z', z_n)$ has exactly m_0 roots in the circle $|z_n| \leq a$.

We denote these roots by $z_1(z', \gamma), z_2(z', \gamma), \ldots, z_{m_0}(z', \gamma)$ taking into account their multiplicity, choosing their numeration so that the functions $z_i(z', \gamma)$ are continuous on z' and γ in $V' \times \mathscr{O}(\gamma_0)$. We can do this according to the Rouché theorem.

Let us consider the function

$$P_{\gamma}(z) = \prod_{i=1}^{m_0} (z_n - z_i(z', \gamma)).$$

For all $z' \in V'$, $\gamma \in \mathscr{O}(\gamma_0)$ the functions $P_{\gamma}(z', z_n)$ and $e_{\gamma}(z', z_n)$, regarded as functions of one variable z_n, have the same roots of the same order in the circle $|z_n| \leq a$. Then in this circle for any $z' \in V'$, $\gamma \in \mathscr{O}(\gamma_0)$, we can define the analytic function of one variable

$$g_{\gamma}(z', z_n) = \frac{e_{\gamma}(z', z_n)}{P_{\gamma}(z', z_n)},$$

and $g_{\gamma}(z', z_n) \neq 0$ for the values of γ, z', z_n considered. Let us note that $g_{\gamma}(z', z_n)$ is continuous on γ and z' when $\gamma \in \mathscr{O}(\gamma_0)$, $z' \in V'$ and $|z_n| = a$, because the functions $e_{\gamma}(z', z_n)$ and $P_{\gamma}(z', z_n)$ are continuous on the arguments γ, z', z_n, and $P_{\gamma}(z', z_n)$ does not equal zero in this set. Using the Cauchy formula,

$$g_{\gamma}(z', z_n) = \frac{1}{2\pi i} \int_{|\zeta|=a} \frac{g_{\gamma}(z', \zeta)}{\zeta - z_n} d\zeta$$

we obtain the continuity of $g_{\gamma}(z', z_n)$ on γ and z' in the set $\gamma \in \mathscr{O}(\gamma_0)$, $z' \in V'$, $|z_n| \leq a$. So, for all $\gamma \in \mathscr{O}(\gamma_0)$, $z \in V' \times \{|z_n| \leq a\}$, we have the representation $e_\gamma(z) = P_\gamma(z)g_\gamma(z)$, where $g_\gamma(z) \neq 0$, $g_\gamma(z)$ is continuous on γ, z. Now we return to real coordinates. Then $e_\gamma(x) = P_\gamma(x)g_\gamma(x)$ when $\gamma \in \mathscr{O}(\gamma_0)$, $x \in \mathscr{O}(0') \times \{|x_n| < a\} = \mathscr{O}(0)$. The continuous function $g_\gamma(x)$ does not equal zero in $\mathscr{O}(0)$, so taking, if we need, this neighborhood smaller, we can assert that $|g_\gamma(x)| > 1/L$ when $x \in \mathscr{O}(0)$.

Now let us estimate $\mu(x \in \mathscr{O}(0) : |e_\gamma(x)| \leq \varepsilon)$ when $\gamma \in \mathscr{O}(\gamma_0)$. If $x \in \mathscr{O}(0)$, $|e_\gamma(x)| \leq \varepsilon$, then $|P_\gamma(x)|/L \leq |g_\gamma(x)||P_\gamma(x)| = |e_\gamma(x)| \leq \varepsilon$, i.e., $|P_\gamma(x)| \leq \varepsilon L$. But then by Proposition A.3, we have

$$\mu(x \in \mathscr{O}(0) : |P_\gamma(x)| \leq \varepsilon L) \leq 2m(\varepsilon L)^{1/m_0} \mu(\mathscr{O}(0')).$$

So, $L_0 = 2mL^{1/m_0}\mu(\mathscr{O}(0'))$, and the proposition is completely proved. □

PROPOSITION A.5. *For any point $\gamma_0 \in \mathbb{S}^{N-1}$ there exists a neighborhood $\mathscr{O}(\gamma_0) \subset \mathbb{S}^{N-1}$ such that for all $\gamma \in \mathscr{O}(\gamma_0)$,*

$$\mu(x \in \Omega : |e_\gamma(x)| \leq \varepsilon) \leq L(\gamma_0)\varepsilon^{1/p_0}.$$

PROOF. By Proposition A.4, for any point $x \in \overline{\Omega}$ there exist a neighborhood $\mathscr{O}(x)$ and a neighborhood $\mathscr{O}_x(\gamma_0) \subset \mathbb{S}^{N-1}$ such that

$$\mu(y \in \mathscr{O}(x) : |e_\gamma(y)| \leq \varepsilon) \leq L(x)\varepsilon^{1/m_0(x,\gamma_0)}$$

for all $\gamma \in \mathscr{O}_x(\gamma_0)$.

From the covering $\{\mathscr{O}(x)\}$ of the set $\overline{\Omega}$, choose a finite subcovering: $\mathscr{O}(x_1), \mathscr{O}(x_2), \ldots, \mathscr{O}(x_M)$. Denote

$$\mathscr{O}(\gamma_0) = \bigcap_{i=1}^{M} \mathscr{O}_{x_i}(\gamma_0).$$

Then

$$\mu(x \in \Omega : |e_\gamma(x)| \leq \varepsilon) \leq \sum_{i=1}^{M} \mu(x \in \mathscr{O}(x_i) : |e_\gamma(x)| \leq \varepsilon)$$

$$\leq \sum_{i=1}^{M} L_i \varepsilon^{1/m_i} \leq L(\gamma_0)\varepsilon^{1/p_0},$$

where $L = \sum_{i=1}^{M} L_i$, because $1/p_0 \leq 1/m_i$ for all i by Proposition A.2. The proposition is proved. □

PROOF OF LEMMA 6.3. For any $\gamma_0 \in \mathbb{S}^{N-1}$ we define the neighborhood $\mathscr{O}(\gamma_0)$ whose existence is stated in Proposition A.5. From the covering of the sphere $\mathbb{S}^{N-1}$ by these neighborhoods, choose a finite subcovering $\mathscr{O}(\gamma_1)$, $\mathscr{O}(\gamma_2), \ldots, \mathscr{O}(\gamma_M)$. Then

$$\mu(x \in \Omega : |e_\gamma(x)| \leq \varepsilon) \leq L(\gamma_i)\varepsilon^{1/p_0}$$

for all $\gamma \in \mathscr{O}(\gamma_i)$. Denoting $L = \max\{L(\gamma_i) : 1 \leqslant i \leqslant M\}$, we see that for all $\gamma \in \mathbb{S}^{N-1}$

$$\mu(x \in \Omega : |e_\gamma(x)| \leqslant \varepsilon) \leqslant L\varepsilon^{1/p_0}.$$

The lemma is proved, and $p = p_0$ is the maximal order of the root of the functions $e_\gamma(x)$. $\square$

References

1. A. V. Babin and M. I. Vishik, *Attractors of partial differential evolution equations and estimates of their dimension*, Uspekhi Mat. Nauk **38** (1983), no. 3, 133–187; English transl. in Russian Math. Surveys **38** (1983), no. 3.

2. _____, *Regular attractors of semigroups and evolution equations*, J. Math. Pures Appl. **62** (1983), 441–491.

3. _____, *Maximal attractors of semigroups corresponding to evolution differential equations*, Mat. Sb. **126** (1985), no. 3, 397–419; English transl. in Math. USSR-Sb. **54** (1986).

4. _____, *Unstable invariant sets of semigroups of nonlinear operators and their perturbations*, Uspekhi Mat. Nauk **41** (1986), no. 4, 3–34; English transl. in Russian Math. Surveys **41** (1986), no. 4.

5. _____, *About unstable sets of evolution equations in a neighborhood of critical points of the equilibrium curve*, Izv. Akad. Nauk SSSR Ser. Mat. **51** (1987), no. 1, 44–78; English transl. in Math. USSR-Izv. **30** (1988).

6. _____, *Spectral and stabilized asymptotic behavior of solutions of nonlinear evolution equations*, Uspekhi Mat. Nauk **43** (1988), no. 5, 99–132; English transl. in Russian Math. Surveys **43** (1988), no. 5.

7. _____, *Attractors of evolution equations*, "Nauka", Moscow, 1989. (Russian)

8. V. V. Chepyzhov, *On unbounded invariant sets and attractors of some semilinear equations and systems of parabolic type*, Uspekhi Mat. Nauk **42** (1987), no. 5, 219–220; English transl. in Russian Math. Surveys **42** (1987), no. 5, 167–168.

9. _____, *Unbounded attractors of some parabolic systems of differential equations and estimations of their dimension*, Dokl. Akad. Nauk SSSR **301** (1988), no. 4, 4–49; English transl. in Soviet Math. Dokl. **38** (1989).

10. _____, *Unbounded attractor of the system of semilinear partial differential equations of parabolic type*, Manuscript No. 4739-1387, deposited at VINITI (1987). (Russian)

11. J.-M. Ghidaglia and R. Temam, *Attractors for damped nonlinear hyperbolic equations*, J. Math. Pures Appl. **66** (1987), 273–319.

12. C. M. Dafermos, *Asymptotic behavior of solutions of evolution equations*, Nonlinear Evolution Equations, Academic Press, New York, 1978, pp. 103–123.

13. C. Foias, G. R. Sell, and R. Temam, *Inertial manifolds for nonlinear evolutionary equations*, J. Differential Equations **73** (1988), no. 2, 309–353.

14. C. Foias and J. C. Saut, *Asymptotic behavior, as $t \to +\infty$, of solutions of Navier-Stokes equations and nonlinear spectral manifolds*, Indiana Univ. Math. J. **33** (1984), 459–477.

15. C. Foias and R. Temam, *Some analytic and geometric properties of the solutions of the evolution Navier-Stokes equations*, J. Math. Pures Appl. **58** (1979), 339–368.

16. _____, *On the Hausdorff dimension of an attractor for the two-dimensional Navier-Stokes equations*, Phys. Lett. A **93** (1983), 431–434.

17. A. Yu. Goritskii, *Unbounded attractor of the hyperbolic equation*, Vestnik Moskov. Univ. Ser. I Mat. Mekh. **1988**, no. 3, 47–49; English transl. in Moscow Univ. Math. Bull. **44** (1988), no. 3.

18. _____, *Asymptotic of unbounded solutions of hyperbolic equations as $t \to +\infty$*, Vestnik Moskov. Univ. Ser. I, Mat. Mekh. **1990**, no. 2, 56–58; English transl. in Moscow Univ. Math. Bull. **46** (1990), no. 2.

19. A. Haraux, *Nonlinear evolution equations — global behavior of solutions*, Lecture Notes in Math., vol. 841, Springer-Verlag, Berlin and Heidelberg, 1981.

20. _____, *Two remarks on dissipative hyperbolic problems*, Nonlinear Partial Differential Equations and Their Applications, Res. Notes in Math., vol. 122, Pitman, Boston and London, 1985, pp. 161–179.

21. J. K. Hale, *Asymptotic behavior and dynamics in infinite dimensions*, Nonlinear Differential Equations, Res. Notes in Math., vol. 132, Pitman, Boston and London, 1985, pp. 1–42.

22. J. K. Hale, L. T. Magallaes, and W. M. Oliva, *An introduction to infinite-dimensional dynamical systems — geometric theory*, Applied Mathematical Sciences, vol. 47, Springer-Verlag, New York and Berlin, 1984.

23. D. Henry, *Geometrical theory of semilinear parabolic equations*, Lecture Notes in Math., vol. 840, Springer-Verlag, Berlin, Heidelberg, and New York, 1981.

24. M. Hirsch, *Differential topology*, Graduate Texts in Math., vol. 33, Springer-Verlag, New York, 1976.

25. O. A. Ladyzhenskaya, *About dynamical systems corresponding to Navier-Stokes equations*, Zap. Nauchn. Sem. Leningrad. Otdel. Mat. Inst. Steklov. (LOMI) **27** (1972), 91–115; English transl. in J. Soviet Math. **3** (1975), no. 4.

26. _____, *The finite-dimensionality of bounded invariant sets for the Navier-Stokes system and other dissipative systems*, Zap. Nauchn. Sem. Leningrad. Otdel. Mat. Inst. Steklov. (LOMI) **115** (1982), 137–155; English transl. in J. Soviet Math. **28** (1985), no. 5.

27. _____, *About attractors of nonlinear evolution problems with dissipation*, Zap. Nauchn. Sem. Leningrad. Otdel. Mat. Inst. Steklov. (LOMI) **152** (1986), 72–85; English transl. in J. Soviet Math. **40** (1988), no. 5.

28. _____, *Finding minimal global attractors for the Navier-Stokes equations and other partial differential equations*, Uspekhi Mat. Nauk **42** (1987), no. 6, 25–60; English transl. in Russian Math. Surveys **42** (1987).

29. J.-L. Lions, *Quelques méthodes de résolution des problèmes aux limites non-linéaires*, Études Math. Coll. Dirigée par P. Lelong, Dunod & Gauthier-Villars, Paris, 1969.

30. J.-L. Lions and E. Magenes, *Problèmes aux limites non-homogènes et applications*, (Travaux et Recherches Mathématiques, 17), vol. 1, Dunod, Paris, 1968.

31. P. Massat, *Limiting behavior for strongly damped nonlinear wave equations*, (Travaux et Recherches Mathématiques, 17), vol. 1, Dunod, Paris, 1968, pp. 334–349.

32. X. Mora, *Finite-dimensional attracting invariant manifolds for damped semilinear wave equations*, Contribution to Nonlinear Partial Differential Equations, Res. Notes in Math., vol. 122, Pitman, Boston and London, 1985, pp. 272–292.

33. X. Mora and J. Sola-Morales, *The singular limit dynamics of semilinear damped wave equations*, J. Differential Equations **78** (1987), no. 2, 262–307.

34. R. Temam, *Attractors for Navier-Stokes equations*, Nonlinear Partial Differential Equations and Their Applications, Res. Notes in Math., vol. 122, Pitman, Boston and London, 1985, pp. 272–292.

Translated by A. YU. GORITSKIĬ

Attractors of Singularly Perturbed Parabolic Equations, and Asymptotic Behavior of Their Elements

M. YU. SKVORTSOV AND M. I. VISHIK

Asymptotic expansions of solutions of singularly perturbed evolution equations on a finite interval $(0, T)$ were considered in many papers (see, for instance, [1, 2, 3]). So the solution $u^\varepsilon(t, x) \equiv u$ of the boundary value problem

$$\frac{\partial u}{\partial t} = -\varepsilon^2 \Delta^2 u + \Delta u - f(u) - g(x), \qquad x \in \Omega, \ \Omega \in \mathbb{R}^n, \tag{0.1}$$

$$u|_{\partial\Omega} = 0, \qquad \left.\frac{\partial u}{\partial \nu}\right|_{\partial\Omega} = 0, \tag{0.2}$$

$$u|_{t=0} = \varphi(x), \tag{0.3}$$

$(0 < \varepsilon \leqslant \varepsilon_0)$ for $0 \leqslant t \leqslant T$ can be written in the form

$$u(t, x) = w(t, x) + v(t, x', \rho/\varepsilon) + O(\varepsilon). \tag{0.4}$$

Here $w(t, x)$ is the solution of the limit (for $\varepsilon = 0$) boundary value problem:

$$\frac{\partial w}{\partial t} = \Delta w - f(w) - g(x), \qquad x \in \Omega, \tag{0.5}$$

$$w|_{\partial\Omega} = 0, \tag{0.6}$$

$$w|_{t=0} = \varphi(x), \tag{0.7}$$

and $v(t, x', \rho/\varepsilon)$ is the boundary layer function which can be represented in the form

$$v(t, x', \rho/\varepsilon) = a(t, x')e^{-\lambda\rho/\varepsilon} \tag{0.8}$$

near the boundary $\partial\Omega \times [0, T]$. Here (x', ρ) are the local coordinates: $x' \in \partial\Omega$, ρ is the distance from the point x to the boundary $\partial\Omega$ along the normal on $\partial\Omega$. Under certain conditions on $f(u)$ the expansion (0.4) can be extended with the aid of two iteration processes (see [1, 2]) to terms of orders $O(\varepsilon^k)$, and the remainder is of order ε^{k+1} in the proper norm.

1991 *Mathematics Subject Classification.* Primary 35B40, 35K22, 58F12.

©1992 American Mathematical Society
1051-8037/92 $1.00 + $.25 per page

In this work we study the structure of elements of the attractors $\mathfrak{A}^\varepsilon$ corresponding to the evolution equations (0.1), (0.2). A compact set $\mathfrak{A}^\varepsilon$ is the maximal attractor of a semigroup $\{S_t(\varepsilon)\}$ if for any bounded set B in the phase metric space the distance between the set $S_t(\varepsilon)B$ and $\mathfrak{A}^\varepsilon$ tends to zero as $t \to +\infty$ (attractive condition) and $\mathfrak{A}^\varepsilon$ is invariant: $S_t(\varepsilon)\mathfrak{A}^\varepsilon = \mathfrak{A}^\varepsilon$ for all $t \geq 0$. For any element $u \in \mathfrak{A}^\varepsilon$ the main term of the asymptotics is constructed. We restrict ourselves to dimension $n = 3$ for brevity. Under certain conditions on $f(u)$ it is proved that for any function $u = u(x) \in \mathfrak{A}^\varepsilon$ the following asymptotic representation, similar to (0.4)

$$u = (u_0 + v_0 - \varepsilon c_0) + \varepsilon(u_1 + v_1 - \varepsilon c_1) + r, \tag{0.9}$$

holds, where u_0 and u_1 are bounded in $H_3(\Omega)$ uniformly for ε, $0 < \varepsilon \leq \varepsilon_0$, and for $u \in \mathfrak{A}^\varepsilon$, v_0 and v_1 are boundary layer terms, which are constructed from u_0 and u_1, while c_0 and c_1 are sufficiently smooth functions, bounded in the proper norms uniformly for ε and for $u \in \mathfrak{A}^\varepsilon$. The remainder r satisfies the following estimate:

$$\|r\|_{H_3(\Omega)} + \varepsilon^{-1}\|r\|_{H_2(\Omega)} + \varepsilon^{-2}\|r\|_{H_1(\Omega)} \leq M, \tag{0.10}$$

where M does not depend on ε and on $u \in \mathfrak{A}^\varepsilon$. Thus it is proved that the boundary layer phenomenon which holds for solutions $u(t, x)$ of the problem (0.1), (0.2), (0.3) on any finite interval $[0, T]$ is inherited by the elements of the attractor $\mathfrak{A}^\varepsilon$ which is an ω-limit set for $S_t(\varepsilon)B_0$, where B_0 is the absorbing set for the semigroup $\{S_t(\varepsilon)\}$ (see [4]).

It should be noted that the boundedness, uniform in ε, of attractors $\mathfrak{A}^\varepsilon$ corresponding to the problem (0.1), (0.2) (for $n = 3$) in $H_{3/2}(\Omega)$ was established in [5–7]:

$$\|\mathfrak{A}^\varepsilon\|_{3/2} \leq M, \tag{0.11}$$

where M does not depend of ε, and the index $3/2$ cannot be increased. Moreover, it was proved that

$$\mathrm{dist}_{H_{3/2-\delta}}(\mathfrak{A}^\varepsilon, \mathfrak{A}^0) \xrightarrow[\varepsilon \to 0]{} 0 \quad \forall \delta > 0, \tag{0.12}$$

where $\mathfrak{A}^0$ is the attractor of the degenerate problem (0.5), (0.6) and in (0.12) δ cannot equal zero. (An example in [6] shows that the distance between the equilibrium points $z_\varepsilon(x)$ of $\{S_t(\varepsilon)\}$ (which are the solutions of a linear ordinary differential equation) and the equilibrium point $z_0(x)$ of the limit semigroup $\{S_t(0)\}$ does not tend to zero as $\varepsilon \to 0$ in $H_{3/2}(\Omega)$. In this case the attractor consists of only one point $z_\varepsilon(x)$, therefore assertion (0.12) is wrong when $\delta = 0$.)

Let us briefly describe the contents of this work. In §1 the problem of asymptotic expansion of elements of the attractors is given more precisely and the main theorems are formulated. In §2 some a priori estimates for the solution of (0.1)–(0.3) are given and used to prove inequality (0.10). Thereby the validity of the asymptotic expansion (0.9) is established. In §3 the proofs of estimates formulated in §2 are given.

§1. Definitions of the asymptotic expansion terms, and basic theorems

We shall be concerned with the model equation (0.1) with boundary conditions (0.2) and initial data (0.3) in the bounded domain Ω in $\mathbb{R}^n$. Here ε is a small parameter, $0 < \varepsilon \leq \varepsilon_0$. Assume for simplicity that $n = 3$ and Ω is the cylindrical domain: $\Omega = T_x^2 \times \{0 < y < 1\}$, where T^2 is the two-dimensional torus whose points are denoted by x ($x = (x_1, x_2)$). It is not difficult to extend our results to any n and to any domain Ω with sufficiently smooth boundary. Let $f(u)$ satisfy the following conditions:

$$f(u)u \geq -C, \tag{1.1}$$

$$f'(u) \geq -C, \qquad |f''(u)| \leq C(|u|+1), \tag{1.2}$$

$$|f^{(l)}(u)| \leq C, \qquad 3 \leq l \leq k \quad (k \geq 7). \tag{1.3}$$

Assume also that

$$-C_1 \leq F(u) \equiv \int_0^u f(\xi)\,d\xi \leq C_2(f(u)u + u^2 + 1). \tag{1.4}$$

It is easy to establish by the methods described, for instance, in [4, 8], that there exists a unique solution $u(t)$ of (0.1)–(0.3) in the corresponding functional spaces. Hence, to the problem (0.1)–(0.3) corresponds the semigroup $\{S_t(\varepsilon)\}$, $0 < \varepsilon \leq \varepsilon_0$,

$$S_t(\varepsilon): H \to H \quad \forall t > 0, \qquad H = L_2(\Omega),$$

defined by $S_t(\varepsilon)\varphi = u(t)$. It is easy to show (see [4]) that for any $\varepsilon > 0$ the semigroup $\{S_t(\varepsilon)\}$ has an (H, H)-attractor $\mathfrak{A}^\varepsilon$, i.e., a compact set in H that satisfies the invariance condition $(S_t(\varepsilon)\mathfrak{A}^\varepsilon = \mathfrak{A}^\varepsilon \ \forall t \geq 0)$ and the attractive condition ($\operatorname{dist}_H(S_t B, \mathfrak{A}^\varepsilon) \to 0$ as $t \to +\infty$ for any bounded set B in H). Moreover, as it is shown in [5, 6], these attractors are uniformly bounded (for $0 < \varepsilon \leq \varepsilon_0$) in $H_{3/2}(\Omega)$ (see (0.11)). For $\varepsilon = 0$, the problem (0.1), (0.2), (0.3) reduces into the limit problem (0.5), (0.6), (0.7), in which only one boundary condition is given. This problem also has an (H, H)-attractor $\mathfrak{A}^0$ and $\mathfrak{A}^\varepsilon \to \mathfrak{A}^0$ in $H_{3/2-\delta}(\Omega)$ $\forall \delta > 0$ as $\varepsilon \to 0$ (see (0.12)).

The key task of this paper is to find the main term of the asymptotics in ε of elements $u \in \mathfrak{A}^\varepsilon$. As will be shown below, the expansion (0.9) is valid for $u \in \mathfrak{A}^\varepsilon$, where $u_0 = u_0(x, y; \varepsilon, u)$, $u_1 = u_1(x, y; \varepsilon, u)$ are uniformly bounded for ε, $0 < \varepsilon \leq \varepsilon_0$, and $u \in \mathfrak{A}^\varepsilon$ in $H_3(\Omega)$, v_0 and v_1 are the boundary layer functions, c_0 and c_1 are sufficiently smooth functions and $r(\varepsilon)$ is the remainder satisfying the estimates (0.10).

At first we define more precisely each term in (0.9) and formulate the main theorem. Let us take any element

$$u = u(x, y) \in \mathfrak{A}^\varepsilon \qquad (x \in T^2,\ 0 \leq y \leq 1)$$

and denote by $u(t) = u(t, x, y)$, $t \in \mathbb{R}$, the trajectory of $\{S_t(\varepsilon)\}$ passing through u when $t = 1$: $u(1) = u$; more explicitly

$$u(1, x, y) = u(x, y) \quad \forall (x, y) \in \Omega.$$

The existence of such a trajectory $u(t)$ ($t \in \mathbb{R}$) follows from properties of the attractor $\mathfrak{A}^\varepsilon$ (see, for instance, [4]). Below we shall consider only the part of this trajectory which corresponds to the interval $0 \leqslant t \leqslant 1$ and $u(0) \in \mathfrak{A}^\varepsilon$. Since $u(t)$ is the trajectory of the semigroup $\{S_t(\varepsilon)\}$ which lies on the attractor $\mathfrak{A}^\varepsilon$, it satisfies the equation (0.1). Therefore we have:

$$L_\varepsilon u(1) \equiv -\varepsilon^2 \Delta^2 u(1) + \Delta u(1) = \partial_t u(1) + f(u(1)) + g \equiv h, \quad (1.5)$$

$h = h(x, y, \varepsilon)$. In order to obtain a first approximation of the function u, we consider the solution u_0 of the following boundary value problem:

$$\Delta u_0 = h \quad \text{(where h is the right-hand side of (1.5))}, \quad (1.6)$$

$$u_0|_{\partial\Omega} = 0. \quad (1.7)$$

Obviously this problem has a unique solution and, as will be shown, this solution $u_0 = u_0(x, y; \varepsilon, u)$ is uniformly bounded for ε and $u \in \mathfrak{A}^\varepsilon$ in $H_3(\Omega)$:

$$\|u_0\|_{H_3(\Omega)} \leqslant M \quad (1.8)$$

(and its derivatives w.r.t. the variables x are uniformly bounded in $H_{k+1}(\Omega)$). But this approximation u_0 for u is not valid in the neighborhood of the boundary $\partial\Omega$, since the second boundary condition (0.2) for

$$\left.\frac{\partial u_0}{\partial \nu}\right|_{\partial\Omega} \equiv \left.\frac{\partial u_0}{\partial y}\right|_{y=0, y=1}$$

is not satisfied. A better approximation of u is to be obtained by adding to u_0 a boundary layer term v_0 (see [1, 2]). In the neighborhood of $\Gamma_0 = \partial\Omega \cap \{y = 0\}$ the function v_0 has the form:

$$\tilde{v}_0(x, y; \varepsilon) = \varepsilon \tilde{c}_0(x) e^{-y/\varepsilon} \quad (1.9)$$

(compare with (0.8)). It should be noted that $\tilde{v}_0$ satisfies the differential equation

$$-\varepsilon^2 \frac{\partial^4 \tilde{v}_0}{\partial y^4} + \frac{\partial^2 \tilde{v}_0}{\partial y^2} = 0$$

and $|\tilde{v}_0(x, y; \varepsilon)|$ exponentially decreases for increasing values of y and for decreasing values of ε ($\varepsilon > 0$). The function $\tilde{c}_0(x)$ is determined so that the second boundary condition (0.2) is satisfied

$$\left.\frac{\partial (u_0 + \tilde{v}_0)}{\partial y}\right|_{\Gamma_0} = 0,$$

i.e.,

$$\left.\frac{\partial \tilde{v}_0}{\partial y}\right|_{y=0} = -\tilde{c}_0(x) = -\left.\frac{\partial u_0}{\partial y}\right|_{y=0}. \quad (1.10)$$

As will be shown below, the function $\tilde{c}_0(\chi)$ satisfies the following estimate:

$$\|\tilde{c}_0(x)\|_{H_{(k+1)/2}(\partial\Omega)} \leq M, \tag{1.11}$$

where M does not depend on ε and $u \in \mathfrak{A}^\varepsilon$. Similarly, the function $\tilde{v}_0$ is determined in the neighborhood $\Gamma_1 = \partial\Omega \cap \{y = 1\}$.

In order to express the boundary layer term as a function defined in the entire domain Ω, we multiply $\tilde{v}_0$ by an infinitely differentiable smoothing function $\chi(y)$:

$$\chi(y) = \begin{cases} 1, & \text{if } y \in [0, \eta] \cup [1 - \eta, 1], \\ 0, & \text{if } y \in [2\eta, 1 - 2\eta], \end{cases} \tag{1.12}$$

where η is sufficiently small. In this way we define the second term in (0.9):

$$v_0 = \chi(y)\tilde{v}_0(x, y; \varepsilon).$$

Now the function $u_0 + v_0$ satisfies (by (1.10)) the second boundary condition (0.2), but does not satisfy the first one, since

$$(u_0 + v_0)|_{\Gamma_0} = \tilde{v}_0|_{\Gamma_0} = \varepsilon\tilde{c}_0(x),$$

where $\tilde{c}_0(x)$ is defined in (1.10). A similar relation holds on Γ_1 when we replace $\tilde{c}_0(x)$ by $\tilde{c}_0^1(x)$. Let $c_0(x, y)$ denote the function which is equal to $\chi(y)\tilde{c}_0(x)$ in the 2η-neighborhood of Γ_0, equal to $\chi(y)\tilde{c}_0^1(x)$ in the 2η-neighborhood of Γ_1 and equal to zero for $2\eta < y < 1 - 2\eta$.

Thus the function

$$u^0 \equiv u_0 + v_0 - \varepsilon c_0$$

satisfies the boundary condition (0.2) and roughly satisfies the equation (1.5) up to order ε. Therefore it may be regarded as the first approximation for u. However, it turns out that this is not enough for obtaining the estimates (0.10) for the remainder $r(\varepsilon)$. Therefore we add to the function u^0 the following terms:

$$\varepsilon u^1 \equiv \varepsilon(u_1 + v_1 - \varepsilon c_1),$$

so that the function $u^0 + \varepsilon u^1$ satisfies equation (1.5) more exactly. Substituting this function into (1.5), using (1.6), and setting the coefficient of ε equal to zero (leaving the boundary layer out of our consideration), we get the differential equation:

$$\Delta u_1 = \Delta c_0. \tag{1.13}$$

We supply this equation with the first of the boundary conditions (0.2):

$$u_1|_{\partial\Omega} = 0.$$

Hence, we have defined the function $u_1 = u_1(x, y; \varepsilon, u)$. It follows from the equation (1.13) that estimates similar to (1.11) are valid for u_1:

$$\|u_1(x, y; \varepsilon, u)\|_{H_{(k+1)/2}(\Omega)} \leq M, \tag{1.14}$$

and M does not depend on ε and $u \in \mathfrak{A}^\varepsilon$. In order to satisfy the second of the boundary conditions (0.2), we add to the function $u^0 + \varepsilon u_1$ a boundary layer function similar to (1.9) (in the neighborhood of Γ_1):

$$\varepsilon \tilde{v}_1 = \varepsilon^2 \tilde{c}_1(x) e^{-y/\varepsilon}.$$

As in (1.10), we obtain:

$$\left.\frac{\partial \tilde{v}_1}{\partial y}\right|_{y=0} = -\tilde{c}_1(x) = -\left.\frac{\partial u_1}{\partial y}\right|_{y=0}. \tag{1.15}$$

Then, as above, we set $v_1 = \chi(y)\tilde{v}_1$, and to satisfy the first boundary condition (0.2), add the function $-\varepsilon^2 c_1(x, y)$. As will be shown in further sections, the following estimate holds:

$$\varepsilon \|c_1\|_{H_{(5k-2)/8}(\Omega)} + \|c_1\|_{H_{(k-2)/2}(\Omega)} \leq M, \tag{1.16}$$

where M does not depend on ε and $u \in \mathfrak{A}^\varepsilon$. Thus all the terms in the asymptotic representation (0.9) have been determined.

Now we formulate our main result:

THEOREM 1. *The remainder $r(x, y; \varepsilon)$ satisfies the estimate (0.10), in which M does not depend on $u \in \mathfrak{A}^\varepsilon$ and ε, $0 < \varepsilon \leq \varepsilon_0$.*

The proof will be given in the next section. We shall now establish some corollaries of this theorem.

THEOREM 2. *Let*

$$\Omega_\gamma = \{(x, y) \in \Omega : \gamma < y < 1 - \gamma\}.$$

Then for any $u \in \mathfrak{A}^\varepsilon$ we have

$$\|u\|_{H_3(\Omega_\gamma)} \leq M, \tag{1.17}$$

where $M = M(\gamma)$ does not depend on $u \in \mathfrak{A}^\varepsilon$ and ε, $0 < \varepsilon \leq \varepsilon_0$.

PROOF. It follows from the expansion (0.9) that

$$\begin{aligned}\|u\|_{H_3(\Omega_\gamma)} &\leq \|u_0\|_{H_3(\Omega_\gamma)} + \|v_0\|_{H_3(\Omega_\gamma)} + \varepsilon\|c_0\|_{H_3(\Omega_\gamma)} \\ &+ \varepsilon(\|u_1\|_{H_3(\Omega_\gamma)} + \|v_1\|_{H_3(\Omega_\gamma)} + \|c_1\|_{H_3(\Omega_\gamma)}) + \|r(\varepsilon)\|_{H_3(\Omega_\gamma)}.\end{aligned} \tag{1.18}$$

The first, third, fourth, and sixth terms on the right-hand side of (1.18) are bounded according to (1.8), (1.11), (1.14) and (1.16). From (1.9) and (1.11), we obtain

$$\|v_0\|_{H_3(\Omega_\gamma)} \leq M\varepsilon \|e^{-y/\varepsilon}\|_{H_3((\gamma, 1-\gamma))} \leq M_1.$$

Similarly, the boundedness of $\varepsilon\|c_1\|_{H_3(\Omega)}$ implies

$$\|v_1\|_{H_3(\Omega_\gamma)} \leq M_2.$$

We finally note that Theorem 1 implies that the last term in (1.18) is also bounded.

REMARK 1. It follows from Theorem 2 that elements of the attractors $\mathfrak{A}^\varepsilon$ are bounded uniformly for $u \in \mathfrak{A}^\varepsilon$ and for ε in $H_3(\Omega_\gamma)$, where $\Omega_\gamma \subset \Omega$ is any interior subdomain, while we have already seen that in the whole domain Ω these elements are bounded uniformly only in $H_{3/2}(\Omega)$ (see (0.11)), and the index $3/2$ cannot be increased.

REMARK 2. It is easily shown (see [4, 6]) that for $\varepsilon = 0$

$$\|\mathfrak{A}^0\|_{H_3(\Omega)} \leqslant M.$$

THEOREM 3. *For any* $\gamma > 0, \delta > 0$

$$\operatorname{dist}_{H_{3-\delta}(\Omega_\gamma)}(\mathfrak{A}^\varepsilon, \mathfrak{A}^0) \xrightarrow[\varepsilon \to 0]{} 0. \tag{1.19}$$

PROOF. At first we remark that

$$\operatorname{dist}_H(\mathfrak{A}^\varepsilon, \mathfrak{A}^0) \xrightarrow[\varepsilon \to 0]{} 0 \tag{1.20}$$

(where $H = L_2(\Omega)$). Indeed, let $\{S_t(\varepsilon)\}$ be the semigroup corresponding to the boundary value problem (0.1), (0.2), (0.3) for $0 < \varepsilon \leqslant \varepsilon_0$ and to the problem (0.5), (0.6), (0.7) for $\varepsilon = 0$. Then on the set

$$X = B_0 \times \Lambda_0 \subset H \times \Lambda_0, \quad \text{where } \Lambda_0 = [0, \varepsilon_0],$$

the semigroup $\{S_t = (S_t(\varepsilon), \varepsilon)\}$ satisfies all the assumptions of Theorem 1 from the book [4, p. 226]: this semigroup is continuous on X in $H \times \Lambda_0$ and it has an H-absorbing (uniformly in $\varepsilon \in \Lambda_0$) set B_0, compact in H (as shown in [6]). Hence, according to Proposition 3 of [4, p. 227], the assertion (1.20) is valid. Since the attractors $\mathfrak{A}^\varepsilon$ are bounded uniformly in $H_3(\Omega_\gamma)$ as shown in Theorem 2, there exists (uniformly in $\varepsilon \in \Lambda_0$) absorbing set B_1, compact in $H_{3-\delta}(\Omega_\gamma)$, $\delta > 0$ (it consists of the functions $u \in \mathfrak{A}^\varepsilon$ restricted to Ω_γ). Then the assertion (1.9) follows from Remark 1 of the book [4, p. 228].

REMARK 3. It was shown in [5, 6] that

$$\operatorname{dist}_{H_{3/2-\delta}(\Omega)}(\mathfrak{A}^\varepsilon, \mathfrak{A}^0) \xrightarrow[\varepsilon \to 0]{} 0 \quad \forall \delta > 0.$$

Theorem 3 implies that $H_{3/2-\delta}(\Omega)$ may be replaced by $H_{3-\delta}(\Omega_\gamma)$ ($\delta > 0$, $\gamma > 0$). This fact shows that the functions $u \in \mathfrak{A}^\varepsilon$ have boundary layer properties near $\partial\Omega$.

REMARK 4. Taking into account the fact that the attractors $\mathfrak{A}^\varepsilon$ are uniformly (in ε) bounded in $H_{3/2}(\Omega)$ (see (0.11)), we obtain that any set

$$\{u_\varepsilon : u_\varepsilon \in \mathfrak{A}^\varepsilon, \varepsilon \to 0\}$$

is compact in H and therefore we can choose a convergent subsequence from it:

$$u_{\varepsilon_m} \to w \quad \text{in } H \quad \text{as } \varepsilon_m \to 0. \tag{1.21}$$

But $\mathfrak{A}^{\varepsilon_m} \to \mathfrak{A}^0$ as $\varepsilon_m \to 0$, hence $w = \lim_{\varepsilon_m \to 0} u_{\varepsilon_m}$ is an element of $\mathfrak{A}^0$.

THEOREM 4. *Let* (1.21) *be valid. Then:*
a) *for any* $\delta > 0$, $\gamma > 0$,

$$u_{\varepsilon_m} \to w \quad \text{in } H_{3-\delta}(\Omega_\gamma) \quad \text{as } \varepsilon_m \to 0; \tag{1.22}$$

b) *in the asymptotic representation for* u_{ε_m}

$$u_{\varepsilon_m} = (u_{0m} + v_{0m} - \varepsilon c_{0m}) + \varepsilon(u_{1m} + v_{1m} - \varepsilon c_{1m}) + r(\varepsilon_m) \tag{1.23}$$

the following assertions concerning u_{0m} *and* c_{0m} *hold*:

$$u_{0m} \to w \quad \text{in } H_{3-\delta}(\Omega), \quad \delta > 0, \tag{1.24}$$

$$c_{0m} \to -\left.\frac{\partial w}{\partial y}\right|_{y=0} \quad \text{in } H_{(k+1)/2-\delta_1}(\Omega), \quad \delta_1 > 0, \text{ near } \Gamma_0, \tag{1.25}$$

and a similar assertion for c_{0m} *is valid in a neighborhood of* Γ_1.

PROOF. Theorem 2 implies that the set $\{u_{\varepsilon_m}\}$ is compact in $H_{3-\delta}(\Omega_\gamma)$ when $\delta > 0$. Then assertion (1.22) follows from (1.21).

Taking into account the expression (1.9) for the boundary layer term v_{0m} and using the estimate (1.11), we obtain

$$\|v_{0m}\|_{H_{3/2-\delta}(\Omega)} \to 0, \quad \varepsilon_m \|c_{0m}\|_{H_{(k+1)/2}(\Omega)} \to 0 \quad \text{as } \varepsilon_m \to 0.$$

Similarly, it follows from (1.16) that

$$\varepsilon_m \|v_{1m}\|_{H_{5/2-\delta}(\Omega)} \to 0, \quad \varepsilon_m^2 \|c_{1m}\|_{H_{(5k-2)/8}(\Omega)} \to 0 \quad \text{as } \varepsilon_m \to 0.$$

From the estimate (1.14) we get

$$\varepsilon_m \|u_{1m}\|_{H_{(k+1)/2}(\Omega)} \to 0 \quad \text{as } \varepsilon_m \to 0,$$

and inequality (0.10) implies

$$\|r(\varepsilon_m)\|_{H_{3-\delta}(\Omega)} \to 0 \quad \text{when } \varepsilon_m \to 0.$$

Hence, from (1.21) and (1.23), we see that

$$\lim_{\varepsilon_m \to 0} u_{0m} = \lim_{\varepsilon_m \to 0} u_{\varepsilon_m} = w,$$

where the limits are taken, for instance, in the metric of $H_{3/2-\delta}(\Omega)$. Since the sequence $\{u_{0m}\}$ is uniformly bounded in $H_3(\Omega)$, it is compact in $H_{3-\delta}(\Omega)$ $\forall \delta > 0$, and we can choose a subsequence converging to the same limit w in $H_{3-\delta}(\Omega)$. Since this assertion is valid for any subsequence, (1.24) is also valid.

It now follows from (1.24) that

$$\left.\frac{\partial u_{0m}}{\partial y}\right|_{y=0} \to \left.\frac{\partial w}{\partial y}\right|_{y=0}, \tag{1.26}$$

for instance, in the metric of $H_{3/2-\delta}(\Omega)$. Taking into account the fact that in a neighborhood of Γ_0

$$c_{0m} = \left.\frac{\partial u_{0m}}{\partial y}\right|_{y=0},$$

(see (1.10)) and the functions c_{0m} are uniformly bounded in $H_{(k+1)/2}(\Omega)$ (see (1.11)), we deduce (1.25) from (1.26). We consider the properties of c_{0m} in a neighborhood of Γ_1 similarly.

REMARK 5. The assertions (1.24) and (1.25) show that the expansion (0.9) and the asymptotic expansion of the solution of the stationary differential equation obtained by the Lyusternik-Vishik procedure are close in a certain sense.

§2. Proof of Theorem 1

We turn now to the proof of the main Theorem 1. At first we shall formulate some estimates for the trajectories of the problem (0.1), (0.2), (0.3). We denote the norms in the Sobolev spaces $H_s(\Omega)$ by $\|\cdot\|_s$, in $H = L_2(\Omega)$ by $\|\cdot\|$.

PROPOSITION 1. *Let the function $f(u)$ satisfy condition (1.1) and $g \in L_2(\Omega)$. Then the following estimate for the solution $u(t)$ of the problem (0.1)–(0.3) holds:*

$$\|u(t)\|^2 + \int_0^t \left(\|u(\tau)\|_1^2 + \varepsilon^2 \|u(\tau)\|_2^2\right) d\tau \leqslant C. \tag{2.1}$$

If, furthermore, condition (1.4) is satisfied, then the following estimate holds:

$$\int_0^t \tau \|u_t\|^2 d\tau + \varepsilon^2 t \|u(t)\|_2^2 + t \|u(t)\|_1^2 \leqslant C. \tag{2.2}$$

In the inequalities (2.1) and (2.2) we have $t \in [0, T]$ and the constants C depend only on $\|u(0)\|$ and T.

PROPOSITION 2. *Let the function $f(u)$ satisfy (1.1), (1.2), and (1.4) and $g \in L_2(\Omega)$. Then the following estimate holds:*

$$\int_0^t \tau^3 \|u_{tt}\|^2 d\tau + \varepsilon^2 t^3 \|u_t(t)\|_2^2 + t^3 \|u_t(t)\|_1^2 \leqslant C, \tag{2.3}$$

where $t \in [0, T]$ and C depends only on $\|u(0)\|$ and T.

PROPOSITION 3. *Let $f(u)$ satisfy conditions (1.1)–(1.4) and the function $g(x)$ and its derivatives $\partial^j/\partial x_i^j$ ($i = 1, 2$; $j = 1, 2, \ldots, k-2$) belong to $H_2(\Omega)$. Denote by $p_l(t)$ the derivative*

$$\frac{\partial^l u(t, x, y)}{\partial x_i^l}, \qquad i = 1 \text{ or } 2.$$

Then the following estimates uniform in ε, $0 \leqslant \varepsilon \leqslant \varepsilon_0$, are valid:

$$\varepsilon^{5/2}\|p_l(1)\|_1 + \varepsilon^{3/2}\|p_l(1)\|_3 + \varepsilon^{1/2}\|p_l(1)\|_2 + \|p_l(1)\|_{3/2} \leqslant C, \qquad (2.4)$$

$$\varepsilon\|\partial_t p_l(1)\|_1 + \|\partial_t p_l(1)\|_1 \leqslant C, \qquad (2.5)$$

where $l = 1, 2, \ldots, k-2$ and the constants C depend only on $\|u(0)\|$.

Propositions 1, 2, and 3 will be proved in §3.

Denote by $W_2^{(l_1, l_2, l_3)}(\Omega)$ the nonisotropic functional space (see [9]) with norm

$$\|u\|_{W_2^{\vec{l}}} = \|u\| + \sum_{i=1}^{3} \|\mathscr{D}_i^{l_i} u\|, \qquad \vec{l} = (l_1, l_2, l_3),$$

where

$$\mathscr{D}_1 = \frac{\partial}{\partial x_1}, \qquad \mathscr{D}_2 = \frac{\partial}{\partial x_2}, \qquad \mathscr{D}_3 = \frac{\partial}{\partial y}.$$

The following embedding theorems are valid (S. M. Nikol'skiĭ [9, 10]):

(1) *If a function u belongs to $W_2^{\vec{l}}(\mathbb{R}^n)$, then its partial derivative satisfies*

$$\mathscr{D}^{\vec{k}} u \in W_2^{\varkappa \vec{l}}(\mathbb{R}^n), \qquad (2.6)$$

where $\varkappa = 1 - \sum_{i=1}^{n} k_j/l_j > 0$;

(2) *for $\vec{l} = (l_1, \ldots, l_n)$, $\vec{l}^m = (l_1, \ldots, l_m, 0, \ldots, 0)$,*

$$W_2^{\vec{l}}(\mathbb{R}^n) \hookrightarrow W_2^{\varkappa \vec{l}^m}(\mathbb{R}^n), \qquad (2.7)$$

where

$$\varkappa = 1 - \frac{1}{2}\sum_{j=m+1}^{n} \frac{1}{l_j} > 0, \qquad m < n.$$

We shall apply these theorems to the terms in the asymptotic expansion (0.9).

PROPOSITION 4. *Under the assumptions of Proposition 3, the following uniform (in ε) estimates for the functions u_0, u_1, c_0, c_1 in (0.9) hold:*

$$\varepsilon\|u_0\|_{W_2^{(k+2,4)}} + \|u_0\|_{W_2^{(k+1,3)}} \leqslant C, \qquad (2.8)$$

$$\varepsilon\|u_1\|_{5(k+2)/8} + \|u_1\|_{(k+1)/2} \leqslant C, \qquad (2.9)$$

$$\varepsilon\|c_0\|_{W_2^{(5(k+2)/8, \infty)}} + \|c_0\|_{W_2^{((k+1)/2, \infty)}} \leqslant C, \qquad (2.10)$$

$$\varepsilon\|c_1\|_{W_2^{(5(k-2)/8, \infty)}} + \|c_1\|_{W_2^{((k-1)/2, \infty)}} \leqslant C \qquad (2.11)$$

(here the first indices show the orders of the derivatives with respect to x_1 and x_2 and the second ones show the orders of the derivatives with respect to y).

PROOF. We consider the boundary value problem (1.6), (1.7) for u_0:

$$\Delta u_0 = \partial_t u(1) + f(u(1)) + g \equiv h(\varepsilon), \qquad (1.6')$$

$$u_0|_{\partial\Omega} = 0. \qquad (1.7')$$

The inequalities (2.4) and (2.5) imply the following estimate for the right-hand side $h(\varepsilon)$:
$$\varepsilon \|h\|_{W_2^{(k,2)}} + \|h\|_{W_2^{(k-1,1)}} \leq C. \qquad (2.12)$$
Indeed, this estimate for the function $\partial_t u(1)$ follows immediately from (2.5), where $l = k - 2$. Further, since
$$\mathscr{D}_{x_i}^l f(u) = f^{(l)}(u) p_1^l + a_{l-1} f^{(l-1)}(u) p_1^{l-2} p_2 + \cdots + f'(u) p_l,$$
the conditions (1.2), (1.3) on the derivatives $f^{(m)}(u)$ and the estimates (2.4) imply estimate (2.12) for $f(u(1))$. Here we use the Hölder inequality for estimating derivatives $\mathscr{D}_{x_i}^k f(u(1))$ and $\mathscr{D}_{x_i}^{k-1} f(u(1))$ and also the Sobolev embedding theorems
$$\begin{aligned} H_{3/2}(\Omega) &\subset L_p(\Omega) \quad \forall p, \\ H_{1/2}(\Omega) &\subset L_3(\Omega), \end{aligned} \qquad (2.13)$$
which are valid for $n = 3$. It follows from the estimate (2.12) that the function u_0, as the solution of the elliptic boundary value problem (1.6), (1.7), satisfies inequality (2.8).

We now consider the functions $c_0(x, y)$ and $c_1(x, y)$. Observe first that their infinite differentiability with respect to y follows from their construction. Since $c_0(x, y) \equiv \tilde{c}_0(x)$ and $c_1(x, y) \equiv \tilde{c}_1(x)$ in a neighborhood of the boundary Γ_0, where $\tilde{c}_0(x)$ and $\tilde{c}_1(x)$ were defined in (1.10) and (1.15), respectively, c_0 and c_1 are defined in a neighborhood of Γ_1 analogously and these functions are equal to zero in the interior subdomain $\Omega_{2\eta}$, then this is enough to prove inequalities (2.10) and (2.11) only for $\tilde{c}_0(x)$ and $\tilde{c}_1(x)$.

We shall estimate
$$\tilde{c}_0(x) \equiv \left. \frac{\partial u_0}{\partial y} \right|_{y=0},$$
applying (2.6) to the function u_0. Putting in (2.6)
$$\vec{k} = (0, 0, 1), \quad \vec{l}_1 = (k+2, k+2, 4), \quad \varkappa_1 = 3/4,$$
$$\vec{l}_2 = (k+1, k+1, 3), \quad \varkappa = 2/3,$$
we get, using the estimates (2.8) for u_0:
$$\varepsilon \left\| \frac{\partial u_0}{\partial y} \right\|_{W_2^{(3(k+2)/4, 3)}} + \left\| \frac{\partial u_0}{\partial y} \right\|_{W_2^{(2(k+2)/3, 2)}} \leq C. \qquad (2.14)$$

We apply now the embedding theorem (2.7) to the function $\partial u_0/\partial y$. Putting in (2.7)
$$\vec{l}_1 = (\tfrac{3}{4}(k+2), \tfrac{3}{4}(k+2), 3),$$
$$\varkappa_1 = 1 - \tfrac{1}{2} \cdot \tfrac{1}{3} = \tfrac{5}{6}, \quad \varkappa_1 \vec{l}_1^m = (\tfrac{5}{8}(k+2), \tfrac{5}{8}(k+2), 0),$$
$$\vec{l}_2 = (\tfrac{2}{3}(k+1), \tfrac{2}{3}(k+1), 2),$$
$$\varkappa_2 = 1 - \tfrac{1}{2} \cdot \tfrac{1}{2} = \tfrac{3}{4}, \quad \varkappa_2 \vec{l}_1^m = (\tfrac{1}{2}(k+1), \tfrac{1}{2}(k+1), 0),$$

we get from (2.14) the following estimate for $\tilde{c}_0(x)$:

$$\varepsilon\|\tilde{c}_0(x)\|_{H_{5(k+2)/8}(\Gamma_0)} + \|\tilde{c}_0(x)\|_{H_{(k+1)/2}(\Gamma_0)} \leq C.$$

This inequality implies (2.1).

Equation (1.13) and inequality (2.10) imply the estimate (2.9) for u_1, from which, in turn, the estimate (2.11) for $c_1(x, y)$ follows (since

$$c_1(x, y) \equiv \tilde{c}_1(x) = \left.\frac{\partial u_1}{\partial y}\right|_{y=0},$$

in a neighborhood of Γ_0, and similarly, in a neighborhood of Γ_1).

REMARK 6. If $k = 7$ in (1.3), then from the estimate (2.11), which in this case has the form

$$\varepsilon\|c_1\|_{33/8} + \|c_1\|_{5/2} \leq C,$$

and from the interpolation inequality

$$\|u\|_{W_p^s} \leq C\|u\|_{W_p^{s_0}}^{1-\theta}\|u\|_{W_p^{s_1}}^{\theta}, \qquad s = (1-\theta)s_0 + \theta s_1,$$

in which we put

$$p = 2, \quad s = 4, \quad s_0 = 5/2, \quad s_1 = 33/8, \quad \theta = 12/13,$$

we get

$$\varepsilon^{12/13}\|c_1\|_4 + \|c_1\|_{5/2} \leq C_1. \tag{2.15}$$

PROOF OF THEOREM 1. Since the functions u, $u^0 = u_0 + v_0 - \varepsilon c_0$ and $u^1 = u_1 + v_1 - \varepsilon c_1$ satisfy the boundary conditions (0.2), we note that the remainder $r(\varepsilon)$ also satisfies homogeneous boundary conditions:

$$r|_{\partial\Omega} = \left.\frac{\partial r}{\partial y}\right|_{\partial\Omega} = 0.$$

Consider the expression

$$\begin{aligned} L_\varepsilon r &\equiv -\varepsilon^2\Delta^2 r + \Delta r \\ &= L_\varepsilon(u - (u_0 + v_0 - \varepsilon c_0) - \varepsilon(u_1 + v_1 - \varepsilon c_1)) \\ &= h + \varepsilon^2\Delta^2 u_0 - \Delta u_0 - L_\varepsilon v_0 + \varepsilon(\varepsilon^2\Delta^2 u_1 - \Delta u_1) - \varepsilon L_\varepsilon v_1 \\ &\quad - \varepsilon(\varepsilon^2\Delta^2 c_0 - \Delta c_0) - \varepsilon^2(\varepsilon^2\Delta^2 c_1 - \Delta c_1) \\ &= \varepsilon^2\Delta^2 u_0 + \varepsilon^3\Delta^2 c_0 - \varepsilon^2(\varepsilon^2\Delta^2 c_1 - \Delta c_1) - L_\varepsilon v_0 - \varepsilon L_\varepsilon v_1 \end{aligned} \tag{2.16}$$

(here we use the equations (1.6), (1.13); the function h is defined in (1.5)).

Multiplying $L_\varepsilon r$ by r in $L_2(\Omega)$, we get

$$|(L_\varepsilon r, r)| = \varepsilon^2(\Delta r, \Delta r) + \|r\|_1^2. \tag{2.17}$$

Substitute the expression for $L_\varepsilon r$ in the right-hand side of (2.16) into (2.17) and estimate the inner products of each term:

$$|\varepsilon^2(\Delta^2 u_0, r)| = |\varepsilon^2(\nabla(\Delta u_0), \nabla r)|$$
$$\leq C\varepsilon^4 \mu^{-1}\|u_0\|_3^2 + \mu\|r\|_1^2$$
$$\leq C_1 \varepsilon^4 + \mu\|r\|_1^2 \qquad (2.18)$$

(using (1.8));

$$|\varepsilon^3(\Delta^2 u_1, r)| \leq C_1\varepsilon^6 + \mu\|r\|^2 \quad \text{(using (1.14), where } k \geq 7\text{)}; \qquad (2.19)$$
$$|\varepsilon^3(\Delta^2 c_0, r)| \leq C_1\varepsilon^6 + \mu\|r\|^2 \quad \text{(using (2.10))}; \qquad (2.20)$$
$$|\varepsilon^4(\Delta^2 c_1, r)| \leq C_2\varepsilon^6 + \mu\|r\|^2 \quad \text{(using (2.11))}; \qquad (2.21)$$
$$|\varepsilon^2(\Delta c_1, r)| \leq C_2\varepsilon^4 + \mu\|r\|^2 \quad \text{(using (2.11))}. \qquad (2.22)$$

Taking into account that $v_0 = \varepsilon\tilde{c}_0(x)\chi(y)e^{-y/\varepsilon}$ (in a neighborhood of Γ_0), we obtain:

$$|(L_\varepsilon v_0, r)| = |\Delta(\varepsilon^2\Delta v_0 - v_0, r)|$$
$$\leq |(\varepsilon^2\partial_{yy}^2 v_0 - v_0, \Delta r)| + \varepsilon^2|(\Delta_x v_0, \Delta r)|$$
$$\leq \varepsilon^3|((\chi'' - 2\varepsilon^{-1}\chi')\tilde{c}_0 e^{-y/\varepsilon}, \Delta r)| + \varepsilon^3|(\chi e^{-y/\varepsilon}\Delta_x \tilde{c}_0, \Delta r)|$$
$$\leq C_3\varepsilon^4 + \mu_1\varepsilon^2\|\Delta r\|^2. \qquad (2.23)$$

We used

$$|\chi^{(k)} e^{-y/\varepsilon}| \leq C_{k,N}\varepsilon^N \qquad \forall k, N > 0$$

(because $\chi^{(k)}(y) \equiv 0$ for $y \in [0, \eta] \cup [1-\eta, 1]$) and the estimate (1.11). Analogous consideration is valid for the function v_0 in a neighborhood of Γ_1. In exactly the same way we can estimate the term involving $L_\varepsilon v_1$:

$$\varepsilon|(L_\varepsilon v_1, r)| \leq C_3\varepsilon^4 + \mu_1\varepsilon^2\|\Delta r\|^2 \quad \text{(using (2.15))}. \qquad (2.24)$$

It follows from the expressions (2.16) and (2.17) for $L_\varepsilon r$ and from the estimates (2.18)–(2.24) that

$$\varepsilon^2\|\Delta r\|^2 + \|r\|_1^2 = |(L_\varepsilon r, r)| \leq C_4\varepsilon^4 + \mu_1\varepsilon^2\|\Delta r\|^2 + \mu\|r\|_1^2.$$

From this estimate, choosing μ and μ_1 sufficiently small, we obtain:

$$\|r\|_2 = \|\Delta r\| \leq C\varepsilon, \qquad \|r\|_1 \leq C\varepsilon^2. \qquad (2.25)$$

Now we shall prove that

$$\|L_\varepsilon r\| = \|-\varepsilon^2\Delta^2 r + \Delta r\| \leq C\varepsilon. \qquad (2.26)$$

Indeed, from (1.8), (1.14), (2.10), and (2.11) we deduce that the norms in H of the first five terms on the right-hand side of (2.16) are of order ε:

$$\varepsilon^2\|\Delta^2 u_0\| + \varepsilon^3\|\Delta^2 u_1\| + \varepsilon^3\|\Delta^2 c_0\| + \varepsilon^2\|\Delta c_1\| + \varepsilon^4\|\Delta^2 c_1\| \leq C\varepsilon.$$

Further, as in (2.23), we obtain

$$
\begin{aligned}
-L_\varepsilon v_0 &\equiv \Delta(\varepsilon^2 \Delta v_0 - v_0) \\
&= \Delta(\varepsilon^2 \Delta_x v_0 + \varepsilon^2 \partial_{yy}^2 v_0 - v_0) \\
&= \varepsilon^3 \Delta(\Delta_x \tilde{c}_0 e^{-y/\varepsilon} \chi) + \varepsilon^2 \Delta_x \tilde{c}_0 e^{-y/\varepsilon}(-2\chi' + \varepsilon \chi'') \\
&\quad + \varepsilon^2 \tilde{c}_0 \partial_{yy}^2 [e^{-y/\varepsilon}(2\chi' + \varepsilon \chi'')].
\end{aligned}
$$

Hence, from (1.11), we have

$$\|L_\varepsilon v_0\| \leqslant C\varepsilon.$$

In a similar manner, using (2.15), we deduce

$$\|L_\varepsilon v_1\| \leqslant C\varepsilon,$$

and (2.26) is therefore valid. It follows from (2.26) and (2.25) that

$$\|\Delta^2 r\| \leqslant C\varepsilon^{-1}.$$

Combining this inequality with the first of the inequalities (2.25) and using the interpolation inequality

$$\varepsilon^k \|u\|_k \leqslant C_{kl}(\varepsilon^l \|u_l\| + \|u\|), \qquad 0 < k < l, \tag{2.27}$$

(see [11]) we conclude that the remainder $r(\varepsilon)$ is uniformly bounded in $H_3(\Omega)$:

$$\|r\|_3 \leqslant C.$$

Combining this result with the estimates (2.25), we arrive at the assertion of Theorem 1.

REMARK 7. By differentiating (2.16) l times with respect to x_i and using the nonisotropic estimates (2.8)–(2.11), in exactly the same way as in the proof of inequality (0.10), we obtain the following estimate (uniform in ε):

$$\|r\|_{3,l} + \varepsilon^{-1}\|r\|_{2,l} + \varepsilon^{-3}\|r\|_{1,l} \leqslant M,$$

where

$$\|r\|_{m,l} = \|r\|_{W_2^{(m+l,m)}(\Omega)}$$

and l satisfies the following condition:

$$(5/8)k - 17/4 - l \geqslant 0.$$

§3. Proof of Propositions 2.1–2.3

We shall now prove Propositions 2.1, 2.2, and 2.3.

PROOF OF PROPOSITION 2.1. Multiplying both sides of the equation (0.1) by u and integrating over Ω, we obtain:

$$\frac{1}{2}\partial_t \|u(t)\|^2 + \varepsilon^2 \|\Delta u\|^2 + \|\nabla u\|^2 + \int f(u)u\,dx \leqslant \mu \|u\|^2 + C\|g\|^2. \tag{3.1}$$

Choosing μ sufficiently small, using (1.1) and the Friedrichs inequality, and then integrating (3.1) with respect to t, we obtain (2.1).

To deduce (2.2), we multiply equation (0.1) by $t\partial_t u$ in $L_2(\Omega)$. Taking into account the relation

$$tf(u)u_t = \partial_t(tF(u)) - F(u),$$

we deduce:

$$t\|u_t\|^2 + \varepsilon^2 \partial_t(t\|\Delta u\|^2) + \partial_t(t\|\nabla u\|^2) + \partial_t\left(\int tF(u)\,dx\right)$$
$$\leq \varepsilon^2\|\Delta u\|^2 + \|\nabla u\|^2 + \int F(u)\,dx + C\|g\|^2. \quad (3.2)$$

Then we integrate both sides of the inequality (3.2) with respect to t. Estimating the right-hand side obtained by (1.4), (2.1), and (3.1), we get the estimate (2.2).

PROOF OF PROPOSITION 2.2. Let us differentiate both sides of equation (0.1) with respect to t:

$$u_{tt} = -\varepsilon^2 \Delta^2 u_t + \Delta u_t - f'(u)u_t. \quad (3.3)$$

Multiplying (3.3) by $t^2 u_t$ in $L_2(\Omega)$ and using the first of the conditions (1.2), we get:

$$\partial_t(t^2\|u_t\|^2) + \varepsilon^2 t^2\|\Delta u_t\|^2 + t^2\|\nabla u_t\|^2 \leq 2t\|u_t\|^2 + Ct^2\|u_t\|^2.$$

Integrating this inequality with respect to t and using the estimate (2.2), we deduce:

$$t^2\|u_t\|^2 + \int_0^t (\varepsilon^2 \tau^2\|\Delta u_t\|^2 + \tau^2\|\nabla u_t\|^2)\,d\tau \leq C, \quad (3.4)$$

$C = C(t)$. Then multiplying both sides of (3.3) by $t^3 u_{tt}$ in L_2, we obtain

$$t^3\|u_{tt}\|^2 + \varepsilon^2 \partial_t(t^3\|\Delta u_t\|^2) + \partial_t(t^3\|\Delta u_t\|^2)$$
$$\leq C(\varepsilon^2 t^2\|\Delta u_t\|^2 + t^2\|\nabla u_t\|^2 + t^3\|f'(u)\|_{L_3}\|u_t\|_{L_6}\|u_{tt}\|)$$
$$\leq C(\varepsilon^2 t^2\|\Delta u_t\|^2 + t^2\|\nabla u_t\|^2 + (1/2)t^3\|u_{tt}\|^2).$$

(We used (1.2), the Hölder inequality, and Sobolev embedding theorems.) Integrating with respect to t, and using (3.4), we obtain the estimate (2.3).

The following lemma (see [5, 6]) plays a basic role in the proof of Proposition 2.3.

LEMMA 1. *Let $z(\varepsilon)$ be the solution of the stationary boundary value problem*:

$$L_\varepsilon z \equiv -\varepsilon^2 \Delta^2 z + \Delta z = h(\varepsilon) \quad \text{in } \Omega \in \mathbb{R}^n, \quad (3.5)$$

$\partial\Omega$ *is sufficiently smooth manifold,*

$$z|_{\partial\Omega} = \left.\frac{\partial z}{\partial \nu}\right|_{\partial\Omega} = 0. \quad (3.6)$$

Suppose the right-hand side of (3.5) *satisfies the following condition:*

$$\varepsilon^2\|h\|_2 + \varepsilon\|h\|_1 + \|h\| \leqslant C, \tag{3.7}$$

where C does not depend on ε. Then the following uniform estimate of $z(\varepsilon)$ holds:

$$\varepsilon^{5/2}\|z\|_4 + \varepsilon^{3/2}\|z\|_3 + \varepsilon^{1/2}\|z\|_2 + \|z\|_{3/2} \leqslant C. \tag{3.8}$$

PROOF. We shall look for the solution z of the linear elliptic equation (3.5) in the form (see [1, 2]):

$$z = z_0 + v + r, \tag{3.9}$$

where z_0 is the solution of the limit problem (for $\varepsilon = 0$):

$$\Delta z_0 = h, \qquad z_0|_{\partial\Omega} = 0,$$

$v = \varepsilon c(x) e^{-\rho/\varepsilon}$ is a boundary layer function of the first order, added to z_0 to satisfy all boundary conditions (3.6) (ρ is the distance to $\partial\Omega$ measured along the normal on $\partial\Omega$, $\rho < \eta$), and r is the remainder. From a priori estimates for solutions of linear elliptic equations, it follows that condition (3.7) implies the following estimate:

$$\varepsilon^2\|z_0\|_4 + \varepsilon\|z_0\|_3 + \|z_0\|_2 \leqslant C. \tag{3.10}$$

The coefficient $c(x)$ in the expression for v is determined so as to satisfy the second boundary condition (3.6):

$$c(x) = \left.\frac{\partial z_0}{\partial \rho}\right|_{\rho=0}.$$

It should be noted that (3.10) implies

$$\varepsilon^2\|c\|_{5/2} + \varepsilon\|c\|_{3/2} + \|c\|_{1/2} \leqslant C_1. \tag{3.11}$$

To satisfy the first boundary condition (3.6), we add to $z_0 + v$ the function $-\varepsilon c(x)$. Finally we multiply the function v_0 (and also the term $-\varepsilon c(x)$), defined in a neighborhood of the boundary $\Omega_\eta = \{\rho < \eta\}$, by an infinitely differentiable smoothing factor $\chi(\rho)$ such as (1.12) to define these functions in the entire domain Ω. It follows from (3.11) that the boundary layer term satisfies the estimate:

$$\varepsilon^{1/2}\|v\|_2 + \varepsilon^{-1/2}\|v\|_1 \leqslant C. \tag{3.12}$$

Applying the interpolation inequality ([11]),

$$\varepsilon^{1-\delta}\|u\|_{1-\delta} \leqslant C_\delta (\varepsilon\|u\|_1 + \|u\|), \qquad 0 \leqslant \delta \leqslant 1, \tag{3.13}$$

we get

$$\|v\|_{3/2} \leqslant C. \tag{3.14}$$

Observe that the remainder $r = z - (z_0 + v - \varepsilon c)$ satisfies homogeneous boundary conditions (3.6). Just as in the proof of Theorem 1 in §2, using (3.10), (3.11) and (3.12), we obtain the following energy estimate:

$$\varepsilon^2 \|\Delta r\|^2 + \|\nabla r\|^2 = |(L_\varepsilon r, r)| \leq (1/2)(\varepsilon^2 \|\Delta r\|^2 + \|\nabla r\|) + C\varepsilon;$$

it implies:

$$\varepsilon^{1/2} \|r\|_2 + \varepsilon^{-1/2} \|r\|_1 \leq C, \qquad \|r\|_{3/2} \leq C. \tag{3.15}$$

Thereby it follows from (3.9), (3.10), (3.11), (3.12) and (3.15) that the solution $z(\varepsilon)$ of the problem (3.5), (3.6) satisfies the following estimate

$$\varepsilon^{1/2} \|z\|_2 + \|z\|_{3/2} \leq C. \tag{3.16}$$

Now rewriting equation (3.5) in the form

$$\Delta^2 z = \varepsilon^{-2}(\Delta z - h)$$

and taking into account (3.7), (3.6), and the interpolation inequality (3.13), we obtain the estimate (3.8).

The proof of Proposition 2.3 is based on this Lemma.

PROOF OF PROPOSITION 2.3. We differentiate the equation (0.1) with respect to x_i. Taking into consideration the boundary conditions (0.2), we get the following boundary value problem for $p_1(t) \equiv \partial u/\partial x_i$

$$\partial_t p_1 = -\varepsilon^2 \Delta^2 p_1 + \Delta p_1 - f'(u) p_1 - g'_{x_i},$$

$$p_1|_{\partial \Omega} = \left.\frac{\partial p_1}{\partial y}\right|_{\partial \Omega} = 0. \tag{3.17}$$

We remark that equation (3.17) differs from equation (0.1) for u only in the term $f'(u)p_1$. Multiplying (3.17) by $t^2 p_1$ in L_2, integrating with respect to t, using the Gronwall inequality and taking into account (2.2), we obtain:

$$t^2 \|p_1(t)\|^2 + \int_0^t (\varepsilon^2 \tau^2 \|p_1(\tau)\|_2^2 + \tau^2 \|p_1(\tau)\|_1^2) d\tau \leq C. \tag{3.18}$$

Multiplying (3.17) by $t^4 \partial_t p_1$ in L_2 and using the estimate (2.2), we get:

$$t^4 \|\partial_t p_1\|^2 + \partial_t (t^4 \varepsilon^2 \|\Delta p_1\|^2 + t^4 \|\nabla p_1\|^2)$$
$$\leq 4t^3(\varepsilon^2 \|p_1\|_2^2 + \|p_1\|_1^2) + Ct^2 \|p_1\|_1^2 + Ct^4.$$

Integrating this inequality with respect to t and taking into account (3.18), we get:

$$\int_0^t \tau^4 \|\partial_t p_1\|^2 d\tau + t^4 \varepsilon^2 \|p_1(t)\|_2^2 + t^4 \|p_1\|_1^2 \leq C, \tag{3.19}$$

where $t \in [0, T]$ and C depends only on $\|u(0)\|$ and T.

Then we differentiate the estimate (3.17) with respect to t:

$$\partial_{tt} p_1 = -\varepsilon^2 \Delta^2 (p_1)_t + \Delta(p_1)_t - f'(u)(p_1)_t - f''(u) u_t p_1,$$

$$(p_1)_t|_{\partial \Omega} = \left.\frac{\partial (p_1)_t}{\partial y}\right|_{\partial \Omega} = 0. \tag{3.20}$$

Multiplying (3.20) by $t^5(p_1)_t$ in L_2 and using the Hölder inequality and the estimates (2.2) and (2.3), we obtain:

$$\partial_t(t^5\|(p_1)_t\|^2) + t^5\varepsilon^2\|\Delta(p_1)_t\|^2 + t^5\|\nabla(p_1)_t\|^2 \leqslant C(t^2\|p_1\|_1^2 + t^4\|(p_1)_t\|^2).$$

Integrating this inequality with respect to t and using (3.18) and (3.19), we get:

$$t^5\|(p_1)_t\|^2 + \int_0^t (\tau^5\varepsilon^2\|(p_1)_t\|_2^2 + \tau^5\|(p_1)_t\|_1^2)\,d\tau \leqslant C. \qquad (3.21)$$

Finally, multiply the equation (3.20) by $t^7(p_1)_{tt}$ in L_2 and then integrate with respect to t. The estimates (2.2), (2.3) and (3.21) imply:

$$\int_0^t \tau^7\|(p_1)_{tt}\|^2 d\tau + t^7\varepsilon^2\|(p_1)_t\|_2^2 + t^7\|(p_1)_t\|_1^2 \leqslant C. \qquad (3.22)$$

Observe that the constants C in (3.21) and (3.22) depend only on $\|u(0)\|$ and T. This inequality implies (2.5) for $l = 1$.

Hence, estimates (3.18), (3.19) and (3.22) for $p_1(x, y, t)$, which are similar to the estimates (2.1), (2.2) and (2.3) for $u(t, x, y)$ (for fixed $t > 0$), are established.

Put $t = 1$ in the equation (3.17) and rewrite it in the form (3.5) with the right-hand side

$$h_1(\varepsilon) \equiv \partial_t p_1(1) + f'(u(1))p_1(1) + g'_{x_i}.$$

We shall prove below that the function h_1 satisfies the condition (3.7) of Lemma 1. Indeed, it follows from (1.2), (0.11), and (3.22) that

$$\|f'(u(1))p_1(1)\| \leqslant C(1 + \|u^2 p_1\|^2) \leqslant C(1 + \|u\|_{L_6}^4 \|p_1\|_{L_6}^2) \leqslant C \qquad (3.23)$$

(we use also the Hölder inequality and the embedding theorems (2.13)). Further, using the estimates (2.2), (3.19), and the embedding $W_2^2(\mathbb{R}^3) \hookrightarrow W_6^1(\mathbb{R}^3)$ we obtain:

$$\|f'(u(1))p_1(1)\|_1^2 \leqslant \sum_{i=1}^3 \|f''(u)p_1\mathscr{D}_i u + f'(u)\mathscr{D}_i p_1\|^2 + \|f'(u)p_1\|^2$$

$$\leqslant \|f''(u)\|_{L_6}^2 \|p_1\|_{L_6}^2 \|u\|_{W_6^1}^2 + \|f'(u)\|_{L_3}^2 \|p_1\|_{W_6^1}^2 + C$$

$$\leqslant C_1(\|u\|_2^2 + \|p_1\|_2^2 + 1) \leqslant C_2\varepsilon^{-2}. \qquad (3.24)$$

Observe that by rewriting equation (3.17) (for $t = 1$) as follows

$$\varepsilon^2\Delta^2 p_1 = \Delta p_1 - \partial_t p_1 - f'(u)p_1 - g'_{x_i},$$

we obtain (from (3.19), (3.21), and (3.23))

$$\|\Delta^2 p_1(1)\| \leqslant C\varepsilon^{-3},$$

and then the interpolation inequality (2.27) implies the following estimate:

$$\varepsilon^3\|p_1\|_4 + \varepsilon^2\|p_1\|_3 + \varepsilon\|p_1\|_2 + \|p_1\|_1 \leqslant C. \qquad (3.25)$$

In exactly the same way, using (2.2) and (3.3), we can prove a similar estimate for $u = u(1)$:

$$\varepsilon^3\|u\|_4 + \varepsilon^2\|u\|_3 + \varepsilon\|u\|_2 + \|u\|_1 \leqslant C. \tag{3.26}$$

We can now estimate the expression $\|f'(u)p_1\|^2$. Using the Hölder inequality, the estimates (0.11), (3.25), (3.26), and the Sobolev embedding theorems, we have

$$\begin{aligned}
\|f'(u)p_1(1)\|_2^2 &= \sum_{i,j=1}^{3} \|f'''(u)p_1\mathscr{D}_i u \mathscr{D}_j u + 2f''(u)\mathscr{D}_i u \mathscr{D}_j p_1 \\
&\quad + f''(u)p_1\mathscr{D}_{ij}u + f'(u)\mathscr{D}_{ij}p_1\|^2 + \|f'(u)p_1\|_1^2 \\
&\leqslant C(\|u\|_{W_6^1}^4\|p_1\|_{L_6}^2 + \|f''(u)\|_{L_6}^2\|u\|_{W_6^2}^2\|p_1\|_{L_6}^2 \\
&\quad + \|f''(u)\|_{L_6}^2\|u\|_{W_6^1}^2\|p_1\|_{W_6^1}^2 + \|f'(u)\|_{L_3}^2\|p_1\|_{W_6^2}^2 + 1) \\
&\leqslant C_1(\|u\|_2^4\|p_1\|_1^2 + \|u\|_1^2\|u\|_3^2\|p_1\|_1^2 \\
&\quad + \|u\|_1^2\|u\|_2^2\|p_1\|_2^2 + \|u\|_1^2\|p_1\|_3^2 + 1) \\
&\leqslant C_2\varepsilon^{-4}.
\end{aligned} \tag{3.27}$$

All the constants in these estimates do not depend on ε. Observe that inequality (3.22) implies that the function $\partial_t p_1(1)$ satisfies (3.7).

Hence we have established that the function $h_1(\varepsilon)$ satisfies the condition (3.7); therefore it follows from (3.8) that inequality (2.4) is valid for $l = 1$.

REMARK 8. In a similar way, taking into account the estimates (2.2), (3.19), and (3.21), we obtain inequalities for the function $t^4 f'(u(t))p_1(t)$ that are similar to estimates (3.23), (3.24) and (3.27). It follows from these inequalities that assertion (2.4) is also valid for $t^4 p_1(t)$, $t \in [0, T]$.

The proof of (2.4) for $l = 2, 3, \ldots$ is quite similar. The equation (3.17) is differentiated with respect to x_i step by step and estimates, similar to (3.18), (3.19), and (3.22), are established:

$$\int_0^t \tau^{m_1}\|\partial_t p_l\|^2 d\tau + t^{m_1}\varepsilon^2\|p_l(t)\|_2^2 + t^{m_1}\|p_l(t)\|_1^2 \leqslant C, \tag{3.28}$$

$$\int_0^t \tau^{m_2}\|(p_l)_{tt}\|^2 d\tau + t^{m_2}\varepsilon^2\|(p_l)_t\|_2^2 + t^{m_2}\|(p_l)_t\|_1^2 \leqslant C. \tag{3.29}$$

Here we use the embedding theorems (2.13) and the boundedness of the derivatives $f^{(l)}(u)$ for $l \geqslant 3$.

For instance, the function $p_2(t)$ satisfies the following equation:

$$\partial_t p_2 = -\varepsilon^2 \Delta^2 p_2 + \Delta p_2 - f'(u)p_2 - f''(u)p_1^2 - g''_{x_i}, \tag{3.30}$$

which differs from equation (3.17) only in the term $f''(u)p_1^2$. We can estimate this term in the following way:

$$t^4\|f''(u)p_1^2\| \leqslant t^4\|f''(u)\|_{L_3}\|p_1^2(t)\|_{L_{3/2}} \leqslant Ct\|u\|_1^2 t^3\|p_1(t)\|_{L_3}^2 \leqslant C$$

(we use (2.2) and inequalites (3.18) and (3.19), which imply $t^{3/2}\|p_1(t)\|_{1/2} \leqslant C$). Then we differentiate equation (3.30) with respect to t. All terms in the expression thus obtained, except $f'''(u)u_t p_1^2$, are similar to the terms in (3.20).

For this new term we deduce:

$$t^6\|f'''(u)u_t p_1^2\| \leqslant Ct^6\|u_t p_1^2\| \leqslant Ct^3\|u_t\|_1^2 t^3\|p_1(t)\|_{L_3}^2 \leqslant C,$$

in accordance with (2.3). Hence, as before, we obtain the estimates (3.28), (3.29) for $l = 2$.

For arbitrary l these estimates are established in a similar manner.

References

1. M. I. Vishik and L. A. Lyusternik, *Regular degeneration and boundary layer for linear differential equations with small parameter*, Uspekhi Mat. Nauk **12** (1957), no. 5, 3–122. (Russian)

2. _____, *Solution of certain perturbed problems in case of matrices and self-adjoint and non-self-adjoint differential equations*, Uspekhi Mat. Nauk **15** (1960), no. 3, 3–80; English transl. in Russian Math. Surveys **15** (1960), no. 3.

3. V. A. Trenogin, *The development and applications of the asymptotic method of Lyusternik and Vishik*, Uspekhi Mat. Nauk **25** (1970), no. 4, 123–158; English transl. in Russian Math. Surveys **25** (1970), no. 4.

4. A. V. Babin and M. I. Vishik, *Attractors of evolution equations*, "Nauka", Moscow, 1989. (Russian)

5. M. Yu. Skvortsov, *The maximal attractor of the semigroup corresponding to the first boundary value problem for a singularly parabolic equation*, Uspekhi Mat. Nauk **42** (1987), no. 2, 243–244; English transl. in Russian Math. Surveys **42** (1987), no. 2.

6. M. Yu. Skvortsov, *Attractors of singularly perturbed dynamical systems*, Manuscript No. 8603, deposited at VINITI, 1986. (Russian)

7. _____, *Attractors of singularly perturbed dynamical systems*, Uspekhi Mat. Nauk **42** (1987), no. 4, 154.

8. J.-L. Lions, *Quelques méthodes de résolution des problèmes aux limites non linéaires*, Dunod & Gauthier-Villars, Paris, 1969.

9. O. V. Besov, V. P. Il'in, and S. M. Nikol'skiĭ, *Integral representations of functions and imbedding theorems*, "Nauka", Moscow, 1975; English transl., Wiley, New York, 1979.

10. S. M. Nikol'skiĭ, *Approximation of functions of several variables and embedding theorems*, "Nauka", Moscow, 1969; English transl., Springer-Verlag, Berlin and New York, 1975.

11. M. S. Agranovich and M. I. Vishik, *Elliptic problems with a parameter and parabolic problems of general type*, Uspekhi Mat. Nauk **19** (1964), no. 3, 53–160; English transl. in Russian Math. Surveys **19** (1964), no. 3.

Translated by M. YU. SKVORTSOV

The Asymptotics of Solutions of Reaction-Diffusion Equations with Small Parameter

V. YU. SKVORTSOV AND M. I. VISHIK

The asymptotic behavior of solutions of systems of quasilinear parabolic reaction-diffusion equations is investigated in this paper. In §§1–3 the following system is considered:

$$\varepsilon \partial_t u_1 = \Delta u_1 - f_1(u_1, u_2) - g_1(x), \quad (0.1)$$
$$\partial_t u_2 = \Delta u_2 - f_2(u_1, u_2) - g_2(x), \quad x \in \Omega \Subset \mathbb{R}^n, \quad (0.2)$$

with boundary conditions
$$u_1|_{\partial\Omega} = 0,$$
$$u_2|_{\partial\Omega} = 0, \quad (0.3)$$

and initial data
$$u_1|_{t=0} = u_{10}(x),$$
$$u_2|_{t=0} = u_{20}(x), \quad (0.4)$$

where $0 < \varepsilon \leq \varepsilon_0$, $g_i(x) \in L_2(\Omega)$ ($i = 1, 2$). If certain conditions on $f_1(\xi)$, $f_2(\xi)$ are satisfied, the problem (0.1)–(0.4) has a unique solution
$$u(t) = (u_1(t), u_2(t)) \quad (u_i(t) \equiv u_i(t, x)),$$
which belongs to the space $H_1 = H_1^0(\Omega) \times H_1^0(\Omega)$ for any $t \geq 0$. Therefore, this system generates a semigroup
$$\{S_t(\varepsilon)\}, \quad S_t(\varepsilon): H_1 \to H_1 \quad \forall t \geq 0,$$
where $S_t(\varepsilon)u_0 = u(t)$ is a solution of the problem (0.1)–(0.4). For $\varepsilon = 0$ the system (0.1)–(0.4) becomes

$$0 = \Delta v_1 - f_1(v_1, v_2) - g_1(x), \quad (0.5)$$
$$\partial_t v_2 = \Delta v_2 - f_2(v_1, v_2) - g_2(x), \quad (0.6)$$

$$v_1|_{\partial\Omega} = 0, \quad v_2|_{\partial\Omega} = 0, \quad (0.7)$$
$$v_2|_{t=0} = v_{20}(x). \quad (0.8)$$

1991 *Mathematics Subject Classification.* Primary 35B40, 35K57.

Equation (0.5) is stationary and, owing to the conditions on $f_1(u_1, u_2)$ (see §1), it has a unique solution $v_1(x) = Bv_2(x)$ for any function $v_2(x) \in H_1^0(\Omega)$. Substituting $v_1 = Bv_2$ in the second equation, one can obtain an evolution equation for v_2, $v_2(t) = S_t v_{20}$. It is assumed that the limit equation so obtained (at $\varepsilon = 0$) for v_2 has a finite number of stationary points and all of them are hyperbolic.

Under the assumption that $(f_1(u), f_2(u))$ is a potential vector and $f_1(u)$, $f_2(u)$ satisfy certain other conditions, the following statement is proved in §3.

Solutions $u(t, \varepsilon) = (u_1(t, \varepsilon), u_2(t, \varepsilon))$ of the problem (0.1)–(0.4) with initial data from the bounded set $B_0 \subset H_1$ can be approximated by piecewise-continuous (with respect to t) solutions $v(t) = (v_1(t), v_2(t))$ of the limit problem (0.5)–(0.8) and moreover $v(t)$ depends on ε ($v(t) = v(t, \varepsilon)$) and satisfies the estimates:

$$\sup_{t \geq 0} \|u_2(t, \varepsilon) - v_2(t)\| \leq C_1 \varepsilon^q, \tag{0.9}$$

$$\sup_{t \geq \tau} \|u_1(t, \varepsilon) - v_1(t)\| \leq C_2 \varepsilon^q, \quad \tau > 0, \tag{0.10}$$

$q > 0$.

Here the constants C_1 and C_2 depend on B_0, while C_2 also depends on τ, q depends on the spectral properties of the operators $S_1'(z_j)$, where z_j are equilibrium points,

$$S_1'(z_j) = S_t'(z_j)\big|_{t=1}$$

is the Frechet derivative of the operator S_t at the point z_j for $t = 1$. It is necessary to note that the continuous pieces of $v_2(t)$, except the first one, lie on finite-dimensional unstable manifolds of the limit semigroup $\{S_t\}$ passing through z_j.

So, the trajectory $v(t) = (v_1(t), v_2(t))$ is the main term of the asymptotics of $u(t, \varepsilon)$ for all $t \geq \tau$. It is called the *stabilized asymptotics* of $u(t, \varepsilon)$. To prove the statement formulated above, a general theorem about the existence of a stabilized asymptotics, proved in [1], is used.

In §§4–6 analogous problems are investigated for a system of equations of the form

$$\varepsilon \partial_t u_1 = \varepsilon d_1 \Delta u_2 - f_1(u_1, u_2) - g_1(x), \tag{0.11}$$

$$\partial_t u_2 = d_2 \Delta u_2 - f_2(u_1, u_2) - g_2(x), \tag{0.12}$$

with boundary conditions

$$u_1\big|_{\partial\Omega} = 0, \quad u_2\big|_{\partial\Omega} = 0, \tag{0.13}$$

and initial data

$$u_1\big|_{t=0} = u_{10}(x), \quad u_2\big|_{t=0} = u_{20}(x). \tag{0.14}$$

In this case, we get a limit (for $\varepsilon = 0$) equation of the form

$$-f_1(v_1, v_2) - g_1(x) = 0. \tag{0.15}$$

As well as in the previous problem, the variable v_1 is a "stable" one here. Owing to this, v_1 is determined via v_2:

$$v_1(x) = \varphi(x, v_2(x)).$$

The limit equation (for $\varepsilon = 0$) for v_2 may have a finite number of equilibrium points, some of them may be unstable. The stabilized asymptotics for solutions $u(t, \varepsilon)$ of problem (0.11)–(0.14) is constructed and satisfies estimates of the form (0.7), (0.8).

It is necessary to note that the Dirichlet boundary conditions in (0.3) and (0.13) can be changed to Neumann conditions. The theorems proved can be generalized to the case when u_1 and u_2 are vectors:

$$u_1 = (u_1^1, \ldots, u_1^m), \qquad u_2 = (u_2^1, \ldots, u_2^k).$$

Finally we should note that in problem (0.1)–(0.4) (respectively (0.11)–(0.14)) the approximate trajectory $v(t)$ lies on M, where M is the manifold determined by the stationary equation (0.5) (respectively (0.15)) that attracts the solution $u(t, \varepsilon)$ of the prelimit equation. In the neighborhood of $t = 0$, the component $u_1(t, \varepsilon)$ has the form of a boundary layer (see, for instance, [5]), which is not investigated here (so $t \geqslant \tau > 0$ in (0.10)).

We restrict ourselves to the case of Dirichlet boundary conditions:

$$u_1|_{\partial \Omega} = 0, \qquad u_2|_{\partial \Omega} = 0.$$

Problems similar to (0.1)–(0.4) or (0.11)–(0.14) were investigated by many authors for systems of ordinary differential equations (see, e.g., [2, 3]).

§1. Formulation of the problem

We consider a system of quasilinear parabolic equations of the form (0.1)–(0.4) with a small parameter at the derivative $\partial u_1/\partial t$.

We denote:

$$u = u(u_1, u_2), \qquad f(u) = (f_1(u), f_2(u)),$$
$$f_i(u) \in C^{1+\alpha}, \quad \alpha > 0 \ (i = 1, 2), \qquad g(x) = (g_1(x), g_2(x)).$$

If we set $\varepsilon = 0$, (0.1) becomes the elliptic equation

$$\Delta u_1 - f_1(u_1, u_2) - g_1(x) = 0. \tag{1.1}$$

We shall assume that the function $f(u)$ satisfies the estimate

$$(f'(\xi)\eta, \eta) \geqslant \mu_1 \eta_1^2 + \mu_2 \eta_2^2, \qquad \mu_1, \mu_2 \in \mathbb{R}, \ \mu_1 \geqslant -(\lambda_1 - \delta), \tag{1.2}$$

$\forall \xi \in \mathbb{R}^2$ and $\forall \eta \in \mathbb{R}^2$, where $\delta > 0$ is an arbitrary constant, and $-\lambda_1$ is the first eigenvalue of the Laplace operator with boundary conditions (0.3) in the domain $\Omega \in \mathbb{R}^n$. The condition (1.2) implies, in particular, that

$$f'_{1\xi_1} \geqslant -(\lambda_1 - \delta), \tag{1.3}$$

$$f'_{2\xi_2} \geqslant \mu_2. \tag{1.4}$$

We shall assume also that the function $f(\xi)$ has the following properties:

$$(f(\xi), \xi) \geq -C + \delta_1^2 |\xi|^2, \qquad f(0) = 0, \tag{1.5}$$

$$|f'_{1\xi_2}(\xi)| \leq C(1 + |\xi|^\eta), \qquad \text{where } 1/\eta \geq (n-2)/2. \tag{1.6}$$

Moreover, let $f(\xi)$ be a potential vector, i.e., suppose that there exists a function $F(\xi_1, \xi_2)$ such that

$$f(\xi) = \operatorname{grad} F(\xi). \tag{1.7}$$

It is assumed that

$$-C \leq F(\xi) \leq C(1 + |\xi|^{p+1}), \qquad \text{where } 1/p \geq (n-2)/n. \tag{1.8}$$

We should note that conditions (1.6), (1.7) imply

$$|f'_{2\xi_1}(\xi)| \leq C(1 + |\xi|^\eta) \tag{1.9}$$

because

$$\frac{\partial^2 F}{\partial \xi_1 \partial \xi_2} = \frac{\partial^2 F}{\partial \xi_2 \partial \xi_1}.$$

We also assume that

$$|f(\xi)| \leq C(1 + |\xi|^p). \tag{1.10}$$

It will be proved below that the equation (1.1) has a unique solution $u_1(x) \in H_1^0(\Omega)$ for any function $u_2(x) \in H_1^0(\Omega)$, $u_1 = B(u_2)$, since $f(\xi)$ satisfies the conditions (1.2)–(1.10).

Moreover, let the function $g_2(x) \in L_2(\Omega)$ satisfy:
1) the set $\mathfrak{N}$ of solutions of the equation

$$\Delta u_2 - f_2(B(u_2), u_2) - g_2(x) = 0$$

(where B is the operator defined in the introduction) is finite,

$$\mathfrak{N} = \{z_1, \ldots, z_N\};$$

2) all the $z_j \in \mathfrak{N}$ are hyperbolic (see [1]).

The existence of a unique solution of the problem (0.1)–(0.4) is proved by using Galerkin's method (see, e.g., [1, 4]). The validity of computations performed below can also be proved simply by Galerkin's method. Thus we restrict ourselves to the formal reasoning.

§2. A priori estimates

We shall denote: $H = (L_2(\Omega))^2$, $H_1 = (H_1^0(\Omega))^2$; let $\{S_t(\varepsilon)\}$ be the semigroup corresponding to the problem (0.1)–(0.4). Operators $S_t(\varepsilon)$ map the initial data $(u_{10}(x), u_{20}(x)) = u_0(x)$ into the solution

$$(u_1(t, x), u_2(t, x)) = u(t, x)$$

of the problem (0.1)–(0.4) at the moment t:

$$S_t(\varepsilon) u_0 = u(t) \qquad (u(t) \equiv u(t, x), \ u_0 \equiv u_0(x)).$$

At first we establish estimates for the component $u_2(t)$.

LEMMA 1. *Let* $u(t) = (u_1(t), u_2(t))$ *be a solution of the problem* (0.1)–(0.4), $0 < \varepsilon \leq 1$. *Then there exist a constant* $C_1 > 0$ *and a function* $C_2(\cdot) > 0$, *independent of* ε, *such that*

1) $\|u_2(t)\|^2 \leq C_1(1 + \|u(0)\|^2) \quad \forall t \geq 0$,
2) $\|u_2(t)\|_1^2 \leq C_2(\|u(0)\|_1) \quad \forall t \geq 0$.

PROOF. 1) We multiply the system (0.1)–(0.2) by u in H and use condition (1.5). Then we get

$$(1/2)(\varepsilon \partial_t \|u_1\|^2 + \partial_t \|u_2\|^2) + \|\nabla u\|^2 = -(f(u), u) - (g, u)$$
$$\leq C - \delta_1^2 \|u\|^2 + M\|g\|^2 + (1/2)\delta_1^2 \|u\|^2 \leq C' - (1/2)\delta_1^2 \|u\|^2. \quad (2.1)$$

Multiplying both sides of the inequality (2.1) by $e^{\delta_1^2 t}$, where δ_1^2 is sufficiently small, and integrating from 0 to t, we obtain

$$\varepsilon e^{\delta_1^2 t}\|u_1(t)\|^2 + e^{\delta_1^2 t}\|u_2(t)\|^2 + \delta_1^2(1-\varepsilon)\int_0^t e^{\delta_1^2 \tau}\|u_1(\tau)\|^2 d\tau$$
$$\leq C''(e^{\delta_1^2 t} - 1) + \varepsilon\|u_1(0)\|^2 + \|u_2(0)\|^2.$$

Hence

$$\|u_2(t)\|^2 \leq C(1 - e^{-\delta_1^2 t}) + \|u(0)\|^2 e^{-\delta_1^2 t}$$

and statement 1) is proved.

2) Integrating the inequality (2.1) from 0 to t, we get

$$\varepsilon\|u_1(t)\|^2 + \delta_1^2 \int_0^t \|u_1(\tau)\|^2 d\tau \leq C't + \varepsilon\|u_1(0)\|^2 + \|u_2(0)\|^2.$$

Since $\|u_1(t)\|^2 \geq 0$, we have $\|u_1(t)\|^2 \leq y(t)$, where $y(t)$ satisfies the equation

$$\varepsilon y(t) + \delta_1^2 \int_0^t y(\tau) d\tau = C''(1 + t),$$

or

$$\varepsilon y'(t) + \delta_1^2 y(t) = C'', \quad y(0) = C''/\varepsilon.$$

Therefore,

$$\|u_1(t)\|^2 \leq y(t) = y(0)e^{-\delta_1^2 t/\varepsilon} + C_1(1 - e^{-\delta_1^2 t/\varepsilon})$$
$$\leq M\varepsilon^{-1} e^{-\delta_1^2 t/\varepsilon} + C_1(1 - e^{-\delta_1^2 t/\varepsilon}).$$

Since $xe^{-x} \leq C_0$, we get

$$\frac{1}{\varepsilon} e^{-\delta_1^2 t/\varepsilon} \leq \frac{C_0}{\delta_1^2} \frac{1}{t}.$$

Hence

$$\|u_1(t)\|^2 \leq M'(1 + \|u(0)\|^2) \quad \forall t \geq 1. \quad (2.2)$$

Multiplying the system (0.1)–(0.2) by $-t\Delta u$ in H, we conclude
$$(1/2)(\varepsilon\partial_t(t\|\nabla u_1\|^2) + \partial_t(t\|\nabla u_2\|^2)) + t\|\Delta u\|^2$$
$$= (1/2)(\varepsilon\|\nabla u_1\|^2 + \|\nabla u_2\|^2) - t(f'(u)\nabla u, \nabla u) + t(g, \Delta u)$$
$$\leqslant (1/2)(\varepsilon\|\nabla u_1\|^2 + \|\nabla u_2\|^2) + t(\lambda_1 - \delta)\|\nabla u_1\|^2$$
$$- \mu_2 t\|\nabla u_2\|^2 + Mt\|g\|^2 + \delta_2 t\|\Delta u\|^2. \tag{2.3}$$

Now let $\delta_2 > 0$ satisfy
$$(1 - \delta_2)\|\Delta u\|^2 \geqslant (\lambda_1 - \delta/2)\|\nabla u\|^2. \tag{2.4}$$

One can also see that, by integrating the inequality (2.1) from 0 to t, we get
$$\int_0^t \|\nabla u(\tau)\|^2 d\tau \leqslant C(1+t), \qquad C = C(\|u(0)\|). \tag{2.5}$$

The estimates (2.3)–(2.5) imply that
$$\varepsilon t\|\nabla u_1(t)\|^2 + t\|\nabla u_2(t)\|^2 + \delta \int_0^t \tau\|\nabla u_1(\tau)\|^2 d\tau$$
$$\leqslant \int_0^t (\varepsilon\|\nabla u_1(\tau)\|^2 + \|\nabla u_2(\tau)\|^2) d\tau - \mu_2 \int_0^t \tau\|\nabla u_2(\tau)\|^2 d\tau + Ct^2$$
$$\leqslant -\mu_2 \int_0^t \tau\|\nabla u_2(\tau)\|^2 d\tau + C'(1+T^2) \quad \text{for } 0 \leqslant t \leqslant T.$$

Hence, using the Gronwall inequality, we get for $0 \leqslant t \leqslant T$,
$$t\|\nabla u_2(t)\|^2 \leqslant C, \qquad C = C(T, \|u(0)\|^2). \tag{2.6}$$

Now multipying the system (0.1)–(0.2) by $-\Delta u$ in H, we obtain
$$(1/2)(\varepsilon\partial_t\|\nabla u_1\|^2 + \partial_t\|\nabla u_2\|^2) + \|\Delta u\|^2$$
$$= -(f'(u)\nabla u, \nabla u) + (g, \Delta u)$$
$$\leqslant (\lambda_1 - \delta)\|\nabla u_1\|^2 - \mu_2\|\nabla u_2\|^2 + M\|g\|^2 + \delta_2\|\Delta u\|^2,$$
where δ_2 satisfies condition (2.4). Therefore,
$$(1/2)(\varepsilon\partial_t\|\nabla u_1\|^2 + \partial_t\|\nabla u_2\|^2) \leqslant -\mu_2\|\nabla u_2\|^2 + C.$$

Integrating over $[0, t]$, we get
$$\|\nabla u_2(t)\|^2 \leqslant C_1 \quad \text{for } 0 \leqslant t \leqslant T, \qquad C_1 = C_1(T, \|\nabla u(0)\|). \tag{2.7}$$

Then we should note that part 1) of this lemma and the formulas (2.2) and (2.6) imply
$$\|\nabla u_2(t)\|^2 \leqslant C(\|u(t-1)\|) \leqslant C_1(\|u(0)\|) \quad \text{for } t \geqslant 2 \tag{2.8}$$
and formula (2.7) implies
$$\|\nabla u_2(t)\|^2 \leqslant C(\|\nabla u(0)\|) \quad \text{for } 0 \leqslant t \leqslant 2. \tag{2.9}$$

Statement 2) follows from estimates (2.8) and (2.9).

Now we establish certain properties of the semigroup $\{S_t(\varepsilon)\}$.

LEMMA 2. *The semigroups* $\{S_t(\varepsilon)\}$ *are*

1) (H_1, H)-*bounded uniformly with respect to* ε, $0 < \varepsilon \leqslant \varepsilon_0$, *and* $t \geqslant 0$, *that is, for any bounded set* B_1 *in* H_1, *there exists a set* B_0, *bounded in* H, *independent of* ε *and* t, $0 < \varepsilon \leqslant \varepsilon_0$, $0 \leqslant t < +\infty$, *such that* $S_t(\varepsilon) B_1 \subset B_0$;

2) (H_1, H_1)-*bounded uniformly with respect to* ε, $0 < \varepsilon \leqslant \varepsilon_0$ *and* $t \geqslant 0$.

PROOF. 1) Multiplying equation (0.1) by u_1 in $L_2(\Omega)$, we get

$$(\varepsilon/2)\partial_t \|u_1\|^2 = -\|\nabla u_1\|^2 - (f_1(u_1, u_2), u_1) - (g_1, u_1).$$

One can see that

$$f_1(u_1, u_2) = f_1(0, u_2) + \int_0^1 f'_{1u_1}(\theta u_1, u_2) d\theta \cdot u_1$$

and (1.3) implies

$$(\varepsilon/2)\partial_t \|u_1\|^2 \leqslant -\lambda_1 \|u_1\|^2 - (f_1(0, u_2), u_1)$$
$$+ (\lambda_1 - \delta)\|u_1\|^2 + M\|g_1\|^2 + (\delta/4)\|u_1\|^2.$$

Then we obtain, using condition (1.10),

$$(\varepsilon/2)\partial_t \|u_1\|^2 \leqslant -(\delta/2)\|u_1\|^2 + C_1 \|f_1(0, u_2)\|^2 + M\|g_1\|^2$$
$$\leqslant -(\delta/2)\|u_1\|^2 + C(1 + \|u_2\|_{0,2p}^{2p})$$
$$\leqslant -(\delta/2)\|u_1\|^2 + C(1 + \|u_2\|_1^{2p}). \tag{2.10}$$

Lemma 1 and the inequality (2.10) imply

$$\varepsilon \partial_t \|u_1\|^2 + \delta \|u_1\|^2 \leqslant C_2, \qquad C_2 = C_2(\|u(0)\|_1).$$

Therefore

$$\|u_1(t)\|^2 \leqslant C_3(1 - e^{-\delta t/\varepsilon}) + \|u(0)\|^2 e^{-\delta t/\varepsilon}, \qquad C_3 = C_3(\|u(0)\|_1),$$

and taking into account Lemma 1, we get statement 1).

2) We now need the following functional

$$\Phi(u) = \int_\Omega \left\{ \frac{1}{2} |\nabla u|^2 + F(u) + g \cdot u \right\} dx, \qquad u \in H_1, \tag{2.11}$$

where $F(u)$ is determined by (1.7). (This functional is the global Lyapunov function of the problem (0.1), (0.2).)

Let us note, that if $u(t)$ is a trajectory of the system (0.1)–(0.2), then

$$\partial_t \Phi(u(t)) = -\varepsilon \|\partial_t u_1\|^2 - \|\partial_t u_2\|^2. \tag{2.12}$$

It follows from relation (2.12) that

$$\Phi(u(t)) \leqslant \Phi(u(0)) \qquad \forall t \geqslant 0. \tag{2.13}$$

Condition (1.8) implies

$$(1/2)\|\nabla u\|^2 - C - \|g\|^2 - \|u\|^2$$
$$\leqslant \Phi(u) \leqslant (1/2)\|\nabla u\|^2 + C(1 + \|u\|_{0,1+p}^{1+p}) + \|g\|^2 + \|u\|^2. \quad (2.14)$$

Now, using the inequalities (2.13) and (2.14) we obtain

$$\|\nabla u(t)\|^2 \leqslant 2\|u(t)\|^2 + 2\|u(0)\|_1^2 + M(1 + \|u(0)\|_1^{1+p}).$$

Hence part 1) of this lemma implies statement 2).

Now we estimate the so-called integral of dissipation, i.e., the integral with respect to t of $\varepsilon\|\partial_t u_1\|^2 + \|\partial_t u_2\|^2$.

LEMMA 3. *Let $u(t) = (u_1(t), u_2(t))$ be a solution of the problem (0.1)–(0.4). Then uniformly with respect to ε, $0 < \varepsilon \leqslant \varepsilon_0$, the following estimates hold*

$$\int_0^\infty (\varepsilon\|\partial_t u_1(\tau)\|^2 + \|\partial_t u_2(\tau)\|^2)d\tau \leqslant C_1, \quad C_1 = C_1(\|u(0)\|_1), \quad (2.15)$$

$$t(\varepsilon\|\partial_t u_1(t)\|^2 + \|\partial_t u_2(t)\|^2) \leqslant C_2(1+t), \quad C_2 = C_2(\|u(0)\|_1). \quad (2.16)$$

PROOF. First we prove the estimate (2.15). Now (2.12) and (2.14) imply

$$\int_0^t (\varepsilon\|\partial_t u_1(\tau)\|^2 + \|\partial_t u_2(\tau)\|^2)d\tau = \Phi(u(0)) - \Phi(u(t))$$
$$\leqslant \|u(t)\|^2 + M(1 + \|u(0)\|_1^{1+p}) + \|u(0)\|_1^2.$$

Hence, using lemma 2, we obtain

$$\int_0^t (\varepsilon\|\partial_t u_1(\tau)\|^2 + \|\partial_t u_2(\tau)\|^2)d\tau \leqslant C_1, \quad C_1 = C_1(\|u(0)\|_1).$$

Since C_1 does not depend on t, we get (2.15).

Then we prove estimate (2.16). If we differentiate the system (0.1)–(0.2) with respect to t and denote the derivative $\partial_t u_i$ by u_i' ($i = 1, 2$) we can deduce

$$\varepsilon\partial_t u_1' = \Delta u_1' - f_{1u_1}'(u)u_1' - f_{1u_2}'(u)u_2',$$
$$\partial_t u_2' = \Delta u_2' - f_{2u_1}'(u)u_1' - f_{2u_2}'(u)u_2'.$$

Multiplying this system by tu' in H, we get

$$(\varepsilon/2)\partial_t(t\|u_1'\|^2) + (1/2)\partial_t(t\|u_2'\|^2) + t\|\nabla u'\|^2$$
$$= (\varepsilon/2)\|u_1'\|^2 + (1/2)\|u_2'\|^2 - t(f'(u)u', u').$$

Then we integrate the previous equality from 0 to t and use condition (1.2)

$$\varepsilon t\|\partial_t u_1\|^2 + t\|\partial_t u_2\|^2 + \int_0^t \tau\|\nabla \partial_t u(\tau)\|^2 d\tau$$
$$\leq (\lambda_1 - \delta)\int_0^t \tau\|\partial_t u_1(\tau)\|^2 d\tau - \mu_2 \int_0^t \tau\|\partial_t u_2(\tau)\|^2 d\tau$$
$$+ \int_0^t \frac{1}{2}(\varepsilon\|\partial_t u_1(\tau)\|^2 + \|\partial_t u_2(\tau)\|^2) d\tau.$$

Note that $\|\nabla v\|^2 \geq \lambda_1 \|v\|^2$. Moreover, taking into account the estimate (2.15), we get

$$t(\varepsilon\|\partial_t u_1(t)\|^2 + \|\partial_t u_2(t)\|^2) \leq |\mu_2|tC_1 + C_1$$
$$\leq C_2(1+t), \qquad C_2 = C_2(\|u(0)\|_1).$$

COROLLARY 1. *From (2.16) it follows that*

$$\varepsilon\|\partial_t u_1(t)\|^2 + \|\partial_t u_2(t)\|^2 \leq C_3 = C_3(\|u(0)\|, \tau) \quad \text{for } t \geq \tau > 0. \qquad (2.17)$$

§3. The stabilized asymptotics of $u(t)$

We need the following lemma.

LEMMA 1. *If*

$$|\varphi(\xi)| \leq C(1 + |\xi|^\eta), \qquad 1/\eta \geq (n-2)/2,$$

then for any $u, w \in H_1$, $v \in L_2$, $\alpha > 0$ *there exists a* $C > 0$ *such that the following estimate holds*:

$$\|\varphi(u(x))v(x)w(x)\|_{0,1} \leq C(1 + \|u\|_1^{2\eta})\|v\|^2 + \alpha\|w\|_1^2.$$

PROOF. One can see that the Hölder inequality implies

$$\|\varphi(u)uw\|_{0,1} \leq \|\varphi(u)\|_{0,p_1} \|v\|_{0,p_2} \|w\|_{0,p_3}, \qquad (3.1)$$

where $p_1^{-1} + p_2^{-1} + p_3^{-1} = 1$. We restrict ourselves to proving the lemma in the case $n > 2$. Let $p_1 = n$, $p_2 = 2$, $p_3 = 2n/(n-2)$. Then

$$\|w\|_{0,p_3}^2 \leq C_1 \|w\|_1^2.$$

Moreover,

$$\|\varphi(u)\|_{0,p_1} \leq C_2(1 + \|u\|_{0,\eta\cdot n}^\eta) \leq C_3(1 + \|u\|_1^\eta).$$

From these estimates and from (3.1) it follows that

$$\|\varphi(u)vw\|_{0,1} \leq C_4 \|\varphi(u)\|_{0,p_1}^2 \|v\|_{0,p_2}^2 + \alpha_1 \|w\|_{0,p_3}^2$$
$$\leq C_5(1 + \|u\|_1^{2\eta})\|v\|^2 + \alpha_1 C_1 \|w\|_1^2.$$

Since $d_1 > 0$ is arbitrary, the lemma is proved.

Now we formulate a theorem proved in [1].

THEOREM 1. *Let $\{S_t\}$ be a semigroup acting in E, where E is a Banach space, and let B_0 be a bounded set in E, $S_t(B_0) \subset B_0$ $\forall t \geq 0$. Let U_ε be a set of functions $u(\cdot, \varepsilon) = u(\cdot) \in U_\varepsilon$ depending on a parameter ε, such that the set of values of these functions*

$$B_\varepsilon = \{u = u(t) : u(t) \in U_\varepsilon\}$$

lies in E: $B_\varepsilon \subset E$. We assume that the following conditions hold:

(1) *The set $\mathfrak{N}$ of equilibrium points of $\{S_t\}$ is finite,*

$$\mathfrak{N} = \{z_1, \ldots, z_N\}, \qquad \mathfrak{N} \subset B_0.$$

(2) $\forall \delta \geq 0$, $\exists T^0 < +\infty$ *such that T^0 is the time of arrival from B_0 to $O_\delta(\mathfrak{N})$. (Recall that T^0 is called the time of arrival from B_0 to $O_\delta(\mathfrak{N})$ if for any $u_0 \in B_0$ there exists a t, $0 \leq t \leq T^0(B_0)$, such that $S_t u_0 \in O_\delta(\mathfrak{N})$.)*

(3) $\forall u_0 \in B_0$ *there exist a numeration $\{z_j\}$ of points $z \in \mathfrak{N}$ and a $\delta > 0$ such that $S_t u_0$ passes $O_\delta(z_j)$ in the order contrary to this numeration. Moreover, it is assumed that $\{S_t\}$ has a global Lyapunov function.*

(4) $\forall j = 1, \ldots, N$, $z_j \in \mathfrak{N}$ *is a hyperbolic equilibrium point.*

(5) $B_\varepsilon \subset B_0$ $\forall \varepsilon \in (0, \varepsilon_1]$.

(6) *There exist positive constants α, c, and q_0 such that*

$$\forall u(t) \in U_\varepsilon, \ \forall v_0 \in B_0, \ \forall t, \tau, \ t \geq \tau \geq 0,$$
$$\|u(t) - S_{t-\tau} v_0\|_E \leq C e^{\alpha(t-\tau)}(\varepsilon^{q_0} + \|u(\tau) - v_0\|_E).$$

(7) $u(t) \in U_\varepsilon$ *is continuous in t for any $t \geq 0$.*

Then there exist $\varepsilon_0 > 0$, $q > 0$, and $c > 0$ such that $\forall \varepsilon \in (0, \varepsilon_0]$, $\forall u(t) \in U_\varepsilon$ there exists a combined limit trajectory $\tilde{u}(t, \varepsilon)$ satisfying the inequality

$$\sup_{t \geq 0} \|u(t) - \tilde{u}(t, \varepsilon)\|_E \leq C \varepsilon^q. \tag{3.1'}$$

Recall that the family of combined limit trajectories (c.l.t.) corresponding to a set of functions U_ε is a family of piecewise continuous in t trajectories $\tilde{u}(t, \varepsilon)$ of the limit semigroup $\{\bar{S}_t\}$ (i.e., $\{\bar{S}_t\}$ corresponds to $\varepsilon = 0$, although trajectories $\tilde{u}(t, \varepsilon)$ in (3.1') of the semigroup $\{S_t\}$ may depend on ε) with the following properties:

(1) $\tilde{u}(t, \varepsilon)$ is continuous in t, except the discontinuity points

$$T_1, \ldots, T_m, \quad m \leq N, \quad T_i = T_i(\tilde{u}), \quad T_1 < \cdots < T_m;$$

(2) the values $\tilde{u}(T_i - 0, \varepsilon)$, $\tilde{u}(T_i + 0, \varepsilon)$ at the discontinuity points T_i lie in a small neighborhood $O_\delta(\mathfrak{N})$ of the set $\mathfrak{N} = \{z_1, \ldots, z_N\}$ of equilibrium points of $\{S_t\}$;

(3) in any sufficiently small neighborhood $O_\delta(z_k)$, there are values $\tilde{u}(T_i \pm 0, \varepsilon)$ at no more than one point of discontinuity T_i. Moreover, $\tilde{u}(T_i+0, \varepsilon) \in M^u(z_k)$ (where $M^u(z_k)$ is the unstable manifold containing z_k), $\tilde{u}(t, \varepsilon) = S_{t-T_i}\tilde{u}(T_i+0, \varepsilon)$, $T_i < t < T_{i+1}$;

(4) $\tilde{u}(0, \varepsilon) = u(0, \varepsilon)$ for some $u(\cdot, \varepsilon) \in U_\varepsilon$ (see [1, p. 246]).

We should note that starting from the second continuous piece, the trajectories $\tilde{u}$ satisfy

$$\tilde{u}(t, \varepsilon) \subset \bigcup_k M^u(z_k).$$

Since the manifold $M^u(z_k)$ is finite-dimensional, these pieces of $\tilde{u}(t, \varepsilon)$ belong to a finite-dimensional family of trajectories.

To prove that the conditions of Theorem 1 hold for the solutions $u(t)$ of the system (0.1)–(0.4) and the solutions $v(t)$ of the system (0.5)–(0.7), we need some auxiliary statements. Recall that $v_1 = B(v_2)$ is a solution of the stationary equation (0.5), and moreover, $B: H_1^0(\Omega) \to H_1^0(\Omega)$ (see Lemma 3 below). The existence of the operator B follows from the properties of the function $f_1(v_1, v_2)$.

LEMMA 2. *Let* $u(t) = (u_1(t), u_2(t)) \in H_1$ *be a solution of the problem* (0.1)–(0.4). *Then*

1) $\|u_1(t) - B(u_2(t))\|_1^2 \leq \varepsilon C_1$, $\quad C_1 = C_1(\|u(0)\|_1, \tau) \quad \forall t \geq \tau > 0$,

2) $\int_0^t \|u_1(\tau) - B(u_2(\tau))\|_1^2 d\tau \leq \varepsilon C_2$, $\quad C_2 = C_2(\|u(0)\|_1) \quad \forall t \geq 0$.

PROOF. Subtracting equation (1.1), where u_1 is replaced by $B(u_2)$, from equation (0.1), we get

$$\varepsilon \partial_t u_1 = \Delta(u_1 - B(u_2)) - (f_1(u_1, u_2) - f_1(B(u_2), u_2)). \qquad (3.2)$$

Multiplying the equation (3.2) by $(u_1 - B(u_2))$ in $L_2(\Omega)$ and using the condition (1.3), we obtain

$$0 = -\|\nabla(u_1 - B(u_2))\|^2 - (f_1(u_1, u_2) - f_1(B(u_2), u_2), u_1 - B(u_2))$$
$$- (\varepsilon \partial_t u_1, u_1 - B(u_2))$$
$$\leq -\delta_0^2 \|\nabla(u_1 - B(u_2))\|^2 - (\lambda_1 - (\delta/4))\|u_1 - B(u_2)\|^2$$
$$- \left(\int_0^1 f'_{1u_1}(B(u_2) + \theta(u_1 - B(u_2)), u_2)d\theta(u_1 - B(u_2)), u_1 - B(u_2)\right)$$
$$+ M\varepsilon^2 \|\partial_t u_1\|^2 + (\delta/4)\|u_1 - B(u_2)\|^2$$
$$\leq -\delta_0^2 \|\nabla(u_1 - B(u_2))\|^2 - (\delta/2)\|u_1 - B(u_2)\|^2 + M\varepsilon^2 \|\partial_t u_1\|^2.$$

In this argument we used the inequality

$$-\left(\int_0^1 f'_{1u_1}(B(u_2) + \theta(u_1 - B(u_2)), u_2)d\theta(u_1 - B(u_2)), u_1 - B(u_2)\right)$$
$$\leq (\lambda_1 - \delta)\|u_1 - B(u_2)\|^2.$$

Hence,
$$\|u_1 - B(u_2)\|_1^2 \leq M'\varepsilon^2 \|\partial_t u_1\|^2. \qquad (3.3)$$
Now we deduce from the estimates (2.17) and (3.3)
$$\|u_1(t) - B(u_2(t))\|_1^2 \leq \varepsilon M' \varepsilon \|\partial_t u_1\|^2 \leq \varepsilon C_1, \qquad C_1 = C_1(\|u(0)\|_1, \tau),$$
for $t \geq \tau > 0$, and from the estimates (2.15) and (3.3)
$$\int_0^t \|u_1(\tau) - B(u_2(\tau))\|_1^2 d\tau \leq \varepsilon M' \int_0^t \varepsilon \|\partial_t u_1(\tau)\|^2 d\tau \leq \varepsilon C_2,$$
where $C_2 = C_2(\|u(0)\|_1)$, $\forall t \geq 0$.

LEMMA 3. Let $v(x) = (v_1(x), v_2(x))$, $w(x) = (w_1(x), w_2(x))$ be solutions of the equation (1.1), $v_1 = B(v_2)$, $w_1 = B(w_2)$. Then
$$\|B(v_2) - B(w_2)\|_1 \leq M \|v_2 - w_2\|, \quad \text{where } M = M(\|v_2\|_1, \|w\|_1).$$

PROOF. We have
$$\Delta(v_1 - w_1) - (f_1(v_1, v_2) - f_1(w_1, w_2)) = 0. \qquad (3.4)$$
Multiplying the equation (3.4) by $v_1 - w_1$ in $L_2(\Omega)$, we get
$$-\|\nabla(v_1 - w_1)\|^2 - \left(\int_0^1 f'_{1u_1}(w_1 + \theta(v_1 - w_1), v_2) d\theta (v_1 - w_1), v_1 - w_1\right)$$
$$- \left(\int_0^1 f'_{1u_2}(w_1, w_2 + \theta(v_2 - w_2)) d\theta (v_2 - w_2), v_1 - w_1\right) = 0.$$
Now using conditions (1.3), (1.6), and Lemma 1, we obtain
$$0 \leq -\delta_0^2 \|\nabla(v_1 - w_1)\|^2 - (\lambda_1 - (\delta/2))\|v_1 - w_1\|^2$$
$$+ (\lambda_1 - \delta)\|v_1 - w_1\|^2 + C(1 + \|v_2\|_1^{2\eta} + \|w\|_1^{2\eta})\|v_2 - w_2\|^2$$
$$+ (1/2)\delta_0^2 \|v_1 - w_1\|_1^2, \qquad \delta > \delta_0^2 > 0.$$
Hence,
$$\|v_1 - w_1\|_1^2 \leq C'(1 + \|v_2\|_1^{2\eta} + \|w\|_1^{2\eta})\|v_2 - w_2\|^2.$$
Recalling that $v_1 = B(v_2)$, $w_1 = B(w_2)$ and denoting
$$M^2 = C'(1 + \|v_2\|_1^{2\eta} + \|w\|_1^{2\eta}),$$
we obtain a complete proof of the lemma.

REMARK 1. Lemma 3 implies that the operator B acts from $H_1^0(\Omega)$ to $H_1^0(\Omega)$, i.e.,
$$B: H_1^0(\Omega) \to H_1^0(\Omega).$$
Actually, it can easily be seen from the condition (1.5), by multiplying equation (1.1) by u_1 in $L_2(\Omega)$, that
$$\|u_1\|_1^2 = \|B(0)\|_1^2 \leq M(1 + \|g_1\|^2).$$

According to Lemma 3, if $v \in H_1^0(\Omega)$, then
$$\|B(v)\|_1 \leq \|B(0)\|_1 + M(\|v\|_1)\|v\| \leq M_0 + M(\|v\|_1)\|v\|.$$

Now we use Theorem 1 for constructing the asymptotics of $u_2(t)$. Let $E = L_2(\Omega)$ and $U_\varepsilon = \{u_2(t): u(t) = (u_1(t), u_2(t))$ is a solution of the problem (0.1)–(0.4), $\|u(0)\|_1 \leq M\}$. Let the semigroup $\{S_t\}$ correspond to the following problem:
$$\partial_t v_2 = \Delta v_2 - f_2(B(v_2), v_2) - g_2(x), \tag{3.5}$$
$$v_2|_{\partial\Omega} = 0, \quad v_2|_{t=0} = v_{20}(x), \quad x \in \Omega. \tag{3.6}$$

The semigroup $\{S_t\}$ acts in $L_2(\Omega)$,
$$S_t: L_2(\Omega) \to L_2(\Omega) \quad \forall t \geq 0.$$

This fact is established as in the proof of Lemma 2.1. Let
$$B_0 = \bigcup_{t \geq 0} S_t(\{u \in L_2(\Omega): \|u\|_1 \leq M_1\}).$$

Since $\{S_t\}$ is (H_1, H_1)-bounded uniformly with respect to $t \geq 0$, B_0 is bounded in H_1 and $S_t(B_0) \subset B_0 \ \forall t \geq 0$.

Let us now check all the assumptions of Theorem 1.

We note that, as was assumed in §1, the conditions 1) and 4) of Theorem 1 hold.

Condition 2) follows from the boundedness of the integral of dissipation (formula (2.15)) and the boundedness of $u_2(t)$ in $H_1(\Omega)$ (see [1, p. 257]).

The Lyapunov function has the form
$$\Phi_1(u_2) = \int_\Omega \{\tfrac{1}{2}|\nabla B(u_2)|^2 + \tfrac{1}{2}|\nabla u_2|^2 + F(B(u_2), u_2) + g_1 \cdot B(u_2) + g_2 \cdot u_2\} dx.$$

Actually, using the system (0.1), (0.2) for $\varepsilon = 0$, it is easy to see that
$$\partial_t \Phi_1(u_2(t)) = -\int_\Omega \partial_t u_2 \cdot \partial_t u_2 \, dx < 0. \tag{3.7}$$

Here $u_2(t)$ is any solution of equation (3.5) different from the stationary one. To deduce (3.7), we can use the fact that $(u_1(t) = B(u_2(t)), u_2(t))$ is a solution of the system (0.1), (0.2) for $\varepsilon = 0$.

Condition 3) follows from the existence of the Lyapunov function, the hyperbolicity of the equilibrium points and the precompactness of the set $\{S_t v_{20}, t \geq 1\}$ in $L_2(\Omega)$, which in turn follows from Lemma 2.1, valid also for $\varepsilon = 0$.

Condition 5) holds by Lemma 2.1.

Condition 7) follows from the finiteness of the dissipation integral (formula (2.15)) and the boundedness of $u_2(t) \in U_\varepsilon$ in $L_2(\Omega)$ (Lemma 2.1).

Now we check condition 6) of Theorem 1. Subtracting equation (3.5) from (0.2), we obtain
$$\partial_t(u_2 - v_2) = \Delta(u_2 - v_2) - (f_2(u_1, u_2) - f_2(B(v_2), v_2)). \tag{3.8}$$

Multiplying (3.8) by $u_2 - v_2$ in $L_2(\Omega)$ and using the conditions (1.4), (1.9) and Lemma 1, we deduce:

$$(1/2)\partial_t \|u_2 - v_2\|^2 + \|\nabla(u_2 - v_2)\|^2$$
$$= -\left(\int_0^1 f'_{2u_1}(B(v_2) + \theta(u_1 - B(v_2))), u_2) d\theta(u_1 - B(v_2)), u_2 - v_2\right)$$
$$- \left(\int_0^1 f'_{2u_2}(B(v_2), v_2 + \theta(u_2 - v_2)) d\theta(u_2 - v_2), u_2 - v_2\right)$$
$$\leq C(1 + \|u\|_1^{2\eta} + \|B(v_2)\|_1^{2\eta})\|u_1 - B(v_2)\|^2$$
$$+ (1/2)\|u_2 - v_2\|_1^2 + \mu_2 \|u_2 - v_2\|^2. \tag{3.9}$$

Note that since $\|u(t)\|_1$, $\|B(v_2)\|_1$ are bounded uniformly with respect to $t \geq 0$ (Lemma 2.2), we have

$$C(1 + \|u\|_1^{2\eta} + \|B(v_2)\|_1^{2\eta}) \leq M.$$

Therefore, integrating (3.9) from 0 to t we get

$$\|u_2(t) - v_2(t)\|^2 \leq \|u_2(0) - v_2(0)\|^2 + M \int_0^t \|u_1(\tau) - B(u_2(\tau))\|^2 d\tau$$
$$+ M \int_0^t \|B(u_2(\tau)) - B(v_2(\tau))\|^2 d\tau$$
$$+ \mu_2 \int_0^t \|u_2(\tau) - v_2(\tau)\|^2 d\tau.$$

Using Lemmas 2 and 3, we obtain

$$\|u_2(t) - v_2(t)\|^2 \leq \|u_2(0) - v_2(0)\|^2 + M_1 \int_0^t \|u_2(\tau) - v_2(\tau)\|^2 d\tau + M_2 \varepsilon.$$

Hence owing to the Gronwall inequality, condition 6) has been proved.

Therefore we have checked all the assumptions of Theorem 1 and the following statement is valid.

THEOREM 2. *For any set B_0 bounded in H_1 and any $\tau > 0$ there exist positive constants C_1, C_2, q, ε_0 such that for any solution of the problem (0.1)–(0.4) $u(t) = (u_1(t), u_2(t))$ with $0 < \varepsilon \leq \varepsilon_0$ and initial data from B_0 there exists a c.l.t. $\tilde{u}_2(t, \varepsilon)$ corresponding to the problem (0.5)–(0.6) which satisfies the estimates*:

$$\sup_{t \geq 0} \|u_2(t) - \tilde{u}_2(t, \varepsilon)\| \leq C_1 \varepsilon^q, \tag{3.10}$$

$$\sup_{t \geq \tau} \|u_1(t) - B(\tilde{u}_2(t, \varepsilon))\|_1 \leq C_2 \varepsilon^{q'}, \qquad q' = \min(q, 1/2). \tag{3.11}$$

PROOF. The estimate (3.10) holds by Theorem 1. We shall show that the estimate (3.11) also holds. We have

$$\|u_1(t) - B(\tilde{u}_2(t, \varepsilon))\|_1^2 \leq \|u_1(t) - B(u_2(t))\|_1^2 + \|B(u_2(t)) - B(\tilde{u}_2(t, \varepsilon))\|_1^2.$$

Using Lemmas 2 and 3 and estimate (3.10), we obtain
$$\|u_1(t) - B(\tilde{u}_2(t,\varepsilon))\|_1^2 \leq C_1'\varepsilon + M^2\|u_2(t) - \tilde{u}_2(t,\varepsilon)\|^2 \leq C_1'\varepsilon + C_1''\varepsilon^{2q}$$
for $t \geq \tau > 0$. Hence the estimate (3.11) follows.

§4. Systems of equations with small parameter at the derivatives of highest order

Let us consider the following problem for a system of quasilinear parabolic equations with small parameter at the highest derivatives in the first equation:
$$\varepsilon\partial_t u_1 = \varepsilon d_1 \Delta u_1 - f_1(u_1, u_2) - g_1(x), \tag{4.1}$$
$$\partial_t u_2 = d_2 \Delta u_2 - f_2(u_1, u_2) - g_2(x), \tag{4.2}$$
with boundary conditions
$$u_1|_{\partial\Omega} = 0, \qquad u_2|_{\partial\Omega} = 0, \tag{4.3}$$
and initial data
$$u_1|_{t=0} = u_{10}(x), \qquad u_2|_{t=0} = u_{20}(x), \qquad x \in \Omega \in \mathbb{R}^n. \tag{4.4}$$
For $\varepsilon = 0$, equation (4.1) turns into
$$f_1(v_1, v_2) + g_1(x) = 0, \tag{4.5}$$
which is not a differential equation. Here $x \in \Omega$ is regarded as a parameter. As in §1, we denote
$$u = (u_1, u_2), \quad f(u) = (f_1(u), f_2(u)), \quad f_i(u) \in C^{1+\alpha}, \quad \alpha > 0 \; (i=1,2),$$
$$g(x) = (g_1(x), g_2(x)).$$
It is assumed that the following conditions hold:
$$(f'(\xi)\nu, \nu) \geq \gamma_1^2 \nu_1^2 - \mu\nu_2^2, \qquad \mu \in \mathbb{R}, \; \gamma_1 \neq 0, \tag{4.6}$$
$$(f(\xi), \xi) \geq -C_1 + \gamma_2^2|\xi|^2, \qquad f(0) = 0, \tag{4.7}$$
$$|f'_{1\xi_2}(\xi)| \leq C_2, \tag{4.8}$$
$$|f(\xi)| \leq C_3 + C_4|\xi|^{p_0}, \qquad p_0^{-1} \geq \frac{n-2}{n+2}. \tag{4.9}$$
It follows from condition (4.6) that
$$f'_{1\xi_1} \geq \gamma_1^2, \tag{4.10}$$
$$f'_{2\xi_2} \geq -\mu. \tag{4.11}$$
Moreover, let $f(\xi)$ be a potential vector, i.e., suppose there exists a function $F(\xi_1, \xi_2)$ such that
$$f(\xi) = \operatorname{grad} F(\xi), \tag{4.12}$$
$$-C_5 \leq F(\xi) \leq C_6(1 + |\xi|^{p_0+1}). \tag{4.13}$$

Since $\partial^2 F/\partial\xi_1\partial\xi_2 = \partial^2 F/\partial\xi_2\partial\xi_1$, we deduce from (4.8) and (4.12) that

$$|f'_{2\xi_1}(\xi)| \leq C_2. \qquad (4.14)$$

It follows from condition (4.10) that for any function $v_2(x)$ equation (4.5) has a unique solution $v_1(x) = \varphi(x, v_2(x))$, where $\varphi(x, \xi)$ is a numerical function. It is assumed that the function

$$g(x) = (g_1(x), g_2(x)) \in H_1^0(\Omega) \times L_2(\Omega)$$

is such that
1) the set $\mathfrak{N}$ of solutions of the equation

$$d_2\Delta u_2 - f_2(\varphi(x, u_2), u_2) - g_2(x) = 0$$

is finite, $\mathfrak{N} = \{z_1, \ldots, z_N\}$;
2) all the $z_j \in \mathfrak{N}$ are hyperbolic equilibrium points.

§5. A priori estimates

As in the previous sections, we denote

$$H = (L_2(\Omega))^2, \qquad H_1 = (H_1^0(\Omega))^2.$$

We shall investigate some properties of the semigroup $\{S_t(\varepsilon)\}$ corresponding to the problem (4.1)–(4.4).

LEMMA 1. *The semigroups $\{S_t(\varepsilon)\}$ are (H, H)-bounded uniformly with respect to ε, $0 < \varepsilon \leq \varepsilon_0$, and $t \geq 0$.*

PROOF. Multiplying the system (4.1)–(4.2) by u in H and using condition (4.7), we obtain

$$\begin{aligned}
&(\varepsilon/2)\partial_t\|u_1\|^2 + (1/2)\partial_t\|u_2\|^2 + \varepsilon d_1\|\nabla u_1\|^2 + d_2\|\nabla u_2\|^2 \\
&= -(f(u), u) - (g, u) \\
&\leq C_1|\Omega| - \gamma_2^2\|u\|^2 + M\|g\|^2 + (1/2)\gamma_2^2\|u\|^2 \\
&\leq -(1/2)\gamma_2^2\|u\|^2 + C.
\end{aligned} \qquad (5.1)$$

Hence, as in Lemma 2.1, we deduce

$$\|u_2(t)\|^2 \leq C(1 + \|u(0)\|^2). \qquad (5.2)$$

Note that conditions (4.8) and (4.10) imply

$$\begin{aligned}
&(f_1(u_1, u_2), u_1) \\
&= \left(f_1(0,0) + \int_0^1 f'_{1u_2}(0, \theta u_2)\,d\theta \cdot u_2 + \int_0^1 f'_{1u_1}(\theta u_1, u_2)\,d\theta \cdot u_1, u_1\right) \\
&\geq -M\|u_2\|^2 - (1/2)\gamma_1^2\|u_1\|^2 + \gamma_1^2\|u_1\|^2 \\
&\geq (1/2)\gamma_1^2\|u_1\|^2 - M_1\|u_2\|^2. \qquad (5.3)
\end{aligned}$$

Multiplying equation (4.1) by u_1 in $L_2(\Omega)$ and using the estimates (5.2) and (5.3), we obtain

$$(1/2)\varepsilon\partial_t\|u_1\|^2 + \varepsilon d_1\|\nabla u_1\|^2 = -(f_1(u_1, u_2), u_1) - (g_1, u_1)$$
$$\leqslant -(1/2)\gamma_1^2\|u_1\|^2 + M_1\|u_2\|^2 + M_2\|g_1\|^2 + (1/4)\gamma_1^2\|u_1\|^2$$
$$\leqslant -(1/4)\gamma_1^2\|u_1\|^2 + M_3, \qquad M_3 = M_3(\|u(0)\|).$$

Hence it follows that

$$\|u_1(t)\|^2 \leqslant C(1 + \|u(0)\|^2);$$

taking into account the estimate (5.2), we obtain a complete proof of the lemma.

LEMMA 2. *The semigroup* $\{S_t(\varepsilon)\}$ *is* $(H, L_2(\Omega) \times H_1(\Omega))$-*bounded for* $t > 0$.

PROOF. Integrating the inequality (5.1) from 0 to t we obtain for all t, $0 \leqslant t \leqslant T$, the relation

$$\int_0^t \|\nabla u_2(\tau)\|^2 d\tau \leqslant C(1 + T), \qquad C = C(\|u(0)\|). \qquad (5.4)$$

It follows from conditions (4.11) and (4.14) that

$$(f_2(u_1, u_2), \Delta u_2) = \left(f_2(0, u_2) + \int_0^1 f'_{2u_1}(\theta u_1, u_2)\, d\theta \cdot u_1, \Delta u_2\right)$$
$$\leqslant -(f'_{2u_2}(0, u_2)\nabla u_2, \nabla u_2) + (1/4)d_2\|\Delta u_2\|^2$$
$$+ M\left\|\int_0^1 f'_{2u_1}(\theta u_1, u_2)\, d\theta \cdot u_1\right\|^2$$
$$\leqslant \mu\|\nabla u_2\|^2 + (1/4)d_2\|\Delta u_2\|^2 + M'\|u_1\|^2. \qquad (5.5)$$

Now we proceed directly to the proof of the lemma. Multiplying equation (4.2) by $-t\Delta u_2$ in $L_2(\Omega)$ and using estimate (5.5) and Lemma 1, we get:

$$(1/2)\partial_t(t\|\nabla u_2\|^2)$$
$$= (1/2)\|\nabla u_2\|^2 - td_2\|\Delta u_2\|^2 + t(f_2(u_1, u_2), \Delta u_2) + t(g_2, \Delta u_2)$$
$$\leqslant (1/2)\|\nabla u_2\|^2 - td_2\|\Delta u_2\|^2 + \mu t\|\nabla u_2\|^2$$
$$+ (1/4)td_2\|\Delta u_2\|^2 + M't\|u_1\|^2 + (1/4)td_2\|\Delta u_2\|^2 + M''t\|g_2\|^2$$
$$\leqslant ((1/2) + \mu t)\|\nabla u_2\|^2 + Ct,$$

where $C = C(\|u(0)\|)$. Integrating this inequality from 0 to t and taking into account estimate (5.4), we obtain (for $0 \leqslant t \leqslant T$):

$$t\|\nabla u_2(t)\|^2 \leqslant C', \qquad C' = C'(T, \|u(0)\|).$$

LEMMA 3. *The semigroups $\{S_t(\varepsilon)\}$ are (H_1, H_1)-bounded uniformly with respect to ε, $0 < \varepsilon \leq \varepsilon_0$, and $t \geq 0$.*

PROOF. At first we prove uniform boundedness of $\|\nabla u_2(t)\|$ with respect to ε, $0 < \varepsilon \leq \varepsilon_0$, and $t \geq 0$. Multiplying the system (4.1)–(4.2) by $-\Delta u$ in H and using the condition (4.6), we get:

$$(1/2)(\varepsilon \partial_t \|\nabla u_1\|^2 + \partial_t \|\nabla u_2\|^2) + \varepsilon d_1 \|\Delta u_1\|^2 + d_2 \|\Delta u_2\|^2$$
$$= (f(u), \Delta u) + (g, \Delta u)$$
$$= -(f'(u)\nabla u, \nabla u) - (\nabla g_1, \nabla u_1) + (g_2, \Delta u_2)$$
$$\leq -\gamma_1^2 \|\nabla u_1\|^2 + \mu \|\nabla u_2\|^2 + M_1 \|g_1\|_1^2$$
$$+ (1/2)\gamma_1^2 \|\nabla u_1\|^2 + M_2 \|g_2\|^2 + (1/2)\|\Delta u_2\|^2.$$

Therefore,

$$\varepsilon \partial_t \|\nabla u_1\|^2 + \partial_t \|\nabla u_2\|^2 + \gamma_1^2 \|\nabla u_1\|^2 \leq \mu \|\nabla u_2\|^2 + C.$$

Hence, owing to the Gronwall inequality, it follows that

$$\|\nabla u_2(t)\|^2 \leq C(T, \|u(0)\|_1) \quad \text{(for } 0 \leq t \leq T). \tag{5.6}$$

Note that Lemmas 1 and 2 imply

$$\|\nabla u_2(t)\|^2 \leq C(\|u(t-1)\|) \leq C_1(\|u(0)\|) \quad \text{(for } t > 1)$$

and owing to the estimate (5.6),

$$\|\nabla u_2(t)\|^2 \leq C(\|u(0)\|_1) \quad \text{for } 0 \leq t \leq 1.$$

Therefore, taking into account Lemma 1, we get

$$\|u_2(t)\|_1^2 \leq C(\|u(0)\|_1) \quad \forall t \geq 0. \tag{5.7}$$

Now we prove the uniform boundedness of $\|\nabla u_1(t)\|$. To do this, we multiply equation (4.1) by $-\Delta u_1$ in $L_2(\Omega)$ and use the conditions (4.8) and (4.10):

$$(1/2)\varepsilon \partial_t \|\nabla u_1\|^2 + \varepsilon d_1 \|\Delta u_1\|^2$$
$$= (f_1(u_1, u_2), \Delta u_1) + (g_1, \Delta u_1)$$
$$= -(f'_{1u_1}\nabla u_1, \nabla u_1) - (f'_{1u_2}\nabla u_2, \nabla u_1) - (\nabla g_1, \nabla u_1)$$
$$\leq -\gamma_1^2 \|\nabla u_1\|^2 + (1/4)\gamma_1^2 \|\nabla u_1\|^2$$
$$+ M\|f'_{1u_2}\nabla u_2\| + (1/4)\gamma_1^2 \|\nabla u_1\|^2 + M\|g_1\|_1^2$$
$$\leq -(1/2)\gamma_1^2 \|\nabla u_1\|^2 + C(1 + \|\nabla u_2\|^2).$$

Using the estimate (5.7), we deduce

$$\varepsilon \partial_t \|\nabla u_1\|^2 + \varepsilon d_1 \|\Delta u_1\|^2 + \gamma_1^2 \|\nabla u_1\|^2 \leq C', \qquad C' = C'(\|u(0)\|_1). \tag{5.8}$$

It follows from inequality (5.8) that

$$\|\nabla u_1(t)\| \leqslant C'', \quad C'' = C''(\|u(0)\|_1),$$

and taking into account Lemma 1 and estimate (5.7), we obtain the complete proof of the lemma.

We now estimate the dissipation integral.

LEMMA 4. *Let* $u(t) = (u_1(t), u_2(t))$ *be a solution of the problem* (4.1)-(4.4). *Then the following estimate holds*:

$$\int_0^\infty (\varepsilon\|\partial_t u_1\|^2 + \|\partial_t u_2\|^2)\,dt \leqslant C(\|u(0)\|_1).$$

PROOF. We consider the functional

$$\Phi_\varepsilon(u) = \int_\Omega \left\{\frac{1}{2}\varepsilon d_1|\nabla u_1|^2 + \frac{1}{2}d_2|\nabla u_2|^2 + F(u) + g\cdot u\right\}dx, \quad (5.9)$$

where $F(u)$ is determined by (4.12). It is easy to see that

$$\partial_t \Phi_\varepsilon(u(t)) = -(\varepsilon\|\partial_t u_1\|^2 + \|\partial_t u_2\|^2).$$

Therefore,

$$\int_0^t (\varepsilon\|\partial_t u_1\|^2 + \|\partial_t u_2\|^2)\,d\tau = \Phi_\varepsilon(u(0)) - \Phi_\varepsilon(u(t)). \quad (5.10)$$

Owing to condition (4.13),

$$(1/2)\varepsilon d_1\|\nabla u_1\|^2 + (1/2)d_2\|\nabla u_2\|^2 - C_5|\Omega| - \|g\|^2 - \|u\|^2$$
$$\leqslant \Phi_\varepsilon(u) \leqslant (1/2)\varepsilon d_1\|\nabla u_1\|^2 + (1/2)d_2\|\nabla u_2\|^2$$
$$+ C_6(|\Omega| + \|u\|_{0,1+p_0}^{1+p_0}) + \|g\|^2 + \|u\|^2. \quad (5.11)$$

Inequalities (5.10) and (5.11) imply

$$\int_0^t (\varepsilon\|\partial_t u_1(\tau)\|^2 + \|\partial_t u_2(\tau)\|^2)\,d\tau \leqslant \|u(t)\|^2 + M(1 + \|u(0)\|_1^2 + \|u(0)\|_1^{1+p_0}).$$

According to Lemma 1, $\|u(t)\|^2 \leqslant C(1 + \|u(0)\|)$. Therefore,

$$\int_0^t (\varepsilon\|\partial_t u_1(\tau)\|^2 + \|\partial_t u_2(\tau)\|^2)\,d\tau \leqslant M'(1 + \|u(0)\|_1^2 + \|u(0)\|_1^{p_0+1}) = C, \quad (5.12)$$

where $C = C(\|u(0)\|_1)$. Since the right-hand side of the inequality (5.12) does not depend on time, by passing to the limit as $t \to +\infty$ we obtain the proof of the lemma.

§6. Asymptotics of $u(t)$

To construct the asymptotics of $u_2(t)$, we use Theorem 3.1. In our case $E = L_2(\Omega)$, and $U_\varepsilon = \{u_2(t) : u(t) = (u_1(t), u_2(t))$ is a solution of the problem (4.1)–(4.4), $\|u(0)\|_1 \leq M\}$. The semigroup $\{S_t\}$ corresponds to the limit problem (for $\varepsilon = 0$)

$$\partial_t v_2 = d_2 \Delta v_2 - f_2(\varphi(x, v_2), v_2) - g_2(x), \qquad (6.1)$$
$$v_2|_{\partial \Omega} = 0, \qquad v_2|_{t=0} = v_{20}(x), \quad x \in \Omega, \qquad (6.2)$$

where the function $\varphi(x, \xi)$ was defined in §4. As in Lemma 5.1, it can be established that the semigroup $\{S_t\}$ acts in $L_2(\Omega)$,

$$S_t : L_2(\Omega) \to L_2(\Omega) \qquad \forall t \geq 0.$$

Let

$$B_0 = \bigcup_{t \geq 0} S_t(\{u \in L_2(\Omega) : \|u\|_1 \leq M_1\}).$$

Since $\{S_t\}$ is (H_1, H_1)-bounded uniformly with respect to $t \geq 0$, it follows that B_0 is bounded in H_1 and $S_t(B_0) \subset B_0$ $\forall t \geq 0$.

Now we check all the conditions of Theorem 3.1.

Conditions 1) and 4) are fulfilled by assumption (§4).

Condition 2) of Theorem 3.1 follows from the finiteness of the dissipation integral (Lemma 5.4) and the boundedness of $v_2(t)$ in $H_1(\Omega)$ (see [1, p. 257]).

The Lyapunov function of equation (6.1) is given by (5.9) where $\varepsilon = 0$, $u_1 = \varphi(x, u_2)$. It is easy to see that

$$\int_0^{u_2} f_2(\varphi(x, \xi), \xi) \, d\xi = F(\varphi(x, u_2), u_2) + g_1 \cdot \varphi(x, u_2) + \text{const},$$

and therefore, the Lyapunov function has the form

$$\Phi_0(u_2) = \int_\Omega \left\{ \frac{1}{2} d_2 |\nabla u_2|^2 + F_2(u_2) + g_2 \cdot u_2 \right\} dx,$$

where

$$F_2(u_2) = \int_0^{u_2} f_2(\varphi(x, \xi), \xi) \, d\xi.$$

Condition 3) follows from the existence of the Lyapunov function, the precompactness of the set $\{S_t v_{20}, t \geq 1\}$ in $L_2(\Omega)$, and the hyperbolicity of the equilibrium points $z_i \in \mathfrak{N}$.

Condition 5) of Theorem 3.1 holds owing to the uniform (with respect to $t \geq 0$) (H, H)-boundedness of the semigroup $\{S_t(\varepsilon)\}$ (Lemma 5.1).

Condition 7) follows from the finiteness of the dissipation integral (Lemma 5.4) and the boundedness of $u_2(t)$ in $L_2(\Omega)$ (Lemma 5.1).

Now let us check condition 6). First we prove some auxiliary lemmas.

LEMMA 1. *Let $u(t)$ be a solution of the problem* (4.1)–(4.4). *Then the following estimates hold*:

1) $\int_\theta^t \varepsilon \|\Delta u_1(\tau)\|^2 d\tau \leqslant C_1(1 + |t - \theta|)$, $C_1 = C_1(\|u(0)\|_1)$,
2) $\int_\theta^t \|u_1(\tau) - \varphi(x, u_2(\tau))\|^2 d\tau \leqslant \varepsilon C_2(1 + |t - \theta|)$, $C_2 = C_2(\|u(0)\|_1)$.

PROOF. 1) Integrating inequality (5.8) over $[\theta, t]$ and using Lemma 5.3, we obtain

$$d_1 \int_\theta^t \varepsilon \|\Delta u_1(\tau)\|^2 d\tau \leqslant \varepsilon \|\nabla u_1(\theta)\|^2 + C'(t - \theta) \leqslant C''(1 + |t - \theta|).$$

Hence statement 1) follows, where $C_1 = d_1^{-1} C''$.

2) Subtracting (4.5) from (4.1), we get

$$\varepsilon \partial_t u_1 = \varepsilon d_1 \Delta u_1 - (f_1(u_1, u_2) - f_1(\varphi(x, u_2), u_2)). \tag{6.3}$$

Multiplying the equation (6.3) by $u_1 - \varphi(x, u_2)$ in $L_2(\Omega)$ and using condition (4.10), we deduce:

$$\begin{aligned}
0 =\ & -(\varepsilon \partial_t u_1, u_1 - \varphi(x, u_2)) + (\varepsilon d_1 \Delta u_1, u_1 - \varphi(x, u_2)) \\
& - (f_1(u_1, u_2) - f_1(\varphi(x, u_2), u_2), u_1 - \varphi(x, u_2)) \\
\leqslant\ & M\varepsilon^2 \|\partial_t u_1\|^2 + (1/4)\gamma_1^2 \|u_1 - \varphi(x, u_2)\|^2 + M\varepsilon^2 d_1^2 \|\Delta u_1\|^2 \\
& + (1/4)\gamma_1^2 \|u_1 - \varphi(x, u_2)\|^2 \\
& - \left(\int_0^1 f'_{1u_1}(\varphi(x, u_2) + \theta(u_1 - \varphi(x, u_2)), u_2)\, d\theta (u_1 - \varphi(x, u_2)), \right. \\
& \hspace{8cm} \left. u_1 - \varphi(x, u_2) \right) \\
\leqslant\ & \varepsilon M_1 (\varepsilon \|\partial_t u_1\|^2 + \varepsilon \|\Delta u_1\|^2) - (1/2)\gamma_1^2 \|u_1 - \varphi(x, u_2)\|^2.
\end{aligned}$$

Now moving the term $(1/2)\gamma_1^2 \|u_1 - \varphi(x, u_2)\|^2$ to the left-hand side of inequality, we integrate the inequality over $[\theta, t]$; using part 1) of this lemma and Lemma 5.4, we deduce the estimate 2)

$$\int_\theta^t \|u_1(\tau) - \varphi(x, u_2(\tau))\|^2 d\tau \leqslant \varepsilon C_2(1 + |t - \theta|), \qquad C_2 = C_2(\|u(0)\|_1).$$

LEMMA 2. *Let* $v(x) = (v_1(x), v_2(x))$, $w(x) = (w_1(x), w_2(x))$ *be solutions of equation* (4.5), *i.e.*, $v_1 = \varphi(x, v_2)$, $w_1 = \varphi(x, w_2)$. *Then*

$$\|v_1 - w_1\| \leq M \|v_2 - w_2\|.$$

PROOF. It is obvious that

$$f_1(v_1, v_2) - f_1(w_1, w_2) = 0.$$

Multiplying this equation by $v_1 - w_1$ in $L_2(\Omega)$ and using the conditions (4.8), (4.10) we obtain:

$$0 = \left(\int_0^1 \{f'_{1u_1}(w_1 + \theta(v_1 - w_1), v_2) \cdot (v_1 - w_1)\right.$$
$$\left. + f'_{1u_2}(w_1, w_2 + \theta(v_2 - w_2)) \cdot (v_2 - w_2)\} d\theta, v_1 - w_1\right)$$
$$\geq \gamma_1^2 \|v_1 - w_1\|^2 - C \left\| \int_0^1 f'_{1u_2}(w_1, w_2 + \theta(v_2 - w_2)) d\theta \cdot (v_2 - w_2) \right\|^2$$
$$- (1/2)\gamma_1^2 \|v_1 - w_1\|^2$$
$$\geq (1/2)\gamma_1^2 \|v_1 - w_1\|^2 - M' \|v_2 - w_2\|^2.$$

Therefore,

$$\|v_1 - w_1\|^2 = \|\varphi(x, v_2) - \varphi(x, w_2)\|^2$$
$$\leq M \|v_2 - w_2\|^2.$$

Now let us derive condition 6) of Theorem 3.1. Let

$$u(t) = (u_1(t), u_2(t))$$

be a solution of problem (4.1)–(4.4), $v_2(t)$ be a solution of problem (6.1)–(6.2). Note that

$$\partial_t(u_2 - v_2) = d_2 \Delta(u_2 - v_2) - (f_2(u_1, u_2) - f_2(\varphi(x, v_2), v_2)). \tag{6.4}$$

Multiplying equation (6.4) by $u_2 - v_2$ in $L_2(\Omega)$ and using conditions (4.11), (4.14), we deduce:

$$(1/2)\partial_t \|u_2 - v_2\|^2 + d_2 \|\nabla(u_2 - v_2)\|^2$$
$$= -\left(\int_0^1 \{f'_{2u_1}(\varphi(x, v_2) + \theta(u_1 - \varphi(x, v_2)), u_2) \cdot (u_1 - \varphi(x, v_2))\right.$$
$$\left. + f'_{2u_2}(\varphi(x, v_2), v_2 + \theta(u_2 - v_2)) \cdot (u_2 - v_2)\} d\theta, u_2 - v_2\right)$$
$$\leq C \|u_1 - \varphi(x, v_2)\|^2 + \|u_2 - v_2\|^2 + \mu \|u_2 - v_2\|^2$$
$$\leq (1 + \mu) \|u_2 - v_2\|^2 + C \|u_1 - \varphi(x, u_2)\|^2$$
$$+ H \|\varphi(x, u_2) - \varphi(x, v_2)\|^2. \tag{6.5}$$

Integrating the inequality (6.5) over $[\theta, t]$ and using Lemmas 1 and 2, we obtain

$$\|u_2(t) - v_2(t)\|^2 \leq \|u_2(\theta) - v_2(\theta)\|^2 + C' \int_\theta^t \|u_2(\tau) - v_2(\tau)\|^2 d\tau$$
$$+ C \int_\theta^t \|\varphi(x, u_2(\tau)) - \varphi(x, v_2(\tau))\|^2 d\tau$$
$$+ C \int_\theta^t \|u_1(\tau) - \varphi(x, u_2(\tau))\|^2 d\tau$$
$$\leq \|u_2(\theta) - v_2(\theta)\|^2 + C' \int_\theta^t \|u_2(\tau) - v_2(\tau)\|^2 d\tau$$
$$+ M_1 \varepsilon (1 + |t - \theta|) + M_2 \int_\theta^t \|u_2(\tau) - v_2(\tau)\|^2 d\tau$$
$$\leq \|u_2(\theta) - v_2(\theta)\|^2 + M_3 \int_\theta^t \|u_2(\tau) - v_2(\tau)\|^2 d\tau$$
$$+ M_1 \varepsilon (1 + |t - \theta|).$$

Hence by the Gronwall inequality, we get condition 6) of Theorem 3.1, where $q_0 = 1/2$, $\alpha = M_3 + 1/2$.

Since all the conditions of Theorem 3.1 are fulfilled, the following theorem has been proved.

THEOREM 1. *For any set B_0 bounded in H_1 there exist positive constants ε, C_1, C_2, C_3, q such that for $0 < \varepsilon \leq \varepsilon_0$ and whenever a solution $u(t) = (u_1(t), u_2(t))$ of the problem (4.1)–(4.4) has initial data from B_0 ($u_0 = (u_{10}, u_{20}) \in B_0$ there exists c.l.t. $\tilde{u}_2(t, \varepsilon)$ corresponding to the problem (6.1)–(6.2), which satisfies the estimates*

$$\sup_{t \geq 0} \|u_2(t) - \tilde{u}_2(t, \varepsilon)\| \leq C_1 \varepsilon^q, \tag{6.6}$$

$$\int_0^t \|u_1(\tau) - \varphi(x, \tilde{u}_2(\tau, \varepsilon))\|^2 d\tau \leq C_2(1 + t)\varepsilon + C_3 t \varepsilon^{2q}. \tag{6.7}$$

PROOF. The estimate (6.6) is a consequence of Theorem 3.1. To obtain estimate (6.7), we note that

$$\int_0^t \|u_1(\tau) - \varphi(x, \tilde{u}_2(\tau, \varepsilon))\|^2 d\tau$$
$$\leq \int_0^t \|u_1(\tau) - \varphi(x, u_2(\tau))\|^2 d\tau + \int_0^t \|\varphi(x, u_2(\tau)) - \varphi(x, \tilde{u}_2(\tau, \varepsilon))\|^2 d\tau.$$

Then we use Lemmas 1 and 2 and the estimate (6.6):

$$\int_0^t \|u_1(\tau) - \varphi(x, \tilde{u}_2(\tau, \varepsilon))\|^2 d\tau \leq C_2(1 + t)\varepsilon + C_3 t \varepsilon^{2q}.$$

REFERENCES

1. A. V. Babin and M. I. Vishik, *Attractors of evolution equations*, "Nauka", Moscow, 1989. (Russian)
2. A. N. Tikhonov, *Systems of differential equations with small parameters*, Mat. Sb. **31** (1952), no. 3, 375–386. (Russian)
3. _____, *Systems of differential equations with small parameters*, Mat. Sb. **27** (1950), no. 1, 147–156. (Russian)
4. J.-L. Lions, *Quelques méthodes de résolution des problèmes aux limites non linéaires*, Dunod & Gauthier-Villard, Paris, 1969.
5. M. I. Vishik and L. A. Lyusternik, *Regular degeneration and boundary layer for linear differential equations with small parameters*, Uspekhi Mat. Nauk **12** (1957), no. 5, 3–122. (Russian)

Translated by V. YU. SKVORTSOV

编辑手记

"苏联数学进展系列"由不同数学领域的一名或多名资深专家作为主编,内容包含来自俄罗斯的世界顶级数学家的论文. 此系列书籍在 21 卷之后作为"美国数学协会译丛 2"的子系列出版,后更名为"苏联数学进展系列".

本书为此系列的第 10 卷《偏微分方程全局吸引子的特性》.

演化方程的全局吸引子是一组描述动态系统在非常大的时间值内的行为轨迹. 值得注意的是,偏微分方程组的吸引子点是某个函数空间的一个元素;这一点是空间变量的函数,也取决于方程中出现的参数. 对于带有耗散的物理系统的任何有限制的系统($as\ t\to+\infty$),被描述为:与存在于吸引子中的轨迹相对应的演化方程. 从物理的角度来看,这种制度往往很有意义. 例如,根据 Landau 和 Ruelle-Takens 的猜想,正是 Navier-Stokes 系统的非平凡动力学确定了湍流的存在. 因此,获得关于吸引子的尽可能完整的信息无论是从物理角度来说,还是从数学问题的趣味性来说都是重要的. 本卷中的文章涉及吸引子的存在及其在解决方案(比如 $t\to+\infty$)行为描述中应用. 然而,关键的一点是对吸引子的函数的详细分析,研究了这些函数对空间变量以及参数的依赖关系.

在论文"小参数反应扩散方程解的渐近性"(作者 V. Yu. Skvortsov 和 M. I. Vishik)中,两个抛物线反应-扩散方程的系统,其中一个具有小参数作为相对于时间的导数系数,即,在该方程中出现项 $\varepsilon \partial_t u_1$. 对于所有 $t \geq 0$,该系统解的 $\varepsilon \to 0$ 的渐近行为用极限系统吸引子的解决方案来描述,其中一个方程是固定的.

论文"演化方程的无限吸引子"(作者 V. V. Chepyzhov 和 A. Yu. Goritskiĭ)研究了无限制吸引集的方程中的吸引子,例如在狭义上不耗散的方程式,这样的方程没有紧凑的全局吸引子. 然而,对于某些足够宽泛的此类方程,有可能引入一个合理的吸引子概念,证明吸引子的存在,并描述它们的性质. 这些吸引子既不是紧的,也不是有界的,它们是局部紧和有限维的,通过具体实例说明一般理论. 作者试图使论述尽可能地自成一体,只提到那些可以在易读的书中找到的事实;对于所有其他的陈述内容,作者都给出了详细的证明.

具体论文包括:"强摄动泊松叶动流无限的渐近展开""演化方程的无限吸引子""奇摄动抛物方程的吸引子及其元素的渐近行为""小参数反应扩散方程解的渐近性".

出版资源目前在中国是一种稀缺资源,如何使用这有限的资源,每个编辑有各自不同的出版理念,所以图书市场也呈现出色彩缤纷的"繁荣". 但笔者的基本判断是:出版物特别是学术出版物,本质上讲是一种知识产品,原创性是首要的,尤其是在当今的"山寨"中国. 然而这种理念知易行难. 正如已故日本作家夏目漱石在散文《草枕》中写到:"发挥才智,则锋芒毕露;凭借感情,则流于世俗;坚持己见,则多方掣肘."

刘培杰

2018 年 9 月 15 日

于哈工大

刘培杰数学工作室
已出版(即将出版)图书目录——高等数学

书 名	出版时间	定 价	编号
距离几何分析导引	2015—02	68.00	446
大学几何学	2017—01	78.00	688
关于曲面的一般研究	2016—11	48.00	690
近世纯粹几何学初论	2017—01	58.00	711
拓扑学与几何学基础讲义	2017—04	58.00	756
物理学中的几何方法	2017—06	88.00	767
几何学简史	2017—08	28.00	833
复变函数引论	2013—10	68.00	269
伸缩变换与抛物旋转	2015—01	38.00	449
无穷分析引论(上)	2013—04	88.00	247
无穷分析引论(下)	2013—04	98.00	245
数学分析	2014—04	28.00	338
数学分析中的一个新方法及其应用	2013—01	38.00	231
数学分析例选:通过范例学技巧	2013—01	88.00	243
高等代数例选:通过范例学技巧	2015—06	88.00	475
三角级数论(上册)(陈建功)	2013—01	38.00	232
三角级数论(下册)(陈建功)	2013—01	48.00	233
三角级数论(哈代)	2013—06	48.00	254
三角级数	2015—07	28.00	263
超越数	2011—03	18.00	109
三角和方法	2011—03	18.00	112
随机过程(Ⅰ)	2014—01	78.00	224
随机过程(Ⅱ)	2014—01	68.00	235
算术探索	2011—12	158.00	148
组合数学	2012—04	28.00	178
组合数学浅谈	2012—03	28.00	159
丢番图方程引论	2012—03	48.00	172
拉普拉斯变换及其应用	2015—02	38.00	447
高等代数.上	2016—01	38.00	548
高等代数.下	2016—01	38.00	549
高等代数教程	2016—01	58.00	579
数学解析教程.上卷.1	2016—01	58.00	546
数学解析教程.上卷.2	2016—01	38.00	553
数学解析教程.下卷.1	2017—04	48.00	781
数学解析教程.下卷.2	2017—06	48.00	782
函数构造论.上	2016—01	38.00	554
函数构造论.中	2017—06	48.00	555
函数构造论.下	2016—09	48.00	680
概周期函数	2016—01	48.00	572
变叙的项的极限分布律	2016—01	18.00	573
整函数	2012—08	18.00	161
近代拓扑学研究	2013—04	38.00	239
多项式和无理数	2008—01	68.00	22

Ⅰ

刘培杰数学工作室
已出版（即将出版）图书目录——高等数学

书　名	出版时间	定　价	编号
模糊数据统计学	2008—03	48.00	31
模糊分析学与特殊泛函空间	2013—01	68.00	241
常微分方程	2016—01	58.00	586
平稳随机函数导论	2016—03	48.00	587
量子力学原理·上	2016—01	38.00	588
图与矩阵	2014—08	40.00	644
钢丝绳原理:第二版	2017—01	78.00	745
代数拓扑和微分拓扑简史	2017—06	68.00	791
半序空间泛函分析.上	2018—06	48.00	924
半序空间泛函分析.下	2018—06	68.00	925
概率分布的部分识别	2018—07	68.00	929
受控理论与解析不等式	2012—05	78.00	165
不等式的分拆降维降幂方法与可读证明	2016—01	68.00	591
实变函数论	2012—06	78.00	181
复变函数论	2015—08	38.00	504
非光滑优化及其变分分析	2014—01	48.00	230
疏散的马尔科夫链	2014—01	58.00	266
马尔科夫过程论基础	2015—01	28.00	433
初等微分拓扑学	2012—07	18.00	182
方程式论	2011—03	38.00	105
Galois 理论	2011—03	18.00	107
古典数学难题与伽罗瓦理论	2012—11	58.00	223
伽罗华与群论	2014—01	28.00	290
代数方程的根式解及伽罗瓦理论	2011—03	28.00	108
代数方程的根式解及伽罗瓦理论(第二版)	2015—01	28.00	423
线性偏微分方程讲义	2011—03	18.00	110
几类微分方程数值方法的研究	2015—05	38.00	485
N 体问题的周期解	2011—03	28.00	111
代数方程式论	2011—05	18.00	121
线性代数与几何:英文	2016—06	58.00	578
动力系统的不变量与函数方程	2011—07	48.00	137
基于短语评价的翻译知识获取	2012—02	48.00	168
应用随机过程	2012—04	48.00	187
概率论导引	2012—04	18.00	179
矩阵论（上）	2013—06	58.00	250
矩阵论（下）	2013—06	48.00	251
对称锥互补问题的内点法:理论分析与算法实现	2014—08	68.00	368
抽象代数:方法导引	2013—06	38.00	257
集论	2016—01	48.00	576
多项式理论研究综述	2016—01	38.00	577
函数论	2014—11	78.00	395
反问题的计算方法及应用	2011—11	28.00	147
数阵及其应用	2012—02	28.00	164
绝对值方程—折边与组合图形的解析研究	2012—07	48.00	186
代数函数论（上）	2015—07	38.00	494
代数函数论（下）	2015—07	38.00	495

刘培杰数学工作室
已出版(即将出版)图书目录——高等数学

书　名	出版时间	定　价	编号
偏微分方程论:法文	2015—10	48.00	533
时标动力学方程的指数型二分性与周期解	2016—04	48.00	606
重刚体绕不动点运动方程的积分法	2016—05	68.00	608
水轮机水力稳定性	2016—05	48.00	620
Lévy噪音驱动的传染病模型的动力学行为	2016—05	48.00	667
铣加工动力学系统稳定性研究的数学方法	2016—11	28.00	710
时滞系统:Lyapunov泛函和矩阵	2017—05	68.00	784
粒子图像测速仪实用指南:第二版	2017—08	78.00	790
数域的上同调	2017—08	98.00	799
图的正交因子分解(英文)	2018—01	38.00	881
点云模型的优化配准方法研究	2018—07	58.00	927
吴振奎高等数学解题真经(概率统计卷)	2012—01	38.00	149
吴振奎高等数学解题真经(微积分卷)	2012—01	68.00	150
吴振奎高等数学解题真经(线性代数卷)	2012—01	58.00	151
高等数学解题全攻略(上卷)	2013—06	58.00	252
高等数学解题全攻略(下卷)	2013—06	58.00	253
高等数学复习纲要	2014—01	18.00	384
超越吉米多维奇.数列的极限	2009—11	48.00	58
超越普里瓦洛夫.留数卷	2015—01	28.00	437
超越普里瓦洛夫.无穷乘积与它对解析函数的应用卷	2015—05	28.00	477
超越普里瓦洛夫.积分卷	2015—06	18.00	481
超越普里瓦洛夫.基础知识卷	2015—06	28.00	482
超越普里瓦洛夫.数项级数卷	2015—07	38.00	489
超越普里瓦洛夫.微分、解析函数、导数卷	2018—01	48.00	852
统计学专业英语	2007—03	28.00	16
统计学专业英语(第二版)	2012—07	48.00	176
统计学专业英语(第三版)	2015—04	68.00	465
代换分析:英文	2015—07	38.00	499
历届美国大学生数学竞赛试题集.第一卷(1938—1949)	2015—01	28.00	397
历届美国大学生数学竞赛试题集.第二卷(1950—1959)	2015—01	28.00	398
历届美国大学生数学竞赛试题集.第三卷(1960—1969)	2015—01	28.00	399
历届美国大学生数学竞赛试题集.第四卷(1970—1979)	2015—01	18.00	400
历届美国大学生数学竞赛试题集.第五卷(1980—1989)	2015—01	28.00	401
历届美国大学生数学竞赛试题集.第六卷(1990—1999)	2015—01	28.00	402
历届美国大学生数学竞赛试题集.第七卷(2000—2009)	2015—08	18.00	403
历届美国大学生数学竞赛试题集.第八卷(2010—2012)	2015—01	18.00	404
超越普特南试题:大学数学竞赛中的方法与技巧	2017—04	98.00	758
历届国际大学生数学竞赛试题集(1994—2010)	2012—01	28.00	143
全国大学生数学夏令营数学竞赛试题及解答	2007—03	28.00	15
全国大学生数学竞赛辅导教程	2012—07	28.00	189
全国大学生数学竞赛复习全书(第2版)	2017—05	58.00	787

刘培杰数学工作室
已出版(即将出版)图书目录——高等数学

书　名	出版时间	定价	编号
历届美国大学生数学竞赛试题集	2009—03	88.00	43
前苏联大学生数学奥林匹克竞赛题解(上编)	2012—04	28.00	169
前苏联大学生数学奥林匹克竞赛题解(下编)	2012—04	38.00	170
大学生数学竞赛讲义	2014—09	28.00	371
普林斯顿大学数学竞赛	2016—06	38.00	669
初等数论难题集(第一卷)	2009—05	68.00	44
初等数论难题集(第二卷)(上、下)	2011—02	128.00	82,83
数论概貌	2011—03	18.00	93
代数数论(第二版)	2013—08	58.00	94
代数多项式	2014—06	38.00	289
初等数论的知识与问题	2011—02	28.00	95
超越数论基础	2011—03	28.00	96
数论初等教程	2011—03	28.00	97
数论基础	2011—03	18.00	98
数论基础与维诺格拉多夫	2014—03	18.00	292
解析数论基础	2012—08	28.00	216
解析数论基础(第二版)	2014—01	48.00	287
解析数论问题集(第二版)(原版引进)	2014—05	88.00	343
解析数论问题集(第二版)(中译本)	2016—04	88.00	607
解析数论基础(潘承洞,潘承彪著)	2016—07	98.00	673
解析数论导引	2016—07	58.00	674
数论入门	2011—03	38.00	99
代数数论入门	2015—03	38.00	448
数论开篇	2012—07	28.00	194
解析数论引论	2011—03	48.00	100
Barban Davenport Halberstam 均值和	2009—01	40.00	33
基础数论	2011—03	28.00	101
初等数论 100 例	2011—05	18.00	122
初等数论经典例题	2012—07	18.00	204
最新世界各国数学奥林匹克中的初等数论试题(上、下)	2012—01	138.00	144,145
初等数论(Ⅰ)	2012—01	18.00	156
初等数论(Ⅱ)	2012—01	18.00	157
初等数论(Ⅲ)	2012—01	28.00	158
平面几何与数论中未解决的新老问题	2013—01	68.00	229
代数数论简史	2014—11	28.00	408
代数数论	2015—09	88.00	532
代数、数论及分析习题集	2016—11	98.00	695
数论导引提要及习题解答	2016—01	48.00	559
素数定理的初等证明.第2版	2016—09	48.00	686
数论中的椭函数与狄利克雷级数(第二版)	2017—11	78.00	837
数论:数学导引	2018—01	68.00	849
域论	2018—04	68.00	884
代数数论(冯克勤　编著)	2018—04	68.00	885

刘培杰数学工作室
已出版（即将出版）图书目录——高等数学

书　名	出版时间	定　价	编号
新编 640 个世界著名数学智力趣题	2014—01	88.00	242
500 个最新世界著名数学智力趣题	2008—06	48.00	3
400 个最新世界著名数学最值问题	2008—09	48.00	36
500 个世界著名数学征解问题	2009—06	48.00	52
400 个中国最佳初等数学征解老问题	2010—01	48.00	60
500 个俄罗斯数学经典老题	2011—01	28.00	81
1000 个国外中学物理好题	2012—04	48.00	174
300 个日本高考数学题	2012—05	38.00	142
700 个早期日本高考数学试题	2017—02	88.00	752
500 个前苏联早期高考数学试题及解答	2012—05	28.00	185
546 个早期俄罗斯大学生数学竞赛题	2014—03	38.00	285
548 个来自美苏的数学好问题	2014—11	28.00	396
20 所苏联著名大学早期入学试题	2015—02	18.00	452
161 道德国工科大学生必做的微分方程习题	2015—05	28.00	469
500 个德国工科大学生必做的高数习题	2015—06	28.00	478
360 个数学竞赛问题	2016—08	58.00	677
德国讲义日本考题. 微积分卷	2015—04	48.00	456
德国讲义日本考题. 微分方程卷	2015—04	38.00	457
二十世纪中叶中、英、美、日、法、俄高考数学试题精选	2017—06	38.00	783
博弈论精粹	2008—03	58.00	30
博弈论精粹. 第二版（精装）	2015—01	88.00	461
数学 我爱你	2008—01	28.00	20
精神的圣徒　别样的人生——60 位中国数学家成长的历程	2008—09	48.00	39
数学史概论	2009—06	78.00	50
数学史概论（精装）	2013—03	158.00	272
数学史选讲	2016—01	48.00	544
斐波那契数列	2010—02	28.00	65
数学拼盘和斐波那契魔方	2010—07	38.00	72
斐波那契数列欣赏	2011—01	28.00	160
数学的创造	2011—02	48.00	85
数学美与创造力	2016—01	48.00	595
数海拾贝	2016—01	48.00	590
数学中的美	2011—02	38.00	84
数论中的美学	2014—12	38.00	351
数学王者　科学巨人——高斯	2015—01	28.00	428
振兴祖国数学的圆梦之旅：中国初等数学研究史话	2015—06	98.00	490
二十世纪中国数学史料研究	2015—10	48.00	536
数字谜、数阵图与棋盘覆盖	2016—01	58.00	298
时间的形状	2016—01	38.00	556
数学发现的艺术：数学探索中的合情推理	2016—07	58.00	671
活跃在数学中的参数	2016—07	48.00	675

Ⅴ

刘培杰数学工作室
已出版(即将出版)图书目录——高等数学

书　名	出版时间	定价	编号
格点和面积	2012—07	18.00	191
射影几何趣谈	2012—04	28.00	175
斯潘纳尔引理——从一道加拿大数学奥林匹克试题谈起	2014—01	28.00	228
李普希兹条件——从几道近年高考数学试题谈起	2012—10	18.00	221
拉格朗日中值定理——从一道北京高考试题的解法谈起	2015—10	18.00	197
闵科夫斯基定理——从一道清华大学自主招生试题谈起	2014—01	28.00	198
哈尔测度——从一道冬令营试题的背景谈起	2012—08	28.00	202
切比雪夫逼近问题——从一道中国台北数学奥林匹克试题谈起	2013—04	38.00	238
伯恩斯坦多项式与贝齐尔曲面——从一道全国高中数学联赛试题谈起	2013—03	38.00	236
卡塔兰猜想——从一道普特南竞赛试题谈起	2013—06	18.00	256
麦卡锡函数和阿克曼函数——从一道前南斯拉夫数学奥林匹克试题谈起	2012—08	18.00	201
贝蒂定理与拉姆贝克莫斯尔定理——从一个拣石子游戏谈起	2012—08	18.00	217
皮亚诺曲线和豪斯道夫分球定理——从无限集谈起	2012—08	18.00	211
平面凸图形与凸多面体	2012—10	28.00	218
斯坦因豪斯问题——从一道二十五省市自治区中学数学竞赛试题谈起	2012—07	18.00	196
纽结理论中的亚历山大多项式与琼斯多项式——从一道北京市高一数学竞赛试题谈起	2012—07	28.00	195
原则与策略——从波利亚"解题表"谈起	2013—04	38.00	244
转化与化归——从三大尺规作图不能问题谈起	2012—08	28.00	214
代数几何中的贝祖定理(第一版)——从一道IMO试题的解法谈起	2013—08	18.00	193
成功连贯理论与约当块理论——从一道比利时数学竞赛试题谈起	2012—04	18.00	180
素数判定与大数分解	2014—08	18.00	199
置换多项式及其应用	2012—10	18.00	220
椭圆函数与模函数——从一道美国加州大学洛杉矶分校(UCLA)博士资格考题谈起	2012—10	28.00	219
差分方程的拉格朗日方法——从一道2011年全国高考理科试题的解法谈起	2012—08	28.00	200
力学在几何中的一些应用	2013—01	38.00	240
高斯散度定理、斯托克斯定理和平面格林定理——从一道国际大学生数学竞赛试题谈起	即将出版		
康托洛维奇不等式——从一道全国高中联赛试题谈起	2013—03	28.00	337
西格尔引理——从一道第18届IMO试题的解法谈起	即将出版		
罗斯定理——从一道前苏联数学竞赛试题谈起	即将出版		
拉克斯定理和阿廷定理——从一道IMO试题的解法谈起	2014—01	58.00	246
毕卡大定理——从一道美国大学数学竞赛试题谈起	2014—07	18.00	350
贝齐尔曲线——从一道全国高中联赛试题谈起	即将出版		
拉格朗日乘子定理——从一道2005年全国高中联赛试题的高等数学解法谈起	2015—05	28.00	480
雅可比定理——从一道日本数学奥林匹克试题谈起	2013—04	48.00	249
李天岩—约克定理——从一道波兰数学竞赛试题谈起	2014—06	28.00	349
整系数多项式因式分解的一般方法——从克朗耐克算法谈起	即将出版		

刘培杰数学工作室
已出版（即将出版）图书目录——高等数学

书　　名	出版时间	定　价	编号
布劳维不动点定理——从一道前苏联数学奥林匹克试题谈起	2014—01	38.00	273
伯恩赛德定理——从一道英国数学奥林匹克试题谈起	即将出版		
布查特－莫斯特定理——从一道上海市初中竞赛试题谈起	即将出版		
数论中的同余数问题——从一道普特南竞赛试题谈起	即将出版		
范·德蒙行列式——从一道美国数学奥林匹克试题谈起	即将出版		
中国剩余定理：总数法构建中国历史年表	2015—01	28.00	430
牛顿程序与方程求根——从一道全国高考试题解法谈起	即将出版		
库默尔定理——从一道IMO预选试题谈起	即将出版		
卢丁定理——从一道冬令营试题的解法谈起	即将出版		
沃斯滕霍姆定理——从一道IMO预选试题谈起	即将出版		
卡尔松不等式——从一道莫斯科数学奥林匹克试题谈起	即将出版		
信息论中的香农熵——从一道近年高考压轴题谈起	即将出版		
约当不等式——从一道希望杯竞赛试题谈起	即将出版		
拉比诺维奇定理	即将出版		
刘维尔定理——从一道《美国数学月刊》征解问题的解法谈起	即将出版		
卡塔兰恒等式与级数求和——从一道IMO试题的解法谈起	即将出版		
勒让德猜想与素数分布——从一道爱尔兰竞赛试题谈起	即将出版		
天平称重与信息论——从一道基辅市数学奥林匹克试题谈起	即将出版		
哈密尔顿－凯莱定理：从一道高中数学联赛试题的解法谈起	2014—09	18.00	376
艾思特曼定理——从一道CMO试题的解法谈起	即将出版		
一个爱尔特希问题——从一道西德数学奥林匹克试题谈起	即将出版		
有限群中的爱丁格尔问题——从一道北京市初中二年级数学竞赛试题谈起	即将出版		
贝克码与编码理论——从一道全国高中联赛试题谈起	即将出版		
帕斯卡三角形	2014—03	18.00	294
蒲丰投针问题——从2009年清华大学的一道自主招生试题谈起	2014—01	38.00	295
斯图姆定理——从一道"华约"自主招生试题的解法谈起	2014—01	18.00	296
许瓦兹引理——从一道加利福尼亚大学伯克利分校数学系博士生试题谈起	2014—08	18.00	297
拉姆塞定理——从王诗宬院士的一个问题谈起	2016—04	48.00	299
坐标法	2013—12	28.00	332
数论三角形	2014—04	38.00	341
毕克定理	2014—07	18.00	352
数林掠影	2014—09	48.00	389
我们周围的概率	2014—10	38.00	390
凸函数最值定理：从一道华约自主招生题的解法谈起	2014—10	28.00	391
易学与数学奥林匹克	2014—10	38.00	392
生物数学趣谈	2015—01	18.00	409
反演	2015—01	28.00	420
因式分解与圆锥曲线	2015—01	18.00	426
轨迹	2015—01	28.00	427
面积原理：从常庚哲命的一道CMO试题的积分解法谈起	2015—01	48.00	431
形形色色的不动点定理：从一道28届IMO试题谈起	2015—01	38.00	439
柯西函数方程：从一道上海交大自主招生的试题谈起	2015—02	28.00	440

刘培杰数学工作室
已出版（即将出版）图书目录——高等数学

书　名	出版时间	定　价	编号
三角恒等式	2015—02	28.00	442
无理性判定：从一道2014年"北约"自主招生试题谈起	2015—01	38.00	443
数学归纳法	2015—03	18.00	451
极端原理与解题	2015—04	28.00	464
法雷级数	2014—08	18.00	367
摆线族	2015—01	38.00	438
函数方程及其解法	2015—05	38.00	470
含参数的方程和不等式	2012—09	28.00	213
希尔伯特第十问题	2016—01	38.00	543
无穷小量的求和	2016—01	28.00	545
切比雪夫多项式：从一道清华大学金秋营试题谈起	2016—01	38.00	583
泽肯多夫定理	2016—03	38.00	599
代数等式证题法	2016—01	28.00	600
三角等式证题法	2016—01	28.00	601
吴大任教授藏书中的一个因式分解公式：从一道美国数学邀请赛试题的解法谈起	2016—06	28.00	656
易卦——类万物的数学模型	2017—08	68.00	838
"不可思议"的数与数系可持续发展	2018—01	38.00	878
最短线	2018—01	38.00	879
从毕达哥拉斯到怀尔斯	2007—10	48.00	9
从迪利克雷到维斯卡尔迪	2008—01	48.00	21
从哥德巴赫到陈景润	2008—05	98.00	35
从庞加莱到佩雷尔曼	2011—08	138.00	136
从费马到怀尔斯——费马大定理的历史	2013—10	198.00	I
从庞加莱到佩雷尔曼——庞加莱猜想的历史	2013—10	298.00	II
从切比雪夫到爱尔特希（上）——素数定理的初等证明	2013—07	48.00	III
从切比雪夫到爱尔特希（下）——素数定理100年	2012—12	98.00	III
从高斯到盖尔方特——二次域的高斯猜想	2013—10	198.00	IV
从库默尔到朗兰兹——朗兰兹猜想的历史	2014—01	98.00	V
从比勒巴赫到德布朗斯——比勒巴赫猜想的历史	2014—02	298.00	VI
从麦比乌斯到陈省身——麦比乌斯变换与麦比乌斯带	2014—02	298.00	VII
从布尔到豪斯道夫——布尔方程与格论漫谈	2013—10	198.00	VIII
从开普勒到阿诺德——三体问题的历史	2014—05	298.00	IX
从华林到华罗庚——华林问题的历史	2013—10	298.00	X
数学物理大百科全书. 第1卷	2016—01	418.00	508
数学物理大百科全书. 第2卷	2016—01	408.00	509
数学物理大百科全书. 第3卷	2016—01	396.00	510
数学物理大百科全书. 第4卷	2016—01	408.00	511
数学物理大百科全书. 第5卷	2016—01	368.00	512
朱德祥代数与几何讲义. 第1卷	2017—01	38.00	697
朱德祥代数与几何讲义. 第2卷	2017—01	28.00	698
朱德祥代数与几何讲义. 第3卷	2017—01	28.00	699

刘培杰数学工作室
已出版(即将出版)图书目录——高等数学

书 名	出版时间	定 价	编号
闵嗣鹤文集	2011—03	98.00	102
吴从炘数学活动三十年(1951～1980)	2010—07	99.00	32
吴从炘数学活动又三十年(1981～2010)	2015—07	98.00	491
斯米尔诺夫高等数学.第一卷	2018—03	88.00	770
斯米尔诺夫高等数学.第二卷.第一分册	2018—03	68.00	771
斯米尔诺夫高等数学.第二卷.第二分册	2018—03	68.00	772
斯米尔诺夫高等数学.第二卷.第三分册	2018—03	48.00	773
斯米尔诺夫高等数学.第三卷.第一分册	2018—03	58.00	774
斯米尔诺夫高等数学.第三卷.第二分册	2018—03	58.00	775
斯米尔诺夫高等数学.第三卷.第三分册	2018—03	68.00	776
斯米尔诺夫高等数学.第四卷.第一分册	2018—03	48.00	777
斯米尔诺夫高等数学.第四卷.第二分册	2018—03	88.00	778
斯米尔诺夫高等数学.第五卷.第一分册	2018—03	58.00	779
斯米尔诺夫高等数学.第五卷.第二分册	2018—03	68.00	780
zeta 函数,q-zeta 函数,相伴级数与积分	2015—08	88.00	513
微分形式:理论与练习	2015—08	58.00	514
离散与微分包含的逼近和优化	2015—08	58.00	515
艾伦·图灵:他的工作与影响	2016—01	98.00	560
测度理论概率导论,第2版	2016—01	88.00	561
带有潜在故障恢复系统的半马尔柯夫模型控制	2016—01	98.00	562
数学分析原理	2016—01	88.00	563
随机偏微分方程的有效动力学	2016—01	88.00	564
图的谱半径	2016—01	58.00	565
量子机器学习中数据挖掘的量子计算方法	2016—01	98.00	566
量子物理的非常规方法	2016—01	118.00	567
运输过程的统一非局部理论:广义波尔兹曼物理动力学,第2版	2016—01	198.00	568
量子力学与经典力学之间的联系在原子、分子及电动力学系统建模中的应用	2016—01	58.00	569
算术域:第3版	2017—08	158.00	820
算术域	2018—01	158.00	821
高等数学竞赛:1962—1991年的米洛克斯·史怀哲竞赛	2018—01	128.00	822
用数学奥林匹克精神解决数论问题	2018—01	108.00	823
代数几何(德语)	2018—04	68.00	824
丢番图近似值	2018—01	78.00	825
代数几何学基础教程	2018—01	98.00	826
解析数论入门课程	2018—01	78.00	827
中正大学数论教程	即将出版		828
数论中的丢番图问题	2018—01	78.00	829
数论(梦幻之旅):第五届中日数论研讨会演讲集	2018—01	68.00	830
数论新应用	2018—01	68.00	831
数论	2018—01	78.00	832

刘培杰数学工作室
已出版(即将出版)图书目录——高等数学

书　名	出版时间	定价	编号
湍流十讲	2018—04	108.00	886
无穷维李代数:第3版	2018—04	98.00	887
等值、不变量和对称性:英文	2018—04	78.00	888
解析数论	即将出版		889
《数学原理》的演化:伯特兰·罗素撰写第二版时的手稿与笔记	2018—04	108.00	890
哈密尔顿数学论文集(第4卷):几何学、分析学、天文学、概率和有限差分等	即将出版		891
数学王子——高斯	2018—01	48.00	858
坎坷奇星——阿贝尔	2018—01	48.00	859
闪烁奇星——伽罗瓦	2018—01	58.00	860
无穷统帅——康托尔	2018—01	48.00	861
科学公主——柯瓦列夫斯卡娅	2018—01	48.00	862
抽象代数之母——埃米·诺特	2018—01	48.00	863
电脑先驱——图灵	2018—01	58.00	864
昔日神童——维纳	2018—01	48.00	865
数坛怪侠——爱尔特希	2018—01	68.00	866
当代世界中的数学.数学思想与数学基础	2018—04	38.00	892
当代世界中的数学.数学问题	即将出版		893
当代世界中的数学.应用数学与数学应用	即将出版		894
当代世界中的数学.数学王国的新疆域(一)	2018—04	38.00	895
当代世界中的数学.数学王国的新疆域(二)	即将出版		896
当代世界中的数学.数林撷英(一)	即将出版		897
当代世界中的数学.数林撷英(二)	即将出版		898
当代世界中的数学.数学之路	即将出版		899

联系地址:哈尔滨市南岗区复华四道街10号　哈尔滨工业大学出版社刘培杰数学工作室
网　　址:http://lpj.hit.edu.cn/
邮　编:150006
联系电话:0451—86281378　　13904613167
E-mail:lpj1378@163.com